# INTERPRETATIONS OF ISLAM

# INTERPRETATIONS of ISLAM

## PAST AND PRESENT

By Emmanuel Sivan

The Darwin Press, Inc.
Princeton, New Jersey

[redacted]



**Library of Congress Cataloging in Publication Data**

Sivan, Emmanuel.
Interpretations of Islam.

Includes index.
1. Arab countries—Historiography—Addresses, essays, lectures. 2. French—Algeria—Addresses, essays, lectures. I. Title.
DS37.S57 1985 909'.097671'0072 84-70415
ISBN 0-87850-049-9

Printed in the United States of America

## CONTENTS

*To My Mother*

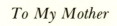

# INTRODUCTION

THERE ARE, it has been said, two types of scholars: the divers who plunge deeper and deeper into the water, turning around the one object they covet, and the explorers who like to furrow the sea, in quest of boundless horizons, describing the various worlds they encounter along the way. It seems that I belong to the second category, hopping back and forth between medieval and contemporary Islamic history, between *Mashriq* and *Maghrib*, between the viewpoint of the Muslim native and that of the European colonizer.

Yet, if there is a *raison d'être* to this activity, other than the sheer fun of exploration, it resides in the one recurring theme of my scholarly concerns—the relationship between the Islamic past and present.

This collection of essays intends to illustrate the diverse aspects of this theme, perhaps in a better focused manner than I could do in my books. I begin by discussing the deep interest of modern Muslims in their past, especially the Middle Ages, which attract them more than Westerners are attracted to their own (Western) Middle Ages. (Half of the Ph.D. dissertations in Egyptian universities, for instance, are devoted to medieval history.)* Two facets of this interest—which one may call "history as a witness for the defense" and "history as a witness for the prosecution"—are discussed in Chapters 1 and 2 respectively. These interpretations illustrate the subjective presence of the past in the minds of contemporary Muslims, the past as represented by the modern observer. But the past has a more "objective" presence in modern realities through the legacies it left and which survive (in various and ever-changing forms), regardless of whether the contemporaries are conscious of it or not. Two such legacies are probed in Chapters 3 and 4. Chapter 5 attempts to place the same *leitmotif* in a broader scope—that of the debate on Orientalism launched by the book bearing this title by Edward Said. The one great merit of Said's book is, undoubtedly, in stressing the "cultural archives" brought by scholars and observers to the study of Islam. Awareness of this fact, i.e., attention to one's own prejudices and predilections, is the best guarantee against falling

* See my "Egyptian Historiography: Quantitative Indicators," *Hamizrah Hehadash* XXIII (Hebrew), 1973.

into the pitfalls of extreme subjectivism, though objectivity will remain, at best, elusive. This is particularly true of the outside observer, and even more so of the Western one whose civilization has long dominated (and in some ways still does) that of Islam. Studying the various representations of Islam by Westerners is one way to enhance such self-awareness. I have chosen to do so not at the level of high culture (discussed by Said and his reviewers, see Chapter 5), but by focusing on Western popular culture in one of the most intensive (and tragic) colonial situations, namely, French Algeria (see Chapters 6, 7, and 8). The lessons to be learned therefrom are all the more poignant, since the Pied Noirs were both a dominant class (in the colonial context) and a subordinate class (in the French context), both "Mediterranean" and "European."

Chapters 1, 2, 6, and 8 are reprinted here, more or less, as they originally appeared in English. Chapter 5 is a greatly expanded version of a 1977 article. Chapters 3, 4, and 7 appear here in English for the first time and were also revised or expanded.

These essays were prepared for publication at the suggestion of my friend and mentor, Charles Issawi, during a year spent at the Institute for Advanced Study, Princeton. My thanks to the Institute and to its staff.

# PART I: HISTORY INTERPRETED

# Chapter 1:

# MODERN ARAB HISTORIOGRAPHY OF THE CRUSADES

REFLECTING ON the character of medieval Arab historiography of the Crusades, F. Gabrieli pointed out that

> the concept of the Crusades as an historical phenomenon in itself with its own characteristics, which might be treated separately, either in a monograph or within the framework of a general periodization of history, is one totally alien to Muslim historiography. The events which took place in Syria, Egypt and Mesopotamia between the end of the eleventh century and the end of the thirteenth by the fact of the Frankish invasion and the Muslim resistance, have never been the object of a special and at the same time comprehensive treatise on the part of the chroniclers. . . . In general, the wars with the Crusaders were for the Muslim historians one element among several others, a thread in the cloth of their history, although naturally this thread at certain times displayed a very special importance and development.[1]

Indeed, medieval Muslim historians did not even coin a new term to distinguish these wars from former wars waged by Europe against Islamic countries, nor did they feel the need to confer upon the Crusaders any specific name, satisfying themselves with the ethnic one "Franks" (*Faranj, Ifranj*), which had already been in use for centuries to designate the inhabitants of the territories once included in the Carolingian Empire.[2] The terms *al-ḥurūb al-ṣalībiyya,* or *ḥurūb al-ṣalībiyyīn* (Crusaders) seem to have appeared only in modern times. They first appear in the middle of the nineteenth century among the Christian intelligentsia in Syria, a fact which certainly attests not only to the emergence of an awareness of the specificity of the Crusaders but also to the growth of interest in them. This awakening of interest was also reflected in literary activity. A *History of the Holy Wars in the East, otherwise called the Wars of the Cross,* translated into Arabic from French, appeared in Jerusalem in 1865, bearing the *imprimatur* of the Patriarch of the Holy City.[3] And there is a short chapter entitled *al-ḥurūb al-ṣalībiyya*[4] in Jirī Yannī's *History of Syria* (Beirut, 1881). These timid and wholly unoriginal beginnings were followed by real attempts at the writing of full-scale Arabic accounts of the Crusades. Yūsuf al-Dibs, Maronite Archbishop of Beirut, who also composed a history of Syria, devoted half of the sixth volume of his work (1901) to the exploits of *"al-Ifranj al-Ṣalībiyyūn."*[5] He was preceded three years earlier, however, by an Egyptian Muslim, Sayyid 'Alī al-Ḥarīrī, author of *The Splendid Story of the Crusading Wars*.[6] Written in classical style and according to the standards of medieval Muslim historiography (from which al-Ḥarīrī also quotes passages at great length), the book aroused a certain amount of interest, attested to by the fact that a second edition was published thirteen years later with the addition of complimentary letters from readers.

Except for this auspicious beginning, research on the Crusader period developed in unspectacular fashion until the end of World War II, though it should be noted that historical studies in general were only just beginning to appear in the Arab world during this period. Nine articles and ten books (biographies, monographs, and general surveys) constitute the entire crop of Arab historiography of the Crusades in the forty-odd years following the publication of al-Ḥarīrī's book, and only about one half of these studies may be regarded as inspired by the standards of modern scientific scholarship and by the findings of modern European historians of the Crusades.[7] It was only in the post-1945 period that the study of the Crusades began to gain momentum, and its rare growth was considerably accelerated from the mid-1950s on. In all, thirty articles and fifty books dealing with the Crusades have appeared in the last three decades, and more than one quarter of these books have been reprinted once or twice. Moreover, some two score books of general or regional Islamic history have devoted long, detailed, and fairly accurate chapters to these Western expeditions and to the states they established in the Middle East.[8]

There exists, therefore, a large and ever-expanding body of modern Arabic historical literature describing and analyzing the Crusades. Its main currents and salient problems undoubtedly deserve closer study.[9]

## THE CRUSADES AS "CONTEMPORARY HISTORY"

There were a number of factors which influenced the genesis, growth, and flowering of the historiography of the Crusades: the influence of French culture with its glorification of the Crusades, especially apparent in Christian circles in Ottoman Syria; the increasing acquaintance with Western historiography both in the original and in translation;[10] the general development in Arab countries of historical studies and public interest therein; and, last but not least, the tireless efforts of several distinguished Egyptian historians (notably Muḥammad Muṣṭafā Ziyāda and ʿAzīz ʿAṭīya), who initiated a whole generation of young scholars into the study of the period. But important as these developments may be, they are overshadowed by another factor—not entirely connected with detached scientific curiosity—namely, the consciousness, common to nearly all Arab historians, that the Crusades are highly relevant to the events and experiences of their own times. If, as G. Barraclough contends, "all history which means anything is contemporary history,"[11] none is more "contemporary," in terms of its relevance, than the historiography of the Crusades.[12]

The sense of relevancy may already be detected in al-Ḥarīrī's introduction to his book: "The sovereigns of Europe nowadays attack our Sublime Empire in a manner bearing a great resemblance to the deeds of these people [i.e., the Crusaders] in bygone times. Our most glorious Sultan, ʿAbd al-Ḥamīd II, has rightly remarked that Europe is now carrying out a Crusade against us in the form of a political campaign."[13] Baylī's biography of Saladin (1920) exalts this ruler's historical role in thwarting the *first* European attempts to subdue the East.[14] ʿInān claims, in *Decisive Moments in the History of Islam* (1934), that "the West today is still waging Crusading wars against Islam under the guise of political and economic imperialism."[15]

References to the "topicality" of the Crusades multiplied considerably by the mid-1940s. Tamīmī's *The Crusades* (Jerusalem, 1945) is dedicated "to the martyrs and combatants for Allāh and for the Arabs, their independence and unity"; the author, a Palestinian educator, implicitly compares the Franks at times to the Zionists.[16] Far more explicit in this respect is *The New Crusade in Palestine* written by Wadīʿ Talḥūq, a Syrian, in 1948 (a little while before the establishment of the State of Israel). Talḥūq regards the Crusades as "a major link in the chain connecting the present to the past."[17] The first half of this book accordingly deals with the Crusades in order to arrive at a better understanding of the essence and development of their modern counterpart, Zionist colonization, to which the second half is devoted. The Arab-Israel War of 1948 gave new impetus to this theme. In

October of the same year 'Abd al-Laṭīf Ḥamza wrote in a preface to his study, *The Literature of the Crusades*: "The struggle against Zionists has reawakened in our hearts the memory of the Crusades; educated youth in all the Arab countries wish to acquire some knowledge of those religious wars." It is noteworthy that this book, dedicated "to the souls of the martyrs who have fallen for Palestine," was composed at the initiative of the Egyptian Royal Academy of the Arabic Language.[18] Many later books echo the same concept. Jūzīf Yūsuf, for instance, entitled his study of the Seventh Crusade, *Louis IX in the Middle East, the Palestine Problem in the Middle Ages,*[19] and Dahhān dedicated an edition of the thirteenth-century treatise on the historical geography of Palestine to the parts of Palestine under Israeli rule.[20] Even Naẓīr Sa'dāwī's Ph.D. thesis, which deals with the somewhat technical subject of the Egyptian army in the time of Saladin, emphasizes that "the present situation very much resembles that of the times when the Crusaders landed on the shores of Syria-Palestine and established their domination there."[21] Elsewhere in the same work, the author likens the *mutaṭawi'a* (volunteers) who joined Saladin's army, to the volunteers of the Arab-Israel War, and the Christian Military Orders to the Stern and Irgun terrorist movements.[22]

This awareness reached new heights in the wake of the Suez War, as even a casual reading of titles and prefaces will suffice to prove. Al-Khūlī studies *The Triple Aggression in the Middle Ages* and Ziyāda—*Our* [i.e., Egyptian] *Struggle against the Aggressors* (mainly in the thirteenth century), while al-Ghatīt endeavors to present a full-scale survey of *East and West from the Crusades to the Suez War.*[23] Abd al-Mun'im Mājid, a biographer of Saladin, claims that

> anyone reviewing the history of Saladin and his times will find that it reminds him of the events of our times. He (i.e., Saladin) appeared at a dark moment for the Muslim Middle Eastern countries: weak and divided among themselves, they attracted the greed of their European enemies, who snatched parts of their territory. Then this hero appeared . . . upon whom devolved the task of fighting the enemies and saving [his coreligionists] from them.[24]

More recently Sa'īd 'Āshūr affirmed in his monumental two-volume *History of the Crusades*: "It is evident that the present state of affairs in the Arab Middle East makes us feel that our condition is very close to that of our ancestors eight and a half centuries ago; it is consequently incumbent upon us to study the movement of the Crusades minutely and scientifically."[25] This concept has gained impetus since the Six-Day War. Thus, an article published in *Majallat al-Azhar* in August 1967 states that Israel, in this war, has avenged the defeat of the Franks by Saladin and the Arabs at the Horns of Ḥaṭṭīn.[26]

The concept of the topicality of the Crusades stems, then, from a belief in a certain parallelism between the twelfth to thirteenth centuries and the last hundred years: in both cases the Islamic (or Arab-Islamic) Middle East was assailed by European forces, which, availing themselves of the state of discord and general weakness prevailing in the region, succeeded in imposing their control upon a large part of it. This parallelism, in the opinion of all Arab scholars, is not fortuitous, since the Crusades as well as current developments are part and parcel of the same historical process—the age long struggle between East and West. Opinions differ, however, as regards the date at which this struggle began, the identity of the two contending forces, and the nature of the conflict between them.

Up to World War II, most Arab historians were committed to the theory depicting the struggle in terms of a contest between Islam and Christendom. Initiated by the Arab conquests, it generated a Christian counter-offensive in the form of the Crusades; Islam responded to this challenge by Ottoman expansion, which gave rise in its turn to modern Western penetration into the Middle East. The best expression of this theory is to be found in the writings of ʻInān. In an article devoted to "The Crusading Idea," he defines it as the idea with which Europe was always imbued, "the idea of a perpetual Islamic peril from the very beginning, the concept of a life-and-death battle between Islam and Christendom."[27] His book, *Decisive Moments in the History of Islam* describes important stages in this conflict, the axis of which remained the Western intention of crushing Islam, an intention first crystallized by the Crusades.[28]

The post-1945 generation, for its part, considers the Crusades as the primary phase of European Colonialism, paving the way for the Bonaparte expedition, the nineteenth-century "Eastern Question," the British conquest of Egypt, and the Mandate system in the Levant. The Crusades are *istiʻmār mubakkar* (imperialism ahead of its time),[29] a sort of *praefiguratio* of the powerful modern movement. Two of the books mentioned above provide us with the clearest expressions of this theory: Talḥūq's *The New Crusade in Palestine,* where Zionism is presented as the culmination of the whole process, and Ghatīt's *East and West,* where this role is assigned to the 1956 war.

The difference between the two theories is not so great as it would seem at first sight. The latter theory is unmistakably much more secular (thus reflecting the change which took place during the 1940s in the orientation of the Arab intelligentsia), yet on the whole it differs from the former mainly in emphasis, and in some respects it may be viewed as a natural outgrowth of it. On the other hand, the first theory, while it considers the conflict to be religious or ideological, does not exclude the existence of materialistic ulterior motives—conquest, pillage, exploitation of natural resources, opening of new trade-routes, and so forth. These materialistic motives are ascribed, however, solely to the Christian (past and present) antagonists; Arab conquests are described as an idealistic campaign destined to spread the Prophet's message and resorting mainly to peaceful means of persuasion.[30] It is but a step from here to conferring upon the Crusades the designation of imperialism and maintaining that their religious ideology—just like its modern counterparts, "the white man's burden" and *la mission civilisatrice*—is nothing but a cynical guise adapted to the prevalent mentality of that age.[31] The concept of ulterior motives obviously assumes a certain "asymmetry" in the conflict; this trait is further accentuated by the claim that the Arab conquest of the seventh century did not constitute real aggression and that it was, consequently, the Crusades which put in motion the whole chain of events reaching to this very day. The imperialistic theory makes the asymmetry sharper: it totally ignores the Arab conquests and simply fixes the beginning of the process at the end of the eleventh century, thus laying the entire blame at Europe's door.

It is somewhat arduous to disentangle the various factors contributing to the elaboration of the two theories. The deepest roots of the idea of Islamo-Christian contest may be discerned in the medieval Muslim vision of the world as clearly divided into two—politically, religiously, and morally—opposed spheres, *Dār al-Islām* and *Dār al-Ḥarb*, and more specifically in the writings of Muslim historians, who regarded the Crusades as part of a wide-ranging European attack upon Islam carried out at different points around the Mediterranean.[32] No less important, in this context, was the influence exerted by a powerful trend in modern European historiography, born in the age of the Enlightenment and surviving to the present day,[33] which defines the Crusades in more explicit terms as a second stage in the centuries-old conflict between the two great world religions. It is from some of the aforementioned Enlightenment historians and from their early nineteenth-century disciples (e.g., Gibbon, Mills, Hallam)[34]—made known to Muslims especially through the medium of *A Short History of the Saracens* by the Indian Muslim scholar Sayyid Amīr 'Alī[35]—that Arab writers borrowed the idea of the materialistic motives of the Franks hidden under the cloak of Holy War. Such a view was to fit in, on the other hand, with the concept, highly typical of modern Islamic apologetics, of the materialism of the West as contrasted with the spirituality of the East.[36]

But how were these concepts concerning a distant past linked with recent and contemporary realities? The primary drive in this direction probably emanated from the French historical school, comprising, among others, Rey, Madelin, and Longnon,[37] which viewed the Crusaders (who were mostly of French stock) as the founders of *la présence française au Levant,* which was to be continued by Napoleon and by modern French imperialism. These ideas were brought to the attention of the Arabo-Islamic intelligentsia and political leadership not only through erudite French scholarly work and literature,[38] but also through the declarations of many French and English advocates of imperialism and empire-builders who used them as historical precedents to support their claims (the English, of course, focusing their interest upon Richard the Lion-Hearted). The public statements of Generals Allenby (1918) and Gouraud (1920), who spoke in terms of re-establishment of the Crusaders' rule in Palestine and Syria, are the outstanding examples.[39] When the image imperialism had of itself was absorbed by the Arab-Muslim community, harrassed and mutilated by the modern West, it underwent a huge transformation. In that "twilight world of popular myths and images"—to borrow B. Lewis' words[40]—the Crusades served to crystallize the mounting antagonism against the West and became a symbol of its domination as well as irrefutable proof of the innately malicious character of Western intentions toward the Arab-Islamic world.[41] Arab writers stressed the economic aspect of the two movements rather than the altruistic motives which pro-colonialist Western writers like to ascribe both to the Crusades (the defense of Oriental Christians, and so forth) and to their modern followers. An enormous arsenal of arguments in favor of this view may be found in the works of Western critics of imperialism of the Hobson-Lenin school and in studies of the Crusades by economically-minded historians influenced by this school.[42]

This phenomenon—the identification of the Crusades with

imperialism—has already been singled out and analyzed by several students of modern Middle Eastern history,[43] and it would be superfluous to discuss it in greater detail. What should be emphasized from the point of view of the present article is that it was not Arab historiography that established this concept in the Middle East. A product of all the influences noted above, it was born in the governing as well as in the cultured circles and only later, and to a large extent under the inspiration of those circles, was it adopted by the historians; witness for example, al-Ḥarīrī's quotation from the speech of 'Abd al-Ḥamīd.[44] The development of the theory of "Islam-Christendom struggle," with its medieval world-picture colored by some modern brush strokes, into the "imperialism-Arab world struggle" theory, formulated in more modern terminology and permeated with stronger animosity toward the Franks (as well as toward their modern counterparts) is above all the result of the general worsening of relations between the Arab-Muslim world and the West. Even the identification of Zionism with the Crusades was by no means created by historiography. One may detect it among Arab Palestinian nationalists in the early thirties (and in a somewhat vaguer manner even on the eve of World War I.)[45]

Nevertheless, the importance of these historiographical theories for the historian of Arab nationalism does not only lie in the fact that they serve as an illustration of the development of the Arab attitude toward the West. There can be no doubt that Arab historians of the Crusades contributed in their turn to the propagation of this attitude, conferring upon it the appearance of an objective, scientific truth. Many of the studies are popular in style and presentation, nor should one forget the historical novels that flourish side by side with historiography proper.[46]

The marked interest of the post-1952 Egyptian regime in this historical literature (many of the studies have been published by official or semi-official publishing houses), may serve as additional proof of its popularity and effectiveness in intensifying the aforementioned sentiments.

One should not fail to note a third theory which is on the margin of the "Islam-Christendom" and the "imperialism-Arab world" theories, but is quite different in sources and character. Expounded for the first time about twenty years ago by the Egyptian historian 'Azīz 'Aṭīya, who has remained its chief spokesman,[47] this theory asserts that the conflict at issue is really a conflict between the civilizations of East and West, whose origins stretch far back into antiquity. It began with the Greco-Persian wars of the fifth century B.C. and conquests of Alexander the Great and was resumed by the Parthian revolt at the time of the Seleucids and the Roman-Sassanid wars. With the advent of the Middle Ages, what had hitherto been a problem of race and culture was transformed into a religious problem, the successive stages of attack and counterattack being: Heraclius' Persian wars; Islamic conquests; Byzantine expeditions of the tenth century; Spanish Reconquest; the Crusades; and Mamluk and Ottoman counter-Crusades. "In modern times, imperialistic colonialism was a logical if remote successor to the Crusades, from the Eastern Question to the present day."[48] 'Aṭīya was certainly inspired by the ideas of the French historian R. Grousset, who spoke of the "frontières spirituelles" between Europe and Asia as the bone of the contention in two millennia of world conflict.[49] It is interesting to note, however, that while Grousset contented himself with situating the Crusades (which constituted his primary interest) in an historical frame of reference extending from the Greco-Persian wars to the battle of Lepanto (1571), 'Aṭīya connects this last phase with modern European expansion in the Middle East. Despite this strong sense of the topicality of the Crusades, it would be a mistake to consider 'Aṭīya's views as essentially similar to the "pre-imperialist-Arab world" theory. Speaking in terms of waves and counter-waves and assuming that at each stage both antagonists were driven by the same kind of motives, the Egyptian scholar categorically rules out any notion of one side being the constant aggressor, and he thus confers upon the conflict an evident symmetry. Although conscious of contemporary problems, 'Aṭīya shuns the arbitrary application of contemporary concepts and terminology to phenomena of the past, and rather seeks to understand them against the background of their own era. Discussing the driving forces of the Crusades, he says for example:

> The Middle Ages was first and foremost an age of faith and war. This becomes quite clear when one studies the element of chivalry and feudalism. The fullest expression of this trend is the Crusade which was a war of religion. This explains the spontaneity of the movement and the readiness of Europe to espouse the new cause.... We must consider this mystical excitement which swept over Europe, according to medieval standards of thinking, and thus accept the good faith of the chronicler who contended that the Crusade was the greatest event since the creation of the world and the mystery of the Crucifixion—that it is the work of God, not of man.[50]

'Aṭīya's views have attracted a small though not insignificant following, including Hitti, Maṭawī, Mājid, and Naqqāsh.[51] It is true that some of the partisans of the "pre-imperialism" concept (especially Zakī, Qal'ajī, Talḥūq, Yūsuf, and al-Kharbūṭlī)[52] have borrowed from 'Aṭīya the idea that the roots of the struggle lie in pre-Islamic times, yet they have deliberately ignored the other (and perhaps more important) components of this thesis. Thus, it was possible for them to fit this idea with the theory of never-ending Western efforts aimed at the subjugation of the East. Qal'ajī writes, for example, that the Crusades marked a new round in a contest inaugurated by the Persians and the Greeks, "the struggle of the West in order to colonize and exploit the East, the struggle of the East for its own liberation and independence; a struggle . . . whose most intensive stage has been reached in the present epoch."[53] Although the historical horizon of such a concept is as wide as 'Aṭīya's there is not a trace here of the symmetry and the intentional absence of moral judgment that characterize his views.

## ANALOGIES AND LESSONS

On considering all three historical theories, one may be moved to ask why Arab historians take such pains to establish that the analogy between the Crusades and the present conditions is not fortuitous. The reason is to be found in their basic concepts regarding the aims and methodology of historical science. The primary aim of nearly all of these historians is to derive some moral lesson from the events they study and to impart it to the reader, so that it may serve him as a source of inspiration, instigate him to action, help him to bear the reverses of fortune patiently and bolster his self-confidence.[54] The history of the Crusades, which bears at least some external resemblance to present conflicts and has for its denouement a total Middle Eastern victory, seemed most suitable from this point of view; it carried the promise of a brighter future for an Arab society in the throes of a structural crisis, brought about by its encounter with the West. One only had to prove that the resemblance was not confined to external features; once this requirement was fulfilled, historians could solemnly pronounce the encouraging conclusion to be drawn therefrom. "The struggle waged today by the leaders of the Arab movement of liberation," claims the literary historian Muḥammad Kamāl Ḥusayn, "is the very same conducted by the Ayyūbids and the Mamluks in order to beat off the Crusaders. As the Arabs gained the victory in the past, so they will gain it nowadays."[55]

Colonel 'Abd al-Raḥmān Zakī, a scholar who has studied the Crusades from the military point of view, states: "Up to this very day we are confronted with a modern brand of Crusades. Nevertheless, confident in ourselves and in the power of Right, we believe that these attacks will be terminated in the same manner as their forerunners. God willing, the East shall end victorious."[56] Even book titles sometimes evoke such inspiring lessons, e.g., Abū Ḥadīd's *Saladin, the Hero Who Vanquished in the West.*[57]

This tendency to regard history as a means of creating specific psychological effects in the mind of the reader is not peculiar, of course, to the scholars discussed in the present article. Its existence has already been observed in other fields of modern Arab historiography.[58] What seems peculiar to the Arab historiography of the Crusades (or at least is more conspicuous there than elsewhere) is that many of these scholars are not content with lessons of this kind and strive to draw others of greater accuracy and of a more practical kind. The underlying assumption behind their endeavor is the predictability of historical developments, based upon inference from scientifically established past experience. It follows that if an historical situation resembles a contemporary one in its esential traits, the methods used to solve the crucial problems of the former are *most likely to* (or, according to a more intransigent view, *must*) indicate the measures one should resort to now in order to find a way out of similar difficulties in the present.

In its crudest form one notes this pragmatic concept of history in brief and categorical affirmations such as "history repeats itself," "history is a master providing us with lessons concerning [future] events," "history is the best guide for rising nations,"[59] or, in a more flowery style, "what happened in Egypt in bygone ages will tell us what is going to happen on the shores of the Nile in the ages to come."[60] These affirmations are usually followed by a more or less detailed discussion of the course of action to be followed in the conflict with the West. Other scholars dwell upon the *historia magistra vitae* theme in a more developed and sophisticated manner. 'Āshūr concedes that it is not quite certain that the exact recurrence of past events may be expected; yet, speaking about the broad lines of historical evolution, he maintains: "The importance of the Crusades lies in their being a gigantic experience, full of lessons and admonitions. Therefore, we should study this subject and reflect on it time and time again, now and in the future, in order to be able to benefit from mistakes committed [by our forefathers] and avoid them, and to face and overcome present perils and obstacles."[61] It is not sheer coincidence that his book bears the motto: "We might make it a memorial (*tadhkira*) unto you, and the retaining ear might retain it" (Koran, LXIX, 12).

In their search for significant (and, consequently, sufficiently accurate) lessons, historians subscribing to such views naturally tend to draw a more minute and systematic comparison between past and present. Geopolitical conditions in the region are shown to be very much the same in both periods (the Middle East as a bridge between the Mediterranean and the Indian Ocean, Egypt as center of gravity of the region, the sanctity of Jerusalem for Christianity and Islam and its political implications). The modes of action of the Crusaders are painstakingly examined in order to single out analogies with the methods employed by the Western powers or by Israel (use of religious-historical claims, *divide et impera* maneuvers, effacing of the national and religious character of the region by continuous European immigration and by drawing on some favored minorities, etc.).[62]

According to some historians, this similarity of the modes of action results from the fact that modern imperialism has learned from the experience of its medieval predecessors, an example the Arabs are called upon to follow.[63] The evolution of Muslim reaction to Frankish challenge is likened, stage by stage, to the development of attitudes toward Imperialism and Zionism: indifference, incomprehension, and collaboration at first, rise of a *jihād* movement that also seeks to restore unity to a divided region, resistance of "reactionary" Islamic princes to this movement and their failure, military victory over the Westerners.[64] Special attention is paid to the State of Israel, the sources of whose strength (technological superiority, Western aid, mystical zeal, and so forth) and of its weakness (tiny territory, lack of internal cohesion, dwindling immigration) are supposed to be identical with those of the Latin Kingdom of Jerusalem.[65]

In contrast to the detailed and realistic character of the analogies, the practical lessons drawn from them are somewhat too general and nebulous: Arab unity as a *sine qua non* for the success of the anti-imperialist struggle, the importance of strong leadership, the imperativeness of shrewd manipulation of Middle Eastern strategic and economic positions, the necessity of creating a spirit of combativeness and self-assurance in the Arab countries, and so forth. The heuristic value of this "comparative method" would in this case appear doubtful, while these lessons, far from giving the clue to new ways of action, serve mainly to corroborate solutions and catchwords that are already well-known in the Arab world. If, for this reason and for many others, the validity of the method is contestable, it should be admitted that their grasp of current problems gives some of these historians valuable insight into the vital problems of the period of the Crusades.

Why is it that so many Arab historians, none of them Marxists, are tempted to employ such methods, to tread such paths, at a time when modern historiography generally falls in with P. Geyl's opinion: "History is not to be searched for practical lessons, the applicability of which will always be doubtful in view of the inexhaustive novelty of circumstances and combination of causes"?[66] In the absence of a comparative study of this phenomenon in other fields of Arab historiography, it would be hazardous to propose any explanation of general bearing, although the persistence of the concept of *'ibra* (lesson) in classical Muslim historiography would certainly have to be taken into account.[67] Whatever the general causes operating there, their influence on the historiography of the Crusades seems to have been greatly strengthened by the intense sensitivity to current problems prevalent in this field—a sensitivity which is surely in part intellectual but does not lack strong emotional components.

M. Bloch remarks in *The Historian's Craft* that "once an emotional chord has been struck, the limit between past and present is no longer regulated by a mathematically measurable chronology."[68] It is just this sort of interpenetration between past and present, and the emotional strain involved therein, which impinges upon the basic beliefs of Arab students of the Crusades. This interpenetration has, moreover, had a powerful effect—as we shall try to prove—upon the way in which these students actually treat the main problems of their research subject, particularly where major themes of Arab nationalism are at stake.

## THE "*JIHĀD* OF THE ARABS"

There is a consensus of opinion among Arab historians that the wars of the Crusades were waged on both sides *in the name* of religion. Yet, as we have noted above, with regard to the Western side they claim to have discovered a deeper level of meaning (or, if one may prefer, ulterior motives)—i.e., imperialism. Do they make similar distinctions between appearance (or propaganda) and true essence in their analysis of the war from the Eastern side? Pre-World War II scholars did not accept such a distinction. In accordance with their general historical scheme, they viewed the twelfth-thirteenth century *jihād* as a single unit; both externally and internally it was an Islamic war. Most historians writing in the last three decades, however, distinguish two levels of meaning therein, although the difference between the two is quite dissimilar to that noted on the Crusader's side. The intrinsic nature of the counter-Crusade is that of a war of Arabhood *('urāba)*. A cursory reading of almost any book will rapidly lead to the conclusion that the terms Islam and Arabhood are interchangeably or conjunctly used to describe the "Middle Eastern" camp, its territory, war aims, leaders, warriors, and so on. Some book titles stress the inner (and, therefore, the most important) meanings: *Saladin and Arab Nationalism* ('Īd), *Al-Manṣūra, the Story of Arab Heroism* (Haddāra), *Arabs, Byzantines and Franks in the First Crusade* (Yūsuf). Āshūr's *The Movement of the Crusades* bears the subtitle: "A Glorious Page in the History of the *Jihād* of the Arabs in the Middle Ages."[69]

Such a use would appear plausible, given on the one hand the fact it was the Arab-speaking countries of Eastern Islam—extending from Mesopotamia to Egypt—which were the theatre of the Crusading wars, and on the other hand, the prevailing tendency of contemporary Arab nationalism to equate Islam with Arabhood, the former being the creation of the latter, a phase in its development and the contents of its culture.

Nevertheless, in the case of the Crusades, there are two arguments against this equation; the first concerns only some of the post-1945 scholars, the other encompasses most of them.

1. As long as historians who hold the aforementioned nationalist doctrine state that any war carried out by Arab-speaking countries in the name of Islam is *ipso facto,* that is to say *objectively,* a war for Arabhood, there can be no argument regarding the historiographical tenets here implied. Some historians, however, go much further and claim that the *jihād* may be regarded even in a *subjective* sense as nationalist warfare; in other words, that the Middle Eastern opponents of the Crusaders were conscious of their being Arabs and fought against them *qua* Arabs. It is no coincidence perhaps that most of the students committed to this idea are also partisans of the pragmatic approach; in both cases they seem to be under the spell of the same process, the blurring of the boundaries between past and present. Ḥamza says that "Muslims hoped to chase the Crusaders away from their land, to purify it from the ignominy of their presence and to render it again wholly Arab."[70] 'Āshūr attributes Muslim final victory to the "national consciousness" of the Arab people and to the "Arabs' belief in their common aims."[71] Sa'dāwī, describing the wave

of protest and criticism against the Egyptian sultan al-Kāmil following his retrocession of Jerusalem to the Franks (1229), writes: "People considered this act to be high treason against Islam as well as against Arabhood."[72] Qalʿajī, in an attempt to clarify the relationship between these two levels of meaning, claims that the Arab *jihād* assumed an Islamic appearance only in order to counter the religious mantle in which the Crusade was clad.[73]

The application of terminology relating to ideas and concepts created by a later age, to concepts and ideas prevalent in a previous period, is, of course, of questionable validity, according to the standards of modern historiography. Those who do so lack (as was said of sixteenth- and seventeenth-century European historians) "an awareness of distance, of a general 'otherness' of earlier ages as regards not only circumstances but also mentality."[74] Many contemporary Arab historians of the Crusades, it is true, use the term "Arab" as an equivalent to "Muslim" only in the objective sense (in the same way that some Arab historians designate the Crusades as "imperialist"). Yet it is rather interesting to note that scarcely any of them ever refer to the use made of this term in a subjective sense by their colleagues, nor do they raise methodological doubts about it. The sole scholar to voice some reservations in this context is Aḥmad Aḥmad Badawī, in his *Literary Life in Egypt and Syria in the Age of the Crusades*, and even he does so in a very cautious and roundabout way.[75]

2. Far more complicated and of wider implications are the problems aroused by the fact that the countries invaded by the Crusades, although Arabic-speaking, were ruled during those centuries by politico-military elites of non-Arab stocks (mostly Turkish, but also Kurdish, Armenian, and so forth) and speaking non-Arabic languages. It was elites that conducted the Holy War against the Crusaders: Turkmen chiefs from the Jazīra (Ilghāzī, Bursūqī) launched the counterattack, the Turkish house of the Zengids and the Kurdish house of the Ayyūbids amplified its scope and conquered most of the territory of the Frankish principalities, and the Turkish Mamluks gave them the *coup de grâce*. Moreover, the armies that were at the disposal of these elites were drawn in the main from the same stock, spoke the same languages, and a good part of them were newcomers to the region. Is there, therefore, scientific warrant for speaking of a "Jihād of the Arabs"?

Contemporary Arab historians, obviously conscious of this problem and yet determined not to allow it to change their concept of the character of the war, usually try to obviate it in various ways. The great pains they take, and the various methods they resort to, testify eloquently as to how important it is for them that this holy war—and particularly a war with such contemporary connotations—be styled a national, i.e., Arab, war.

The first method employed aims at the "Arabization" of conspicuous sections of the elites, especially Saladin and his Ayyūbid successors. On the one hand, it appears that it was impossible to deny the foreign origin of *all* the leaders of the *jihād* (although two historians even try to Arabicize Zenki, Nūr al-Dīn, and Baybars).[76] On the other hand, following in the wake of Muslim historiography of the time of the Crusades and of popular tradition elaborated in the course of ages, modern Arab historians have always tended to minimize (quite unjustly) the role played by the Zengids, predecessors of Saladin.[77] They regard the latter as the real architect of Middle Eastern coalescence and moral regeneration as well as the anti-Frankish *jihād*. The dimensions of this hero-worship are thrown into relief by the fact that Saladin is the subject of twenty biographies, i.e., about one-quarter of the modern Arab historical output concerning the Crusades, and that substantial sections of all general surveys of the Crusades are dedicated to him. By proving the Arabhood of this sultan (and *ipso facto* of his house as well), the *jihād*, symbolized by his person and directed for four-score years by his dynasty, could be in some way "Arabicized."

The arguments in favor of this view by no means hinge on the ethnic factor, as even the most zealous nationalist historians allow that Saladin was of Kurdish origin. In accordance with the predominant concepts of Arab nationalism, emphasis is laid upon linguistic and cultural factors. The intensive activity of Saladin and the Ayyūbids as patrons of letters is evoked as major proof of their deep attachment to Arab culture; some scholars even contend (though without producing any definite evidence) that all of them were Arab-speaking.[78] The great sultan's renowned virtues—tolerance, bravery, gallantry, and the like—are attributed to "the Arab chivalry."[79] Badawī argues, in addition, that Saladin and his successors were so strongly stamped by Arab culture that they wished they had been of Arab stock, as one can judge from the fact that they pretended to be the descendants of the Umayyad Caliph Marwān II. Reflecting on this claim, another historian writes enthusiastically about the assimilatory power of Arabhood upon those who settled in its sphere of influence.[80]

Not many scholars have recourse to this method, but it is interesting to note that it is rarely criticized by their colleagues. The latter, if they belong to the "nationalist school," either note Saladin's origin casually, without trying to adapt it to their general theory, or omit mentioning it. The three post-1945 historians who openly oppose the "Arabization" of the Ayyūbids belong to that small group depicting the counter-Crusade in terms of religious consciousness, for whom the non-Arab origin of Saladin's dynasty presents no difficulty. Bayyūmī and Mājid refute the arguments of the "Ayyūbids' Arab descent" showing it to be the invention of some sycophants from among the jurists of that period, an invention flatly rejected by the great majority of the Ayyūbids, including Saladin.[81] Mājid further proves that the resistance of the Egyptians to the conquest of their country by the Kurdish general Shīrkūh and his nephew Saladin was motivated, at least in part, by a powerful ethnic antagonism towards the two commanders and their Turco-Kurdish army. Concurrent views are held by al-'Arīnī who points out the "strong Kurdish qualities and sentiments" predominating in Saladin's family and among his confidants, their consciousness of their origin, and their animosity towards non-Kurds.[82]

Most scholars of the "nationalist school" try to "Arabicize" the counter-Crusade by quite different means: magnification of the role played in the *jihād* by the Arab people, at the expense of the role attributed to the regular armies (*but not*—be it noted—*at the expense of the leaders,* or at least the most famous among them, Nūr al-Dīn, Saladin, Baybars). These attempts converge with, and receive a strong impetus from, that mounting tendency in contemporary Arab nationalist thought to regard the people as one of the principal forces shaping history, and the one assuring the continuity of Arab history through all the vicissitudes it has undergone. Some of the theoretical expositions of this concept (e.g., those of al-Dūrī and Lacheraf) try to apply it to the counter-Crusade, which they depict—though in vague terms and without the support of factual proof—as a "popular movement."[83]

In historical literature two versions of the "populist" interpretation are to be distinguished. The first asserts that it was really the people who carried the burden of the *jihād*. The role of local (i.e., Arab) volunteers, notably in the decisive campaigns of Saladin, is overemphasized.[84] Eulogizing accounts are given of the exploits of Arab emirs such as Usāma b. Munqidh (who, however, in the earlier part of his career, according to his own memoirs, collaborated with the Franks).[85] Historians make the most of the few episodes of general mobilization of civil population decreed when some large Islamic center was directly attacked (for example, in Cairo during the fifth and seventh Crusades). Special attention is paid to the battle of al-Manṣūra (1250), where Muslim victory (which saved Cairo from being conquered by St. Louis, King of France) is ascribed not to the Mamluk Baḥrī regiment, as all medieval chroniclers maintain unequivocally,[86] but to the Egyptian volunteers. The claim appears for the first time in 1949, in Ḥabashī's study of the Crusade of St. Louis,[87] yet it did not become widespread until after the Suez war. This was probably under the inspiration of the efforts exerted by official propaganda in order to extol the idea of popular Egyptian resistance to imperialistic invasions throughout history. One perceives this source of influence in Ḥusayn's *The Al-Manṣūra Campaign and the Victory of the People* (semiofficial edition), as well as in the bibliography of the Crusades published by the Ministry of Culture and National Guidance, which devoted special attention to this battle with the subtitle, "Prepared on the Occasion of the Celebration of the People's victory at Al-Manṣūra."[88]

The shift in emphasis in Egyptian historiography comes out most clearly when one compares the two editions of Colonel Zakī's study of this campaign. In the 1945 edition, the Mamluks alone are regarded as responsible for the victory, while the 1960 version exalts the contribution of *al-sha'b* (the people) in no less ardent a manner. The introduction to the latter edition is a word-by-word copy of the former; yet, when speaking of the great heroes of the *jihād* (Saladin, Baybars, and so on), the author adds the words "and all the other unknown soldiers, sons of the people, who have fallen as martyrs in the campaigns for the defense of the sacred fatherland."[89] One of the most exuberant nationalist historians goes even further and argues that the bulk of the Muslim army in the time of Saladin was composed of Arabs. In the absence of textual evidence he finds himself constrained to resort to a very curious *argumentum ex silentio*: "If some of the ancient historians do not mention the Arab element at all, this is due to the fact it was so self-evident that [the Arabs] constituted the great majority, that it sufficed to mention the rest in order that their [the Arabs'] role be thrown into relief. It has thus been established beyond any doubt that the backbone of Saladin's army consisted of Arabs from all over the Arab East."[90]

Again, one must note that those historians of the Crusades who do not ignore the preponderance of the non-Arabs in twelfth- and thirteenth-century armies,[91] still avoid any frontal attack on the populist thesis; if there is any controversy, it is implicit. It was a Syrian scholar specializing in later periods, 'Abd al-Karīm Gharāybeh, who undertook a systematic refutation of these views in a book of a much wider scope, *The Arabs and the Turks; a Study of the Development of Their Relations During One Thousand Years.* In his introduction, Gharāybeh claims to have been convinced of the urgent need for the composition of such a study by seven-years' experience as lecturer in the University of Damascus. His students generally thought that Arab-Turkish relations dated only from the Ottoman conquest and considered the Turkish contribution to Arab history to have been, on the whole, rather negative and the main cause for Arab backwardness and cultural decline; their ignorance was especially great regarding the part played by the Turks in the struggle against the Byzantines and the Franks.[92] Such views, one should remark, are by no means surprising; they only echo the widely-diffused ideas of modern Arab historiography (owing their origin, it seems, to the first Muslim Reformist thinkers),[93] which tend to belittle and disparage the role of the Turks in the history of Islam generally and of the Arab-speaking countries in particular. With regard to the Crusades, the students' ignorance bears the clear mark of the nationalist historians mentioned above. Combating these views, Gharāybeh stresses first and foremost the importance of Turkish soldiers, commanders, and princes in the defense of the Arab East as early as the pre-Ottoman era (from the ninth to the sixteenth century). One of their most prominent exploits in this respect was, as the author seeks to establish with the aid of rich evidence, the decisive part they played in driving away the Franks.[94] Gharāybeh considers himself a sincere Arab nationalist, yet he sees no contradiction between this conviction and his general historical theory. Nationalism, for him, does not mean exclusiveness and does not dictate refusal to admit the interpenetration of Arab history with that of other nations and the debt the former has incurred towards the latter.[95]

The second version of the "populist" interpretation lays emphasis upon the moral rather than upon the military aspect. The thesis proposed is that it was public opinion which intervened at certain times of crisis—exerting heavy pressure on the princes to take part in the Holy War and promoting active resistance to rulers who collaborated with the Franks—and turned the scale in favor of the movement for unity and *jihād*. Saʻdāwī cites as proof of the existence of what he calls "a popular liberation front" the case of the delegation sent from Aleppo to Baghdad (1110) in order to arouse the people against the Caliph's indifference toward the Crusades.[96] ʻĀshūr mentions other instances: the opposition of the inhabitants of Damascus to their pro-Frankish Atabeks and their covert support, and ultimately open welcome, of their city's annexation by the prince of Aleppo and leader of the *jihād*, Nūr al-Dīn (1148-1154); the choir of protest raised all over the Middle East against the surrender of Jerusalem (1229); the protest and resistance in Damascus to the pact signed with the Latin Kingdom by al-Ṣāliḥ Ismāʻīl, ruler of that city (1240).[97] Yūsuf holds that it was popular indignation that brought about the breakdown of the peace negotiations between St. Louis and the Mamluks (1250-1253).[98] Except for this last case, all the instances singled out above are factually true; yet, the decisive character attributed to them is contestable and the sweeping generalization drawn, on the basis of this assumption, with regard to the character of the whole counter-Crusade seems most doubtful.

A somewhat mitigated form of this version is advanced by ʻAbd al-Laṭīf Ḥamza. He attributes to public opinion not so much an active and direct role as an indirect one: it was public opinion, he asserts, which created a moral atmosphere propitious to the rise and subsequent strengthening of the *jihād* movement. In order to prove the existence of this atmosphere, he draws mainly upon twelfth- and thirteenth-century poetry, which abounds in patriotic and combative verses. Unlike works in rhymed prose (letters, patriotic epistles, and so forth), which are nothing but official propaganda, the poetry, claims Ḥamza, "expresses the feelings of the people."[99] This theory was severely criticized by another historian of the literature of that period, Aḥmad Aḥmad Badawī. He pointed out that almost all the poets lived in the courts of the princes or benefited from their patronage, and that very many of the poems of *jihād* took the form of panegyrics (*madīḥ*) or were composed according to explicit instructions of the poets' patrons and served the latter's immediate political purposes. Their style was no more comprehensible to the masses than that of the profuse and elaborate sentences of the official *rasāʼil*. A real expression of the feelings of these masses, says Badawī, should have been looked for in popular literature (written partly in colloquial Arabic), of which, unfortunately, only few works are extant.[100] These sound methodological doubts were expressed in 1954. Six years later, however, in his study of the poetry of the age of Saladin, Badawī seems to have completely ignored them. It is impossible to ascertain whether he was convinced by his colleagues or felt himself bound to retract from his former views because his second book was published under the auspices of the Egyptian Ministry of Cultural and National Guidance. The salient theme of this book is that "the poets represent to us truthfully the people's sentiments towards Saladin, and many of their *qaṣā'id* were on everyone's lips."[101] He therefore regards the portrait of the sultan, which he draws on the basis of these poems, not as an official image created by propagandists, as he would have asserted in 1954, but as a popular and spontaneous image.

## THE HISTORIC ROLE OF EGYPT

The pioneers of the study of the Crusades were mostly Syrian Christians, but by the 1920s and early 1930s the majority of students of this period were Egyptian Muslims, and their relative weight continued to increase. It was natural for Muslims, whose civilization was the victim of the Crusades, to display keen interest in them, but Egyptian interest is somewhat difficult to explain. The theatre of the Crusades was unmistakably Syria and Palestine: it was there that most expeditions landed, that all the Frankish states were established, and nearly all the stages of the *jihād* took place.The sheer preponderance of Egyptian literary output in the Arab world can by no means account in itself for the fact that more than four-fifths of all the studies of the Crusades have been published in Egypt and that Egyptian books dealing with Islamic and general history devote so much space to the anti-Frankish wars. It is certain that antagonism toward the West has something to do with the development of Egyptian interest in the Crusades, but it would be difficult to prove that this antagonism is much stronger in Egypt than in Syria, for instance.[102]

It appears that a satisfying explanation can be arrived at by approaching the problem from another angle, namely that of studying the reasons, both manifest and covert, which in each case induced a particular Egyptian writer, as Egyptian, to interest himself in the period of the Crusades. In the 1920s and early 1930s, one finds, above all, the belief that this period (or rather, some parts of it, notably the reign of Saldin) constitutes a critical phase in the development of Egypt as a distinct and independent entity.

Abū Ḥadīd (1927) says that he chose Saladin for the object of his study

> since he is the founder of a mighty Egyptian state which may be considered the first great state established in Egypt whose Egyptianhood is wholly certain. None of its predecessors was purely Egyptian. The states of the Ṭūlūnids and the Ikhshīdids were not real states but mere experiments [in this direction]. The Fāṭimid state did not constitute a national state in the full sense of the word. The Fāṭimids had founded their original principality in the Maghrib and only afterwards did they conquer Egypt. Having made Egypt the center of their state, their Shī'ism impeded them from being totally fused with the native Egyptians in order to create a national state.[103]

'Inān, in an article published in 1926, claims that this "Egyptian revival" in the age of Saladin was the challenge which brought about the Third Crusade. Three years later, in his chapter on the Seventh Crusade in *Decisive Moments in the History of Islam,* he stresses that "Egypt was the target of many a Crusading campaign. Its armies repelled the invaders faster and in a more violent manner than any other Muslim army."[104] Similar views imply that the only Crusades worthy of study are those which threatened the independence or integrity of Egyptian territory, or which (like the Third) were closely related to the evolution of the Egyptian state. In history books written in these years there is an evident lack of interest in the larger Middle Eastern context within which the Crusades operated, as well as in the role that Egypt was called upon to fulfill in the struggle of the region against the Franks. A most revealing expression of this state of mind, which is obviously inspired by the "pharaonic" tendency prevalent in Egyptian nationalism of that era, is to be found in the first biography of Saladin, composed in 1920 by Baylī. Commenting upon the Sultan's decison to put an end to the attempts to conquer the Sudan (1172-3), Baylī writes that it would have been much better, if, instead of devoting his energies to the war against the Franks in Syria and Palestine, Saladin had conquered the Sudan, that natural extension of Egypt, "thus creating a powerful Empire reaching from the sources of the Nile to the Mediterranean.[105]

As a result of the change in the orientation and content of Egyptian national consciousness, which occurred from the late 1930s onward, scholars began to view the Crusades within a much wider frame of reference—that of the history of the Arab world, of which Egypt came to be considered a part. Her role appeared to them more important than that of any other Arab country. Consequently, the Crusades are depicted as one of the major embodiments of the historic role of Egypt, destined, by virtue of its geopolitical position, large population, and natural resources (to mention material factors only) to be the leader of the entire Arab East. Some of the early Arabhood-oriented Egyptian thinkers, e.g., Mirrīt Ghālī,[106] who created the concept of *al-risāla al-miṣriyya* as a link between Egyptianhood and Arabhood, already cited the Crusades in support of their theory. Yet the elaboration of this new conception of the Crusades was mainly the work of historians. Mu'nis conceded that most of the actual fighting occasioned by the Crusades took place in Syria, but he alleged that Egypt supplied the main part of the war effort, particularly from the financial and logistic point of view but also with regard to manpower.[107] Surūr (1938), a biographer of the Mamluk Sultan Baybars, described the latter's reign as that in which Egypt, having completed the conquest of the Frankish states and driven the Mongols away, became the power center of the whole region. The services she rendered to the neighboring countries even justified their coming under her direct control; Surūr considers the annexation of Syria by the Mamluks, for instance, as a prerequisite for the struggle against the Mongols and the Crusaders.[108]

These themes gained ground steadily during the 1940s and early 1950s, bringing with them a rise in Egyptian interest in the Crusades. In 1942, and later in 1948, Muḥammad Muṣṭafā Ziyāda spoke of the historical role allotted to Egypt to be the "axis of the defensive and the offensive campaigns against the Crusades," uniting around it, for that purpose, the whole Middle East.[109] Ḥabashī writes in his study of St. Louis (1949) that this country "took upon herself in the Middle Ages the task of saving the Arab East from the peril of European imperialism."[110] Time and time again he claims in his study—and this claim is severely criticized by Qusṭanṭīn Zurayq—that had Egypt failed, "the first line of defense of all the Arab states would have been broken and all the Fertile Crescent might have become a French colony to this very day."[111] This image of Egypt's pivotal role in the counter-Crusade and of her subsequent claim to Arab leadership has in later years received semiofficial and then official sanction, reflected in Nasser's *Philosophy of the Revolution* (1954), Mu'nis' *Egypt and Her Mission* (1955), and finally the National Pact of 1962.[112] It has also become omnipresent in historical literature published in this country.[113] One could hardly imagine a more propitious climate for the study of the Crusades. Several scholars even go so far as to contend that from its very beginning (or, at least, from the moment it landed in the Levant) the Crusade had for its primary aim the conquest of Egypt, "the key to the East."[114]

While these last assertions are clearly far-flung and groundless, the Egyptian-centered theory is borne out, to a great extent, by historical evidence. It is certain that but for the harnessing of Egyptian economic resources, the *jihād* could not have been carried on as a long drawn-out contest of endurance on a Middle Eastern scale. The supreme command during the major stages of the struggle was held by rulers based in Egypt (though not necessarily Egyptian-born), and the Egyptian regular army constituted an important part (sometimes even the majority) of the *mujāhidūn*. Though Egypt was attacked much less frequently than Syria and was much less seriously damaged, it is certain that the fact that she withstood these attacks (particularly in 1218-21 and 1249-50) dealt a heavy blow to the Frankish states and helped to produce in Europe a widespread disenchantment with the whole idea of Eastern-bound military expeditions.

It behooves us, however, to state three principal reservations, which, without calling in question the essential veracity of this theory, should have impelled historians to modify the generalizations in some way:

1. Egypt's effort in terms of manpower will appear much smaller if we remember that its army was composed almost entirely of imported Mamluks.

2. Egypt was a latecomer to the anti-Frankish *jihād*. During the First Crusade, its Fāṭimid caliphs abstained from aiding their co-religionists, the Seljūqid rulers of Syria, and availed themselves of the furious combats waged in northern Syria in order to recapture Jerusalem from a vassal of the Seljūqids in 1098 (only to lose it one year later to the Crusaders). The Fāṭimids even tried (without success) to propose to the European invaders a *modus vivendi* based upon a partition of Seljūqid territories in Syria-Palestine. During the following decades, Egyptian indifference and ineffective aid were largely to blame for the Frankish conquest of the Palestinian ports, which were under the Fāṭimid protectorate (1100-24), and finally, for the loss of the "strip of Ascalon" governed directly by Egypt (1154). It was only as a result of the expeditions of Amalric, King of Jerusalem, against Egypt (1164-68), the subsequent conquest of this country by Shīrkūh and Saladin (1169), and the fall of the Fāṭimids (1171) that Egypt began to play an active role in the counter-Crusade.

3. Yet another period that would be difficult to interpret in the light of the theory of a "persistant Egyptian *jihād*" is that of the Ayyūbids (1193-1250). The successors of Saladin, greatly enfeebled by the Sultan's wars against the Latins and by the fragmentation of his empire after his death and the ensuing dissensions among its different parts, strove for a non-military solution of the Frankish question. Their chief aim (which was not attained because of the arrival of new Crusaders) was to establish peaceful coexistence with the Frankish states on the basis of the status quo. In their eagerness to ensure the continuation of peace and of the economic (especially commercial) benefits they reaped, they were sometimes disposed to make substantial territorial concessions to the Franks (parts of Galilee, Jerusalem, and so on). Although this policy was practiced by all the heads of the Ayyūbid states, the largest share of the responsibility for it should be assigned to the Egyptian sultans as the moral as well as political leaders of the Ayyūbid "federation." Particularly responsible were al-'Ādil (1200-18), who inaugurated the policy of coexistence, and al-Kāmil (1218-37), whose treaty of Jaffa constitutes perhaps the peak of these efforts.

How do Egyptian historians cope with these difficulties? The remarks made in the previous chapter are valid, on the whole, with regard to the first problem. We shall deal, accordingly, only with the other two problems. Not all historians, of course, dealt with them. Much of the scholarly effort is concentrated, as we have already noted, upon the semi-legendary figure of Saladin; one should further exclude the studies dealing with Crusading campaigns fought on Egyptian soil, notably that of St. Louis (ten monographs). Nearly all other studies, comprising more than one half of the whole Egyptian output concerning the Crusades, as well as general surveys of the Fāṭimid and Ayyūbid periods, inevitably face the task of reconciling theory with reality.

Egyptian historians are generally more prone to find fault with the Fāṭimids than with the Ayyūbids. This is due, in part, to the fact that the Fāṭimids were Shī'īs and hence constituted a deviation from the deep attachment to Islamic orthodoxy considered one of the essential traits of the "Egyptian personality." On the other hand, in comparison with the golden age of Saladin which followed it, Fāṭimid rule (especially in the twelfth century) appears decadent and disorderly. One historian even likens it to the pre-1952 monarchic regime.[115] The Ayyūbids, on the contrary, benefit from the military halo investing Saladin, the founder of their dynasty, while the intense literary activity which Egypt witnessed under their rule makes them resemble in some manner the great Caliphs-maecenes of the early 'Abbāsid age.

Nevertheless, most of the historians here discussed seem averse to condemning the Fāṭimids for their role in the counter-Crusade.[116] Many of the facts we have expounded above (and in particular the conquest of Jerusalem, the inadequate aid given to the ports, and the neglect of Ascalon) are suppressed. The facts, when conceded, are usually reinterpreted so as to appear in a more favorable light. Thus the 1098 negotiations are explained as Egyptian misunderstanding of the Crusaders' aims, because of deliberately misleading Frankish declarations.[117] On the other hand, in order to counterbalance these still inconvenient points, excessive importance is accorded to the isolated feats of arms accomplished by the Fāṭimids in Palestine: the raids of the vizier al-Afḍal (1100-1105) and others more restricted in scope of the vizier Ṭalā'i' b. Ruzzīk (1118-60), yet magnified by sycophantic court poets.[118]

As could be expected, the treatment accorded to the Ayyūbids is even milder. Rare are the scholars who concur with Ziyāda's clear-cut statement: "[al-'Ādil] made a *volte-face*, changing from top to bottom the political line laid down by Saladin. In order to save Egypt from imminent crusades, he and his successors intended to ensure peace at whatever cost."[119] Most scholars, while they readily admit the misdeeds of the Syrian Ayyūbids (for example, their collaboration with the Franks in 1239-40), never attribute like actions or intentions to the Egyptian sultans. Al-'Ādil is described as a staunch *mujāhid* (although, as one writer allows, "his reign did not see any gigantic campaign in the manner of his brother, Saladin);"[120] al-Kāmil is, for them, first and foremost the defender of Dimyāṭ against the Fifth Crusade. His pact with Frederick II is not ignored, but they try to justify it (or plead extenuating circumstances for it) by pointing out the exceptional personality of the German Emperor: a reluctant Crusader, a tolerant and liberal-minded ruler, and an admirer of Islam.[121] One can barely find a mention of the fact that it was really al-Kāmil who invited Frederick to the Levant as an ally in the struggle against his brothers, the sultans of Syria and Mesopotamia. Just as in the case of the Fāṭimids, the writers throw into relief the actual campaigns of the Ayyūbids (against the Fifth and Seventh crusades), campaigns of undeniable importance but which, in the final analysis, were forced upon the rulers of Egypt and were by no means due to any change of policy on their part.

## THE REPERCUSSIONS

So much for the way Arab historians view the causes, nature, and evolution of Crusade and counter-Crusade. How do they conceive the short- and long-range repercussions of this historical phenomenon?

Common to most of them is the belief that of the two belligerents, it was the West which gained greater benefits. Using a play on words, the Tunisian historian Maṭawī puts this concept succinctly: "All the profit *(ghunm)* of these wars fell to the lot of the Crusaders, all the damage *(ghurm)* was the share of the Muslims."[122] Although Arab historians do not make any distinction, the *ghunm* they speak of consists actually of two distinct categories.[123] In the first place, it is asserted, the Crusades served to convey to Europe ideas, institutions, and material assets of Islamic civilization. Much of Western knowledge of Greco-Muslim philosophy, natural sciences, mathematics, and medicine is due to the contacts established in Frankish Syria. The European institution of chivalry owes much to the *furūsiyya* and particularly to the influence of those paragons of chivalry who commanded the counter-Crusade (Saladin, al-Kāmil, Usāma). Many aspects of Western military architecture and the art of war gained from the experience accumulated during two centuries of war in the Levant. Returning Crusaders and Frankish merchants disseminated Eastern products, foods, plants, and the like in the West and introduced many Arab loan-words still extant in European (mainly Romance) languages. In the second place, Arab scholars attribute nearly all the developments which Europe underwent in the late Middle Ages to the impact of the movement of the Crusades, regarded as a catalytic *internal* factor in European society, a factor which simultaneously was born from this society and reacted vigorously upon it. The principal developments mentioned in this context are: decrease in the power and prestige of Church and Papacy, rise of religious scepticism and heresy (and, ultimately, appearance of the Reformation), breakdown of feudalism in all its aspects (economic, political, social), growth of urbanization and manufacturing, widening of international trade, and creation of a money-economy.[124]

The views outlined above are by no means peculiar to Arab historiography. As a matter of fact, they are mainly inspired by an important trend in European historiography in the late nineteenth and early twentieth century, whose leading protagonists were L. A. Sédillot, H. Prutz, G. Jacob, and, on a more popular level, G. Lebon.[125]

These scholars tended to emphasize the cultural supremacy enjoyed by the Muslim world in the Middle Ages as well as the immense debt the West incurred towards it. The Crusades figured in this concept as one of the major (if not the most important) channels of Eastern influence upon Europe. These opinions were readily borrowed by the modern Islamic Apologetic School, which was intent on enhancing the Muslim pride in their past and uprooting the inferiority complex created as a result of their encounter with the modern West.[126] It is in part through the medium of these Muslim thinkers, and in part directly from the European historians (especially from Lebon and Jacob),[127] but under the inspiration of the tenets of the Apologetic school, that Arab students of the Crusades, from al-Ḥarīrī and Baylī to the present day, have drawn their views of the repercussions of this movement in the continent which gave it birth.

During the last half-century, however, Western historiography has revised its opinion on this subject as a result of a clearer understanding of the Middle Ages as well as of more detailed and specific studies of the Crusades. The second category of the presumed influence is now totally discarded. It has been proved that it was founded upon nothing except what one scholar pertinently calls "the fallacy of *post hoc ergo propter hoc*";[128] i.e., upon the assumption that simply because certain developments occur subsequent to the Crusades the latter may be considered as one of their causes, if not as their single cause. On the whole, the role the Crusades played in the evolution of Europe is shown to have been rather circumscribed and subsidiary, and in some respects even marginal. Their only major contribution seems to have been in the field of Levantine commerce, which they greatly expanded but by no means created. The progress of European research has led concurrently to a reevaluation of Islam's direct influence. It is now generally admitted that the intellectual legacy of Islam passed to Europe through Sicily and Spain, their cosmopolitan courts and schools of translators, and not through the Frankish colonies, whose intellectual activity was, in all spheres, almost nonexistent.[129] Crusaders and Levant traders helped, to be sure, in making Islamic material culture known to Europe, but scholars are nowadays much more conscious of the difficulties involved in ascribing specific contributions to this channel rather than to one of the others (Spain, Sicily, Byzantium, northwest Africa).

These revised beliefs can be found in the European historical literature of the past quarter of a century, yet the great bulk of Arab historiography goes on repeating the old-fashioned thesis. This fact is rather astonishing, since post-1945 Arab specialists on the Crusades generally have been receptive to the research of their Western counterparts and since one of the best accounts of the new theory—E. Barker's article "The Crusades" in *The Legacy of Islam*—was long-ago translated into Arabic.[130] It seems that the reason for this phenomenon is to be found in the persistence of that didactic and apologetic tendency which induced Arab thinkers and historians, especially between the two world wars, to accept the theories of Prutz, Lebon, and Jacob so enthusiastically. It is quite obvious that the new discoveries of European historians could not serve these apologetic ends, or at any rate would do so much less efficaciously.

The attachment Arab historians felt to the old thesis was all the more powerful since the Crusades are considered the counterpart (and prior stage) of modern imperialism. Modern Western civilization is superior, in many respects, such as in technology, to that of the Arab Middle East. Its penetration into this region was in many ways beneficial to the Arabs (although the latter could legitimately argue that the price exacted for them was exorbitant). The importance Arab writers attribute nowadays to the question of the "balance of profits" of modern imperialism and their uneasiness about it explain why their preferences go to a theory describing the balance of medieval imperialism as wholly in favor of the West. The West, it is claimed, had nothing to teach and much to learn, since it had hardly emerged from the Dark Ages when it met a ripe and sophisticated Islam during the Crusades. This theory has provided its Arab partisans with what a psychologist might term "compensatory gratification," offsetting the inferiorities and insufficiencies of the present by the glories of the past. "Is it possible to imagine," asks Maṭawī, "any substantial advantage that the Islamic world has drawn from the Crusades? Indeed, how could Islam benefit from contacts established with an inferior, backward civilization?"[131] What he and his like were bound to overlook in their quest for compensatory gratification was, of course, that the difference in cultural level, which did in fact really exist, did not necessarily mean that the Crusaders *necessarily* learned from the Muslims. The starting point of modern European research was precisely this consideration, which was subsequently put to a meticulous empirical test.

The same test was also applied to the problem of the dimensions of the above-mentioned "cultural gap," which was found to be much smaller than they had been assumed to be. It was only natural that the conclusions arrived at by European scholars were not to the liking of many Arab historians. What was to be deplored is that the latter chose to ignore these conclusions totally and did not even try to refute them in the sole way appropriate for the purpose, that is to say, empirically. Instead, they go on shielding themselves behind general expositions regarding the "cultural gap" and cursory lists of Islamic contributions to European civilization, none of which are expressly proved to have been due to the Crusades.[132] The handful of historians who do mention the new European thesis dismiss it summarily. Their arguments reveal quite clearly the emotionally charged preconceptions that underly their reluctance to accept the thesis as well as their aversion to (or fear of) dealing with it in the proper scientific manner. Naqqāsh, for example, maintains categorically that the divergencies between the views expounded by Barker and those of Prutz and Lebon stem from differing views as to the value of Islamic civilization. While the latter "tend to appraise it according to its real merit," Barker and his followers "are disposed to underestimate it." The detailed arguments put forward in Barker's article are further discarded as "a manifestation of a biased attitude."[133]

Not all Arab scholars share these "maximalist" opinions about the repercussions of the Crusades. Hitti, 'Inān, Sa'dāwī, and 'Āshūr display serious doubts about the Crusaders' role in the transmission of the Greco-Islamic intellectual legacy.[134] Hitti even probes the deep-lying causes for the absence of fertilizing intellectual contact and concludes that "linguistic and religious barriers together with a general climate of mutual hostility militated against exchange."[135] Tamīmī and 'Aṭīya speak in prudent and qualified terms about the impact of the Crusades on socioeconomic evolution in Europe.[136] The writings of these historians are unfortunately not quite exempt from an apologetic vein. Circumspect and skeptical as his attitude may be, Hitti nevertheless terminates his article, "The East's Contribution to the Civilization of the West in the Middle Ages," with this ringing phrase: "The Crusades constituted for Europe a sort of school where her inhabitants progressed gradually from the state of infancy to the state of manhood."[137] Sa'dāwī, who assigns to the Crusades a most limited role in the evolution of European culture, winds up his discussion of the subject with a wholly irrelevant quotation from G. Lebon, in which the French writer lauds in most general terms "the scientific and literary influence of the Arabs . . . which contributed to the development of Europe and helped eventually to bring about the

Renaissance."[138] This he labels "a just evaluation of the Arabs and their civilization."

The passive side of the "balance of profits" of the Crusades consists, according to Arab historians, in the major role they played in the process of the decline of Islamic civilization. Kurd 'Alī puts this idea rather bluntly: "From the Frankish point of view, one of the principal benefits they derived from the Crusades was the obstruction of Muslim progress."[139] How did the Europeans succeed in dealing such a heavy blow to their opponents? Kurd 'Alī as well as the later exponents of this view respond by pointing out the vast destruction the Franks left in their wake wherever they ruled or fought as well as the sapping of the material resources of Muslim countries by the long, bitter, and costly counter-Crusade.[140] One must note, however, that this question attracts only slight interest among Arab scholars, who treat it concisely and perfunctorily, wishing only, so it seems, to complement with its help the black-and-white picture of "medieval imperialism." They obviously prefer to focus their concern upon the brighter pages of the history they relate.[141] Suffice it, therefore, to outline here the main shortcomings of the thesis they put forward:

1. Even assuming that the factual basis of the thesis is both exact and complete, it touches only on the material aspect of Muslim decline. One has still to indicate by what mechanism the material losses reacted upon other aspects of the process of decline, such as the political and social, and most particularly, upon those aspects considered as primary by Muslim historiography: the moral, religious, and cultural.

2. As for the facts themselves, one might pose the question whether in comparison with the havoc wrought by the Mongols the damages due to the Franks do not seem but a marginal factor in accelerating economic decline. And were not the damages partially offset by the profits gained from the expansion of the Levant trade, whose principal ports were Alexandria and Dimyāṭ (and not Frankish-dominated Acre and Tyre)? On the other hand, how do scholars reconcile the presumed decline with their own affirmation of Muslim coalescence, renewed military vigor, and literary efflorescence in the age of the Crusades, and may not these latter phenomena have something to do with the Frankish challenge thrust upon Islam?

None of the scholars here discussed even tries to answer these questions, in however sketchy a way. The few historians who concede some of the facts mentioned above simply juxtapose them with the "decline thesis," failing (or feigning to fail) to notice their incompatibility with it.

The only serious attempt to arrive at a synthesis of all the disparate elements and produce a deeper, more balanced and more comprehensive interpretation of Muslim decline and of the Crusades' role in it, is made by Nabīh Amīn Fāris in an article entitled "The Arab Civilization in the Twelfth Century."[142] The writer, who based his arguments upon careful analysis of rich source material, revolts against the tendency to "externalization of guilt" characteristic of Arab specialists on the later Middle Ages, as well as against concepts dating the inception of the process to the twelfth century. Fāris defines Muslim decline as "that drying-up of the creative forces of Arab society," mainly in the cultural sphere, and traces its origin back to the growing restriction of freedom of thought during the ninth to eleventh centuries: persecution of the Mu'tazila by al-Mutawakkil, definitive formulation of Muslim dogma by al-Ash'arī, anti-Shīite decrees of the caliphs. These internal developments were soon followed by others: decline of creativity in the economic sphere and breaking up of the unity of the Islamic body politic as a result of the exacerbating Sunnite-Shīite struggle and of ethical (Arab-Turkish), regional, and social discords. The Crusades found in the East an already declining civilization which was just at this time severely assailed from within by the Ismā'īlis.

The effect of the Crusades upon this civilization was in two diametrically opposed directions; it was, in Fāris' terms, a benefit (*minḥa*) as well as a misfortune (*miḥna*). On the one side, the Crusades "shook Arab society for some time out of its stagnation"; commerce was given a strong momentum and in its turn stimulated agriculture and manufacture; the kaleidoscope of small principalities was forced to reunite against the Christian foe, and cultural activity attained renewed vigor (at last quantitatively), largely aided by the new masters of the Islamic Middle East. On the other hand, the twofold effort against Franks and Ismā'īlis alike contributed in the long run to the definitive petrification of Muslim culture. Seeking to fortify itself against those attacks, Islamic society considered it incumbent "to follow in the tracks of the Worthy Ancestors (*al-salaf al-ṣāliḥ*) . . . making emulation a strict duty and originality an error." Fāris points out that cultural activity in the age of the Crusades, for all its intensity, consists mostly of works which are either compilations or the exact reproduction of literary patterns consecrated by age-long usage. If the effort to preserve Islamic civilization proved successful, the price paid for it was heavy, not so much in human lives and material losses as in the exhaustion of the little energy left in this declining civilization. "Progress means being in perpetual movement," asserts Fāris; bringing itself to a standstill in order to weather the storm, Islamic civilization inevitably regressed.

## AN INTELLECTUAL REPORT?

J. Huizinga defined history as "the intellectual form in which a civilization renders account to itself of its past."[143] Arab historiography of the Crusades hardly conforms to this definition. The account it renders is essentially an emotional one. Emotion here serves not only as legitimate drive, directing the historian's interest toward a particular problem or period. It exceeds this role by far and imposes upon the historian the manner in which he is to proceed in treating his subject and even the conclusions he will arrive at. All the phenomena singled out in the present article: the conscious or unconscious methods of evasion and distortion, the rough-hewing of the past into preconceived patterns, the superficial explanations and pseudo-scientific arguments—all of them stem from the unintellectual approach characterizing the bulk of the scholarly effort concerning the Crusades. These phenomena are not peculiar, of course, to this branch of Arab historiography. European and Arab writers have noted in other branches as well that lack of sane and rational methodology, of unflinching devotion to truth, of readiness to accept all verified facts and the conclusions these facts will inexorably lead to, and, finally, of self-consciousness about the pitfalls of subjectivity lurking everywhere for the historian as for all imperfect mortals.[144]

The situation seems, however, to be particularly grave in the case of the historiography of the Crusades, because of the acuteness with which the relevancy of this period to current problems (most of which contain powerful emotional charges) is felt. And yet it is precisely this acuteness which renders an intellectual approach to the history of the Crusades all the more desirable. Such an approach could possibly, to use Von Grunebaum's words, "strike historical situations, which examination of the sources . . . has proven unsuited for the purpose, from the dossier of arguments marshalled in support of one's aspirations."[145] Some promising progress toward this goal has already been made. The studies of Fāris, Bayyūmī, and 'Arīnī, as well as the socioeconomic monographs of Rabie and El-Beheiri,[146] bear the stamp of scrupulous intellectual approach. Otherwise, Arab historiography of the Crusades might only serve to corroborate Paul Valéry's famous diatribe against the study of history:

History is the most dangerous product ever concocted by the chemistry of the intellect. Its properties are well known. It causes dreams, inebriates nations, saddles them with false memories, exaggerates their reflects, keeps their old sores running, torments them when they are not at rest, and induces in them megalomania and the mania of persecution. It makes them bitter, arrogant, and full of vanity.[147]

## FOOTNOTES

1. F. Gabrieli, "The Arabic Historiography of the Crusades," in B. Lewis and P. M. Holt (eds.), *Historians of the Middle East,* London, 1962, p. 98.
2. Cf. *EI,* new edition, Vol. 2, p. 64.
3. M. Monrond, *Ta'rīkh al-Ḥurūb al-Muqaddasa fī-l-Mashriq al-Mad'uwwa Ḥarb al-Salīb,* trans. by Muḥammad Maẓlūm, Jerusalem, 1865.
4. Jirī Yannī, *Ta'rīkh Sūriya*, Beirut, 1881, pp. 673-82.
5. Yūsuf al-Dibs, *Ta'rīkh Sūriya,* vol. 6, Beirut, 1901, pp. 1-309.
6. 'Alī al-Ḥarīrī, *Al-Akhbār al-Saniyya fi-l-Ḥurūb al-Ṣalībiyya,* Cairo, 1899. The only non-Muslim source utilized by the author was Maẓlūm's translation of Monrond (see note 3 above).
7. We have not taken into account historical romances nor brief notices concerning sources of the period or Crusader castles (which appeared mainly in *Majallat Ma'had al-'Ilm al-'Arabī* of Damascus). For further bibliographical details, see note 8.
8. There exist two bibliographies of Arab studies of the Crusades: The one published by the Ministry of Culture and National Guidance of the U.A.R. (*Nashra bi-Marāji' 'an al-Ḥurūb al-Ṣalībiyya wa-Ḥamlat Lūwīs al-tāsi' wa-Ma 'rakat al-Manṣūra,* Cairo, 1960) is superficial and insufficient. An excellent bibliographical list is to be found in the appendix to Qusṭī Zurayq's article (see note 9) in *al-Abhāth,* Vol. 12, 1959, pp. 286-92.
9. Zurayq's article, "Mā sāhama bihi al-mu'arrikhūn al-'arab fi-l-mi'a al-sana al-akhīra fī dirāsat al-ta'rikh al-'arabī 'an fatrat al-ḥurūb al-ṣalībiyya," *al-Abḥāth,* Vol. 12, 1959, pp. 232-59 is only a bibliographic survey, although scattered throughout are most judicious remarks about the general characteristics of this branch of historiography.
10. a) *Translations of Western Studies:* E. Barker, "Al-Ḥurūb al-Ṣalībiyya," trans. 'Īsā, in *Turāth al-Islām* (*Legacy of Islam,* ed. T. Arnold and A. Guillaume, Oxford, 1931) Cairo, 1939; idem, *Al-Ḥurūb al-Ṣalībiyya* (another study, originally published as an article in the *Encyclopedia Britannica* and then by Oxford University Press, London, 1923) trans. by Sayyid al-'Arīnī, Cairo, 1960.
    b) *Translations of Western Sources:* Ḥasan Ḥabashī translated the anonymous *Gesta Francorum* (first edition, Cairo, 1947); and Robert de Claris', *La conquête de Constantinople (Fatḥ al-Qusṭanṭīna 'Alā yad al-Ṣalībiyyīn*, Cairo, 1964).
11. G. Barraclough, *History in a Changing World,* Oxford, 1957, p. 63.
12. The same feeling of relevancy applies to other periods as well. See e.g., Nabīh

Amīn Fāris, "Taṭawwur Kitābat al-Ta'rīkh 'Inda-l-Arab al-Muḥdathūn," *al-Abḥāth,* Vol. 16, 1963, p. 403.

13. Al-Ḥarīrī, p. 6.
14. Aḥmad Baylī, *Ḥayāt Ṣalāḥ al-Dīn al-Ayyūbī,* Cairo, 1920, p. 3.
15. Muḥammad 'Abdallāh 'Inān, *Ma'ārik Ḥāsima fī Ta'rikh al-Islām,* second edition, Cairo, 1934, p. 98.
16. Rafīq Tamīmī, *al-Ḥurūb al-Ṣalībiyya*, Jerusalem, 1945, p. 103. It is interesting to note that his article, "al-Ḥurūb al-Ṣalībiyya," published four years earlier in *al-Risāla*, Vol. 9, 1941, pp. 1035-8, 1066-9, contains no such allusions.
17. Wadī' Talḥūq, *Al-Ṣalībiyya al-Jadīda fī Filasṭīn,* Damascus, 1948, p. 1. The date of composition is indicated by the author's analysis of the political situation (ibid., pp. 158-63). The book is dedicated to the "fighters of the third Arab conquest who hasten . . . to liberate the First *qibla* and the Third Sanctuary" (i.e., Jerusalem).
18. 'Abd al Laṭīf Ḥamza, *Adab al-Ḥurūb al-Ṣalībiyya,* Cairo, 1949, pp. 3-4.
19. Jūzīf Yūsuf, *Lūwīs al-Tāsi' Sharq al-Awsaṭ, qaḍiyyat Filasṭin, fī'l-'uṣūr al-wusṭā*, Cairo, 1956. Cf. also idem, *al-'Arab wa'l-Rūm wa'l-Lātīn fi'l-Ḥarb al-Ṣalībiyya al-'Ūlā,* Cairo, 1963, pp. 247-8.
20. 'Izz al-Dīn b. Shaddād, *al-A'lāk al-khaṭīra—ta'rīkh Lubnān wa'-l-Urdunn wa-Filasṭīn,* Damascus, 1963.
21. Naẓīr Sa'dāwī, *Jaysh Miṣr fī Ayyām Ṣalāḥ al-Dīn,* second edition, Cairo, 1959, introduction, p. 4.
22. Ibid., pp. 20, 62.
23. Muḥammad al-Ghatīt, *al-'Udwān al-Thulāthī fī'l-'Uṣur al-Wuṣṭā*, Cairo, n.d. [after 1967]; *Kifāḥunā ḍidda al-Ghuzā,* Cairo, 1957; *al-Sharq wa'l-Gharb min al-Ḥurūb al-Ṣalībiyya ilā ḥarb al-Suways,* 3Vols., Cairo, 1963. See also Muḥammad 'Urayān and Ibrāhīm al-Shayyāl, *Qiṣṣat al-Kifāḥ Bayna al-'Arab wa'l-Isti'mār,'* Cairo, 1960.
24. 'Abd al-Mun'im Mājid, *al-Nāṣir Ṣalāḥ al Dīn al-Ayyūbī,* Cairo, 1958, p. 7.
25. Sa'īd 'Āshūr, *al-Ḥaraka al-Ṣalībiyya, Ṣafḥa Mushriqa fī Ta'rikh al-Jihād al-'Arabī fi'l-'Uṣūr al-Wusṭā,* Vol.1., Cairo, 1963, p. 6.
26. Aḥmad Ḥasan al-Zayyāt, "Khawāṭir min waḥy al-ma'raka," *Majallat al-Azhar,* vol. 41, 1967, p. 226. At the Sixth Congress of Arab Writers (Cairo, March 1968), the Egyptian 'Abbās Khiḍr delivered a lecture about the "Literature of the Struggle from the Time of the Crusades to [modern] Filasṭīn." Cf. the introduction in the same vein by Islamic fundamentalist leader S. Hawwa to 'A. N. 'Alwān's biography of Saladin (Beirut, 1983). H. M. al-Qā'ūd, in *al-Ḥarb al-Salībiyya al-'Āshira* (Cairo, 1981) depicts the Lebanese civil war as a "Maronite Crusade" against Islam. Cf. Dh. Qarqūt "The Twelfth Crusade," *Shu'ūn 'Arabiyya 26* (April 1983), on Israel's invasion of Lebanon.
27. Muḥammad 'Abdallāh 'Inān, "Fikrat al-Ḥurūb al-Ṣalībiyya," *al-Hilāl,* Vol. 34, 1925/26, p. 713.
28. The idea is repeated by 'Inān in all the editions of the book to this day: *Mawāqif Ḥāsima,* first ed., 1929, pp. 53-4; second ed., 1934, p. 95; third ed., 1952, p. 4; fourth ed., 1962, pp. 3-4. W. C. Smith rightly remarked that "one can see in the successive Arabic introductions [of 'Inān's book] an increasing firmness of the sense of Western antagonism" (*Islam in Modern History,* Princeton, 1957, p. 101, note 8)—a remark accepted by the author himself in a later edition (Cairo, 1962, p. 4, note 1). Cf. S. Zakkār, *al-I'lām wa-l-Tabyīn fi Khurūj al-Faranj al-Malā'īn 'ala Bilād al-Muslimin*, Damascus, 1981.
29. Niqūlā Ziyāda, *'Alam al-'Uṣūr al-Wusṭā fī Ūrūbbā,* Jaffa, 1947, p. 138. Cf. Ḥasan Ḥabashī, *al-Sharq al-'Arabī,* Cairo, 1949, p. 35.
30. Cf. for instance, Baylī, p. 17; 'Inān, 4th ed., p. 89; Muḥammad Farīd Abū Ḥadīd,

*Ṣalāh al-Dīn wa-'Aṣruhu,* Cairo, 1927, p. 6; 'Abd al-Raḥmān Zakī and Muḥammad 'Īsā, *al-Ḥurūb Bayna al-Sharq wa'l-Gharb fi-l-'Uṣūr al-Wuṣtā,* Cairo, 1947, p. 4. A recent anti-Israeli article claims, however, that in contrast to Israel, who fights out of greed and love of power, the Crusaders were motivated by Christian and chivalric ideals (al-Zayyāt, p. 225).

31. Some scholars, however, attribute "imperialistic" intentions only to the leaders of the Crusades and to the noblemen who took part in them, while they admit that the common people participating in these expeditions (or, at least, in the First Crusade) were motivated by pure religious zeal (Ziyāda, pp. 138-42; Ḥasan Ḥabashī, *al-Ḥarb al-Ṣalībiyya al-Ūlā,* Cairo, 1947, p. 33). For another attempt to draw a balanced picture, see *Yūsuf, al-'Arab wa-l-Rūm wa-l-Lāṭīn,* pp. 50-8.
32. See, for example, Ibn al-Athīr, *al-Kāmil fi'l-Ta'rikh,* Vol. 10, Cairo, 1303 H., p. 94.
33. For contemporary historians holding these views, cf. A. Toynbee, *A Study of History,* Vol. 2, London, 1948, pp. 362-4; S. Runciman, *History of the Crusades,* vol. 1, Cambridge, 1951, chap. 1; R. W. Southern, *Western Views of Islam and the Middle Ages,* Cambridge, Mass., 1962; N. Daniel, *Islam, Christendom and the Empire,* London, 1966.
34. E. Gibbon, *Decline and Fall of the Roman Empire,* ed., J. B. Bury, Vol. 2, London, 1898, pp. 362-4; idem, *History of the Crusades,* London, 1899, pp. 371-4; N. Mills, *History of the Crusades,* London, 1828, Vol. 1, pp. 58-78; M. Hallam, *History of Europe During the Middle Ages,* vol. 1, New York, 1900, passim.
35. Amīr 'Alī, *A Short History of the Saracens,* fourth ed., London, 1924, pp. 320-8.
36. Cf., for instance, Aḥmad Amīn, *al-Sharq wa-l-Gharb,* Cairo, 1955, pp. 135-46.
37. E. G. Rey, *Les colonies franques en Syrie,* Paris, 1833; L. Madelin, *L'Expansion française,* Paris, 1918; idem, "La Syrie franque," *Revue des Deux Mondes,* Vol. 38, 1917, pp. 314-58; J. Longnon, *Les Français d'outremer au moyen âge,* Paris, 1929.
38. The direct influence of French historians can be clearly perceived, for instance, in Sa'īd 'Āshūr, *al-Ḥaraka al-Ṣalībiyya,* pp. 1054, 1060-1.
39. Cf. Talḥuq, pp. 75-7.
40. B. Lewis, *The Middle East and the West,* London, 1964, p. 135.
41. See for instance, ibid., p. 28; Zakī and 'Īsā, p. 4.
42. Cf. J. W. Thompson, *Economic and Social History of the Middle Ages,* New York, 1959, pp. 392-4; 'Inān, *Mawāqif Ḥāsima,* first ed., 1929, pp. 50, 55; Qadrī Qal'ajī, *Ṣalāḥ al-Dīn al-Ayyūbī,* third ed., Beirut, 1956, p. 16; 'Āshūr, pp. 35-7; S. Zakkār, *Al-I'lām wa-l-Tabyīn fī Khurūj al-Faranj al-Malā'īn,* Damascus, 1981.
43. Lewis, *The Middle East and the West,* pp. 134-6; Smith, *Islam in Modern History,* pp. 101 (note 8), 106 (note 13).
44. *Supra,* p. 112.
45. See the caricature published by the satirical newspaper *Al-Ḥimāra* of Beirut (7 April 1911) showing Saladin defending Arab lands in the Valley of Jezreel against the acquisitiveness of the Zionists headed by Joshua Ḥankin. For the celebration of the "Day of Ḥaṭṭīn" by Palestinian nationalists in the early 1930s, see *Sefer Toldot ha-Hagana* (History of the Hagana Organization), Vol. 2, Tel Aviv, 1959, p. 449.
46. Some of the historical novels were composed by professional historians: 'Abd al-Laṭīf Ḥamza, *Ṣalāḥ al-Dīn baṭal Ḥaṭṭīn,* Cairo, 1942 (second ed., 1958); Jamāl al-Dīn al-Shayyāl, *Miṣr wa-l-Shām Bayna Dawlatayn,* Cairo, 1947; Muḥammad Haddāra, *al-Manṣūra, Qiṣṣat al-Buṭūla al-'Arabiyya,* Cairo, 1962.
47. Review by 'Azīz 'Aṭīya of Grousset's *L'Empire du Levant, al-Majalla al Ta'rīkhiyya al-Miṣriyya,* Vol. 1, 1948, pp. 314-5; idem, "The Crusades: Old Ideas and New Conceptions," *Journal of World History,* Vol. 2, 1954, p. 470; idem, *Crusade, Commerce, and Culture,* Bloomington, Indiana, 1962, pp. 19, 23-6.

48. 'Aṭiya, *Crusade, Commerce and Culture,* p. 253.
49. R. Grousset, *L'Empire du Levant, histoire de la question d'Orient,* Paris, 1946. 'Aṭīya himself admits the debt he incurred toward Grousset (cf. his review "The Crusades: Old Ideas and New Conceptions," p. 470; *Crusade, Commerce and Culture,* pp. 55-6.)
50. 'Aṭīya, "The Crusades: Old Ideas and New Conceptions," p. 470.
51. P. Kh. Hitti, *Islam and the West,* New York, 1962, pp. 78-82; M. 'A. Maṭawī, *al-Ḥurūb al-Ṣalībiyya fī-l-Mashriq wa-l-Maghrib,* Tunis, 1854, pp. 10-12; 'A. M. Mājid, *al-Nāṣir Ṣalāḥ al-Dīn al-Ayyūbī,* Cairo, 1958; pp. 151-5; Zakī Naqqāsh, *al-'Alāqāt al-Ijtimā'iyya wa-l-Thaqāfiyya wa-l-Iqtiṣādiyya bayna al-'Arab wa-l-Faranj khikāla al-Ḥurūb al-Ṣalībiyya,* Beirut, 1958, pp. 9-10.
52. Zakī and 'Īsā, *al-Sharq wa-l-Gharb,* pp. 3-4; Qal'ajī, p. 13; Talḥūq, pp. 7-13; Yūsuf, *al-'Arab wa-l-Rūm wa-l-Lāṭin,* pp. 30-3; 'Alī al-Kharbūṭlī, *Miṣr al-'Arabiyya al-Islāmiyya,* Cairo, 1963, p. 283.
53. Qal'ajī, p. 13.
54. There are, however, some historians, notably Sayyid al-'Arīnī, author of the monumental study *al-Sharq al-Awsaṭ Wa-l-Ḥarūb al-Ṣalībiyya,* Cairo, 1963, who show complete indifference regarding such (and other) lessons. It is no mere coincidence that al-'Arīnī also never speaks of analogies between the object of his study and the modern Middle East.
55. Muḥammad Kamāl Ḥusayn, *Dirāsāt fī-l-Shi'r fī Asr al-Ayyūbiyyīn,* Cairo, 1957, p. 4.
56. Zakī and 'Īsā, p. 4; Cf. Ḥasan Ḥabashī, *Nūr al-Dīn wa-l-Ṣalībiyyūn,* Cairo, 1948, p. 6; Sayyid al-Ahl, *Ayyām Ṣalāh al-Dīn,* Beirut, 1961, pp. 27-28.
57. Muḥammad Darīd Abū Ḥadīd, *Ṣalāh al-Dīn, al-Baṭal Alladhī Intaṣara 'Alā al-Gharb,* second ed., Cairo, 1959. In its first edition published in 1927 the book's title was *Ṣalāḥ al-Dīn wa-'Aṣruhu*; the change surely bespeaks the rising antagonism toward the West. For Saladin's lifework as an edifying example, cf. Mājid, p. 8; Q. J. Jurdāq, *Ṣalāḥ al-Dīn wa-Rikārdus Qalb al-Asad,* Beirut, 1974. Cf. Yusuf Shahin's film *Saladin* (1963), discussed in *Shu'ūn 'Arabiyya* 26 (1983), p. 84.
58. A. J. Chejne, "The Use of History by Modern Arab Writers," *MEJ,* vol. 14, 1960, No. 4, pp. 386-92; G. E. von Grunebaum, *Modern Islam,* Berkeley and Los Angeles, 1962, pp. 101, 119-22.
59. Talḥūq, p. 88; Sayyid al-Ahl, p. 12; Mājid, p. 7; Ḥabashī, *Nūr al-Dīn wa-l-Ṣalībiyyūn,* p. 7; Sa'dāwī, *Jaysh Miṣr,* introduction, p. 2.
60. 'Abd al-Raḥmān Zakī, *Ma'ārik Ḥāsima fī Ta'rīkh Miṣr,* Cairo, 1945, p. 3. Cf. H. Gh. Abū Sa'īd, *Al-Jabha al-Islāmiyya fī 'Asr al-Ḥurūb al-Ṣalībiyya,* Cairo, 1971. B. 'Asalī, *Al-Ayyām al-Ḥāsima fī-l-Ḥurūb al-Ṣalībiyya,* Beirut, 1978.
61. Sa'īd 'Āshūr, *al-Ḥaraka al-Ṣalībiyya,* vol. 1, pp. 3, 6.
62. For example, Ghatīt, pp. 7-8.
63. Talḥūq, pp. 3-5, 14, 79-84; 'Inān, pp. 140-1; Ghatīt, pp. 84-8; 'Āshūr, p. 7; Yūsuf, *al-'Arab wa-l-Rīum wa-l-Lāṭin,* p. 255.
64. 'Āshūr, pp. 7-8, 661-71; Talḥūq, pp. 52-4, 67-9.
65. 'Āshūr, p. 6; Talḥūq, pp. 4-5, 25, 84.
66. P. Geyl, *Use and Abuse of History,* New Haven, 1955, p. 84; cf. Barraclough, p. 26.
67. For this concept, cf. F. Rosenthal, *A History of Muslim Historiography,* Leiden, 1952, p. 122; M. Mahdi, *Ibn Khaldūn's Philosophy of History,* London, 1957, pp. 142-4; G. E. von Grunebaum, *Modern Islam,* pp. 109-10, idem, *Islam: Essays in the Nature and Growth of a Cultural Tradition,* London, 1961, pp. 113, 122-3.
68. M. Bloch, *Apologie pour l'histoire ou métier d'historien,* fifth ed., Paris, 1964, p. 10; cf. E. J. Hobsbawm, "The Social Function of the Past," *Past and Present,* May 1972, p. 15.

69. 'Abdallāh 'Īd, *Ṣalāḥ al-Dīn al-Ayyūbī wa-l-Qawmiyya al-'Arabiyya,* Cairo, 1961. Muḥammad Haddāra, *al-Manṣūra: Qiṣṣat al-Buṭūla al-'Arabiyya,* Cairo, n. d. Jūzīf Yūsuf, *al-'Arab wa-l-Rūm wa-l-Lāṭīn fi-l-Ḥarb al-Ṣalībiyya al-Ūlā',* Cairo, 1963.
70. 'Abd al-Laṭīf Ḥamza, *Ṣalāh al-Dīn, Baṭal Ḥaṭṭīn,* second edition, Cairo, 1958, p. 14. It should be remarked that eleven years earlier the very same scholar rejected the use of the term "nationalism" before modern times and held that in the Middle Ages religious consciousness was of much greater importance than ethno-national consciousness (*al-Ḥaraka al-Fikriyya fī Miṣr fi-l-'Aṣrayn al-Ayyūbī wa'l-Mamlūkī al-Awwal,* Cairo, 1947, pp. 21-2, 361.
71. Sa'īd 'Āshūr, *al-Ḥaraka al-Ṣalībiyya,* p. 9; cf. idem, "al-Imbarāṭūr Frīdrīk al-Thānī wa-l-Sharq al-'Arabi," *al-Majalla al-Ta'rikhiyya al-Miṣriyya,* vol. 11, 1983, p. 198.
72. Naẓīr Sa'dāwī, *al-Ḥarb Wa-l-Salām Zamān al-Udwān al-Ṣalībī,* Cairo, 1961, p. 97.
73. Qal'ajī, p. 71.
74. Geyl, p. 11.
75. Aḥmad Aḥmad Badawī, *al-Ḥayāt al-Adabiyya fī 'Asr al-Ḥurūb al-Ṣalībiyya bi-Miṣr wa-l-Shām,* Cairo, 1954, p. 120. This phenomenon is all the more surprising since one of the most prominent Arab nationalist thinkers, Sāṭī' al-Ḥuṣrī, in conformity with the well-known distinction he drew between Arabhood, which is everlasting, and the spirit of Arabhood, which is only of recent birth, explicity maintained: "The Crusades took place in an age when national consciousness was non-existent and where and when religion exercised a dominant and all-pervasive influence." See *Ārā' wa-Aḥādīth fī-l-Waṭaniyya wa-l-Qawmiyya,* Cairo, 1944, p. 44.
76. Sayyid al-Ahl, pp. 51-2; Sa'īd 'Āshūr, *al-Ẓāhir Baybars,* Cairo, 1963, pp. 3-4. The argument used by them is the cultural one expounded further on.
77. Iraqi historians, however, give Zenkī (who came from Mosul) and his son their full due. See, for instance, 'I. Khalīl, *Imād al-Dīn Zankī,* Beirut, 1972; idem, *Nūr al-Dīn Maḥmūd,* Damascus, 1980.
78. Sayyid al-Ahl, p. 51; Qal'ajī, p. 53; Badawī, p. 36; idem, *Ṣalāḥ al-Dīn al-Ayyūbī bayna Shu'arā' Aṣrihi wa-Kuttābihi,* Cairo, 1960, pp. 32-6; Muḥammad Ḥamawī, *Dimashq fi-l-Aṣr al-Ayyūbī,* Damascus, 1946, p. 22.
79. 'Āshūr, *al-Ḥaraka al-Ṣalībiyya,* p. 583; Qal'ajī, pp. 25, 31, 77; Sayyid al-Ahl, ibid; Ḥamawī, ibid. Baylī, on the contrary, in a biography of Saladin written in 1920, attributes all these virtues to his Kurdish descent (*Ḥayāt Ṣalāh al-Dīn al-Ayyūbī,* pp. 42-3, 47).
80. Badawī, *Ḥayāt Adabiyya,* p. 36; idem, *Ṣalāh al-Dīn,* p. 36; Sayyid al-Ahl, pp. 51-2.
81. 'Ālī Bayyūmī, *Qiyām al-Dawla al-Ayyūbiyya fī Miṣr,* Cairo, 1952, pp. 57-8; Mājid, pp. 43-4.
82. Mājīd, pp. 52, 74-6; Sayyid al-'Arīnī, *al-Sharq al-Awsaṭ wa-l-Ḥurūb al-Ṣalībiyya,* vol. 1, Cairo, 1963, p. 771 (and ibid, note 2). Cf. Ṣalāḥ al-Dīn al-Munajjid, *A'midat al-Nakba,* Beirut, 1967, chap. 2.
83. 'Abd al-'Azīz Dūrī stresses "the role of the masses in the struggle for freedom . . . against the Mongols as well as against the Crusades" (*al-Judhūr al-Ta'rikhiyya li-l-Qawmiyya al-'Arabiyya,* Beirut, 1960, p. 55); M. Lacheraf claims that the heroism of Saladin, Baybars, and other leaders was dependent on the "unknown and necessary efforts of the common people who ceaselessly sacrificed their life and property" ('al-Buṭūla al-'Arabiyya wa-'Awāmil Nash'atihā, Bayna al-Wāqī' wa-l-Mithāliyya', *al-Fikr,* vol. 5, 1960, no. 4, p. 321). Lacheraf, an Algerian F.L.N. leader, evidently tries here to reconcile hero-worship with the "popular warfare" thesis. Cf. in the same vein the film *Shajarat al-Durr and the Mongols* (1962), discussed in *Shu'ūn 'Arabiyya* 26 (1983), pp. 83-84.
84. Sayyid al-Ahl, pp. 19-21; Qal'ajī, pp. 25, 73, 76. Cf. however, H. A. R. Gibb, "The Armies of Saladin," in *Studies on the Civilization of Islam,* Boston, 1962, p. 83.

85. Muḥammad Kamāl Ḥusayn, *Usāma b. Munqidh, Ṣafḥa min Ta'rikh al-Ḥurūb al-Ṣalībiyya,* Cairo, 1946; Nikūlā Ziyāda, "Usāma fāris min Shayzar," in *Shakhṣiyyāt 'Arabiyya,* Jaffa, 1945, pp. 43-83.
86. See, for instance, the contemporary evidence of Ibn Wāṣil, *Mufarrij al-Ḥurūb,* Ms. Paris, 1703, fols. 62b, 63b, 81a-b, 87a.
87. Ḥasan Ḥabashī, *al-Sharq al-'Arabī Bayna Shaqqāy al-Raḥā, Ḥamlat al-Qadīs Lūwīs 'alā Miṣr wa-l-Shām,* Cairo, 1949.
88. Muḥammad Kamāl Ḥusayn, *Ma'rakat al-Manṣūra wa-Intiṣār al-Sha'b,* al-Mansura, 1960. For the bibliography, cf. *supra,* note 8. Lacheraf (note 83) wrote during the Algerian war.
89. The two editions of 'Abd al-Raḥmān Zakī's study appeared under different titles: *Ma'ārik Ḥāsima fī Ta'rikh Miṣr,* Cairo, 1945, introduction and p. 27; *Ma'rakat al-Manṣūra wa-Āthāruhā fī-l-Ḥurūb al-Ṣalībiyya,* Cairo, 1960, introduction and p. 76.
90. Sayyid al-Ahl, p. 17. Cf. Gibb, "The Armies of Saladin," pp. 74-84.
91. CF. Muḥammad Muṣṭafā Ziyāda, *al-Dawla al-Islāmiyya, Ta'rikhuha wa-Ḥaḍāratuha,* Cairo, 1954, p. 275; Tamīmī, p. 146; Naẓīr Sa'dāwī, *al-Ta'rikh al-Ḥarbī al-Miṣrī fī 'Ahd Ṣalāḥ al-Dīn al-Ayyūbī,* Cairo, 1957, introduction, p. 4; Mājid, p. 106; 'Āshūr, *al-Ḥaraka al-Ṣalībiyya,* p. 1069.
92. 'Abd al-Karīm Gharāybeh, *al-'Arab wa-l-Atrāk, Dirāsa li-Taṭawwur al-'Alāqāt bayna al-Ummatayn khilāla Alf Sana,* Damascus, 1961, introduction, p. 6.
93. Cf. for instance, Rashīd Riḍā, "al-Turk wa-l-'Arab," *al-Manār,* vol. 3, 1900, p. 172.
94. Gharāybeh, pp. 226-56.
95. Ibid., introduction, pp. 6-7.
96. Sa'dāwī, *al-Ḥarb wa-l-Ṣalām,* pp. 12-13.
97. 'Āshūr, *al-Ḥaraka al-Ṣalībiyya,* pp. 7, 9, 661-71, 1012, 1037-8.
98. Jūzīf Yūsuf, *Luwīs al-Tāsi' fī-l-Sharq al-Awsaṭ,* Cairo, 1956, p. 163.
99. 'Abd al-Laṭīf Ḥamza, *Adab al-Ḥurūb al-Ṣalībiyya,* p. 19; and cf. ibid., pp. 20, 174, 176, 202, 252, 257-8, 263.
100. Badawī, *Ḥayāt Adabiyya,* pp. 5, 23-31, 560-2. Somewhat similar views were expounded, in less clear terms, by Muḥammad Kaylānī, *al-Ḥurūb al-Ṣalībiyya wa-Āthāruhā fī-l-Adab al-'Arabī fī Miṣr wa-l-Shām,* Cairo, 1949, p. 208.
101. Badawī, *Ṣalāḥ al-Dīn,* p. 162; and cf. ibid., p. 3.
102. Most of the non-Egyptian students of the Crusades are Syrian and Lebanese.
103. Abū Ḥadīd, introduction, p. 8. A similar idea was expressed in 1952 by al-Bayyūmī (p. 238).
104. Muḥammad 'Abdallāh 'Inān, "Fikrat al-Ḥurūb al-Ṣalībiyya," *al-Hilāl,* vol. 34, p. 713; idem, *Ma'ārik Ḥāsima,* first ed., p. 62.
105. Baylī, p. 24.
106. Mirrīt Ghālī, Siyāsat al-Ghadd, Cairo, 1938, pp. 157-8.
107. Ḥusayn Mu'nis, *al-Sharq al-Islāmī fī-l-'Aṣr al-Ḥadīth,* second ed., Cairo, 1938, p. 23. The first edition, published in 1935, was unfortunately unavailable.
108. Muḥammad Surūr, *Dawlat al-Ẓāhir Baybars fī Miṣr,* Cairo, 1938, pp. 7, 74; cf. M. 'Alī, *Abṭāl al-Waḥda al-Sūriyya al-Misriyya fī-l-Ḥurūb al-Ṣalībiyya,* Damascus, 1958.
109. Muḥammad Muṣṭafā Ziyāda, *Miṣr wa-l-Ḥurūb al-Ṣalībiyya,* Cairo (lecture delivered in 1942); and his introduction to Ḥasan Ḥabashī, *Nūr al-Dīn,* Cairo, 1948, p. 2.
110. Ḥasan Ḥabashī, *al-Sharq wa-l-Gharb,* p. 9 and cf. ibid., pp. 12, 13, 14.
111. Ibid., pp. 9, 11-12, 79. For Zurayq's criticism see his article on the historiography of the Crusades, *al-Abḥāth,* vol. 12, 1959, p. 248.
112. Jamāl 'Abd al-Nāṣir, *Falsafat at-Thawra,* Cairo (ed. *Ikhtarnā Laka*), p. 43; Ḥusayn Mu'nis, *Miṣr wa-Risālatuhā.* Cairo, n.d., pp. 107-9; *al-Mīthāq al-Wāṭanī,* chap. 3, p. 16. See also the popular historical tract published for soldiers: Muḥammad 'Abdallāh, *Dimyāṭ wa-Kifāḥuhā Ḍidda al-Isti'mār* (in the series *Ikhtarnā li-l-Jundi*).

113. For an extreme formulation thereof, cf. 'Alī Kharbūṭlī, *Miṣr al-Arabiyya al-Islāmiyya,* Cairo, 1963, p. 4; 'Inān, *Mawāqif Ḥāsima,* fourth ed., p. 131.
114. Sa'dāwī, *al-Ḥarb wa-l-Salām,* pp. 64-5; Ghatīt, *al-Sharq wa-l-Gharb,* pp. 7-8; Kharbūṭlī, pp. 263, 266; and in less categorical terms, 'Āshūr, *al-Ḥaraka al-Ṣalībiyya,* pp. 961-3.
115. Sa'dāwī, *Jaysh Miṣr fī Ayyām Ṣalāḥ al-Dīn,* introduction, pp. 2, 4.
116. The only two scholars who explicitly state that Egypt's role in the *jihād* dates from the time of Saladin (although they do not condemn the Fāṭimids) are Ziyāda (*Miṣr wa-l-Ḥurūb al-Ṣalībiyya,* pp. 2-3) and 'Ashūr (p. 705).
117. 'Āshūr, pp. 197-9; Muḥammad Surūr, *al-Nufūdh al-Fāṭimi fī Bilād al-Shām wa-l-'Irāq,* Cairo, 1959, pp. 66-7.
118. Baylī, p. 22; Badawī, *Ḥayāt Adabiyya,* p. 14; Bayyūmī, pp. 46-9; Muḥammad Surūr, *al-Dawla al-Fāṭimiyya,* Cairo, 1960, pp. 128-9; Ḥasan Ibrāhīm Ḥasan, *al-Mujmal fī-l-Ta'rikh al-Miṣrī,* Cairo, 1942, p. 165; Kharbūṭlī, p. 169; Kaylānī, *al-Ḥurūb al-Ṣalībiyya,* pp. 81-8; 'Arīnī, *al-Sharq al-Awsaṭ wa-l-Ḥurūb al-Ṣalībiyya,* pp. 612 (note 4), 632-3, 658-9.
119. Ziyāda *al-Dawla al-Islāmiyya,* p. 269; cf. Ḥāfiẓ Ḥamdī, *al-Sharq al-Islāmī qubayla al-Ghazw al-Mughūlī,* Cairo, 1950, pp. 127-32.
120. Aḥmad Badawī, *Ma'mūn Banī Ayyūb, al-Mu'aẓẓam 'Īsā,* Cairo, 1953, pp. 6-7. Cf. Kharbūṭlī, pp. 252, 274-5; 'Abd al-Laṭīf Ḥamza, *Ṣalāh al-Dīn Baṭal Ḥaṭṭīn,* Cairo, 1959, p. 148; 'Alī Ibrāhīm Ḥasan, *Miṣr fī-l-'Uṣūr al-Wusṭā,* Cairo, 1954, pp. 311-3; Muḥammad 'Abdallāh, *Dimyāṭ wa-Kifāḥuha Ḍida-l-Isti'mār,* passim.
121. Cf., for instance, " Āshūr, 'al-Imbarāṭūr Fridirik al-Thānī," pp.198-9, 211-2; 'Abd al-Laṭīf Ḥamza, *Ṣalāḥ al-Dīn Baṭal Ḥaṭṭīn,* pp. 152-3; Ḥasan, p. 315. A real criticism of the pact is to be found only in Sa'dāwī, *al-Ḥarb wa-l-Salām,* pp. 89-90. Full exposure of Fāṭimid-Ayyūbid negligence is to be found in the writings of a Palestinian amateur historian, former P.L.O. leader Aḥmad al-Shuqayrī (*Ma'ārik al-'Arab,* Beirut, 1975), who stresses the analogy with the indifference of the Arabs to the Palestinian cause.
122. Maṭawī, *al-Ḥurūb al-Ṣalībiyya,* p. 121.
123. The only one to distinguish clearly between them is P. Kh. Hitti, "Tuḥfat al-Sharq li-Madaniyyat al-Gharb fī-l-'Uṣūr al-Wusṭā," *al-Kitāb al-Dhahabī li-'Id al-Muqtaṭaf al-Khamsīnī,* Cairo, 1926, pp. 141-2.
124. The main passages dealing with both categories of influence: al-Ḥarīrī, p. 408; Baylī, p. 26; Kurd 'Alī, *Khiṭaṭ al-Shām,* Vol. 2, Damascus, 1925, pp. 129-31; Hitti, "Tuḥfat al-Sharq," pp. 142-51; Tamīmī, pp. 65, 105, 270-3; Nīqūlā Ziyāda, *'Alam al-'Uṣūr al-Wusṭā,* pp. 156-9; Ḥabashī, *al-Ḥarb al-Ṣalībiyya al-'Ūlā,* p. 89; Maṭawī, pp. 97, 108-9, 111-21; Zakī and 'Īsā, *al-Ḥurūb Bayna-l-Sharq wa-l-Gharb,* p. 4; Sa'dāwī, *al-Ḥarb wa-l-Salām,* pp. 199-209; Qal'ajī, pp. 21-3; 'Āshūr, pp. 1271-81; A. Zaqlama, *al-Mamālik fī Miṣr,* Cairo, 1947, p. 41; 'Atīya, *Crusade, Commerce and Culture,* pp. 121-47; Zakī Naqqāsh, *al-Alāqāt al-Ijtimā'iyya wa-l-Thaqāfiyya wa-l-Iqtiṣādiyya bayna al-'Arab wa-l-Faranj Khilāla al-Ḥurūb al-Ṣalībiyya,* Beirut, 1958, pp. 131-217.
125. L. A. Sédillot, *Histoire des Arabes,* vol. 6, Paris, 1854; idem, *Des emprunts faits pas le français à la langue arabe,* Paris, 1871; idem, *Un dernier mot sur les Arabes,* Paris, 1871; H. Prutz, *Kulturgeschichte der Kreuzzüge,* Leipzig, 1894; pp. 206-56; G. Jacob, *Der Einfluss des Morgenlands auf das Abendland, vornehmlich während des Mittelalters,* Hannover, 1924, passim; G. Lebon, *La civilisation des Arabes,* Paris, 1884, pp. 345-50, 661-3.
126. See, for instance, 'Abbās Maḥmūd al-'Aqqād, *Athar al-'Arab fi-l-Ḥaḍāra al-Urūbbiyya,* Cairo, 1946, pp. 62, 110. Cf. the reader-letter appended to al-Ḥarīrī's study (p. 407), and the declaration of Egyptian nationalist leader Ismā'īl Ṣidqī Bāshā cited by Baylī (p. 26).

127. Both were translated into Arabic: Lebon by Muḥammad Zu'aytar, *al-Ḥaḍāra al-'Arabiyya,* Cairo, 1945; Jacob by Fu'ād Ḥasanayn, *Athar al-Sharq fī-l-Gharb, Khāyyatan fī-l-'Uṣūr al-Wusṭā,* Cairo, 1946.
128. E. Barker, "The Crusades," in Th. Arnold and A. Guillaume (ed.), *The Legacy of Islam,* Oxford, 1931, p. 51.
129. It should be noted that Lebon expounded similar views (ibid., pp. 350-1).
130. By 'Alī Aḥmad 'Īsā, in *Turāth al-Islām,* Vol. 1,Cairo, 1936, pp. 81-147.
131. Maṭawī, p. 121.
132. This phenomenon was noted, in another context, by N. A. Fāris, "The Arabs and Their History," *MEJ,* Vol. 8, 1954, no. 2, p. 157.
133. Ibid., pp. 124-5, 196.
134. Hitti, "Tuḥfat al-Sharq," pp. 149-50; idem, *History of Syria,* London, 1951, pp. 662-70; idem, *Islam and the West,* pp. 81-2; 'Inān, *Mawāqif,* first ed., p. 55; Sa'dāwī, *al-Ḥarb wa-l-Salām,* pp. 182-3; 'Āshūr, pp. 1269-70; idem, *al-Madaniyya al-Islāmiyya wa-Atharuha fī'l-Ḥaḍāra al-Urūbiyya,* Cairo, 1963, pp. 56-60.
135. Hitti, *Islam and the West,* pp. 81-2.
136. Tamīmī, p. 270; 'Aṭīya, *Crusade, Commerce and Culture,* pp. 127-8.
137. Hitti, "Tuḥfat al-Sharq," p. 151.
138. Sa'dāwī, *al-Ḥarb wa-l-Salām,* p. 209 (the quotation is from Lebon, *La Civilisation des Arabes,* p. 352).
139. Kurd 'Alī, *Khiṭaṭ al-Shām,* Vol. 2, p. 129.
140. Cf. ibid., pp. 129-30; Baylī, p. 25; Hitti, *History of Syria,* p. 622; Mu'nis, *al-Sharq al-Islāmī fī-l-'Aṣr al-Ḥadīth,* pp. 23-4, 28-9; Muḥammad Kaylānī, al-*Ḥurūb al-Ṣalībiyya wa-Atharuhā fī-l-Adab fi Miṣr wa-l-Shām,* Cairo, 1949, p. 38.
141. A tendency common to most Muslim historians, cf. Smith, *Islam in Modern History,* p. 120 (note 26).
142. Nabīh Amīn Fāris, "Ḥaḍārat al-'Arab fī-l-Qarn al-Thānī 'Ashar," *al-Abḥāth,* Vol. 17, 1964, especially pp. 411-22, 426, 438-41.
143. J. Huizinga, "Definition of the Concept of History," in *Philosophy and History,* Essays presented to E. Cassirer, Oxford, 1936, p. 9.
144. H. A. R. Gibb, *Modern Trends in Islam,* Chicago, 1947, pp. 76, 124-6; Smith, pp. 95, 115-20, 152; Von Grunebaum, *Modern Islam,* pp. 110, 112-14, 123-7; Ch. A. Julien, *L'Afrique du Nord en marche,* Paris, 1952, pp. 290-4; Fāris, "The Arabs and Their History," pp. 156-9; H. Sharabi, "The Crisis of the Arab Intelligentsia in the Middle East," *The Muslim World,* vol. 46, 1957, p. 191; Qusṭanṭīn Zurayq, *Ma'nā al-Nakba,* Beirut, 1948, p. 48; idem, *Naḥnu wa-l-Ta'rikh,* Beirut, 1959, pp. 206-7, 215-18, Fāris Sāmir, "Naḥwa ta'rikh jadīd," *al-Thaqāfa al-Jadīda,* Vol. 5, 1958, pp. 9-17; 'Abd al-Raḥmān al-Bazzāz, "Islam and Arab Nationalism," trans. by S. G. Haim in *Die Welt des Islam,* N. S. Vol. 3, 1954, pp. 127-8; P. Shinar, "The Historical Approach in the Reformist 'Ulamā' in the Contemporary Maghrib," *Asian and African Studies,* Vol. 7, 1971, pp. 181-120.
145. Von Grunebaum, ibid., p. 101.
146. H. Rabie, *The Financial System of Egypt (1169-1341),* Oxford, 1972; S. El-Beheiri, *Les Institutions Ayyubides,* Lille, 1972.
147. P. Valéry, *Regards sur le monde actuel et autres essais,* Paris, 1945, p. 43.

# Chapter 2:

# ARAB REVISIONIST HISTORIANS

## HISTORIOGRAPHY AND THE SECOND *NAHḌA*

Strictly speaking this began around the years 1963-1965. It arose in the context of an enquiry into the structure of those progressive Arab countries in which anti-capitalism coexisted with an Islamic ideology. It was also nourished by discussions on the formation, psychology and choices of the petite bourgeoisie. . . . Some saw in it merely the reflection of a class-oriented polity, itself conditioned by insurmountable difficulties in the sphere of economic development. . . others concentrated their energies on the ideological debate, maintaining on the contrary that class-oriented reductionism. . . was a flight from ideological confrontation that would only result, as in the past, in the perpetuation of the traditionalist illusion and a preparing of the way for even deadlier regressions.[1]

This is the admirably penetrating manner in which Abdalla Laroui presents the "second *nahḍa*" (Renaissance, Awakening) —that Arab intellectual movement, loosely situated on the left, and dedicated to the rethinking and reassessment of the ideology, program, and actual behavior of the almost century-old "first *nahḍa*," which had come into being as a result of the modern encounter between the Arabs and the West.

Curiously enough, Laroui (as well as others who treated the same phenomenon,[2] sometimes dubbed the New Arab Left) concentrates—as the quoted paragraph already enunciates—upon the sociological, economic, and ideological production of the "second *nahḍa*." Its contribution to history-writing is barely mentioned, even though, as Laroui himself notes,

behind this questioning lies a concept of history as the sole reality. Secularization, the liberation of thought, democratization, development—all these notions and the political choices that proceed from them are lumped together in an inclusive historicism. . . .[This] is perhaps the real beginning of a truly adult thought that is wary of its own tendencies and for the first time unfolds outside tradition, in the sense that it does not regard its backwardness as a virtue.

The second *nahḍa* rejects the nationalist credo "that presents the recent past as an undeserved decadence and the future as a promise that will sooner or later be fulfilled.[3] After all, the first *nahḍa* attached great importance to historiography and to historiosophy, intent as it was upon rebuilding the shattered Arab-Muslim identity. A critique of the first *nahḍa* was thus bound to respond in kind.

This apparent negligence of second *nahḍa* historiography is to be explained by the fact that its forerunners were for the most part philosophers (N. al-Bīṭār, S. Amīn, M. Hussein). History was touched upon in their writings only at the level of broad generalizations or as a study of the very recent (post-World War II) past, which is actually enmeshed in the present. It is only by the late 1960s and early 1970s that the second *nahḍa* perceived that one of its weaknesses was "being so distant and removed from the study of Arab heritage —in its religious, historical, and literary aspects—which remains the virtual monopoly of the [traditionalist] school, even though these subjects are of vital importance for us."[4] This importance was brought home to these intellectuals by a growing awareness of the role of the past, especially the Islamic past, in Arab society.

> The past. . . lives in us and among us, it permeates our behavior in private and in public, in our interpersonal relationships, in customs of marriage and divorce, in rituals of birth and death, in all that immense heritage of traditions accumulated for thousands of years. A reinterpretation of this past is in order, for this will better enable us to elucidate the present and to look at the future.[5]

This is even more true since the impact of the past came to be seen as one of the major obstacles on the road to that overall revolutionary transformation preached by the second *nahḍa*; an obstacle both by virtue of its very presence and by virtue of the shrewd manipulation of "Islamic heritage" by the ruling class. No wonder that Iraqi historian Hādī al-ʿAlawī sets two goals to progressive students of the heritage *(al-turāthiyyūn al-taqaddumiyyūn)*: scholarly research and struggle against the "policy of commerce in religion carried out by [Arab] regimes. . . which tends to perpetuate backwardness."[6] The sense of relevance and urgency of the historian's task conveyed by this phrase as well as the virulence of tone and highly critical outlook, are all quite typical of the revisionist historians. The past (above all the Islamic one) is indeed inseparable for them from religion, and dealing with it is an oblique way of treating this pillar of Arab society which is Islam. "The non-secular character of Arab regimes makes approaching the question of religion much like crossing a minefield,"[7] as Ḥaydar puts it, drawing perhaps the lessons of difficulties encountered by al-'Aẓm's *Critique of Religious Thought* (1969). Not that reinterpreting the past is such a safe path. "To deal with the *negative* [my italics] aspects of our heritage is to break a taboo and to hazard into a forbidden ground. For how could it be permitted to discuss such a sacrosanct object, our eternal heritage, which is the guarantor of so many dominating class and political interests?"[8] Traditionalist historians, in fact, dub the revisionists as those transgressors of hallowed norms, *mustashriqūn*, or Orientalists, that ultimate term of scholarly abuse.[9]

In spite of the attacks of which it is the object—and but for the continued tendency in certain circles of the second *nahḍa* to concentrate on the present—the revisionist historical school is growing, dedicated to the idea that "a renaissance *(nahḍa)* presupposes a re-reading of the past; whereas the past is a living and indomitable force among us, if we know how to use it, it can be a powerful agent of progress, but if we ignore it, it persists to be a burden drawing us backwards" (A. Maqdisi, a Syrian).[10] This essay intends to take stock of the revisionist school, ten years after its inception; admittedly, not a very long period but sufficient to gain an idea of its characteristics, achievements, and limitations.

## APOLOGETICS IN THE DOCK

As in other revisionist schools, much of the effort is exerted in the critique of the established nationalist historiography, tagged for shorthand *salafī* (fundamentalist) by the revisionists; this term (though obviously polemical and derogatory) is not unwarranted. The characteristics of the mainstream nationalist school which are so vituperatively attacked owe their origin and inspiration to that Islamic reformism of the late nineteenth and early twentieth century, the *salafiyya*.[11] In revisionist parlance, *salafī* means first and foremost apologetic *(tawfīqī, tabrīrī* and even *talfīqī* being its recurrent synonyms). "Infatuated with the glories of the past, drawing a sense of conceit from the endless repetition of its achievements and legends," "depicting our heritage in glowing terms bordering on canonization"[12]—this is how the revisionists describe the nationalist historians. Theirs is certainly not an intellectual pursuit of the truth; the analytical approach is virtually non-existent, the narrative manner is dominant, with an unmistakable bent toward the laudatory. "At least, history writing is an instrument for amusement or distracttion. . . a mere pleasure-hunting after anecdotes"; more often it is intended to bolster the "hankering after the *salaf al-ṣāliḥ*, the Arab Golden Age,"[13] which serves as inspiration. In the words of Lebanese historian A. 'Ulabī: "There is a clear-cut distinction between scholarly research and the search for inspiration in the heritage. The former approach seeks the truth, whatever it may be and regardless of the use it may be put to, while the apologetic approach pays no heed to details and nuances, for its main interest is the present, which it wishes to justify in the name of the past."[14] Another less virulent scholar concurs that the "eulogizing stance played a useful role, given the humiliations and the injustice inflicted upon the Arab in modern times. . . in rebuilding our self-esteem." Yet if "singing the praises of the past was a psychological need of the defeated, . . . one must now go beyond this phase, if we actually wish to understand ourselves; for progress is possible only when the past is used to throw light upon the present in order for the latter to push us towards the future."[15]

The most obvious trait of apologetic historiography is its preoccupation with the question of precedence *(mas'alat al-awwaliyya)*, that cornerstone of the claim that "We, the Arabs, are the best of nations *(khayr umma)*." "We are a nation of noble lineage, rooted in a very old and eternal civilization, we got everything and thank God we do not lack anything"; "we pioneered most modern discoveries in psychology, astronomy, mathematics, medicine, nay even technology." These ideas indeed were found by one critic to be the *leitmotif* of the papers presented at the All-Arab Historical Congress (1975).[16] Antoine Maqdisī, in the same sarcastic vein, scoffs at those who argue that Ibn Khaldūn, rather than having been a giant in the medieval context, "actually preceded Comte and Durkheim in founding sociology, an argument presupposing that our personality is made significant only if it can match the personality of the Other."[17] "In the final analysis," writes the Egyptian scholar F. Zakariya, "this approach is counterproductive: instead of glorifying past Arab scientists and thinkers who are supposed to have preceded those of the West, it makes the accomplishments of the West the sole criterion for measuring achievement, thereby unwittingly glorifying the West and belittling our civilization."[18] In brief, the approach is inherently ahistorical, refusing to interpret phenomena in their true historical context, and lacking a sense of historical relativity. At times this leads to an unmistakable falsification of facts. ʻAṭīf Aḥmad proves this, for instance, with regard to Muṣṭafa Maḥmud's widely read *The Koran: A Contemporary Interpretation.* Maḥmud systematically demolishes the spurious arguments according to which Copernicus', Darwin's, and Freud's theories, among others, are prefigured in the Muslim Holy Book, while Zakariya ridicules the "discovery" of nuclear physics and modern biology in these very scriptures.[19] More often than not such a frame of mind implies that the present is measured solely in comparison with glorious chapters of the past (less-than-glorious chapters being either ignored or, if possible, painted in glowing terms). "It is insufficient," says B. Tībī, "to have Ibn Sīna and Ibn Khaldūn as my ancestors for me to have the right to live; I have to achieve this right on my own;" and S. ʻAbd al-Ṣabbūr adds: "Actually, there is no nation like we Arabs to disdain our present. . . . Why is it that whenever we establish a new university . . . we have to glorify *dār al-ḥikma* of ancient Baghdad" [Caliph Ma'mūn's ninth-century institution, where Greek works were translated into Arabic. In this manner, much of this heritage managed to reach Renaissance Europe].[20]

If the sins of ahistorical thought are particularly flagrant concerning *awwaliyyah*, the revisionists find them in abundance in other domains of nationalist-apologetic scholarship, especially with regard to the study of the so-called classical period (seventh to eleventh century). The laudatory stance *(mawqif al-taghannī)* vis-à-vis this period necessitates whitewashing or disregarding darker historical pages, and in particular adopting the viewpoint of the ruling classes of those eras. History is not written "from the bottom up" even under progressive-populistic regimes, for this would have entailed telling the story of the governed and the exploited. ʻUlabī, for example, criticizes a study of the Persian Gulf under the ʻAbbāsids because it paints a picture of prosperity, whereas in fact it was depicting only the way of life of the merchant class; "those who created the comfort for their masters, immersed as they were in a life of misery," were disregarded. Nationalist historians continued a strain typical of the elitist bent of classical Muslim historiography, written by *ʻulamā'* subservient to the ruling class and who "blotted out many a truth in order to keep the glorious façade of the past" (Y. al-Khawrānī).[21] Instead of demystifying, the nationalist historian tries to bolster long-accepted myths, be it to defend a class-view or for other reasons. Thus, an Arab historian of the Crusades attempted to preserve the myth of Islamic solidarity by speaking of caliphal "aid" to the defense of Muslim Syria; as this aid was practically non-existent, he had to grossly exaggerate the importance of the perfunctory dispatches sent from Baghdad to Syria.[22]

Those demerits of the past, which cannot be erased altogether, are ascribed solely to exogenous forces: imperialism or, in earlier periods, Crusaders, Mongols, Mamluks, and Ottomans. Ṣādiq al-'Aẓm retorts (in a manner reminiscent of the Algerian thinker Malek Bennabi) that to be colonized one has first to become *colonizable*, and Aḥmad Bahā' al-Dīn elaborates on this theme:

> At a certain stage, it may have been easy for many Arab thinkers to put the blame upon the outside world for all the aspects of the Arab crises. They may have done it in order not to have to face up to causes existing within Arab society itself, thus avoiding head-on collision with values, beliefs and sequels of the past which dominate our society. This externalization of guilt further helped the Arab regimes, as it diminished their responsibility and justified their impotence. In fact, Arab society had begun to disintegrate and decline long before the advent of the various foreign invasions which vanquished it. . . . The disintegration of the Caliphate to tiny states is not the only cause of this decline, but it is surely an important symptom. Already long before the actual invasions took place, the values of liberty, justice, and free research were pushed aside by despotism and intolerance.[23]

Not that the revisionists deny there are brilliant pages in Arab history. Their grief against established historiography is that, in its quite legitimate wish to put these aspects in relief, it commits three grave methodological sins.

1. *Anachronism,* or lack of a sense of the "otherness of times past."[24] They arbitrarily apply modern terms to bygone phenomena, seeking thereby to glorify them. Modish terms such as economic development, socialism, nationalization, are read into medieval situations in order to render them more respectable or relevant. "This scientific method," sums up a critical survey of papers presented to the 1973 Arab historical Congress, "leads to distortion of the historical truth. . . it commits treason vis-à-vis the past in the name of false contemporaneity."[25]

2. *Pragmatism (historia magistra vitae)*, drawing concrete lessons from past experience, and *didacticism*, e.g., lessons drawn from the counter-Crusade experience for the conduct of the Arab-Israel conflict are rejected out of hand as methodologically unsound, "the assumption behind it being that the thought of another era can

solve the problems of our times or that tactics of long bygone periods can be applied to modern warfare" (Zakariya). Didacticism is frowned upon at least to the extent that it brings about hero worship (e.g., Caliph 'Umar II as a model Islamic ruler) and is anachronistic (e.g., Caliph 'Umar I's land policy in Iraq is a model of, and an argument for, modern-day reform).[26]

3. *Ethnocentrism* (dubbed *shūfīniyya*, chauvinism), a sin encountered in connection with *awwaliyya* but present elsewhere as well. As with the (originally Koranic) notion of *khayr umma*, a continuity is detected by the critics between medieval Islamic historiography —which had the Islamic world for its sole subject or which kept it at the center of the narrative, as in the case of Mas'ūdī, one of the few universal historians—and modern Arab historiography. The proclivity of the latter to deal with its own culture alone leads to a "simplistic perception" of oneself and of others (e.g., the supposed antinomy between Western materialism and Eastern, or Arab, spiritualism) and to the erroneous view that others' actions vis-à-vis oneself are merely reactive and not autonomous (e.g., the Crusades presented as a reaction to Islamic conquests rather than explained against the background of the Investiture Wars and the economic and demographic growth of Europe). Nationalist historians also lack almost completely the comparative angle, so important for self-awareness even when dealing with civilizations not in direct contact with one's own.[27] Worse than that, the implicit denial of the existence of a world culture entails belittling the role of exogenous influences such as Hellenism in Islam and the legitimation of modern ideas by excavating historical precedents in Islam; only once found in conformity with the original heritage *(aṣāla)*, the stigma of *dakhīl* (alien) is removed from these ideas. "As an Arab intellectual, operating within the modern context, if I want to discuss the building up of Socialism, my encounter is with Marx and not with Ibn Sīna," writes Maqdisī, "if I deal with the question of rationality and scientific method, my encounter is with Descartes and not with al-Kindī (d. 873). Only had I wanted to dwell on the problem of the relationship between human reason and Holy Scriptures would I have to get guidance from medieval *kalām* philosophy or from the chapter on science and religious belief from Ghazālī and Ibn Rushd."[28] M. Ṭālbī draws the lesson of this critique: "We should by no means content ourselves, as we do today, with the study of our own history, but rather study the history of other cultures and nations, with whom

we are in ever-growing interaction. We should have Occidentalists, specializing in the affairs of the West, modelled on (Western) Orientalists."[29]

The sins of nationalist apologetics are not confined, however, to mainstream and rightist-fundamentalist circles. The revisionists do not spare their rod from leftist apologetics, whose values and ultimate goals they may share, albeit disputing their methods. The left "distorted the heritage out of the same reckless desire to find in it an echo of present preoccupations. . . discovering there socialism, existentialism, dialectics, etc."[30] The revisionists thus criticize the Egyptian left-wing historian M. 'Imāra for making Caliph 'Umar II into a socialist (because of his commitment to social justice) and the *zuhd* ascetics into revolutionaries; the Lebanese M. al-Ṣulḥ, of the editorial board of the leftist periodical *Mawāqif*, is excoriated for reading into early Islam the thematics of a "national liberation" movement. A lecture by the Marxist philosopher Garaudy in Cairo sponsored by the left-wing monthly *al-Talī'a* (1970) is painstakingly demolished both with regard to the compatibility of Islamic heritage with Socialism and Marxism (based on such flimsy ground as Ibn Rushd's dialectics, Ibn Khaldūn's materialism, etc.) and with regard to the excessive glorification of Islam's contribution to modern Europe.[31] One of Garaudy's critics stopped to ponder the question of why the Cairo audience reacted with such enthusiasm to Garaudy and so coolly (nay even adversely) a month later to a lecture by M. Rodinson, delivered under the same auspices. Rodinson, he claims, did not cater to their predjudices and applied razor sharp criticism to medieval Islam, while Garaudy "delivered a speech in the defense of Islamic civilization, and the reactions thereto were in the same vein: defense of the past, not an inquiry into it as a history which is to be interpreted, elucidated and whose impact upon the present has to be evaluated."[32]

The last two lines indeed sum up the ideal preached by revisionist historiography. It is not, however, an idea of "neutral" history writing, for they deny the value of such an effort. Taking as their point of departure present-day preoccupations, as indicated in these lines, the revisionists are great believers in committed historiography, which has its sense of relevance and topicality, yet is disciplined by a sane methodology. Theirs is thus to be an *histoire-problème* (to borrow *Annales*' terminology). No wonder they treat with utter disdain that branch of the nationalist historical school that eschews overt apologetics, yet concentrates on antiquarianism: the faithful descriptive recording of events past or editing of ancient manuscripts, whatever their significance. This *histoire-histoire* or *histoire-evenementielle* is not as devoid of ideological bent as it pretends to be. Its very slogan, *iḥyā' al-turāth* (resurrection of the heritage) subsumes the same respect for the past, every part of which deserves to be excavated and embalmed for eternity.[33]

It is in fact this basic attitude towards the past that is the major grief of the revisionists vis-à-vis nationalist apologists. This is how Fu'ād Zakariya argues it:

We are alienated from our present and fraught with nostalgia for our past. This is the most negative phenomenon of our cultural life. Our consciousness is so much oriented towards the past, so inextricably intertwined with it that it expects the past to do the impossible, namely to solve the problems of the present. Suffice it to mention the great importance attached by Egyptian and Arab writers to the question of our cultural heritage *(aṣāla)* and the glory of our past. The past is for us a living phenomenon competing with the present. Our excruciating dilemma is how to accommodate both. This dissension with the past is most evident when we speak of the "return of the spirit" whenever we accomplish something of magnitude such as the October War. Present accomplishment is thus intended to resuscitate and vindicate the past. Had we wished to give the present its due share, we would not have interpreted it always from the viewpoint of the "comeback" to past glory. Our press and literature do not cease, in fact, to make comparisons between past and present events. They tend to link up a modern-day military exploit and another feat of arms dating back several centuries, or a twentieth-century revolution and a revolution which took place in antiquity. Such comparisons and analogies have particular significance in our country, because when many of us pride ourselves—quite legitimately, of course—for being the descendants of ancient civilizations, we tend to believe in the existence of latent mystical relationships through which the past influences the present. We claim that he who traces his ancestry to an ancient civilization is bound today to be better, wiser and nobler than the descendant of a more recent civilization. Truly enough, unity in this vein may be quite agreeable at a purely literary level and may contribute to boost public morale. But can it really stand the test of sober and rational analysis? This would be much like claiming that because twenty-five centuries ago the Greeks had a magnificent civilization, modern-day Greeks are better men than the Norwegians, who are the descendants of the lawless Viking pirates.

. . . The voice of the past submerges the voice of the present in our thought, literature and art. We speak of our past more than any other people on earth. The fault is not with our pride in the past, for indeed it is glorious. What calls for soul-searching is that tendency to revert to the past whenever we encounter complex situations in the present, deluding ourselves into believing that solutions inspired by the spirit of bygone days can best tackle contemporary problems.[34]

## HISTORY AS WITNESS FOR THE PROSECUTION

For all their criticism of nationalist historiography, the revisionists have several common traits with it, notably the concentration of their efforts on two major chunks of history, the most recent past (post-World War I and especially post-World War II) and classical Islam, disregarding completely the period of "decadence." As the former topic is too closely interrelated with politics, we would examine here their production on the so-called Golden Age, attitudes toward which are a sensitive litmus test. The limits of this period are, however, different in revisionist parlance; while both nationalists and revisionists view the rise of Islam as the *terminus post quem*, the *terminus ante quem* is the eleventh century for the revisionists (except in intellectual history, where they are more supple) and the fourteenth to fifteenth century for the mainstream nationalists. The reason seems to be the aversion of the revisionists to study the Crusades or the Mongol and Mamluk periods, once used by the old school to put the blame for the "undeserved decadence" (in Laroui's apt formula)[35] on exogenous forces. Moreover, foreign policy and military history, which dominate the later Muslim Middle Ages, do not interest the revisionists, who are keen on dissecting Muslim society from within. Yet, here another common trait appears: notwithstanding their criticism of nationalist preoccupation with Arab history, the "new historians" in the final analysis deal with barely anything else save history; in this they are typical of the New Arab left whose focus of interest is the Arab World and not even the Third World. In all fairness, one should add that the "new historians" try to enlarge their vision through a comparative angle, and at least on intellectual history take into consideration a wider canvas than that of the Arab (or Muslim) scene.

The difference between the revisionist and the old nationalist approaches becomes more evident with regard to the substance of the discussion of classical Islam. What for the mainstream historians was the Golden Age *(al-'aṣr al-dhahabī)* is for some revisionists "that long and dark night of our history," "those Middle Ages we are still living in"[36]; others, more charitable, state that "Islam had, at its very early period, some positive aspects" or that "our history, like any other, encompasses both lean and fat years." Their interest is undeniably in the less attractive (and hitherto neglected) chapters, "that taboo area," the exploration of which is a *sine qua non* for self-knowledge and intellectually honest criticism. One such revisionist borrows his motto from Jean Jaurès: "a heritage should not be accepted lock, stock and barrel; one should keep the living flame of the ancestors but not the dead ashes."[37] There is no mistaking the general brunt of their discourse, as was demonstrated in the 1974 Kuwait Symposium on the "Crisis of Arab Cultural Development," when Shākir Muṣṭafā created a virtual scandal with a (relatively moderate) paper on the "Historical Dimensions" of that crisis, discussing "the dregs and wounds" left by history on Arab social structure. This paper, which according to one observer "marked with its heavy stamp all Symposium debates in the following days," triggered a number of indignant rejoinders to its focusing on the "negative" and "laying the blame for present defects and deficiencies on the past."[38] In a word, the revisionists (to borrow A. Besançon's phrase on Soviet historiography) invoke "the historical past as witness for the prosecution."[39] The witness is no more *al-aṣr al-dhahabī* but *'uṣūr al-ẓulūmāt* (the Dark Ages). The trial, as Muṣṭafā's critics aptly point out, is that of present Arab society.

The most salient count against Arab history is despotism; a saliency undoubtedly tied up with the Arab intellectuals' great preoccupation with the lack of democracy in their countries, especially in the so-called progressive ones, where all the "revolutions" have ended up with the establishment of military regimes even less tolerant of basic liberties than were the corrupt "feudal bourgeois" regimes that preceded them.[40] The importance of Arab political tradition is evident in phrases like: "The contemporary Arab state is a legitimate heir to the traditions of Arab medieval tyranny," or "notwithstanding the distance in time, public opinion in Arab lands takes the same negative view of the rulers with their excessive luxury and splendor that it used to do in (Islamic times)."[41]

Unbridled (sometimes dubbed "Oriental") despotism and its major corollary, the alienation of the governed,[42] are indeed the basic characteristics of the Muslim state, "ruled by scourge and sword, while its main title for glory is the gold amassed," according to a quotation from thirteenth-century historian Ibn Khallikān.[43] A spate of similar quotations from the sources is marshalled by the revisionists to prove that at least ever since the Umayyad period (or rather from the days of the third Caliph 'Uthmān, 644-658), the state was one of "internal repression," curbing freedom of thought (the *irhāb fikrī* so lamented today), laying oppressive "non-Koranic" taxes on the lower classes, and operating through a powerful yet corrupt bureaucracy, which was the mainstay of the regimes. Particular attention is given to the ruthless security services and their elaborate intelligence branches. The single and autocratic ruler who is at the apex, and his immediate entourage, are depicted as physically and mentally cut off from their subjects—and that long before the military regimes of the tenth century and onward would dig an even wider chasm, cut off by place of residence, opulent life style, retinues of servants, soldiers, and clerks.[44] The perception of these realities by the alienated lower classes is analyzed by the Egyptian scholar Kh. A. Khalīl in his study of the *One Thousand and One Nights*, and other scholars with the help of popular proverbs; suspicion and latent hostility held in check by a sense of powerlessness and a resultant passivity is the popular mood,[45] prefiguring a much deplored trait of the Arab masses today, which accounts, according to the Left, for the failure of all attempts to establish participatory regimes as well as of revolutionary agitation.

The major trait of this Oriental Despotism was the notion that the ruler (and his repressive apparatus) is above the law, which means in fact that the Islamic state disregarded the *sharī'a*, that very foundation of Islam as a normative relgion. This trait goes back once again to Umayyad days, antedating by far Mamluk and Ottoman times (those *bêtes noires* of nationalist apologists), although rendered more blatant with the rise of praetorian guards under still nominal Arab rulers in the ninth to eleventh centuries. If the early Islamic polity (Muḥammad, Abū Bakr, and 'Umar, and perhaps also 'Alī) is presented as based upon the rule of the Law, some revisionists have doubts as to whether it had the making of a democracy, as the *salafiyya* (Muslim or nationalist) would have it. In his study *Islamic Politics: Theory and Practice,* Hādī al-'Alawī claims that the celebrated *shūrā* (election of the Caliph) was actually limited to a small body of notables even when put into practice under the Orthodox Caliphs and thus was a guarantee against tyranny, but was not an ingredient of democracy (for which one cannot, hence, find a *praefiguratio* in Islamic history). The disappearance of the *shūrā* practice by the mid-seventh century was nonetheless a grave loss for the principle of the rule of the Law.[46] "This state of Oriental Despotism was closed towards any measure of democracy and dialogue," writes 'Afīf al-Akhḍar,

> power did not emanate from a council of notables or cardinals, but was based upon the edge of the sword and palace-engineered *coups d'état*. The caliph would pick up his successor according to his own whim, unbound by any custom, and would have him obtain an oath of allegiance from his own entourage, i.e., army commanders, men of religion and the executioners. All through Arab history power has thus always been—and still is—beyond the law. . . and no opposition, past or present, has ever succeeded in subjecting the rulers to the Law.[47]

The Umayyad and 'Abbāsid caliphs take most of the blame for this development, influenced as they were by the Caesarean and Sassanid traditions of the occupied territories (through the locally-recruited bureaucracy) and later by praetorian elites. The responsibility of Muslim intellectuals *('ulamā')* is, however, set almost on a par with that of the politicians. For it was the former, above all the jurists *(fuqahā')*, who were supposed to be the custodians of the *sharī'a* as the governing principle of the polity, interpreting it in order to adapt it to changing circumstances, admonishing the rulers when they trespassed its bounds, sitting in judgment (as *qāḍīs*) on deviating officials. That none of this actually came into effect was the upshot of the cosy relationship that came into being between the rulers and the intellectuals: in return for plump jobs in the bureaucracy and in the state-financed madrasas, for large endowments and privileges, the *'ulamā'* allowed the regime to do whatever it saw fit with the *sharī'a*, accepting a subservient role as *qāḍīs* (hired and fired by the ruler) and on the whole considering matters of state and administration to be the exclusive domain of the caliph, governor, or autonomous local potentate. Not that the bargain was merely utilitarian. Shocked by the civil war between 'Alī and Mu'āwiya, the *'ulamā'* resolved that any kind of Muslim rule was better than anarchy, hence the notion that one should obey even an *imām fāsiq* (sinful ruler). Permeated by an "elitest outlook," the *'ulamā'* was not concerned with the masses, and the price the latter had to pay for such a rule seemed irrelevant. It was easy for the *'ulamā'*, beginning with the *jabariyya* under the Umayyads, to become the "cornerstone of caliphal autocracy": they relinquished the development of constitutional law, renounced their right to operate the *shūrā ahl al-'aqd wa'l-ḥall*, put up with the curbing of the autonomy of the *qāḍīs* and with the limitation of the *sharī'a* to personal status and religious rituals. Their energy was devoted to justify or condone caliphal transgression of the Law (even on sensitive matters such as sex and religious observance), instilling in the common people blind obedience and fatalism and offering them comfort in the after-life as a refuge from, and compensation for, the hardships of the present.[48]

The virulence of this attack upon the medieval *'ulamā'* is to be explained by the unbroken pattern the revisionists see between this alliance with the rulers and the role of men of religion in modern Arab regimes (even "progressive" ones). Indeed, in recent years, one of the major preoccupations of the Left came to be the use made by the state of religion (in the educational system, in the media, etc.) and of men of religion as mediating agents among the Islam-permeated masses in order to legitimize its actions and manipulate public opinion as they see fit (especially against revolutionary tendencies). The part of the *'ulamā'* in this bargain is said to be their rich *waqfs*, wide powers for *sharī'a* courts, teaching jobs, etc.[49]

In a wider perspective, this attention paid to medieval *'ulamā'* is linked to the meditation on the *trahison des clercs* of present-day Arab intellectuals in general, who do not fulfill their critical function vis-à-vis the regime and society and prefer either to serve the rulers or to retreat from public life. The medieval *'ālim* (subservient or withdrawn) was the prototype and originator of that behavior. The underlying elitist frame of mind, disdainful of the *'āmma* and oblivious of intellectuals' responsibilities toward them, is detected even among Mu'tazila, Ibn Rushd, and Ibn Khaldūn, who used to be deemed relatively "progressive," let alone with regard to villains of the piece such as al-Ghazālī (taken to task, *inter alia*, for failing to react to the Crusader invasion even though he had lived in Jerusalem).[50]

Shākir Muṣṭafā, in his controversial landmark study, defined political power in Islam (at least in the last millennium) as based upon the alliance of foreign military cliques (former praetorians who usurped the authority of the caliphs and their governors), men of religion, and feudal landowners.[51] Quite surprisingly, and inexplicably for historians many of whom are avowedly Marxist, the economic angle receives scant attention. Descriptions of the evolution and nature of Islamic feudalism are summary though not inaccurate, sometimes paying homage to the concept of the Asiatic mode of production without actually demonstrating the way in which the relationship between the two operates. What is elucidated rather clearly is the role of the Islamic conquests in the creation of a huge block of state-held lands later to be given out as fiefs by the caliphs, who considered them private property, and the later transformation of the *iqṭā'* into the economic basis of the medieval military regimes. Greater notice is paid to the condition of the fellah, "that most exploited and oppressed creature in the world of the caliphate," and the process whereby he came to lose his private property and to "find refuge" *(lujū', iljā')* in serfdom. The one-way exploitative relationship between town and countryside, the former being the seat of the absentee feudal lords as well as of government, is vividly portrayed with the help of proverbs and folk tales.[52]

Urban economy is barely discussed (perhaps because its relationship to present structures is less self-evident than the rural economy). The one socioeconomic chapter where the revisionists actually stand out with regard to mainstream historiography is that of slavery. Barely wasting space on the tattered apologetics of how Islam greatly improved the status of slaves, Bū 'Alī Yāsīn states that "Islam remains, however, a product of its own age" and thus retained the institution of slavery, developing it further in some respects (e.g., the military enslavement of the Mamluks). The abjection and cruelty of the slaves' condition in the production sector (e.g., the East African *zanj* in the plantations of ninth-century southern Iraq) is depicted with great detail, accounting for—nay even justifying—the violent reaction of the *zanj* revolt. The centrality of the function of the slave in Islamic society is further highlighted by their saliency in popular myths and tales; the recurrent folk anecdotes on the slave's one-upmanship over his master being a sort of compensatory mechanism for present status. The revisionists find slavery not only relevant because it still survives to some extent, but because it represents a blatant example of the exploitative nature of the Islamic system as a whole. Several revisionists even venture into a more dangerous terrain and speak of racial prejudices underlying this institution: the color bar being obvious in the case of the black slaves at the bottom of the ladder (menial household and city jobs; plantation *zanj*) and implicit in the case of the not-so-white (Slavs, Southeastern Europeans) of a slightly higher status (servants, tutors, etc.), and even in that prime of the breed, the Turkish Mamluks.[53]

The freeman/slave dichotomy was, as is well known, one of the three major cleavage-lines in Islam, together with the Muslim/non-Muslim and male/female lines. The abject condition of the non-Muslim *dhimmī* barely engages the interest of the revisionists (although they do not rehash pieties about him being tolerated, prosperous, etc.). Those who mention the phenomenon in passing speak of "oppression" and of the "non-democratic" fact that the *dhimmī* was outside of the polity.[54] Of the three major cleavage-lines, it is, however, the status of women that seems to draw most of the attention of the "new historians." The reason is to be found once again in the sense of topicality: the status of women is taken to be the linchpin of the extended patriarchal family, that elementary cell of traditional society and a major mediating agent of that society's values to its new members during their crucial formative years. A growing number of leftist thinkers came, of late, to see the transformation of the family as a *sine qua non* of social change, which may deal a heavy blow to the values it both reflects and upholds: authoritarianism; religion as a refuge from reality and justification of the *status quo*; overdependence vis-à-vis the social milieu; conformity; helplessness as regards the rulers; and lack of personal initiative.[55] Small wonder that the triad—extended family/woman/sex—occupies so much space in revisionist history. The extended patriarchal family as a microcosm of society where authority is absolute and based upon sex and seniority is traced to its origins in early Islam (when some tribal influence could still be felt) and its full crystallization in the 'Abbāsid era. The woman as sex object, procreative and productive tool confined to home, was by law and practice the mainstay of this structure, with sex made by religion to be the ultimate taboo, serving as a vigorous disciplining factor in child-rearing (especially when eliciting feelings of guilt and shame). "Women," wrote Kh. A. Khalīl, "were the most exploited social group" and "sexual relations were the worst case of exploitation." Analyzing the female theme in *The Thousand and One Nights*, he interprets it as "the epitome of [the] story of oppression in medieval Arab times." The role of the *sharī'a*—through its chapters on personal status, which, unlike those on the *shūrā*, were among its most effective—is demonstrated to have been crucial in giving religious (and hence, political) sanction to the extended family and to the female role in society.

Not that the *'ulamā'* carry all the burden of responsibility in this respect. 'Aṭīf Aḥmad dissects the Koran and finds all this *in embryo* there: a society based on kinship relations, where "the relationship between the sexes presupposed a closed social structure whose women do not participate in the life of society at large, their tasks being circumscribed to conjugal obligations." Small wonder that Bū 'Alī Yāsīn excoriates *al-muḥarramayn* (the two taboos), religion and sex, as the most detrimental legacy of the past, each part of the diptych fortifying the other. The noxious impact of the family is not limited to exploitation and the rule of religion. Serving as a primary reference group, it catalyzed the centrifugal tendencies: the helpless individual retreating from an oppressive and non-participatory society into the family shell, the local alliance of families given prime importance to a far away and weakening caliphate. The *'ashā'iriyya* (clannishness) was thus in a dialectical relationship with the Islamic *umma* it was supposed to serve, hampering integration into a greater whole, inasmuch as today—and contemporary considerations are at the back of the minds of revisionist historians—they are a roadblock on the way to an authentic Arab national integration.[56]

## HEROES AND VILLAINS

The act of indictment, sketched above, is extremely harsh; the revisionist overall view of Islamic history, rather bleak. But could it be that there were no spots of light, no heroes and only villains? Wary of repeating the didactic, moralist mistakes of nationalist historians, some revisionists point out that morally-repugnant Umayyad and 'Abbāsid caliphs wrought astounding feats: establishing a wide empire, developing economy and culture, etc., though they did it at a steep price; and it is this price or obverse of the coin that the historian should elucidate.[57] Yet was not there in Islam a counter-tradition, with real heroes combatting for ideals somewhat akin to those dear to the heart of the Arab Left?

Here a certain tension can be detected in the writings surveyed in this essay: between the tendency to seek in the past a prefiguration of present ideals and historical criticism prone to emphasize the negative. One notes, for instance, on the one hand, 'Alawī's criticism of M. Rodinson—who is otherwise highly respected by the Arab Left—for "divesting the long Islamic era of any significant stand against class exploitation,"[58] and, on the other hand, historians who reject as spurious the "discovery" of a long Islamic revolutionary tradition, devoted to social justice, nay even to democracy and socialism, encompassing all sorts of oppositionary movements, and ascetic, mystic, and rationalist intellectuals.[59] "This is a *Thousand and One Nights* story," scoffs the Lebanese historian 'Alī Ḥamdān.[60] The conflict between these two tendencies is tenuously resolved by saying with T. Tīzīnī that there was a minor tradition, revolutionary for its times yet barely having an impact upon them, quite restricted in scope and lacking real continuity.[61] Literary historians among the revisionists are thus interested in the anti-caliphal poetry of Kumayt b. Zayd and the Ṣa'ālīk under the Umayyads and early 'Abbāsids or in agnostic poets of the Jāhiliyya.[62] Political and social historians (and they are the majority) accept the Zanj (868-882) and Bābak (835-837) revolts and the Qarmaṭī movement (late ninth to eleventh centuries) as major proponents of that tradition by virtue of land and property distribution reforms of the latter two (presented in a somewhat exaggerated form as "proto-Communist") and the Zanj frontal assault against a pillar of the exploitive structure.[63] A very minor tradition indeed, for the Qarmaṭīs were dubbed heretic and thrown outside the pale, and the Zanj slaves were a marginal social factor that, according to the revisionists 'Ulabī and al-Sāmir, had a very limited social program. Beyond that hard core there is no agreement: some revisionists would annex the whole Ismā'īlī movement (especially its terrorist branches such as the Assassins) into the revolutionary fold; others would rather have the Kharwārij (at least under the Umayyads), or the Mukhtār revolt (685-687).[64] Not only are definitions rather vague and one revisionist historian's "revolutionary" can be rejected by another (who uncovers the former's anachronistic or apologetic reading of the sources), but even grouped together, their revolutionaries are few and far between, disappearing completely toward the eleventh century.

The tension between hero worship—the propensity to see the historian's ideals epitomized by a great figure of the past—and the critical approach is even more remarkable with regard to the very core of Muslim *historia sacra:* the era of Muḥammad and the four Orthodox Caliphs (until 660). While the Koranic message is scrutinized within its historical context, on many a chapter (family, slavery, attitude towards ethnicity), the revisionists are reticent about pronouncing an overall judgment. They evidently shy away from the *salafī* eulogizing of the so-called Muslim revolution and tend to present Muḥammad as progressive for his own times in his craving for social justice and commitment to the rule of the Divine Law.[65] The stumbling block is the problem of what went wrong. If Islam had begun so well—and no revisionist interprets the rise of Islam as a negative phenomenon or, *a fortiori*, Muḥammad as a villain—how did it happen that most of its subsequent history is so dark? There is, of course, more than hero worship involved here; being men of the

Left, hence pan-Arabists, who accept Muslim history (if not religion) as a component of Arabhood, the revisionists cannot vituperate the totality of this history (whence the search for "revolutionary" prefigurations), nor touch too heavily its founding father and his immediate associates.[66]

The way out of this dilemma is to present Muḥammad as progressive (some revisionists would even go so far as to dub him *yasārī*, leftist), yet add that at some point he made compromises with the Meccan *ancien régime*, which blunted the edge of his mission, leading to further compromises after his death. The cut-off date suggested is the Ḥudaybiyya Treaty (628) between the Prophet and Quraysh, which brought about a sharing of power with the Meccan "Right"; Muḥammad was henceforward less able to care for the needs of the oppressed (poor, slaves, aliens, etc.).[67] The second turning point was the death of the Prophet, who could still hold the Qurayshī plutocracy in check; then a power struggle erupted between Left and Right, this being the real significance of the Civil War. The Left, carrying the banner of the *shūrā*, social justice (only rarely is it claimed to be Socialism), and the rule of Law, is represented by Abū Dharr, Salmān, and other early followers of the Prophet; the villains on the Right are led by the caliph 'Uthmān. As for the other Orthodox Caliphs, there is a consensus for tagging 'Alī as Left (though admitting his weakness as a leader), Abū Bakr as "Center" (a compromise candidate after Muḥammad's death), while 'Umar's significance is controversial. Tīzīnī, for instance, considers him to be a proponent of social reform, while A. 'A. Ṣāliḥ and H. al-'Alawī view him as a sort of center politician operating in alliance with the Qurayshīs, out of necessity though without enthusiasm. 'Uthmān's period prefigures most of the Umayyad evils: Social polarization (through an unequal distribution of the spoils of conquest), a caliph cut off from the masses by a growing bureaucracy and acting as though superior to the Law, the *shūrā* discarded, and so forth.[68]

Beneath the power struggles, the revisionists detect deeper forces in operation. The Ḥudaybiyya treaty was not so much a tactical mistake as a stategic decision: Muḥammad opted for making Islam both a political structure and a religion, thus necessitating compromises. Had he kept it a religious movement, it is implied, Islam would have been able to maintain its progressive bent—a view which of course tends to substantiate the Left's plea for separation of state and religion. The failure of the concept of the rule of the

Law was largely due to lack of institutional guarantees in the Muḥammadan period it rendered almost inevitable when the conquest made the state stronger, required a vast administration and a large standing army, and introduced Sassanid and Byzantine influence. Law and religious doctrine were not sufficiently developed to act as countervailing forces, especially as their moralistic zeal was undermined by the riches (in land and other assets) falling into the hands of the state and the conquering Arabs. In a way, hint the revisionists, Islam was successful too early for its own good: Muḥammad was tempted by the victory over Mecca to transform a movement of have-nots into a ruling theocracy, while the conquests, too vast and too quick to be digested, were to some extent a curse in disguise.[69]

The intellectual arena seems to provide the revisionists with better objects of admiration, particularly rationalist thinkers and scientists who prefigure or actually pioneer the modern approach. They are set off by those very masters of "obscurantist theory"—such as al-Ash'arī, al-Ghazālī and Ibn Taymiyya—who are the villains of the piece.[70] Yet the same tensions recur. "Arab science and thought knew a golden age reaching the utmost point of progress *attainable in the Middle Ages* [my italics]; the Arabs were then the teachers and cultural leaders of all humanity," writes F. Zakariya, adding, however: "Yet this glorious period soon lost its luster, progress stopped, and rationality was discarded."[71] Adulation of past achievements, in a style reminiscent of the *salafiyya*, is indeed coupled here and elsewhere in revisionist writings with an attempt to put it in its historical context. The creative period is circumscribed to the eighth and ninth centuries, with the tenth and eleventh witnessing a loss of creative momentum; henceforward (i.e., *before* foreign invasions and military rule, though the latter catalyzed the process) decline set in. Moreover, scientific achievements consisted above all in the preservation and further elaboration in the applied fields of the Greco-Roman heritage; chemistry continued to evolve around the search after the Philosopher's Stone; astronomy was circumscribed within the Ptolemean perceptions and anatomy within those of Galienus.

All this was an important feat for the times (especially when compared to Europe of the Dark Ages), but one which had no sequel in the Islamic world, its fruits being reaped by modern Europe. The same is true of Arab thinkers like Ibn Rushd or Ibn Khaldūn, who did not succeed in establishing a real following, which would have been able to further develop their epoch-making ideas, nor did they succeed in filtering down these ideas to the masses. "The truth of the matter is that Ibn Rushd was alien to his age, contradicting rather than representing it," writes M. I. Ismā'īl. "Viewed by his contemporaries he was a heretic, he had less affinity to Islamic thought than to that of Europe, which welcomed his ideas and carried them further." Can one argue, notes F. Zakariya, that he and like-minded thinkers "shaped the mentality and daily behavior of the Arabs in the same way that one can say today the mentality of the Frenchman is Cartesian?"[72]

When further scrutinizing the texts of their undisputed heroes, the revisionists try to avoid the pitfall of excessive adulation: Ibn Khaldūn's work is shown, for all its originality, to have been permeated by metaphysical assumptions (on the role of miracles in history or on occult sciences), and he is scored for having failed to apply the theories of the *muqaddima* to the on the whole deceivingly conventional world history which followed it. Ibn Rushd is shown not to have broken the circle of the apologetic striving to reconcile science and religion.[73] A much harsher judgment is pronounced on the Mu'tazila, who are rather cast in the role of villains: their mode of thought was blatantly apologetic, intolerant toward other schools, submissive to the rulers.[74] A trait common to them and to the former two "pioneers without followers" (as well as to other relatively advanced thinkers like al-Fārābī) is their elitist (*'ulamā'*-like) outlook and lack of concern with social problems.[75]

How uneasy the revisionists feel with such findings is shown by the apologetic note appended by Muṣṭafā to the published version of his controversial article: "This is by no means meant to deny the important Arab contribution to the scientific and philosophical heritage of humanity during the (medieval) era; we merely wish to point out that this contribution did not endure and did not further develop in scope and depth."[76] Explanations of this death in early age are rather summary: (a) the existence of a strong obscurantist, irrational, and past-oriented strand in Islam, which combatted the innovatory, open, and rationalist one till it succeeded in the eleventh century "to strangle it and nip in the bud whatever potentialities there were in it"; (b) social repression of free thought, "a phenomenon closely intertwined with sexual repression, socioeconomic exploitation and political despotism" all designed to defend the *status quo*.[77] The persecution of innovative thinkers is shown to be one of the hallmarks of political power in Islam, employing a continuum of measures: from censorship, banishment, sacking, to official trial and execution. This atmosphere of *irhāb fikrī* (intellectual terror)—presented as much akin to the one prevailing today in the Arab world—had never been conducive to the flourishing of thought and grew more and more stifling as the alliance between the *'ulamā'*, the proponents of obscurantism, and the ruling class grew stronger in the later Middle Ages. "Baghdad fell as a cultural capital not in 1258 (with the Mongol conquest) but in 1150, when the caliph al-Mustanjid ordered burnt in public all scientific books; Arab civilization fell in Spain not in 1492 but in the late twelfth century, when Caliph al-Manṣūr burnt Ibn Rushd's books."[78]

The inadequacy of this explanation is pointed out by F. Zakariya in a candid revisionist autocritique. Medieval Europe was even more immersed that Islam in mythological irrational mentality, and freedom of inquiry was curbed there as ruthlessly (a phenomenon that extends into the early modern era as well, witness the cases of Giordano Bruno, Galileo, Spinoza, etc.). "In the final analysis, scientific knowledge is not an aggregate of truths which we are to discover one by one, but an aggregate of errors to overcome, one by one. Myths, superstitions, and other forms of belief in the supernatural are an inevitable phase on the long road towards knowledge; the crucial thing is whether other phases will follow suit."[79] In other words, there is nothing astounding in the medieval characteristics of Islamic history. The real question, for which Zakariya has no answer, is why (and how) these characteristics succeed in perpetuating themselves, albeit in varying degrees in different fields, well into our own times.

## LESSONS ON A SAD NOTE

"The closing note of this study is rather sad,"[80] says Zakariya when he comes to draw the lessons of inquiry into the past. For the lessons, as could be expected from praxis-oriented intellectuals, has to do with the reading of the present. And this present is found to be much more permeated by the past—in basic structures, attitudes, and patterns of behavior—than the Left has once been prone to think; and not by a recent past (Muslim yet alien, i.e., Ottoman, or alien and imperialist), but by the very glorious Arab-Islamic past, whose impact has been discovered to be not only long-standing, but largely negative. The findings of the revisionist historians thus fortified and gave deeper dimension to those of left-wing social scientists who had been the first to draw attention to the persistence of traditional molds.[81]

The first lesson to be drawn was obviously that the task of the revolutionaries was far more difficult and the resilience of conservative forces much greater than one used to imagine. Once again a feedback relationship was in operation: because of the close relationship between historians and other leftist thinkers, this tended to further reinforce the already sad mood on the Left, bred out of its failures in the 1970s, of the rise in prestige of the established regimes (after 1973) and of the resurgence of a fundamentalist Islam as a mass movement (contrary to the belief that its fortunes are dependent upon Arab military and political defeats). Leftist setbacks and rightist Islamic successes were due to structural, not conjectural, causes.[82] This was the lesson propounded by the historians.

The second lesson had to do with the future. The task of the revolutionaries was to bring about "transformational change" (in Barakāt's term) by attacking root causes, such as changing traditional affiliations by putting an end to the hegemony of familial and religious institutions and replacing them by national and class affiliations."[83] Yet this attack should by no means be aimed at a "cultural revolution" of the type preached by some people on the Left in the 1960s, i.e., complete rejection of history, heritage, and religion.[84] The Left came to be much more cognizant of the hold of Islam over the masses, of the dangers to their collective personality if such an element be brutally eliminated. The extent to which Arab nationalism (to which the Left is firmly committed) is anchored in historical perceptions makes a complete break with the past an even more impossible or hazardous prospect; one has to live with the dichotomy of *'urûbat al-ṭalā'i' wa-islām al-jamāhīr* ("the vanguard is Arab, the masses Muslim") in M. al-Ṣulḥ's phrase.[85] Otherwise the existent chasm between the perceptions of the former and the latter would never be bridged. Thus, while there is a contradiction (not to be whitewashed) between religion and revolutionary ideology, "it is none of the Left's business to propagate atheism" (H. al-'Alawī, quoting Togliatti).[86] It is only the negative social impact of religion and history that should be combatted. The best way to carry on this long and difficult fight is by acquiring self-knowledge, i.e., *inter-alia*, a better knowledge of the past. "An authentic historical analysis may bring about a revolution in our mentality. . . as it operates in the manner of pruning dry and ugly branches which impede further growth" (Ṭālbī). History is thus a sort of exercise in exorcism or, if one prefers, in collective psychotherapy. Getting to know the past accurately and to interpret it in its real context makes it easier to shed those elements once useful or understandable, but now irrelevant or detrimental. "It is one thing to trace one's ancestry to the past; it is quite another to relive this past" (I. Khūrī). A heritage, parts of which die out while serving as bases for further growth, "lives through its death" (F. Zakariya); better to have the past as a "point of departure" than as a "vast prison" (A. 'Abd al-Ghānī).[87]

If the historians helped redefine the tasks of the revolution, these in turn define more sharply the role of the revisionist historian: to create a collective self-image which will bear, in G. von Grunebaum's apt term, much more *richtigkeitsrational*,[88] and to study the past in order to liberate oneself from its stranglehold and help a past-oriented society become more future-oriented. It was the Tunisian M. Ṭālbī who, although much more moderate in political outlook than other revisionists, put this conviction in the most clearcut terms:

> One cannot disentangle oneself from the net of history as long as one is unaware or ignorant of it. As long as we carry it in our subconscious without subjecting it to a process of reassessment, we continue to drag behind us chains, outmoded beliefs, obsolete sediments which disrupt our personality, paralyse or impede our movement. We can liberate ourselves from their hold only through penetrating and fearless examination which will enable us to sort out what should be consigned to the realm of the past. Only thus shall we reshape our personality in the present, rejuvenate it without cutting off all ties to the past.[89]

## FOOTNOTES

1. A. Laroui, *The Crisis of Arab Intellectuals,* trans. D. Camell, University of California Press, 1976, p. 92.
2. E.g., A. Daher, *Current Trends in Arab Intellectual Thought,* Rand paper RM-5979-EFE, 1969; W. W. Kazziha, *Revolutionary Transformation in the Arab World,* London, 1975; T. Y. Ismael, *The Arab Left,* Syracuse University Press, 1976.
3. Laroui, *Crisis,* pp. 91, 96.
4. I. Khūrī, "Al-Islām, al-'Urūba wa-l-Ajwiba al-Radī'a." *Mawāqif,* Summer 1974, p. 96; cf. Gh. Shukrī, *al-Turāth wa-l-Thawra,* Beirut, 1973.
5. H. Sharābī, *Muqaddimāt li-Dirāsat al-Mujtama' al-'Arabi,* Beirut, 1975 (especially, pp. 13-29, which describe the author's intellectual itinerary); F. Ṣāliḥ, "Hawla al-Mafhūm al-Ummī fi-l-Qur'ān," *Dirāsāt 'Arabiyya* (henceforward *DA),* February, 1978, p. 127.

6. H. al-'Alawī, *Fi-l-Dīn wa-l-Turāth,* Beirut, 1973.
7. Ḥ. Ḥaydar, "Naqd Fikr al-Mu'tazila," *Qadāyā' 'Arabiyya,* April 1975, p. 111.
8. Sh. 'Abd al-Ḥakīm, *Madkhal li-Dirāsat al-Fulklūr wa-l-Asāṭīr al-'Arabiyya,* Beirut, 1978, p. 221.
9. Ṣ. Qudsī, "Arab wa-Lakin Mustashriqūn," *al-Ma'rifa,* May 1976, pp. 145-148.
10. A. Maqdisī, "Fi Ma'nā al-Turāth," *Mawāqif,* Sept.-Oct. 1970, p. 38; M. Ṭālbī, "Al-Ta'rīkh wa-Mashākil al-Yawm wa-l-Ghadd," *'Ālam al-Fikr,* April-June 1974, p. 26.
11. The point is made with particular vigor by T. Tīzīnī, *Min al-Turāth ila-l-Thawra,* Beirut 1976, pp. 77, 95; H. al-'Alawī, *Fi-l-Siyāsa al-Islāmiyya: al-Fikr wa-l-Mumārasa,* Beirut 1974, pp. 5-6; Sh. Muṣṭfā, "Al-Ab'ād al-Ta'rīkhiyya li-Azmat al-Taṭawwur al-Ḥaḍārī," *al-Ādāb,* May 1974, p. 14. Cf. B. Lewis, *History—Remembered, Recovered, Invented,* Princeton, 1975.
12. Maqdisī, p. 20, H. Barakāt, "Al-Taghyīr al-Taḥawwulī fi-l-Mujtama' al-Arabī," *Mawāqif,* Summer 1974; cf. T. Khālidī, *Dirāsāt fī-Ta'rikh al-Fikr al-'Arabī wa-l-Islāmī,* Beirut 1977, p. 13; Y. al-Ḥafiẓ, "Al-Judhūr al-Fikriyya li-l-Ḥazīma," *DA,* May 1973, pp. 25-9; 'A. Zi'ūr, *Al-Taḥlīl al-Nafsī li-l-Dhāt al-'Arabiyya,* Beirut, 1977, pp. 160-1.
13. H. al-Alawī, "Kayfa Naqifu min al-Turāth al-īslāmī," *Mawāqif,* Sept.-Oct. 1969, p. 58; T. Tīzīnī, pp. 34, 73; B. Ṭībī, "Al-Kitāba al-Waṣfiyya wa-l-Kitāba al-Thawriyya," *Mawāqif,* Feb. 1968.
14. A. 'Ulabi, "Al-Manhaj wa-l-Turāth wa-l-Ghaybiyya," *al-Ādab,* Jan. 1974, p. 54.
15. G. Zaynātī, "Ibn Rushd bayna-l-'Arab wa-l-Gharb," *al-Bāḥith,* May-June 1978, p. 39.
16. T. Raḥma, "Al-Asāla wa-l-Tajdid fi-l-Mu'tamar al-Ta'rīkhī al-Awwal," *DA,* April 1975, pp. 137-40; cf. Tīzīnī, pp. 37, 42, 58. *Khayr umma* refers, of course, to the celebrated Koranic verse (cx, 3).
17. Maqdisī, p. 27.
18. F. Zakariya, "Al-Takhalluf al-Fikrī wa-Ab'āduhu al-Ḥaḍāriyya," *al- Ādāb,* May 1974, p. 33; 'Ulabī, p. 33.
19. A. Aḥmad, *Naqd al-Fahm al-'Aṣrī li-l-Qur'an,* Beirut 1972; idem, "Mulāḥaẓāt Ḥawla al-Fahm al-'Aṣrī li-l-Qur'an," *Mawāqif,* July-Aug. 1971, pp. 136-47; Zakariya, pp. 31-33; cf. 'U. al-Ṣāfī, *'Alā Hamish Naqd al-Fikr al-Dīnī,* Beirut, 1970, p. 42. M. Maḥmūd's book was printed in 80,000 copies and is most popular among Egyptian students.
20. Ṭībī, p. 94. 'Abd al-Ṣabbūr's interview with *al-Thaqāfa al-'Arabiyya,* February 1975.
21. 'Ulabī, p. 25; Y. al-Khawrānī in *Kayfa Naktubu Ta'rīkhana al-Qawmī,* Damascus, 1966, p. 161. Cf. Khālidī, p. 14-15; F. al-Sāmir, "Naḥwa Ta'rīkh Jadīd." *al-Thaqāfa al-Jadīda,* 5 (1958), pp. 14-17; 'Alawī, p. 60. It should be noted that both 'Ulabī and al-Sāmir studied the Zanj slave rebellion (note 63), while Khālidī published (in his *Dirāsāt*) an inquiry into the social origins of the *'ulamā'* and of heretic movements in Islam and later (*al-Mawāqif,* 49, Winter 1984) a study of Muslim traditions of punishment and torture.
22. 'Ulabī, p. 22.
23. Al-'Aẓm's interview with *al-Thāqafa al-'Arabiyya,* April 1974; A. Bahā' al-Dīn, 'Ta'-līq', *al-Ādāb,* May 1974, p. 104.
24. P. Geyl, *Use and Abuse of the Past,* Yale University Press, 1955, p. 11.
25. 'Ulabī, pp. 22-5; cf. Tīzīnī, p. 34; Zakariya, pp. 35-6.
26. 'Ulabī, pp. 22-5, 54; Zakariya, p. 36; 'Alawī, p. 62; Tīzīnī, p. 34; Ṭālbī, p. 23.
27. Raḥma, pp. 139-42; N. Naṣṣār, "Mafhūm al-Umma fī Naẓrat al-Mas'ūdī ilā-l-Ta'rīkh," *DA,* January 1978, p. 43; 'Ulabī, pp. 21, 23, 51.
28. Maqdisī, p. 27; cf. 'Ulabī, pp. 51-5; Tīzīnī, p. 54.
29. Ṭālbī, p. 24. For statistical data on ethnocentrism in Egyptian M.A. and Ph.D. dissertations in the last forty years cf. E. Sivan, "Trends in Egyptian Historiography" (Hebrew), *Hamizrah he-Ḥadash,* XXIII (1973), p. 80 ff.

30. Maqdisī, p. 30.
31. H. al-Zu'bī, "Al Wāqi' al-'Arabī wa-Ru'yat al-Idiyūlūjiyya li-Shakhṣiyyāt al-Turāth al-'Arabī," *al-Ādāb,* Nov. 1977, pp. 57-8; Khūrī, *loc. cit.* "A Ḥamdān, Ḥiwār Marqsī-Islāmī fī Dār al-Ahrām," *DA,* May 1970, pp. 74-8; M. I. 'Abd al-Rāziq, "Garaudy wa-l-Islām wa-l-Istirākiyya," *al-Fikr al-Mu'*āṣir, Feb. 1970, pp. 54-9.
32. Ḥamdān, May 1970, p. 75; June 1970, p. 116.
33. Tīzīnī, pp. 174-5; 'Ulabī, p. 18; Bahā' al-Dīn, *loc. cit.*
34. F. Zakariya, "Ilā Matā Naghtaribu 'an Ḥāḍirina," *al-Ahrām,* 28 November 1973; for rejoinders see Gh. Ḥalsa in *al-Kātib,* January 1974, pp. 94-103; Ḥ.S. Labīb in *al-Adīb,* February 1974, p. 33.
35. Laroui, *Crisis,* p. 96.
36. 'A. al-Akhḍar, "Min Naqd al-Samā' ilā Naqd al-Arḍ," in *Lenin-Nuṣūṣ Ḥawla al-Mawqif min al-Dīn,* Beirut, 2nd edition, 1978, p. 81; N. al-Mannā', "Kayfa Nuzaḥziḥ Qurūnana al-Wusṭā," *Maqāqif,* September 1972.
37. Tīzīnī, p. 115; it should be noted that in another book of his the author designated the Islamic past by the derogatory code-word "medieval": *Mashrū Ru'ya Jadīda li-l-Fikr al-'Arabī fi-l-'Aṣr al-Wasīṭ,* Damascus 1971; Maqdisī, p. 20; Sh. 'Abd al-Ḥakīm, p. 221; 'Ulabī, p. 54.
38. Muṣṭafā, p. 19; for the debates see *al-Thaqāfa al-'Arabiyya,* June 1974, pp. 20-1, 30-1.
39. A. Besançon, "Soviet Present and Russian Past," *Encounter,* March 1978, p. 80.
40. Sh. 'Abd al-Ḥakīm, p. 226.
41. Akhḍar, p. 79; H. al-'Alawī, "Al-Ḥukkām al-Muslimūn bayna a-l-Zuhd wa-l-Taraf," DA, Sept. 1973, pp. 26-7.
42. For these two phenomena as present preoccupations see *Abḥāth 'Arabiyya,* May-July 1978, pp. 117-8; M. Ḥijāzī, *Sikūlūjiyyat al-Insān al-Maqhūr,* Beirut, 1977; Ḥ. Barakāt, "Al-Ightirāb wa-l-Thawra fī-l-Ḥayāt al-'Arabiyya," *Mawāqif,* July-Aug. 1969.
43. 'A. al-Akhḍar, p. 47.
44. Ibid, pp. 41-51; Sh. Muṣṭafā, p. 17; H. al-'Alawī, *Fi-l-Dīn wa-l-Turāth,* pp. 44-54, 81-1; idem, *al-Siyāsa al-Islāmiyya,* pp. 33-4, 71-5; idem, "al-Ḥukkām al-Muslimūn," pp. 22-4; A. 'Ulabī, *Thawrat al-Zanj,* Beirut, 1961; pp. 64-74; 'Āmil, *Āzmat al-Ḥaḍāra al-'Arabiyya,* Beirut, 1974, pp. 8-12.
45. Kḥ. A. Khalīl, *Maḍmūn al-Usṭūra fi-l-Fikr al-'Arabī,* pp. 118-21, 130-5; 'A. al-Khalīlī, *al-Turāth al-Filasṭīnī wa-l-Ṭabaqāt,* Beirut 1977, pp. 47-9. 'A. al-Wardī, "Ḥawla Ṣirā' al-Qiyam fi-l-Mujtama' al-'Arabī," *Mawāqif,* Summer 1974; M. Rabī', "Al-Ru'ya al-Mustaqbaliyya min Khilāl Wāqi' 'Arabī Mutakhallif," *al-Ādāb,* May 1974, p. 108; K. A. Khalīl, "Anmāṭ al-Qiyāda," *DA,* Jan. 1979.
46. H. al-'Alawī, *Al-Siyāsa al-Islāmiyya,* pp. 34-43, 95-7; idem, *Fi-l-Dīn wa-l-Turāth,* pp. 28-34; Khalīl, pp. 131-2; 'Ulabī, *Tawrat al-Zanj,* pp. 30 ff. 112; al-Akhḍar, pp. 53-5.
47. Al-Akhḍar, p. 46.
48. B.Yāsīn, *Al-thālūth al-Muḥarram,* Beirut, 1973, pp. 149-50; T. al-Khālidī, pp. 14, 16; 'Ulabī, "al-Manhaj wa-l-Turāth," p. 51; Sh. Muṣṭafā, pp. 17-18, 23-4; 'Alawī, *Al-Siyāsa al-Islāmiyya,* pp. 41-52, 59-60; 100-111, 142-4; idem, "Al-Ḥukkām al-Muslimūn," pp. 24-5; al-Akhḍar, pp. 43, 66; Khalīl, pp. 134, 152, 159; Khalīl, *art. cit.* pp. 49 ff.
49. B. Yāsīn, pp. 95-144, idem, "Muḥarramān: al-Dīn wa-l-Jins," *DA,* Nov. 1970, p. 2 ff.; H. al-'Alawī, "Ashyā' min Fuṣūl al-Masraḥ al-Dīnī fī-l-Waṭan al-'Arabī," *Mawāqif,* May-June 1972, pp. 57-67; idem, "Kayfa Naqifu," p. 58; Khalīl, pp. 152-7; Sh. 'Abd al-Ḥakīm, pp. 222-4, 128; M. Kāmil, "Ḥiwār al-Turāth wa-l-'Aṣr," *al-Ādāb,* Jan. 1973, p. 69; Khūrī, pp. 70, 95.
50. I. Sarkīs, "Al-Adīb al-'Arabī wa-l-Iltizām," *DA,* Aug. 1977, pp. 143-5; B. Yāsīn, "Yanābī' al-Ihaqāfa wa-Mashārib al-Muthaqqafīn," *DA,* Dec. 1977, pp. 86-102. Ḥ.

Barakāt, "Al-Kātib al-'Arabī wa-l-Sulṭa," *Mawāqif*, July-Aug. 1970, pp. 28-48; Ḥ. Ḥaydar, "Naqd Fikr al-Mu'tazila," S. J. al-'Aẓm, interview with *al-Thaqāfa al-'Arabiyya*, April 1975.

51. Mustafa, *art. cit.*, p. 20.
52. N. Ballūz, "Ba'd al-Malam̄iḥ al-Ḥadāriyya li-l-Iqṭā'iyya al-Sharqiyya fī Ẓill al-Khilāfa al-'Arabiyya," *DA*, Nov. 1972, pp. 4 ff.; Yāsīn, *al-Thālūth al-Muḥarram*, pp. 77-85; Tīzīnī, *Mashr' Ru'yā Jadīda*, p. 185 ff.; al-Khālīlī, pp. 47 ff., 56 ff., 86 ff.; Sh. Muṣṭafā, pp. 16-17; 'Alawī, *Fī-l-Dīn wa-l-Turāth*, p. 21 ff.; Akhḍar, pp. 49, 67-8.
53. Al-Khalīlī, pp. 83-5, 109-10, 120, 140; A. 'Ulabī, *Thawrat al-Zanj*, Beirut, 1961; F. al-Sāmir, *Thawrat al-Zanj*, Beirut, 1971; Tīzīnī, *Mashrū' Ru'yā Jadīda*, p. 149; Ballūz, p. 7; Yāsīn, *al-Thālūth al-Muḥarram*, pp. 75-7. The left-wing publishing house of Beirut, Dar al-Ṭalī'a, broke the taboo subject of contemporary slavery in the Arab world by translating into Arabic Sean O'Callaghan's *The Slave Trade (Tijārat al-Raqīq*, 1962).
54. 'Alawī, *al-Siyāsa al-Islāmiyya*, p. 42; al-Akhḍar, p. 46.
55. Cf. N. al-Sa'dāwī, *al-Mar'ah al-'Arabiyya wa-l-Jins*, Beirut, 1972; Ḥ. Barakāt, "al-Taghyīr al-Taḥawwulī"; Zī'ūr, passim. Kh. A. Khalīl, "Al-Mar'ah al-'Arabiyya wa-l-Taghayyurāt al-Ra'īsiyya fī 'Aṣrina," *DA*, June 1973; R. al-Samān, "Al-Usra al-Abawiyya . . . wa-Naḥnu," *DA*, Jan. 1974, pp. 113-16; G. Tarābīsī, *Sharq wa-Gharb Rujūla wa-Anūsa*, Beirut, 1977; 'A. Farrāj, *al-Ḥuriyya fī Adab al-Mar'ah*, Beirut, 1975; H. Shārabī, *Muqaddimāt*, p. 31 ff.
56. Yāsīn, "Muḥarramayn: al-Dīn wa-l-Jins," pp. 9-10, 12-13; idem, *al-Thālūth al-Muḥarram*, chap. 3; Khalīl, *Maḍmūn al-Usṭūra*, chap. 4 (especially, pp. 119-20); H. Mannā', "Al-Usra al-Abawiyya fī-l-Islām," *DA*, Oct. 1973, pp. 42-59; 'A. Aḥmad, *Naqd al-Fahm al-'Asrī li-l-Qur'an*, pp. 37-9, 31-2; Sh. Muṣṭafā, pp. 19-22; Sh. 'Abd al-Ḥakīm, chaps. 10, 11; 'Alawī, "Al-Masraḥ al-Dīnī," pp. 61-2; G. Tarābīshī. "Takhalluf Wa'y al-Takhalluf," *DA*, June 1974, pp. 29-32; S. al-Khammāsh, *Al-Mar'ah al-'Arabiyya wa-l-Mujtama' al-Taqlīdī al-Mutakhallif*, Beirut, 197(6)?, pp. 16-18, 32-4; 'A. al-Khālīlī, "Al-Mar'ah fī-l-Turāth al Sha'bī al-Filasṭīnī," *al-Ādāb*, July 1977, pp. 52-7.
57. 'Ulabī, "Al-Manhaj wa-l-Turāth," pp. 25-6; 'Alawī, *Fī-l-Siyāsa al-Islāmiyya*, p. 63 ff.
58. Idem, "Ma'a Rodinson, fi-l-Islām wa-l-Ra'smāliyya," *DA*, Nov. 1974, p. 67.
59. Cf., e.g., M. Ismā'īl, *al-Ḥarakāt al-Sirriyya fi-l-Islām*, Beirut, 1973; Kh. Muhyī al-Dīn, *Al-Dīn wa-l-Ishtirākiyya*, Cairo, 197(6)?; Ḥ. Marwah, "Al-Thawriyya fi-l-Turāth," *al-Ādāb*, May 1975, pp. 17-26; F. Darrāj, "Al-Dīn wa-l-Ṣirā' al-Ṭabaqī," *al-Ṭarīq*, April, 1978, pp. 114-25.
60. 'A. Ḥamdān, "Ḥiwār Marqsī-Islāmī," *DA*, May 1970, p. 78. Cf. Introduction (by N. al-Ḥakīm) to the Arabic translation of *Islam et Capitalisme* (2nd edition, Beirut, 1974, p. 8); H. Zu'bī, "Al-Wāqi' al-Arabī," pp. 57-8.
61. Tīzīnī, *al-Turāth wa-l-Thawra*, p. 60 ff.
62. H. 'Aṭwān, *Al-Shu'arā* al-*Ṣa'ālīk fi-l-'Aṣr al-'Abbāsī al-Awwal*, Beirut, 1977; M. al-Jūzū, *al-A'shā al-Kabīr*, Beirut, 1977; 'Alawī, *Fi-l-Dīn wa-l-Turāth*, pp. 139-54.
63. F. al-Sāmīr. *Thawrat al-Zanj*, Beirut, 1971; 'Ulabī, *Thawrat al-Zanj*, Beirut, 1963; Alawī, "Ma'a Rodinson," pp. 69-70; Akhḍar, pp. 56, 63 ff.
64. See, e.g., Khālidī, *Dirāsāt*, pp. 24-9; 'Alawī, *Siyāsā*, pp. 83-4; Akhḍar, p. 58 ff.; Sh. Muṣṭafā, p. 23; Ḥaydar, p. 119ff.
65. Cf. the articles by 'A. Aḥmad and H. Mannā'.
66. For instance, F. Ṣāliḥ, "Al-Islam wa-l-Qawmiyya," *al-Ādāb*, Aug.-Sept. 1977, pp. 9-13; M. Shafīq, "Al-Waḥda al-'Arabiyya fi-l-Turāth al-'Arabī," *DA*, June-July 1977, pp. 55-72; I. Khūrt, *art. cit.*, N. Abū Niḍāl, "Radd 'alā al-Qā'ilīn bi-Wujūd Umam wa-Qawmiyyāt 'Arabiyya," *DA*, Jan. 1978, pp. 92-110.
67. A. 'A. Ṣāliḥ, *Al-Yamīn wa-l-Yasār fi-l-Islām*, Beirut, 1972, pp. 44-55; Tīzīnī, *Mashrū'*

*Ru'ya Jadīda,* pp. 149-59; 'Alawī, *al-Siyāsa al-Islāmiyya,* chap. 1. A criticism of the hazy definitions underlying this approach was voiced in Bārūt's article on Tīzīnī (*DA,* Feb. 1978, p. 138 ff.).

68. Tīzīnī, *Mashrū',* p. 161 ff; Ṣāliḥ, pp. 56-88, 118-23; Ḥaydar, "Naqd Fikr al-Mu'tazila," pp. 109-10; 'Alawī, *Al-Siyāsa al-Islāmiyya,* pp. 37-41, 64-82; idem, *Fi-l-Dīn wa-l-Turāth,* pp. 28-30.
69. 'Alawī, *Al-Siyāsa al-Islāmiyya,* pp. 55-8, 64-71, 85; Ṣāliḥ, pp. 113-14; 133-5, 142, 152-8; Yāsīn, *Al-Thālūth al-Muḥarram,* pp. 58 ff., 77 ff., 85 ff., 146 ff.; Akhḍar, p. 46 ff.
70. Cf. Tīzīnī, *Min al-Turāth ilā-l-Thawra,* pp. 52, 71; N. Naṣṣār, "Al-Milla wa-l-Umma 'Inda al-Shahrastānī," *DA,* April 1978, pp. 27, 32.
71. F. Zakariya, "Al-Takhalluf al-Fikrī wa-Ab'āduhu al-Ta'rikhiyya," pp. 33-4.
72. Sh. Muṣṭafā, pp. 22-3; Zaynātī, "Ibn Rushd," pp. 37-47; M. I. Ismā'īl, "Garaudy . . . wa-l-Islām wa-l-Ishtirākiyya," pp. 55 ff.; Zakariya, p. 34; Ḥamdān, "Ḥiwār Marqsī-Islāmī," p. 77; *al-Bāḥith,* March-June 1979 (the whole issue).
73. M. I. Ismā'īl, p. 57 ff.; Ṭālbī, p. 23; Tīzīnī, *Min al-Turāth ilā-l-Thawra,* pp. 43, 48; 'Alawī, 'Masraḥ Dīnī, pp. 66-7.
74. Ḥaydar, *art. cit.*; Akhḍar, pp. 34, 50; I. al-Sharqāwī, "Azmat al-Falsafa al-Islāmiyya," *al-Fikr al-Mu'āṣir,* Sept. 1970, pp. 98-9; For a sample of left-apologetic approach see M. 'Imāra, *al-Māddiyya wa-l-Mithāliyya fi Falsafat Ibn Rushd,* Cairo, 1971; Ḥ. Marwa, *al-Naz'āt al-Māddiyya . . . al-Islāmiyya,* Beirut, 1978.
75. Ḥaydar, pp. 124-5; H. al-Zu'bī, "Waḥdat al-Wujūd," pp. 102-3; Khālidī, pp. 14, 17.
76. Sh. Muṣṭafā, p. 23 (n).
77. Ibid., pp. 23-4.
78. Zaynāti, p. 46 (and pp. 43-7).
79. Zakariya, pp. 30-1.
80. Ibid., p. 36.
81. Cf. N. al-Bītār, *Min al-Naksa ilā al-Thawra,* Beirut, 1969, pp. 36 ff., 201 ff.; Ḥ. Barakāt, "Al-Taghyīr al-Taḥawwulī"; H. Sharābī, *Muqqadimāt li-Dirāsat al-Mujtama' al-'Arabī,* Beirut, 1975.
82. Cf. M. Kāmil, "Ḥiwār al-Turāth wa-l-Aṣr," pp. 69-70; N. 'Allūsh, "Awda ilā Mawḍū'āt al-Thawra al-'Arabiyya," *al-Kātib al-Filasṭīnī,* Feb. 1978, pp. 4-7; Ṣ. 'Īsā, "al-Mas'ala al-Thiyūqrātiyya," *al-Mustaqbal al-'Arabī,* May 1978. H. Qaram, "al-Ittijāhāt al-Jadīda," *al-Bāḥith,* July-Sept. 1978. M. A. al-'Ālim, "Min al-Maḥdūdiyya al-lā Maḥdūdiyya," *Mawāqif,* Spring 1975, pp. 54ff.
83. Barakāt, art. cit.
84. 'Afīf al-Akhḍar is a prominent proponent of this view in the 1970s (article cited above). For a critique of this approach cf. Maqdisī, p. 26 ff.
85. 'A. Zi'ūr, *al-Taḥlīl al-Nafsī li-l-Dhāt al-'Arabiyya,* Beirut, 1977; T. Tīzīnī, *Ḥawla Mushkilāt al-Thawra wa-l-Thaqāfa fi-l-Ālam al-Thālith,* 2nd edition, Damascus, 1973; M. al-Ṣulḥ, *al-Islām wa-Ḥarakat al-Taḥarrur al-'Arabiyya,* Beirut, 1973; L. al-Khūlī, "Mulāḥaẓāt Ḥawla al-Waḍ' al-Rāhin," *Shu'ūn Filasṭīniyya,* Dec. 1977, p. 27.
87. Ṭālbī, p. 26; Khūrī, p. 94; Zakariya, p. 36; A. 'Abd al-Ghanī, "Tasā'ulāt Ḥawla Azmat al-Fikr al-'Arabī," *Abḥāth 'Arabiyya,* May-July 1978, pp. 5-6. Cf. Sh. 'Abd al-Ḥakīm, p. 221.
88. G. Von Grunebaum, *Modern Islam,* University of California Press, 1962, p. 101.
89. Ṭālbī, p. 26; Cf. 'U. Farrūkh, *Tajdīd al-Ta'rīkh al-Arabī,* Beirut, 1981; Sh. Muṣṭafā, "The Crisis of Arab Historiography," *al-Majalla al-Kuwaytiya li-l-'Ulūm al-Insāniyya* 3(1981); M. al-Nuwayhī, *Naḥwa Thawra fi-l-Fikr al-Dīnī,* Beirut, 1983.

# PART II: IMPACT OF THE PAST UPON THE PRESENT

# Chapter 3:

# THE SANCTITY OF JERUSALEM IN ISLAM

IN 1968, a young Syrian philosopher, Ṣādiq Jalāl al-'Aẓm pondered the reasons for the recent Arab defeat in the Six-Day War. The book, *Autocritique After the Debacle*, was widely read and discussed at the time. No point was more hotly debated than the author's claim that the hold of religion upon Muslim minds was a major reason for the defeat. The reasons he adduced were to serve as guidelines about what to do and what to avoid in the struggles to come. Thus, on the chapter on religion, al-'Aẓm tackled Arab preoccupation with the fall of Jerusalem into the hands of the Israelis:

> Why did we raise a particular outcry about the conquest of Jerusalem? We do not prefer one part of the Arab homeland to another. Jerusalem is no better than the grains of sand in Sinai, than Nablus, Quneitra, Haifa, or Jaffa. One may, of course, expect to reap important propaganda benefits abroad because of the religious character of Jerusalem, but the struggle for the liberation of Palestine does not boil down to the return of mosques and churches, which are tourist attractions.[1]

While al-'Aẓm's book had some impact, his critique of the cult of Jerusalem failed completely to convince his readership. Even secularist leaders and thinkers refused to secularize (in al-'Aẓm's terms, "politicize") the issue of Jerusalem; whether out of opportunism or sincere belief, they persisted in rallying support for their religious claims to the Third Most Sacred City of Islam.

Ironically enough, this occurrence had its analogy on the other side of the barricade. Some thirty-eight years before, the philosopher and historian, Gershom Scholem, was requested to advise a committee established by the Zionist authories to present evidence to the British commission investigating the Wailing Wall riots (1929). Scholem's biographer recounts:

The committee asked Scholem, as the university expert on Kabbala (Jewish mysticism), for Kabbalistic sources concerning the Wall, presumably to strengthen the Jews' historical and religious claims. Scholem refused to make books from his private library available to the committee. . . . [He was attacked in the Hebrew press] for his refusal to cooperate and portrayed as a rabid anti-Zionist. In his response Scholem argued that he did not believe the question of the Wall should be decided by a judicial body, but should be a matter for political negotiation. Behind Scholem's refusal to lend his expert authority to the Jewish defense of Wailing Wall rights was his belief that the political disputes with the Arabs should be resolved on the plane of politics, irrespective of religious considerations.[2]

Scholem had enjoyed a broader following than al-'Aẓm but, in the end, it was not his view which won the day.

To understand al-'Aẓm's failure one should probe the past. Perhaps the best way may be to concentrate upon the era when Jerusalem—a latecomer to the Islamic set of notions about sanctity— became accepted as a holy place; that is, the era of the Crusades. The circumstances, the ways and means through which this was accomplished, may shed some light upon the contemporary predicament.

## INDIFFERENCE

Jerusalem fell into the Crusaders' hands on July 15, 1099, an event considered a mystical apotheosis of their long and arduous march. Muslim reaction could have been expected to be a mirror image of that Christian exaltation. Yet, strangely enough, one does not detect either shock or a sense of religious loss and humiliation. Contemporary Muslim chroniclers report the fall of the city in a dry, matter-of-fact manner, quite often in passing, as they do for other Syrian and Palestinian cities taken by the Franks.[3] The poetry produced by Muslim refugees lamenting their misfortune never mentions the fall of Jerusalem.[4] Even the great theologian al-Ghazālī, who stayed in Jerusalem in the late 1090s, never alludes to its fall. Then, how are we to explain such an indifference to the loss of the Third Most Sacred City of Islam?

The peripeties of that turbulent era certainly had something to do with it. Jerusalem, hitherto held by the Shīite dynasty of the Fāṭimids, was taken by the Sunni Turkomen warriors in 1070 and reconquered by that Egyptian dynasty in 1098. Both events were greeted in Syria with total indifference.[5] The Frankish conquest coming barely a year later seemed no more than another change of rulers, which, like the former two, might not last long. One glimpses this state of mind in a letter dated 1100 and found in the Cairo Geniza; its author, a North African Jew then living in Egypt, expects the city soon to be reconquered by the Fāṭimid army.[6]

A second, and supplementary explanation, points to the fact that the Muslims have not as yet perceived the uniqueness of the Crusade. It was viewed as a sort of sequel to the Byzantine invasions of Syria, designed to repossess lost territories in which (with one exception in the mid-tenth century) religious themes played no role.[7] The fact that the Crusaders came by way of Constantinople and Byzantine Anatolia tended to bolster that image and, indeed, contemporary Arab sources usually call them *Rūm* (Byzantians).[8]

While these two explanations have some validity, at least for the first few years after the conquest, they are far from being sufficient. On the one hand, it soon became clear that Egypt had neither the force nor the will to recover the territories occupied by the Crusaders. All it did was to launch a few limited and abortive incursions, which ceased altogether after 1105. The other major Muslim power in the region, the city-state of Damascus, did not exert even such a minimal effort. Muslim opinion had thus to learn to view the Frankish occupation of Jerusalem as quasi permanent. Nevertheless, all through the fiirst half of the twelfth century, Muslim public opinion persists in its indifference to the fate of Jerusalem. On the other hand, the absence of any religious antagonism on the part of the Muslims with regard to the Crusaders could not last long. Muslims came to be fully aware of the Frankish *(faranj)* efforts designed to confer upon Jerusalem a distinctly Christian character: the profanation of mosques and synagogues, many of which were later made into churches, the prohibition of non-Muslims to live in the city, etc. Nor were the Muslims oblivious of the fact that the city was both the ultimate goal of the First Crusade (as well as of the later ones), and at the same time the capital of the Frankish state to which it gave its name: The Latin Kingdom of Jerusalem.[9]

All this could be expected to shake Muslim indifference; yet this was not the case. Even those few Muslim circles that from the beginning considered the Franks as infidels and called upon their countrymen to wage *jihād* (Holy War) against them did not allude to the Holy City in their sermons and writings (with the exception of jurist ʻAlī b. Ṭāhir al-Sulamī, of Damascus, who will be discussed later).

In consequence, one should look for another, more profound, explanation for Muslim indifference. In the previous paragraph I used the term "Holy City" as a synonym for Jerusalem, but it was this very sanctity that was in doubt, its ascendancy over Islamic minds being quite weak. The idea of the sanctity of Jerusalem made its first —and short-lived—appearance in Islam when the Prophet Muḥammad, as part of his pact with the Jews of Medina, consented to make Jerusalem the direction of prayer *(qibla)*. But when, after eighteen months, the pact was discarded and war broke out between Muslims and Jews, the *qibla* and the notion of sanctity it stood for were banished from Islam (Muslims henceforward turning in prayer toward the Black Stone, the *Ka'ba*, of Mecca). Indeed, when Jerusalem was captured by the Muslims a few years after the death of the Prophet, no religious significance was attributed to that event and no new Arabic name given to it. *Īlīya* was merely a rendering of the Roman (and secular) name, Aelia Capitolina, which it had borne for over five centuries.

It was more than half a century after the conquest that two new names with markedly religious connotations appeared: *al-Quds* (the Holy) and *Bayt al-Maqdis* (The Temple). At the same time, Muslims began to go on pilgrimages to Jerusalem, staying for a few months or a few years in its "sacred precincts." This sudden interest in Jerusalem came from three quarters: converts to Islam (such as the Jew Ka'b al-Akhbar), who carried a few ideas of their old religion into the new; the edifying example of Christian hermits, who were revered by the Muslims, with their special attachment to Jerusalem; and last but not least, the Umayyad caliphs, particularly 'Abd al-Malik (685-705) and Walīd (705-15), who used the city in order to confer sanctity, and hence legitimacy, upon the whole of the land of *Shām* (Syria-Palestine), which now replaced the Arabian Peninsula as the center of the empire. The Umayyads would therefore combine a propaganda effort on behalf of Jerusalem and an extensive building campaign (e.g., the Dome of the Rock). The idea of Jerusalem's sanctity soon became popular, at least in Syria-Palestine, among believers who, like others in holy places elsewhere in *Dār al-Islām*, found in this city direct access to the deity—an access so rare in Islam with its puritan distaste for intercessory powers. Acculturation of new converts and the needs of believers, hungry for the sacred, thus combined with the blessing of the Umayyads to enhance the city's prestige. Yet, an important social group, the *'ulamā'*, looked askance at this novelty and called it *bidʿa*, a term of opprobrium in Muslim lingo. Not only was this worship new, hence suspect, and related to folk customs of intercession, but it was also of a distinctly non-Muslim provenance (Jews of Medina, converts, monks) at a time when a maturing Islam was more conscious—and jealous—of its uniqueness, less malleable, and no longer ready to absorb easily exogenous religious themes, be they of other monotheistic religions.

The efforts of the Umayyads to encourage pilgrimages to Jerusalem in place of the *ḥajj* to Mecca and Medina at a time when the Arabian Peninsula was held by rebels made such a theme even more suspect. For all the Umayyad protests that this was but a temporary measure and that Jerusalem was only the "third most sacred city," the suspicion lingered that they were about to make it equal to the twin cities of Arabia, all the more so as pilgrimage to Jerusalem was quite attractive to the believers—less onerous and less dangerous than the long hazardous journey to Arabia.

*ʿUlamāʾ* polemics against the sanctity of Jerusalem grew fiercer under the ʿAbbāsids, who toppled the Umayyads (750); the blessing of the new dynasty—which moved its center to Iraq and thus did not care for Syrian prestige—strengthened the hand of puritan experts in Islamic law and further pushed the idea to the margins of official Islam. There was, however, one group of men of religion who espoused the idea of Jerusalem, namely the ascetics *(zuhhād)* and mystics *(ṣūfī)*, then just beginning to emerge, with their special predilection for finding routes of direct, corporeal access to Allah in order not to abandon the believer to confront Him alone, as the jurists and theologians would have it. Furthermore, the mystics, with their underlying pantheism, were much more receptive to outside influence, especially that of the hermits of Syria-Palestine.[10]

But the *ʿulamāʾ*, enjoying as they did the support of the rulers, had the upper hand in the controversy about Jerusalem. The Ṣūfīs were then far less influential than in the later Middle Ages. The memory of the Umayyads and their exploits were not cherished beyond the land of *Shām*, and even there it tended to fade out with the passage of time. No wonder that belief in the sanctity of Jerusalem cannot be said to have been widely diffused nor deeply rooted in Islam on the eve of the Crusades. The small weight Jerusalem carried as a population, administrative, or intellectual center further dminished its prestige.[11] The cult of Jerusalem—unlike that of Mecca and Medina—was, as a result, a local phenomenon, circumscribed to Palestine, perhaps also to certain parts of southern Syria. This is borne out by the observation of the Iranian traveler Nāṣir-i-Khusraw on the geographical origin of pilgrims to Jerusalem (in 1046) and by the fact that all the authors of *Faḍā'īl al-Quds* ("In praise of Jerusalem") treatises were inhabitants of Jerusalem and of its immediate vicinity.[12]

Small wonder that public opinion in the lands of Islam, never particularly sensitized to the idea of Jerusalem, was not deeply shocked by its fall.

There were, no doubt, a few Muslims who reacted more sharply to the Crusader conquest of Jerusalem. But if we are to eliminate a number of so-called prophecies about the Muslim recapture of the city—attributed to the 1120s and 1130s, yet unmistakably apocryphal and dating from the post-1187 (the Saladin reconquest) era[13]—all we are left with are three early twelfth-century pieces of evidence, and even those are difficult to interpret.

The first testimony can be found in an obituary for Abu-l-Qāsim al-Samarqandī (d.1142), a Baghdad *'ālim* of Syrian origin. According to him, the Prophet Muḥammad appeared in his dream (before 1096) and announced that a calamity was going to fall upon Islam. "Sometime later," added al-Samarqandī, "Jerusalem was lost."[14] It is impossible to determine, however, at what exact date (between 1099 and 1142) this theologian came to see the fall of Jerusalem in that light.

The second article of evidence comes from the pen of a *qāḍi* of Seville, Abū Bakr b. al-'Arabī, who was traveling in the Middle East at the time of the Frankish invasion and returned to Muslim Spain in 1102. Describing the first Crusade he stresses the fall of "the third most sacred place" of Islam, namely the *al-Aqṣā* Mosque in Jerusalem.[15] Here, at least, there is no doubt that the reaction came immediately following the event, but much like in the case of al-Samarqandī, it is impossible to say whether we are dealing with the opinions of an individual or with one representing a certain milieu; the problem is further complicated by the fact that both *'ulamā'* lived far from the battlefield, in Iraq and in Spain.

The last article of evidence is more precise, originating this time from a jurist, al-Sulamī of Damascus, who lived in the area struck by the Crusaders. In his *Book of Jihād* (ca. 1105), he maintains that Jerusalem was the "ultimate goal" of the First Crusade, without betraying, however, any sign of profound shock at its fall. The author expresses the wish to see it return soon to the hands of Islam, yet does not set its reconquest as the major aim of the anti-Frankish *jihād* he calls for.[16]

However interesting these three testimonies are, they do not indicate the existence of a significant sense of religious loss vis-à-vis Jerusalem.

## RESURGENCE

The silence of the rulers on the chapter of *al-Quds* in the early twelfth century was no doubt total. However, it was from these very circles that the momentous change in Muslim attitude towards Jerusalem was to come in the middle of that century. Much as at the time of Caliph ʿAbd al-Malik, it was an initiative from above or, if you will, the irruption of politics into the realm of religious beliefs that carried the day.

In 1144, Zenki, the Turkish ruler of the state of Mosul-Aleppo, having conquered the first Crusader principality, Edessa, declared *jihād*, war to the hilt against the Frankish presence in the Middle East. Jerusalem was anointed the ultimate goal of this grandiose campaign: "Zenki is going to turn tomorrow towards Jerusalem," announces one of his poets. Another poet wrote:

> Tell the infidel rulers to surrender not only Edessa but their other territories too,
> For the whole of this land is his,
> If the conquest of Edessa is the open sea, Jerusalem and the *Sāḥil* [the coast, the Frankish territories] are its shore.[17]

Zenki's motives for declaring an all-out war (and he was the first Muslim sovereign to do so) were mixed: the quest for political aggrandizement and a sincere attachment to *jihād* of a Turkish frontier-warrior *(ghāzī)*. The same holds for his reasons for choosing Jerusalem as the symbol: while it was the capital of the Latin Kingdom he wanted to terminate, it could also confer upon his *jihād* a distinct aura of sanctity, i.e., bring forth its religious character. In all probability this idea was first hatched by his two court poets, Ibn Munīr and Ibn al-Qayṣarānī, both refugees from coastal cities, Tripoli and Caesarea, taken over by the Franks.[18] It was to the merit of Zenki, however, that he perceived the utility of their suggestion and adopted it, putting his whole propaganda machinery (of which they were part) at its service.

The moment that the state came to take an interest in the idea of Jerusalem marked a turning-point. Hitherto amorphous and isolated, a certain undercurrent in public opinion was endowed with force and coherence. One detects this already in the fact that Zenki was the first to spell out the need to liberate the city and grant it a major role in his holy war. Yet in order for the new idea to become really galvanizing, it had to be reiterated in a systematic and variegated manner; moreover, its underlying premise—public consciousness regarding the sanctity of Jerusalem—had to be consolidated.

Zenki died two years after the conquest of Edessa and did not have the time to exert a significant effort in these directions; it was his son and successor, Nūr al-Dīn, who undertook the task. From the outset, Nūr al-Dīn gave priority to the idea of Jerusalem in his propaganda, helped by the two refugee-poets who had served his father. Thus, Ibn Munīr adjures his young master in 1149 to pursue the war against the Crusaders "till you see Jesus flee from Jerusalem." The appeals for the re-conquest launched in the early years of the reign develop the theme of the sacred character of the city: they harp upon the significance of its names *(al-Quds, Bayt al-Maqdis, Bayt al-Muqaddas)*, and allude constantly to the *al-Aqṣā* Mosque sanctified by traditions dating to the Umayyad era, which made it the "umbilical point" of the globe and the launching pad for Muḥammad's "nightly ascent to heaven." Both city and mosque stood for all the Frankish territories that should be liberated. Here is Ibn al-Qayṣarānī exclaiming:

> Let Jerusalem be purified by a blood bath!
> Let the *Sāḥil* make its ablutions for (Muslim) prayer with its own sand!
> Nūr al-Dīn's decision is irrevocable always.
> Tomorrow his spear will be directed towards *al-Aqṣā*.[19]

As prime goal and symbol of the *jihād*, the conquest of Jerusalem soon became one of the major arguments employed in Nūr al-Dīn's campaign for Syrian unification under his aegis—unity designed, according to him, to serve as a power base for destroying the Crusader entity. Thus, in his drawn-out struggle against the city-state of Damascus (1154-57), he considered the treaty concluded by the latter with the Franks in order to guarantee its independence as a huge obstacle on the road to realizing his overriding goals. One of his poets even went so far as to claim that by aiding the Crusaders the rulers of Damascus "humiliated and defiled the *al-Aqṣā* Mosque, treading upon it with their sullied feet." Only by breaking that treaty and going over to Nūr al-Dīn's camp can Damascus help bring Jerusalem back to Islam. "Damascus! Damascus!"[20]

In the late 1150s, the *al-Quds* theme became less salient, due perhaps to the death of the two refugee-poets (1154) who were its paragons, but above all because of the grave internal crisis that shook the Zengid state and because of the imminent Byzantine invasion (1157/58). Once the two crises were resolved, Nūr al-Dīn took special pains to show that he did not lose sight of the grand design he had set himself. At the end of his declaration announcing the capture of the Crusader castle of Tibnīn (1162), he expresses the wish that "God willing, the next good news to be announced will be that of the re-conquest of Jerusalem."[21]

The campaigns against Fāṭimid Egypt (1164-69) were soon to absorb all his energies, shelving yet again the re-conquest of the Holy City. But, as in the case of Damascus, Nūr al-Dīn used the re-conquest theme to undermine Egyptian morale. The fall of the Fāṭimids and the annexation of Egypt finally enabled him to prepare for the "ultimate assault" against the Crusaders. It is then that the *al-Quds* propaganda blossomed. Its major protagonist was the famous court poet and historian ʻImād al-Dīn al-Iṣfahānī. "Expurgate Jerusalem sullied by the Cross, hurl yourself against these (infidel) rebels against Allah," he calls upon Nūr al-Dīn, exhorting in like manner his Kurdish generals, Shirkūh and Saladin, who toppled the Fāṭimids.[22] A chorus of other poets (some of the *ʻulamā'*) joined their voices to his, adding a new notch to the scale of recompense for the warriors of the Faith, crowning all others, that of the "sublime reward" set in store for the conquerors of Jerusalem."[23]

The importance of the re-conquest theme is brought forth in Nūr al-Dīn's letter to the Caliph (1173), consecrated to his grand design. His principal aim, he writes, "is to banish the worshippers of the cross from *al-Aqṣā* . . . to take over *al-Quds* . . . and to recapture the *Sāḥil*."[24] In a symbolic gesture to underline these goals he had the craftsmen of Aleppo make a special pulpit designed to be placed in the *al-Aqṣā* Mosque after the conquest. The pulpit (which was indeed brought to *al-Aqṣā* in 1187 and served there for weekly sermons until it was destroyed in the 1969 arson) carried an inscription begging for divine succor to hasten that day.[25] That all is neither mere bluster nor empty sloganeering can be attested by the famous historian Ibn al-Jawzī, an intimate friend of Nūr al-Dīn who was never dependent on him materially or otherwise. One cannot suspect him of a courtesan's flattery when he writes that Nūr al-Dīn "was preparing for the re-conquest of Jerusalem but death took him by surprise."[26] Not without reason, then, does 'Imād al-Dīn lament his master (1174):

> Did you not promise Jerusalem
> that its re-conquest is impending. . . .
> And now, when will you be able
> to liberate it from the opprobrium of
> its enemies?

If the rulers gave the impetus to the *al-Quds* campaign, men of religion, their consciousness raised, came to join it on their own, operating through the resuscitation of the *Faḍā'īl al-Quds* literary genre. Such books, which were disseminated at public readings in mosques, made their appearance in the early eleventh century. Their last protagonist, Abū-l-Qāsim al Rumaylī, perished during the Crusader conquest of Jerusalem.[27] During the first half century of Frankish occupation no new *Faḍā'īl* treatises were written —yet another indicator of the overall Muslim indifference to the fate of the city. (Its former inhabitants, who had produced almost all such treatises, were for the most part massacred in 1099.) A recently discovered manuscript of the most ancient *Faḍā'īl* tract (ca. 1019) is even more revealing. This manuscript of Abū Bakr al-Wāsiṭī's tract carries numerous *ijāzāt* (certificates for auditors present at public readings of this work). The last reading in the eleventh century was held in A.H. 482/1089-90. There are no certificates for more than five decades; they make their appearance again in January 1147 (public reading in Damascus) and June 1152 (in Baghdad).[28] This reappearance of the genre, barely two years after the slogan of the re-conquest of *al-Quds* was launched, is by no means fortuitous. Moreover, it indicates the reception the slogan had and the favorable climate in which Nūr al-Dīn operated (for instance, when trying to win the hearts of the population of Damascus).

A few years later, the Damascene historian and *ḥadīth* scholar Thiqat al-Dīn b. al-'Asākir, a long term proponent of *jihād* and close friend of Nūr al-Dīn, authored the first *Faḍā'īl* treatise dating from the era of the Crusades.[29] Unfortunately no manuscript was found, but the very title is eloquent, linking the city as it does to the two holiest places of Islam: *"In praise of Mecca, Medina, and Jerusalem."*[30] One can catch a glimpse of its contents through the traditions of Jerusalem reported in the first volume of 'Asākir's *History of Damascus*, consecrated almost in its entirety to the praises of *al-Shām* (Syria-Palestine).

The *ḥadīths* either praise the city in general ("Allah loves *al-Shām* more than any other country; Jerusalem is the place he loves the best in *al-Shām*"), or recall the virtues of particular places therein (the Dome of the Rock, *al-Aqṣā*, the fountain of Silwān, and the like).[31] It is no coincidence that the author quotes in this context a (no doubt) spurious *ḥadīth*, where the Prophet Muḥammad is supposed to have said that of all the calamities which could befall Islam, the second in gravity—the first being his own death—is the conquest of Jerusalem by the infidels;[32] this could well be an indicator of the way the Christian occupation came to be perceived in the mid-twelfth century.

This volume of *The History of Damascus* had a number of public readings in this city from 1164 on, well-packed by the standards of the time (seventy to eighty auditors in each). The latter, as well as the auditors of al-Wāsiṭī's works, were for the most part *'ulamā'* notables and merchants who transmitted the message to their own students, families, clients, and neighbors.[33] The reawakening of Jerusalem in religious circles is corroborated by the resumption of Muslim pilgrimages to that city, especially by the *'ulamā'* and Ṣūfīs.[34] Such pilgrims, too, have become agents propagating, by act and words, the notion of the sanctity of *al-Quds*, contributing to the rise of that two-pronged sentiment which the official propaganda had promoted —anger at infidel domination over the city and hope for its return to Islam.[35]

## APOTHEOSIS

Arousal of that sentiment through constant drumming was further accelerated under Saladin, who took over the united Syrian-Egyptian state after the death of Nūr al-Dīn and claimed to be his spiritual heir. This was facilitated by the fact that (much like after the death of Zenki) the new ruler could avail himself of the services of a poet-propagandist of the former ruler, in this case 'Imād al-Dīn al-Iṣfahānī. "March towards Jerusalem, capture it and spill there rivers of blood to purify *al-Quds*,"[36] he writes to his new benefactor in 1177. Very little thematic evolution can be detected in his (and other propagandists') writings on this issue during the following decade. The divine calling of the reconquest was, of course, transferred from Nūr al-Dīn to Saladin, or even depicted as the heritage of his whole family, the 'Ayyūbids.[37]

The only real change to occur concerned the function of that theme in the propaganda setup. It became the major argument in the long struggle of Saladin, who in the beginning only ruled Egypt, to take over the entire Zengid state, thus emulating his former master and expanding the use of his slogan—unity for *jihād*. In the wake of the seizure of southern Syria, he strived to legitimize this operation in a letter to the caliph (1175): "Syria could not find order with its (present government), nor did it have a sovereign capable of carrying out the capture of *al-Quds*," for which Syria is the natural operational basis. The caliph, apparently convinced, did indeed award him with an "investiture parchment" for this area.[38]

Turning his aspirations toward the rest of the Zengid kingdom (Aleppo and Mosul), Saladin upbraided its rulers who "shirk contributing to the reconquest of Jerusalem," as he put it in one of his letters, "and are blatantly indifferent to revenging its humiliation." Subjecting these two city-states to the Ayyūbid general was justified because the latter, as he argues in another letter, "prefers consecrating his brief stay upon earth to combat the Infidel who had transformed the Holy City into an abode of impurity."[39] It is this close relationship between unity and *jihād* that the *qāḍī* Muḥī al-Dīn was to celebrate in the first Friday sermon *(khuṭba)* pronounced in the liberated city (1187): "It is for her that Allah has unified your ranks, till then in disarray, and made your armies, which served nothing but your whims, His own army.[40]

The preponderant role played by Jerusalem in the internecine wars of 1174-86 increased its prestige and created in the aroused public consciousness a climate of tense expectation to its re-conquest. This climate accounts for the numerous "predictions" of that event, which appeared in the decade preceding the final assault.[41] Even foreign visitors could not avoid being affected by that atmosphere. Thus, the Spanish Muslim traveler, Ibn Jubayr, who passed through Syria in 1185, refers to Jerusalem: "May Allah, the Omnipotent, make it return to Islam and deliver it from the impure unbelievers."[42]

When Mosul, the last Zengid principality, was finally annexed by Saladin (February 1186), Jerusalem became the immediate goal. The propaganda machinery was put in motion to prepare the spirits for the great exploit. A letter composed by 'Imād al-Dīn later that year says, for instance: "The swords of *jihād* clatter gaily in their sheaths, the cavalry of Allah is ready to charge. The Dome of the Rock rejoices at the good news that the Koran, of which it has been deprived, is about to come back."[43]

As 1187 wore on, the crescendo of activity accelerated, especially after the knights of the Latin Kingdom were routed in Ḥiṭṭīn (3 July, 1187). Saladin's letter announcing this victory declared: "We will promptly lay siege to Jerusalem. . . the night of infidelity has enveloped this city for too long: now the dawn of deliverance is going to shine." Similar terms were used to announce the conquest of Acre (10 July) and Ascalon (4 September). Public readings of *Faḍā'īl al-Quds* were held.[44] In order to elucidate the sacred character of that eminent event, the Sultan called upon Syrian and Egyptian *'ulamā'* to be present there; that so many did flock to join his camp on the Palestinian coast bears witness to the reverberations of the long-awaited assault.[45]

The mounting climax peaked with the conquest, on 2 October, 1187. The propaganda campaign indeed attained its paroxysm: seventy-six letters were dispatched to the various provinces and to all corners of the Islamic world to announce the exploit and at least a dozen poems and two official Friday sermons celebrated it. This was more than the total output of the propaganda apparatus for the rest of the 1187 campaign (the battle of Ḥiṭṭīn, militarily far more decisive, received merely six letters and four poems). All the cities in the Ayyūbid sultanate were decked with flags, and the governors were ordered to proclaim the news "with great pomp and fanfare."[46] It is, of course, the religious importance of the event—and hence, the prestige one could capitalize on—that made Saladin concentrate all his propaganda effort on Jerusalem.[47]

This effort is distinguished not by any thematic modifications, but rather by its solemn, nay even grandiose, tone—the intent being no doubt to bring forth the historical nature of the event. It is even endowed with a sort of halo, for it took place on the day when Muḥammad was supposed to have ascended to heaven from Jerusalem (the date may have been deliberately chosen by the Sultan with an eye to that effect). Moreover, as with other (past and future) victories in the history of Islam, public rumor soon had it that angels were present in the city at this moment.[48] The whole Islamic world, claimed the propagandists, was delighted to hear the news—"The Ka'ba rejoices at the deliverance of her brother, *al-Aqṣā*, for "the Faith, which had been uprooted of its sanctuary, returns to its native soil."[49] Such a re-conquest is the pinnacle of grandeur. "Were you not the elected of Allah. . . He would have given you the opportunity to accomplish this precept, an act whose recompense is virtually unsurpassed," said the preacher Muḥī al-Dīn to Saladin's soldiers in Jerusalem.[50] Even more exalting is the glory bestowed upon the Sultan himself, who had seen a new addition to his official titles: "Liberator [or: Servant] of Jerusalem." A new court poet exclaims: "No other human being deserved to save Jerusalem. . . for you are as pure and as sacred as this city."[51]

The impact of the conquest upon Muslim *mentalités* can be gauged by the letters of congratulation dispatched to Saladin by other Muslim rulers. (Almost none did so with regard to the victories of his earlier campaigns.) Folk legends were soon woven around the conquest, even during Saladin's lifetime. One of them recounts, for example, that when "astrologists told him that he was fated to lose an eye when entering Jerusalem, the Sultan cried: 'I would gladly become blind provided I take this city.' "[52]

The interest in Jerusalem did not abate throughout the remainder of Saladin's reign. The impact of that exalted moment of the conquest was felt for some time. Thus, in the *Faḍā'īl* treatise composed by Ibn-Jawzī in the early 1190s a vibrant homage was paid to Saladin's exploit and to the *jihād* in general.[53] The city became the coveted goal of the Third Crusade, which twice almost recaptured it; in consequence Saladin had to invest an intensive effort in its defense, fortification, and settlement as well as in attracting pilgrims. Propaganda, insisting on the merits of the city, was a useful tool to that effect, and one indeed finds his poets and his chancellery mobilized for the task. They were helped (whether recruited or on their own accord) by men of religion, prominent among whom was Bahā' al-Dīn b. 'Asākir, the son of the person who resuscitated the *Faḍā'īl* genre, who held public readings of his father's work and delivered conferences in this city in its praise (later collected in book form).[54]

It is the propaganda of the late 1180s and early 1190s that offers the first Islamic composite portrait of Jerusalem dating from the Crusader era. It is an image consisting of four major elements:

1. The sanctity of the city is based above all, on the two mosques, particularly on *al-Aqṣā*, exalted (following Jewish tradition) as the "first piece of earth created by Allah" and as one of the most ancient mosques, built upon the foundation of the temple of Solomon. Of secondary importance are other holy places located here: the Oratories of David and Mary, the Gate of Mercy, and the Silwān spring.[55]

2. The major Muslim tradition celebrating the history of the city is the one concerning the Night Journey of Muḥammad, based on a Koranic verse (XVII, 1): "Praise be unto him, who transported his servant by night from the Sacred Temple of Mecca to the furthermost temple [*al-Masjid al-Aqṣā*]," but dating from the late seventh century. Thus, in Saladin's letter to Richard the Lion-Hearted (1191), Saladin cites the Night Journey as the prime proof of the Muslim title to the city besieged by the English king.[56] It is around this central tradition that the peripheral ones are placed: Jerusalem is one of the three oldest cities upon earth (with Mecca and Medina) and one of "the four cities of Paradise" (the fourth being Damascus); the Biblical Patriarchs, Moses, Mary, and Jesus lived in it; Joshua conquered it; Solomon built his temple and the prophets received their revelation there; and finally Muḥammad designated it as the first *qibla* (direction of prayer).[57]

3. Important in the past, the city will be even more so in the End of Days: it is there that Resurrection and Final Judgment are to take place; the narrow bridge *(ṣirāṭ)* upon which all humanity must pass will be suspended from the Mount of Olives to the Temple Mount.[58]

4. The last category of "virtues" served three specific and pragmatic aims and were, hence, particularly salient:

*a. Fortification and Defence:* When the first phase of the fortification of the city was accomplished in late 1191—with the participation of Saladin and his entourage—'Imād al-Dīn wrote: "This was done for the sake of Allah. . . to protect His abode and safeguard His religion. . . our sole desire is to get recompense in heaven and absolution of our sins."[59] It is such propaganda that must have brought many *'ulamā'* and other volunteers to join in his ongoing effort and made the sovereign of Mosul dipatch a special team of stone-carvers.[60] Bahā' al-Dīn, friend and future biographer of the Sultan, celebrated the defence of the city in a speech to army commanders during the Crusader siege (1191) exalting it as the "purest place in the world"; numerous poets emulated him in epics and psalms of praise destined to preserve the morale of the troops. Ibn al-Sa'ātī, for instance, eulogizes Saladin:

Had it not been for you this sacred place
Would have shed tears of blood
When in its halls
Church bells would have been heard anew

Ibn al-Mujāwir addresses the enemy:

Tell this Englishman, this dog:
Quit this madness!
You cannot take over Jerusalem!
For God's Light will never die out here![61]

*b. Settlement.* In order to repopulate the city where Muslims were forbidden to live under the Franks, the *'ulamā'* took to praise the merits of living there, linking this precept with the *jihād* with the help of the *ḥadīth*: "He who resides in Jerusalem is taken to be a Warrior of Faith." Those who settle there were promised divine recompense: "Seventy thousand angels intercede for every inhabitant of *al-Quds*"; "living in Jerusalem is tantamount to living in heaven." So dire was the need for settlers that even temporary residence was deemed virtuous: "He who lives a whole year there, despite all adversities, Allah is bound to provide his daily bread and make him enter Paradise."[62]

*c. Pilgrimage.* Rewards were promised to those who accomplish this precept. An oft-quoted *ḥadīth* already at the moment of the conquest was the one celebrating *al-Aqṣā* Mosque (together with the holy places of Mecca and Medina) as the "only three mosques one should set out to [in pilgrimage]." Other traditions are cited in corroboration, e.g., "He who visits Jerusalem motivated by piety inherits paradise."[63] Ibn 'Asākir devoted a whole chapter in his treatise to "the praise of prayer at Jerusalem, of pilgrimage to Mecca and of prayer at the mosques of Medina and *al-Aqṣā* during the same year"; the author's aim was, probably, to have Jerusalem profit from the annual pilgrims' caravans in the neighboring *Darb al-Ḥajj*.

When enumerating the virtues of all these precepts he puts special emphasis upon the virtues of prayer in Jerusalem: "He who makes his ritual ablutions and prays in *al-Quds* has all sins absolved and becomes as innocent as he was on the day of his birth." Moreover, small acts of piety attain heights of virtuousness due to the fact that they are made in Jerusalem: "To give there a loaf of bread in alms is tantamount to giving the weight in gold of all the mountains upon earth."[64]

It should be pointed out that care was taken not to interfere with the hierarchy of the holy places in Islam; the city is never depicted as superior to Mecca and Medina. Even during the euphoria of the re-conquest, 'Imād al-Dīn stresses in a letter to the governor of Yemen that the two cities of the Arabian Peninsula remain at the apex: "Jerusalem is third after *Ḥaramayn* (the twin holy places, Mecca and Medina) and does not constitute a trinity with them (i.e., is not on an equal footing)." In the same vein Muḥī al-Dīn postulates in his first sermon in *al-Aqṣā*: "There is no other mosque towards which one should set out [in pilgrimage] after the two mosques (of Mecca and Medina) but this one."[65] All *Faḍā'īl al-Quds* treatises make the distinction between *ḥajj* (pilgrimage) proper, namely the one to Mecca and Medina, which is one of the five Pillars of the Faith (major precepts) and the *ziyāra* (visitation) to Jerusalem, which is a highly recommended but superogatory act. The point is even made in quantitative terms in the *ḥadīths* quoted: "A prayer in Mecca equals ten thousand (regular) prayers, a prayer in Medina equals a thousand, a prayer in Jerusalem equals five hundred."[66]

## THE IMPACT

This propaganda barrage was accompanied by a series of practical measures taken by Saladin. Construction projects, contributions, and endowments to religious establishments, monetary incentives to settlers, special facilities for pilgrims, and so on.[67] What was their combined impact?

Whereas Ṣūfīs, *'ulamā'*, and other Muslims came to inhabit Jerusalem, their number was rather limited. Even with the Oriental Christians (who unlike the Catholics were permitted to continue to live there) and even with the Jews (banned by the Crusaders and now granted permission by the Sultan), the population was smaller than in the Frankish period. The Sultan had greater success in the domain of pilgrimage: a regular influx of people "on visitation" was maintained, including a good many Muslims on their way to the *ḥajj* to Mecca.[68] An interesting indicator of how widespread was the idea of pilgrimage to Jerusalem was found in the memoirs of a vizier of

Mosul. Describing his journey to Palestine at the head of the reinforcement troops sent from Mosul to Saladin (1190), he says that the double aim of that "blessed voyage" was: "*Jihād* for the sake of Allah and the visitation of Jerusalem, may God protect her." When these and other such pilgrims (such as ambassadors to Saladin) returned to their home countries, they probably became agents of diffusion for the worship of *al-Quds*.[69]

It is there indeed that we find the greatest achievement of Saladin's propaganda: the idea of Jerusalem intertwined with the idea of *jihād*; it ceased to be controversial and suspect and occupied henceforth an important place in the consciousness of the devout and of the population at large.

One may gauge the real strength of this idea of Jerusalem under Saladin's successors, the Ayyūbids: it became the driving force of a serious political crisis in their empire. In a dialectical manner, the idea owed some of its continued power to active backing on the part of the rulers whose very prestige was predicated upon the image of Saladin, founder of the dynasty, and of his exploits in the Holy War. Paying homage to *jihād* and *al-Quds* was thus a legitimating factor of no mean importance. Homage was paid not only in declarations, panegyrics of court poets and the like, but also by active Ayyūbid policy: building many *madrasas* (religious colleges) and *khānqas* (Ṣūfī monasteries), in an attempt to woo settlers and help pilgrims.[70] Many rulers of the Ayyūbid successor states made the point of visiting Jerusalem and its holy places, thereby enhancing the prestige of *ziyārat al-Quds*.[71]

Men of religion had their own share in keeping Jerusalem paramount in Muslims' minds. The most active center was no doubt the Banū 'Asākir family of Damascus: Bahā' al-Dīn b. 'Asākir held public readings of the first part of *Ta'rīkh Dimashq*; two of his cousins, Tāj al-Umanā' and Niẓām al-Dīn, wrote treatises on *Faḍā'īl al-Quds* of their own. Their compatriot, the jurist Sibṭ b. al-Jawzī, preached in Jerusalem "eulogizing its glory founded on piety."[72] The "praises of Jerusalem" owed their continued popularity to the efforts of two *'ulamā'*, also known as propagandists of the Holy War. The first, Ḍiyā' al-Dīn al-Maqdisī, consecrated a third of his *jihād* book to Jerusalem;[73] the second, 'Izz al-Dīn al-Sulamī, wrote a treatise "to encourage Muslim settlement in *al-Shām*"; he ends his enthusiastic chapter on Damascus with the words: "It is thus established with complete certainty that Damascus has more virtues than any other place in *al-Shām*, with the exception of Jerusalem."[74] Biographies of Saladin, favorite reading (and reading aloud) material in this era, emphasized the hero's Jerusalem campaigns, [75] and many new folk legends about the 1187 conquest appeared.[76] At this level of folk culture, the most popular epic of these times was the *Futūḥ al-Shām* (conquest of Syria), a work attributed to an early Islamic author (al-Wāqidī) but actually composed toward the end of the twelfth century. The *Futūḥ* recount in length the first Muslim conquest of Jerusalem, that of Caliph 'Umar I, embellishing it with many a descriptive detail taken from Saladin's operation.[77] Last but not least among these popular works is the *Guide to Holy Places* by al-Harawī, where a recondite chapter deals with "Jerusalem and its Merits."[78]

The Jerusalem idea thus continued to develop, prodded both by the rulers and the men of religion. But whereas in the past the two circles cooperated—the ruler initiating and the *'ulamā'* collaborating of their own accord—during the Ayyūbid period tensions flared up between them. If public opinion, led by the *'ulamā'*, owed its rekindled interest to the rulers, it soon developed an autonomous consciousness. Sensitivity to the fate of the reconquered city was acute, and already Saladin was aware of it. In a letter to Richard the Lion-Hearted during the armistice negotiations (late 1191), Saladin affirms that even had he been personally disposed to cede the city to the King, as the letter demanded, "let the King not imagine that such surrender would not have been impossible; we would not have dared pronounce that word before the Muslims."[79]

This does not seem a mere diplomatic stratagem. The Sultan was aware of the fact that even if an ideological emphasis on Jerusalem had rendered him great services, it was also by now a factor with a life of its own, imposing constraints on his freedom to act vis-à-vis the city. Disposing of Jerusalem as a mere pawn on the political chessboard would have sparked sharp reactions. Saladin's successors as paragons of *Realpolitik* were conscious of their military weakness and looked for a way to establish peaceful coexistence with the Franks. In this quest they underestimated the "Jerusalem constraint." The mistake was to exact its political price.

## PROTEST AND REVOLT

The military balance was for the first time heavily tilted in favor of the Franks during the Fifth Crusade. The Ayyūbid Sultan of Damascus, al-Muʿaẓẓam, had every reason to fear that the hilly area of Palestine might fall into the hands of the Crusaders. He decided, then, to dismantle Jerusalem lest it be captured fortified, or else he would have to cede it to them in terms of the accord negotiated in exchange for the evacuation of the Egyptian port city of Damietta. The mere mention that *al-Quds* might be lost elicited a wave of indignation. In Jerusalem, writes a contemporary historian, "there was as much fright and panic as on Judgment Day; women and girls, old men, adolescents and infants, all took refuge in the Dome of the Rock and in *al-Aqṣā*, cut their hair and tore their clothes."[80] Many others fled from the city to Egypt, Damascus, and Iraq and spread the general outcry well beyond the confines of Palestine. Chastised and upbraided from within his Sultanate and from without, al-Muʿaẓẓam tried to justify his order: "We do not defend cities with ramparts but with swords and bows."[81] Yet public opinion, suspicious and overexcited, was not calmed. Popular poets, its spokesmen, wrote satirical ballads about the Sultan, reproving his policies and even cursing his entire rule. One such anonymous jeremiad bemoans:

> In the month of Rajab
> The Sacred was profaned
> In the month of Muḥarran
> The Holy City of Jerusalem was destroyed.

Another ballad is attributed to the pen of Muḥī al-Din, the last *qāḍī* of the castle of Mount Tabor before al-Muʿaẓẓam evacuated and demolished it out of fear of the Franks (1217); from then on he taught in a madrasa in Damascus famous for the close relationship it entertained with Jerusalem. The *qāḍī* had, thus, no reason to softpedal his critique:

> I passed near the noble city of *al-Quds*
> Hailing its devastated dwellings. . .
> My eyes shed hot tears
> At the memory of our glorious past
> The barbarian (Crusader) wants to wipe out its ruins,
> To lay on it his impious and criminal hand.
> I say unto him: "Let your right arm wither!
> Spare this city for those who want to pray and meditate."
> Were he ready to accept it,

I would have given him my life to redeem the city,
And all Muslims would have done the same.[82]

These reactions were but warnings of the great crisis which was to unfurl in 1229 when the Sultan al-Kāmil of Egypt ceded the city to Frederick II of Germany, in the framework of an armistice agreement with the crusading emperor. If, a decade earlier, the Ayyūbids did not foresee the possibility of a head-on clash with public opinion, this time al-Kāmil awaited such reactions, though he had underestimated their scope. In a letter to his estranged brother al-Ashraf, of Transjordan (summer 1228), the Sultan claims that he entered Palestine not in order to fight him but in order to defend Jerusalem (which he had already offered to the emperor!), and adds:

You know that our uncle, Sultan Saladin, recaptured Jerusalem and that this victory bestowed upon us a glory which is bound to endure for centuries. The fall of the city in the hands of the Franks is liable to tarnish our reputation and to make us the butt of villainous censure, so that all the grandeur gathered by our uncle will vanish and we will not be able to save our face and confront God and men.[83]

Reconciled a few months later, al-Kāmil and al-Ashraf concluded the Treaty of Jaffa with Frederick II (February 1229). Muslim territorial concessions included Jerusalem. As an Egyptian historian was to remark later, the immediate crisis the treaty provoked between the sultans and public opinion was much more violent than al-Kāmil had anticipated.

It was from Jerusalem, once again, that the shock waves were diffused. The *muezzins* and *imāms* of *al-Aqṣā* Mosque and of the Dome of the Rock went to al-Kāmil's encampment near Gaza and called for prayer at the wrong time before the Sultan's tent—as a sign of protest. Al-Kāmil, determined to nip the opposition in the bud (he had already imprisoned an emir who criticized the treaty), punished these *'ulamā'* most severely.[84]

The latter were, however, undeterred. During the visit of the German emperor to Jerusalem, the chief *muezzin* pronounced a special call for prayer, adding to the traditional formula two anti-Christian polemical verses of the Koran: "The Lord has not begotten a son" (XXIII, 93); "This way Jesus, son of Mary; the Word of truth, concerning whom they doubt" (XIV, 34). This two-fold challenge, to emperor and sultan alike, crystallized the growing bitterness at that voluntary surrender of the Holy City to the detested infidels. The incident soon became well-known throughout the Ayyūbid principalities, greatly embarrassing al-Kāmil.[85]

As the news of the treaty spread all over the Middle East, the outcry grew louder and sharper. Dozens of popular poems and ballads joined the choir of protest. Some were elegiac:

> How painful it is to see Jerusalem a shambles,
> Its splendor fading out.
> All our tears would not suffice to mourn
> The demise of the city.

Others were openly reprobatory of the rulers, for instance that by an anonymous mystic who makes Jerusalem say:

> If few are ready to defend me in *al-Shām*
> If my walls are in ruins
> If devastation persists,
> Thence will I see
> On the morrow of my destruction
> The sign of shame
> On the forehead of rulers.[86]

Anger erupted with particular vigor in Damascus, to which al-Kāmil and al-Ashraf were at that very moment laying siege. Religious and political struggles became interlaced. The inhabitants were jealous of their independence and took pride in their Ayyūbid Sultan, al-Naṣīr Dā'ūd, a paragon of *jihād*. This two-pronged commitment accounts for the implacable struggle waged by the population, aiding the regular army, during the siege; it would also, later, explain the grief and sorrow which enveloped the city when it ultimately had to surrender and witness the entrance of the Egyptian army into the citadel.[87] Hatred was thus reinforced through the Sultans' relinquishment of *al-Quds*, all the more so as al-Nāṣir Dā'ūd had an interest in using the *al-Quds* affair to rally public opinion. Yet the religious factor was no sheer catalyst of the political struggle, neither was it heavily manipulated by the rulers. All indicators point out that the religious factor had been spawned and developed quite independently of the political one, and that the relationship between them was based rather on reciprocity and feedback.

In fact, the ferment concerning Jerusalem, at least in the circles of the devout, preceded the Treaty of Jaffa. Thus the historian Abū Shāma, then teaching in a madrasa in Damascus, tells us of the sense of foreboding which he experienced—much like the jurist 'Izz al-Din al-Sulamī, a famous apostle of *jihād*—with regard to the secret negotiations held between Frederick II and al-Kāmil; and those who experienced anxiety probably shared it with their friends. Once fears and premonitions became reality in February 1229, furor and rage erupted against the Egyptian Sultan and his brother. Abū Shāma writes: "This surrender was one of the most anguishing disgraces which befell Islam; it alienated the inhabitants of Damascus from al-Kāmil."[88] The historian and popular preacher, Sibṭ b. al-Jawzī, poured oil on the fire in a sermon delivered in the Umayyad Mosque during the worst moments of the siege: "Multitudes of pilgrims can no longer visit *al-Quds*. . . . How many prayers have been said there in the past! How many tears shed! This shameful disaster rends our hearts and we heave deep sighs."[89]

It is true that the sermon also helped the cause of al-Nāṣir Dā'ūd, but given Sibṭ b. al-Jawzī's past commitment to Jerusalem, one cannot doubt his sincerity when he says that he preached not only upon the instigation of his master but also because he "thought it a religious duty to defend the honor of Islam." Indeed, he had taught for ten years in a madrasa in Jerusalem and was one of the propagators of its *Faḍā'il*. Apart from the sermon, he wrote a poem that year lamenting that "at the place of the Ascension (for the Night Journey) and on the (Dome of the) Rock. . . there are no madrasas anymore and Koranic verses are not read."[90]

Other hostile reactions, less virulent perhaps, were heard from places as far apart as Egypt, Jazīra, Mosul, and even Baghdad, both among the *'ulamā'* and in the lower and middle class.[91] One can even detect a certain malaise in parts of the Ayyūbid elite. The Sultan of Irbil, al-Muẓaffar, sent a special emissary to al-Kāmil advising him to apologize to the Caliph for the treaty. This suggestion, which intimated disapproval, was certainly not motivated by political hostility. Al- Muẓaffar, Saladin's brother-in law and a loyal ally of his successors, seems to have been persuaded to take this initiative by his devotion to certain *'ulamā'* of his entourage (who had already made him redeem Muslim prisoners of war from the Crusaders). Ṣalāḥ al-Dīn al-Irbilī, the ambassador sent by al-Kāmil to Frederick II, wrote a venomous poem against the "accursed emperor" expressing doubt as to his intentions to uphold the treaty.[92]

While al-Kāmil reckoned, at first, on being able to gag the enraged public through repressive measures, he soon found himself constrained—given the force and scope of the outcry—and gave way to some extent. Neither the chief *muezzin* of Jerusalem nor the former ambassador to the Emperor were punished. The Sultan could not envision abrogating the treaty, but he judged it necessary to launch an information campaign to pacify the "relevant public opinion" (i.e., above all *'ulamā'*, nobility, and minor princes). A long letter was dispatched to all the Ayyūbid principalities where, on top of the political agreements for the treaty, the Sultan attempted to minimize the religious deprivation caused by the loss of Jerusalem. The Islamic character of the city would not be wiped out, he said, for *al-Aqṣā* would be kept in its present splendor, Muslim worship would be held there, and the pilgrims had free access to the Temple Mount and other holy places.[93]

Having thus justified the Treaty of Jaffa, al-Kāmil sought to prove that no precept had been violated. It is in this spirit that he retorted to the ambassador of Irbil: "We and our ancestors are devoted servants of Jerusalem; the services we rendered it are known to one and all. Our commitment to *al-Quds* contains not a grain of hypocrisy." The reference to Saladin's honorific title ("servant of Jerusalem") was not fortuitous, of course. It is, in effect, the prestige (and legitimacy) of the dynasty predicated upon Saladin's tradition that he intends to keep intact. Such protestations of fidelity to the tradition notwithstanding, al-Kāmil finally had to acquiesce to al-Muẓaffar's proposal and sent a high-ranking emissary to the court of the Caliph in order to clear his name. His brother al-Ashraf sent an emissary of his own, which was also supposed to pacify the disgruntled public in the Jazira.[94]

The storm did not abate so soon, particularly not in the besieged city of Damascus; nor did it in Jerusalem and its immediate vicinity, in which region the unrest swelled several months after the city was ceded to the Franks, to the point where simple protest, designed to put pressure upon the rulers, was replaced by direct action, independent of the rulers. Incited by the *'ulamā'* of Hebron and Nablus, thousands of *fellahīn* from the hilly areas of central Palestine assembled and declared, according to a contemporary Frankish source, that they "cannot suffer to see Jerusalem in Christian hands and not be able to visit the Temple Mount which is the abode of the Lord." Brandishing their arms, the peasant bands succeeded in forcing their way into the city and occupying it for a few days before being chased out. They suffered heavy losses by the local garrison, which was reinforced by troops dispatched from Acre.[95]

Cognizant of the fact that his information campaign did not bear the expected fruits, al-Kāmil tried to repair the damage done to his prestige by exploiting his own (rather limited) military operations. Thus, his propagandists celebrated the Sultan's campaign against Krak des Chevaliers (which was not included in the Treaty of Jaffa). Al-Kāmil was presented as the true *mujāhid* against the "Blond-haired-men" *(Banū-l-Aṣfar,* the Franks), while all other rulers (such as al-Nāṣir Dā'ūd) "indulge in the pleasures of hunting."[96]

The multiple means of propaganda employed by al-Kāmil testify to the ferocity of the storm unleashed by the Treaty of Jaffa. One should point out, however, that much like in 1229, the public was unable to change the policies of the sultans. The latter were compelled to justify themselves before public opinion—not a usual occurrence in those times. For al-Kāmil, given his rough-shod attitude as the crisis began to unfold, this constituted a certain defeat. Nevertheless, despite the vituperations and the loss of prestige, al-Mu'aẓẓam did not rebuild the ramparts and al-Kāmil did not abrogate the Treaty of Jaffa. The Holy City remained for a decade (1229-39) in the hands of the Franks, public agitation subsiding little by little.

Echoes of the 1229 crisis, however, could still be heard. Thus, when Nāṣir Dā'ūd recaptured the city (1239), he saw to it that in all the letters and poems celebrating his exploit allusions would be made to his two uncles who defiled the patrimony of Saladin. One court poet exclaims:

> *Al-Aqṣā* has a long-standing custom:
> Whenever it is sullied by infidel rule
> God sends it a *Nāṣir* [defender, savior]
> It was a *Nāṣir* [Saladin] who purified it once,
> It is a *Nāṣir* [Dā'ūd] who rendered it pure again.[97]

## SEQUELS

The fall of the Ayyūbids and the seizure of power by a new dynasty, the Mamluks (1250), gave a stong impetus to the war against the Crusaders, with special emphasis on its religious significance. Yet neither during the four decades of the final assault to liquidate the Frankish presence nor during the following two centuries of Mamluk rule did Jerusalem occupy again the prominent position it had under Saladin (and in an intermittent manner under the Ayyūbids, too).

The reason lies primarily in the fact that the city was not to be conquered again and was no longer in danger of losing its Muslim character. On the one hand, Mamluk *jihād*, pursuing the re-conquest strategy of Saladin, concentrated upon the recapture of Acre, capital of the Second (thirteenth-century) Crusader Kingdom as the final objective (achieved in 1291).[98] No dangerous Crusaders arrived, on the other hand, at the shores of Syria-Palestine, and thus public opinion had no particular incentive to rally collective commitment to Jerusalem (be it also against its own rulers). Furthermore, the Mamluks had no particular interest to cultivate the memory of Saladin and of his 1187 campaign, all the more so as they had their own *jihād* exploits to base their prestige upon: the battles of Manṣūra against Louis IX of France (1250) and the battle of 'Ayn Jālūt (1260) against the Mongols.[99]

Still the monumental change wrought in the position of Jerusalem due to the counter-Crusade proved enduring. The city had its place assured in Islamic doctrine and popular consciousness alike.

The controversy about the sanctity of Jerusalem, which had raged for four centuries, could not be revived. The doubts were laid to rest by the anti-Frankish *jihād*. Islam had finally come to accept Jerusalem and did so on its own terms—not as a mere part of the Judeo-Christian heritage, but as a response to the need of believers for intercessory mechanisms with a foreboding deity. It was a city strongly coveted by the enemies of the faith, and thus became, in a sort of mirror-image syndrome, dear to Muslim hearts.

Few and far between were the jurists, usually rigorists of the neo-Ḥanbalite school (e.g., Ibn Taymiyya and Ibn Kathīr in the fourteenth century), who persisted in doubting the authenticity of the traditions pertaining to *al-Quds*. And even these critics and their twentieth-century disciples (such as the Syrian Ḥanbalite jurist al-Albānī) do not deny the city all the attributes of sanctity; Ibn Taymiyya seems to be motivated by the fear that Jerusalem's appeal may eclipse that of Mecca and Medina and not by opposition to its present rank in the hierarchy of holy places.[100]

Such fears proved, by the way, to be groundless. The *jihād* propaganda, as we have seen, left the contents of the classical Muslim theology regarding Jerusalem unchanged, including its third place on the sacred ladder. It is indeed as such—with the title *Thālith al-Ḥaramayn* (third after the two holy places of Arabia)—that the city was to be venerated under the Mamluks and the Ottomans.[101]

The literature of *Faḍā'īl al-Quds* continued to flourish; at least thirty such works were composed under the Mamluks: by Ṣūfīs as well as by jurists of all four schools including the Ḥanbalites.[102] Pilgrimage to Jerusalem, always called *ziyāra*, never *ḥajj*, became frequent, with pilgrims (rarely notable jurists or Ṣūfīs) even settling there. The Mamluks, especially, built madrasas and *khānqas*, and *waqfs* endowed existing establishments.

The city did not escape the scourge of the economic decline of Palestine, which began in the fourteenth century and never became under the Mamluks or the Ottomans a political or an intellectual center. Nevertheless, in one of those rare enduring impacts of the Crusaders upon Islam, Jerusalem was firmly ensconced in Muslim religiosity; all the more so, or perhaps just because, it took such a long struggle to be accepted.

One understands, thus, why Ṣādiq Jalālal-'Aẓm's call to make Jerusalem into a purely political issue was of no avail. It ran against heavy odds. The long controversy about the purported sacred character of this city had ended unequivocally. The city came to be integrated into Islamic learned and folk religion in the course of the religious drama of the counter-Crusade and in part as a response to the sanctity of this city in Crusader lore.

When, in the late 1920s, the mufti of Jerusalem, Hajj Amīn al-Ḥusaynī, looked for means to spread nationalism among the traditionalist strata (e.g., the peasant majority of the Palestinians, still wary of such modern ideas), he hit upon the idea of making its focal point the struggle to preserve the Muslim character of Jerusalem, noting, for instance, the Zionist alleged "plot" to demolish *al-Aqṣā* and to rebuild the Third Temple. The making of Palestinian nationalism into a mass movement was thus closely intertwined with the symbol of *al-Quds*. The same holds for Pan-Arabism in relation to Palestine. More was involved here than a mere propaganda ploy or "mirror image syndrome" in response to the role of Jerusalem (Zion) in the Zionist endeavor. Underlying it all was the impact of a long history which made religion and politics so intimately interlaced in Islam. The small top crust of completely modernized (i.e., secularized) intelligentsia could escape, perhaps, this political influence, but this is after all the Age of the Masses—religious-minded masses, including, according to recent surveys,[103] the bulk of the middle class—and the masses bear the impact of Islamic history in a most palpable manner.

Zionism, grounded on a somewhat analogous historical tradition, was no more willing to heed Scholem's advice (delivered, ironically enough, a few months after the mufti launched his initiative), than would Palestinian (or Pan-Arab) nationalism heed that of al-'Aẓm. The latter's attempt was all the more condemned to fail as it came after 1967, when the loss of Jerusalem (and the concomitant euphoria in Israel with its strong religious sentiment) made the memory of the anti-Crusader struggle more poignant than ever. When one reads, for instance, the text of the Friday sermon at *al-Aqṣā* of February 1976, one is immediately struck by the strong affinities to the arguments of the era of Saladin: the same combination of claims to the title over the city antedating the Muslim conquest and refutation of the present occupier's "allegations," down to the use of the very same *ḥadīths* on specific holy places and the merits of the city in this world and in the hereafter.[104] The sanctity of *al-Quds* as a political symbol was thus given a renewed, and rather vigorous, lease on life.

## FOOTNOTES

1. S.J. al-'Aẓm, *Al-Naqd al-Dhātī ba'da-l-Hazīma,* Beirut 1968, pp. 49-50.
2. D. Biale, *Gershom Scholem: Kabbala and Counter-History,* Harvard University Press, 1979, p. 179.
3. Ibn al-Qalānisī, *Dhayl Ta'rīkh Dimashq,* Ed. Amedrot, Leiden 1908, p. 134; al-'Azīmī, "La chronique abrégée de-," ed. Cl. Cahen, *Journal Asiatique* 230 (1938), p. 373.
4. Cf. 'Imad al-Dīn al-Iṣfāhānī, *Kharīdat al-Qaṣr* (Shu'arā' al-Shām), ed. Sh. Faysal, vol. 2, Damascus 1959, passim.
5. Ibn al-Qalānisī, op. cit., p. 99, Sibṭ b. al-Jawzī, *Mir'at al-Zamān,* ms. Paris 1506, fols. 146a-146b.
6. S. D. Goitein, "Contemporary Letters on the Capture of Jerusalem by the Crusaders," *Journal of Jewish Studies* III (1952), pp.169-70.
7. Cf. M. Canard, "La guerre sainte dans le monde islamique et dans le monde chrétien," *Revue Africaine* LXXIX (1936), pp.616-20; P. Lemerle, "Byzance et la Croisade," *Relazioni del X cong. Int. di Scienze storiche,* Firenze 1955, vol. 3, pp. 615-8; G. E. Von Grunebaum, "Eine Poetische Polemik zwischen Byzanz und Bagdad im X. Jahrhundert," *Analecta Orientalia,* XIV (1937), pp. 49-50.
8. Compare my *L'Islam et la Croisade*, Paris 1968, chap. 1.
9. Ibn al-Qalānisī, op. cit., p. 171; al-'Azīmī, op. cit., P. 369; Usāma b. Munqidh, *Kitab al-I'tibar,* ed. Hitti, Princeton 1930, pp. 69, 139.
10. Cf. S. D. Goitein, "The Sanctity of Jerusalem and of Palestine in Early Islam," *Studies in Islamic History and Institutions,* Leiden 1966, pp. 135-8; H. Busse, "The Sanctity of Jerusalem in Islam," *Judaism* XVII (1968), pp. 441-68; M. J. Kister,

"You Shall Only Set Out for Three Mosques: A Study of an Early Tradition," *Muséon* 1969, pp. 173-96.

11. S. D. Goitein, "Jerusalem in the Arab Period" (in Hebrew), *Yerushalayim* IV (1952), pp. 82-103.
12. Nāṣiri-i-Khusraw, *Relation de voyage*, trans. Ch. Scheffer, Paris, 1881, p. 67; E. Sivan, "The Beginnings of the *Fadā'il al-Quds* Literature," *Israel Oriental Studies* I (1971), pp. 263-71.
13. Abū Shāma, *Kitāb al-Rawḍatayn*, Vol. 1, Cairo, A.H. 1287/8, pp. 104, 113; Yunīnī, *Dhayl Mir'āt al-Zamān*, Vol. 4, Hyderabad, 1961, p. 173.
14. Sibṭ b. al-Jawzī, *Mir'āt al-Zamān,* Hyderabad, 1959. Al-Samarqandī, it should be noted, was one of the mentors of Ibn al-'Asākir, the future renovator of the *Faḍa'il al-Quds* literature (see infra, p.r.).
15. *Kitāb al-'Awāṣim mina-l-Qawāsim,* Constantine 1928, Vol. 2, pp. 212-13.
16. Edition and partial translation in "Genèse de la Contre-Croisade," *Journal Asiatique* (1966), pp. 197 ff.
17. Abū Shāma, op. cit., Vol. 1, p. 40; 'Imād al-Dīn, op. cit., Vol. 1, p. 110.
18. Abū Shāma, op. cit., Vol. 1, p. 57; Cf. "Réfugiés syro-palestiniens à l'époque des Croisades," *Revue des Etudes Islamiques* 25 (1967) pp. 141-3.
19. 'Imād al-Dīn, op. cit.,Vol. 1, p. 158.
20. Abū Shāma, op. cit., Vol. 1, pp. 78-9.
21. Ibn al-Furāt, *Ta'rikh*, ms. Vienna 814, vol. 3, fol. 159a.
22. 'Imād al-Dīn, op. cit., Vol. 1, p. 175; cf. pp. 159, 179.
23. Ibid., p. 277; Abū Shāma, op. cit., vol. 1, p. 182.
24. Ibid., Vol. 1, p. 215.
25. Ibn al-Athīr, *Al-Kāmil fī-l-Ta'rīkh*, Vol. 11, Cairo, A.H. 1303, p. 209; Ibn Wāṣil, *Mufarrij al-Kurūb,* Vol. 2, Cairo, 1957, p. 229; *Répteroire Chronologique d'Épigraphie Arabe* (RCEA), Vol. 9, no. 3281.
26. *Kitāb al-Muntaẓam,* Vol. 10, Hyderabad A.H., 1359, p. 249.
27. Abū Shāma, op. cit, Vol. 1, p. 215.
28. Cf. "Beginnings of the *Fada'il al-Quds* Literature" *IOS* (1971); I. Hasson's introduction to his edition of Abū Bakr al-Wāsiṭī's *Fadā'il al-Bayt al-Muqaddas,* Jerusalem 1979; al-Wāṣitī Ms. at al-Jazzār Mosque, Acre, pp. 66-7.
29. Cf. al-Munajjid's edition of *Ta'rīkh Dimasq,* Damascus 1951; 'Imad al-Dīn, op. cit., Vol.1, p. 548 (n.l.). Cf. also his treatise on *jihād,* drafted in 1169/70 and dedicated to Nūr al-Din (ms. Damascus Ẓāhiriyya, Lugha 54).
30. Sibṭ b. al-Jawzī, op. cit., p. 336.
31. Ed. al-Munajjid, Vol. 1, p. 110, 129, 134, 141-2, 211, 224, 228, 240, 270.
32. Ibid., p. 323.
33. Auditor's certificates on the ms. (ibid., p. 629).
34. Abū Shāma, op. cit., Vol. 1, pp. 13-4; al-Harāwī, *Kitab al-Ishārāt ilā Ma'rifat al-Ziyārāt*, Damascus, 1953, p. 24; A. J. Arberry, *An Introduction to the History of Sufism*, Oxford, 1944, p. 68.
35. Cf. p. ex. Abū Shāma, op. cit., Vol. 2, p. 48; al-Qāḍi al-Fāḍil, *Rasā'il*, ms. Paris 6024, fols. 21a-21b.
36. Abū Shāma, op. cit., Vol. 1, p. 269; Ibn al-Sa'ātī, Beirut, 1938, p. 384.
37. Abū Shāma, op. cit., Vol. 2, pp. 72, 116.
38. Ibid., Vol. 1, p. 243, Al-Qalqashandī, *Ṣubḥal-A'sha*, Cairo, 1919, p. 146.
39. Abū Shāma, op. cit., Vol. 1, p. 254; Vol. 2, p. 23.
40. Ibid., p. 111.
41. Ibid., pp. 45, 104.
42. *Riḥla,* Cairo 1908, p. 292; Cl. Cahen, "Indigènes et Croisés," *Syria XV* (1934), pp. 351-60.

43. Abū Shāma, ibid, Vol. 2, p. 66.
44. Ibid, p. 85, 87, 72, 116; Wāsiṭī, ms. Acre, p. 67.
45. Bahā al-Dīn, *Sīrat Salāḥ al-Dīn*, Cairo, A.H. 1357.
46. Cf. Saladin's letter to the governor of Western Egypt quoted *in extenso* in *Siyar al-Āba' al-Baṭārika,* ms. Paris 302, p. 262.
47. Cf. the observations of Ibn al-Athīr (op. cit., Vol. 11, p. 206).
48. Abū Shāma, op. cit., Vol. 2, pp. 97, 99, 101, 105; Qalqashandī, op. cit., Vol. 6, p. 500.
49. Abū Shāma, op. cit., Vol. 2, pp. 98, 110; cf. Qalqashandī, Vol. 6, p. 497.
50. Abū Shāma, op. cit., Vol. 2, pp. 110-11.
51. Ibid, p. 101; *RCEA*, Vol. 9, nrs. 3347, 3464; vol. 10, no. 3916.
52. Abū Shāma, op. cit., Vol. 2, pp. 92, 94, 119-20.
53. Ms. Princeton, 586, *Faḍā'il Bayt al-Muqaddas al-Shāmī*; al-Silafī, ms. Cambridge 736.
54. The book, *Al-Jāmi' al-Mustaqṣa fī Faḍā'īl al-Masjid al-Aqṣā,* is lost, but sections thereof are included in the early fourteenth century's author Ibn al-Firkāḥ, *Bā'ith al-Nufūs ilā Ziyārat al-Quds al-Maḥrūs* (edited by C.D. Matthews in *Journal of the Palestine Exploration Society* [1936] pp. 57-81). On the public readings see *Ta'rīkh Dimashq,* vol. 1, p. 629.
55. Ibn al-'Asākir (in Ibn al-Firkāh), pp. 79-80; 'Imad al-Din, *Al-Fatḥ al-Qussi,* Ed. Landberg, Leiden 1888, pp. 48-9; Abū Shāma, op. cit., vol. 2, pp. 93-4, Ibn al-Jawzī, ms. Princeton, fols. 13b-14a, 29a-30a, Cf. J. W. Hirschberg, "The Sources of Muslim Traditions Concerning Jerusalem," *Rocznik Orientalistyczny* XXVII (151/2), pp. 314-50; G. Vajda, "La Description du Temple de Jerusalem . . . ses élements bibliques et rabbiniques," *Journal Asiatique* 247 (1950), pp. 193-202; A. N. Poliak, "The Ombilical Point of the Globe" (in Hebrew), *Dinaburg Festschrift,* Jerusalem, 1949, pp. 165-75.
56. 'Imād al-Dīn, op. cit., p. 413; Abū Shāma, op. cit., Vol. 2, pp. 94-99, 110; Bahā' al-Dīn, op. cit., p. 187; Ibn al-Jawzī, fols. 20b-23b, 31a-31b, Hirschberg, article cited, pp. 338-9.
57. Ibn 'Asākir (in Ibn al-Firkāḥ), pp. 74-6, 80; Ibn al-Jawzī, fols 13b, 23b-24b.
58. Ibn 'Asākir (in Ibn al-Firkāḥ), pp. 72, 80;ibn al-Jawzī, fols. 28a-29a; Abū Shāma. Vol. 2, p. 94.
59. 'Imād al-Dīn, *Fatḥ*, pp. 413-8. Cf. 'Abd al-Laṭīf quoted by al-Dhahabī, *Ta'rikh al-Islām,* ms. Paris 1582, fol 46a.
60. 'Imād al-Dīn, *Fatḥ,* p. 400; Abū Shāma, Vol. 2, p. 194.
61. Bahā' al-Dīn, op. cit., p. 212; Abū Shāma, Vol. 2, p. 204.
62. Ibn 'Asākir (in Ibn al-Firkāḥ), pp. 79-80; Ibn al-Jawzī, fols. 11a-11b.
63. Abū Shāma, vol. 2, p. 94; Ibn al-Jawzī, fol. 9b, 10a. Cf. Kister, article cited.
64. Ibn 'Asākir (in Ibn al-Firkāḥ), p. 80; Ibn al-Jawzī, fols. 11a-11b; Cf. Hirschberg, art. cit., pp. 315-7.
65. 'Imād al-Dīn, *Fatḥ*, p. 100; Abū Shāma, Vol. 2, p. 94. On attempts in the past to make Jerusalem the first holy place of Islam, cf. Poliak, article cited.
66. Ibn 'Asākir (in Ibn al-Firkāḥ), p. 59; Ibn al-Jawzī, fol. 11a.
67. E. Ashthor, "Jerusalem in the Latter Middle Ages" (in Hebrew), *Yerushalayim* V (1955), pp. 79-80, 84, 88.
68. Ibn al-Athīr, op. cit., Vol. 11, p. 212; 'Abd al-Laṭīf quoted by al-Dhahabī, fol. 48a; Abū Shāma, *Dhayl al-Rawḍatayn,* Cairo 1947, p. 7: al-Yunīnī, *Dhayl Mir'at al-Zamān,* Vol. 3, Hyderabad, 1960, p. 60.
69. Quoted by Ibn al-'Adīm, *Bughyat al-Ṭalab,* ms. Paris 2138, fol. 27a. Cf. 'Imād al-Dīn, *Fatḥ*, p. 101.
70. Ashthor, article cited, pp. 83-4; al-'Umari, *Masālik al-Abṣār,* Vol. 1 Cairo 1924, p.

145; Ibn Duqmāq, *Nuṣrat al-Anām,* ms. Paris 1597, fol. 68a; Cl. Cahen, "Les mémoires de Sa'd al-Din Ibn Ḥamawiya," *Bullétin de la Faculte des lettres,* Université de Strasburg 28 (1950), p. 330.

71. Sibṭ B. al-Jawzī, op. cit., ms. Paris 5866, fol. 237a; ibid., Ed. Hyderbad, p. 517; Ibn al-'Adīm, op. cit., ms. Paris 2138, fol. 55b; Ibn Wāṣil, *Mufarrij al-Kurūb,* ms. Paris 1702, fols.224a, 246a; Ibn al-Sa'i, al-Jāmi', *al-Mukhtaṣar,* Vol. 9, Baghdad, 1934, p. 155; al-Subkī, *Ṭabaqāt al-Shāfi'iyya al-Kubrā,* Vol. 5, p. 101.
72. Al-Maqdisi, *Muthīr al-Gharām,* ms. Damascus, Ẓāhiriyya, (Ta'rīkh 720), fols. 295-6; ibid., ed. Khālidi, Jaffa, 1946, p. 46; Subkī, op. cit., vol. 4, p. 213; Ḥājji Khalīfa, *Kashf al-Ẓunūn,* Vol. 1, p. 454; Sibṭ, op. cit., Ed. Hyderabad, p. 517; Ibn 'Asākir, op. cit., Vol. 1, p. 629.
73. Ms. Damascus, Ẓāhiriyya 34 (Um. 29) Majm. 48, Cf. Ibn Rajab, *Ṭabaqāt al-Ḥanābila,* Cairo 1952/3, vol. 1, p. 372; vol. 2, p. 239.
74. *Targhīb Ahl al-Islam fi Suknā al-Shām,* ed. Khālidi, Jerusalem, 1940, p. 13.
75. Apart from the famous biographies of Bahā' al-Dīn and 'Imād al-Dīn, there were two others, which are unfortunately lost, by Ibn Mammātī and Ibn Abi Tayyī (v. Abū Shāma, *Rawḍatayn,* Vol. 1, p. 43; Maqrīzī, *Khiṭaṭ,* Ed. Būlāk, Vol. 2, p. 160).
76. P. ex. Abū Shāma, op. cit., Vol. 2, pp. 85, 215; Sibṭ b. al-Jawzī, op. cit., p. 430; Michel le Syrien, *Chronique,* Venice 1868, p. 327; al-Maqdisī, *Muthīr al-Gharām,* ms. Damascus, p. 295, ibid., ed. Khālidī, pp. 63-4; al-Harāwī, *Ishārāt,* p.16.
77. Pseudo-Wāqidī, *Futūḥ al-Shām,* Vol.1, Cairo A.H. 1373, pp.133-45; B. Hanenberg, *Eröterungen über pseudo-Wakidi's Geschichte,* Munich 1960. On popular interest in these legends in the early thirteenth century see Harāwī, *Tadhkir,* in *Bullétin d'Études Orientales, Institut de Damas* (BEOID) 17 (1961/62) pp. 231, 242.
78. *Ishārāt,* Damascus 1953, pp. 24-8.
79. Baha' al-Dīn, op. cit., p. 187.
80. Abū Shāma, *Dhayl al-Rawḍatayn,* p. 116; cf. Ibn Taghribirdī, *Al-Nujūm al-Ẓāhira,* Vol. 6, Cairo, 1935, p. 244; S. Humphreys, *From Saladin to the Mongols,* S.U.N.Y. Press, 1977, pp. 164-5.
81. Yāqūt, *Mu'jam al-Buldān,* Vol. 5, Beirut, 1957, p. 171.
82. Sibṭ b. al-Jawzī, op. cit., Ed. Hyderabad, p. 601; Abū Shāma, *Dhayl,* p. 116; cf. Ibn Shaddād, *Al-A'lāq al-Khaṭīra (Ta'rīkh Dimashq),* Damascus, 1956, p. 216.
83. Ibn al-Athīr, *Al-Kāmil,* Vol. 12, p. 198.
84. Ibn Shaddād, *al-A'laq al-Khaṭīra (Ta'rīkh Lubnān),* Damascus 1963, p. 224; Ibn al-'Amīd, *Akhbar al-Ayyūbiyyīn,* in *BEOID* 15 (1955/57) p. 138.
85. Sibṭ b. al-Jawzī. op. cit., p. 656; Maqrizi, *Al-Sulūk li-Ma'rifat Duwal al-Mulūk,* vol. 1, Cairo, 1934, p. 231.
86. Al-'Ayni, *Iqd al-Jumān* in *Recevil des Historiens des Croisades (RHC) Historiens Orientaux,* Vol. 2a, pp. 190-1; Sibt b. al-Jawzī, op. cit., p. 655.
87. Ibn Wāṣil, op. cit., ms. Paris 1702, fols. 253a, 256a; cf. Humphreys, op. cit., chap. 6.
88. Abū Shāma, *Dhayl al-Rawḍatayn* pp. 38, 158.
89. Sibṭ b. al-Jawzī, op. cit., p. 654. (Actually, the Treaty of Jaffa guaranteed free access to Muslim holy places.)
90. Ibid., ms. Paris 5866, fol. 237a; Maqrizi, *Sulūk,* Vol. 1, p. 233.
91. Egypt: Ibn Taghībirdī, Vol.6, p. 272; Mosul—Ibn al-Athīr, Vol. 12, p. 187: Jazīra and Baghdad—Ibn Naṭīf, *al-Ta'rīkh al-Manṣūrī,* Ed. Moscow, 1960, fols. 182b, 185a.
92. Ibid; Ibn Wāṣil, ms. Paris 1702, fols. 288b-289a; ibid., ms. Paris 1703, fol. 4a.
93. Quoted by H.A.R. Gibb from the Chronicle of Ibn Abī-l-Damm (ms. Oxford) in K.M. Setton (ed.) *History of the Crusades* Vol. 2, Philadelphia, 1962, p. 702. Cf. Maqrīzī, *Sulūk,* Vol. 1, p. 230; idem. *Khiṭaṭ,* Vol. 2, p. 377.
94. Ibn Naṭīf, op. cit., fol. 182b, 185a-185b; Cf. Maqrīzī, *Sulūk,* Vol. 1, p. 231.

95. *L'Estoire d'Éracles* in *RHC Historiens Occidentaux* vol. 2, pp. 383-5.
96. Al-'Aynī, op. cit., p. 195; cf. E. Quatremer, *Histoire des Sultans Mamelouks*, vol. 2, Paris 1847, p. 127 (note 14).
97. Ibn Maṭrūḥ, *Dīwān*, Istanbul A.H. 1299, pp. 182-3, Saladin's official title was *al-Malik al-Nāṣir*. Cf. Ibn Shaddād, op. cit. *(Ta'rīkh Lubnān)*, pp.226-33.
98. Ibn 'Abd al-Ẓāhir, *Sīrat al-Malik al Manṣūr (Qalā'ūn)*, Cairo, 1961, p. 83; Yunīnī, op. cit., vol. 2, p. 375; 'Ayni, *RHC Historiens Orientaux*, vol. 2a, p. 243.
99. Cf. D. Ayalon, "Studies on the transfer of the Abbasid Caliphate from Bagdad to Cairo (I)," "*Arabica*, VII(1960), p. 58-9.
100. V. C. D. Mathews, "A Muslim Iconoclast (Ibn Taymiyyah) on the Merits of Jerusalem and Palestine," *JAOS*, LVI (1936), pp. 1-21; Ibn Kathīr, *Al-Bidāya wal-Nihāya*, vol. 8, p. 280; N. al-Albānī, *Hujjat al-Nabī*, Damascus, 3rd Ed., 1967, pp. 157-60; H. Lazarus-Yaffe, "The Sanctity of Jerusalem in Islam" in her *Some Religious Aspects of Islam*, Leiden, 1981, p. 71.
101. P. ex. Al-Kanji al-Ṣūfī, *Faḍa'īl Bayt al-Maqdis*, ms. Tübingen 26, fols. 65b, 74a-74b; Shihāb al-Dīn al-Maqdisi, *Muthīr al-Gharām*, ms. Damascus, Ẓāhiriyya, Ta'rīkh 720, p. 2; al-Suyūṭī, *The History of the Temple of Jerusalem*, trans. Reynolds, London 1836, pp. 270-1.
102. C. V. Brocklmann, *Geschichte der Arabische Literatur*, vol. 2, pp. 130, 136, 162, 163, 169; ibid. (Supplement), vol. 1, p. 876; vol. 2, pp. 128, 164, 214.
103. Cf. my "Intellectual Blues," *The Jerusalem Quarterly 20* (1981), p. 136.
104. *Khuṭbat al-Jum'a: Al-Marjid al-Aqṣā bayna-l-Dīn wa-l-Ta'rīkh* (delivered on 13 Feb. 1976), Jerusalem, 1976.

# Chapter 4:
# 'ULAMĀ' AND POWER

## *'ULAMĀ'* AS TRAITORS?

The term "treason of the clerics" *(trahison des clercs)*, coined by Julien Benda to characterize the failure of French intellectuals in the 1920s to do their duty as the conscience of society, has now been adopted by the Islamic world. The intellectuals in question cover the entire political spectrum, but particular scorn is reserved for the *'ulamā'*, a loose term covering jurists *(fuqahā')*, religious judges *(qāḍīs)*, theologians, teachers in religious schools *(madrasas)*, other religious functionaries (such as *imāms* and *muezzins* of mosques), and mystics (Ṣūfīs).

Why the *'ulamā'* in particular? Perhaps because unlike modern Muslim intellectuals, a class which began to burgeon only in the late nineteenth century and whose real growth can be dated to the 1950s (with the expansion of the university system), the *'ulamā'* span fourteen centuries of Islam. They are taken to task for contemporary failures as well as for those in the faraway past; they can be held responsible not only for the evils of present society but also for the evils of Muslim society throughout history. They are, to some, the prototype of the intellectual in Muslim lands and thus foreshadow the frailties and sins of the modern secular intellectual too: his abject subservience to the ruling class out of fear or greed, his lack of candor and consistency, the intellectual flabbiness that makes him evade tough questions, his preference for the detailed and the technical rather than important issues, his predilection for bloated rhetoric and hair-splitting speculations. Here is how a leading modern thinker judges his fellow intellectuals:

> Dependence is an ancient type of relationship, perhaps thousands of years old. Whatever its roots, suffice it to say that contemporary Arab thought does not lead or inspire political power but is a tributary thereof. It does not initiate moves but follows the rules. The *sulṭān* orders and the *'ulamā'* give their blessing, the *amīr* sets the law and *qāḍīs* judge accordingly—such a dependency is not only related to external constraints, e.g., censor-

ship of the press and the electronic media, but is internalized and thus breeds a feeling of powerlessness, a lack of will and drive to launch a new intellectual initiative or to present a novel analysis of reality regardless of the directives of the people in power.[1]

We have already seen how crucial the role of the *'ulamā'* was considered in the revisionist historiography of the liberals and the leftists (Chapter 2). The judgment pronounced by Muslim radicals, and even by milder fundamentalists, is not different in essence. This refers not only to *'ulamā'* opportunism and servility nowadays but also to the notorious "*fuqahā'* of the palaces" upbraided by Khomeini (in his *Islamic Government*). It is true that under the twentieth-century military regimes the *'ulamā'* sank particularly deep: "Many are the *'ulamā'*, men of religion; few of the latter are really men" as one radical put it.[2] This harsh verdict is amply borne out by the record: slavish acceptance of the Free Officers, who were topplers of the *ancien régime* that the *'ulamā'* had so praised in the past, their contribution being the personality cult, enthusiasm for the status quo, or more rarely silence when the new regimes developed into police states.

Yet the abdication of the *'ulamā'*, as Muslim reformers argued already in the early twentieth century, harks back many centuries, perhaps even to early Islamic times. If the Muḥammad 'Abduh school detected the roots of the *'ulamā'* conservatism in their opposition to the ninth-century rationalism of the *mu'tazila*, Muslim Brethren Leader Ḥasan al-Banna in the 1930s and 1940s and Sayyid Quṭb, father of present-day radicalism, saw a continued, thirteen-century-old tradition of pusillanimous *'ulamā'*, shirking their duty to set polity and society aright.[3] Muḥammad 'Alī Ḍinnāwī, a major Lebanese fundamentalist writer, summed up the thinking of this school by tracing the *'ulamā'* conservatism to the trauma of the First Civil War (mid-seventh century), the following struggle between Shīites and Umayyads, and the tremors and ravages of the 'Abbāsid Revolution: "All this made the *'ulamā'* shudder at the specter of internecine strife and eschew fighting against injustice and deviation."[4]

Moreover, *'ulama'* (especially jurists and other practitioners of the *sharī'a*, or Islamic Law, such as muftis and *qāḍīs*) were assigned a primordial duty in Islam. Like Judaism and unlike Christianity, Islam is a religion interested above all in shaping Man's behavior rather than beliefs; a religion cherishing *orthopraxis* before *orthodoxy*. Behavior was to be shaped by the law, rudiments of which were left by Muḥammad and developed into a systematic corpus by the *'ulamā'* during the first three centuries of Islam. They, and not the rulers, were also entrusted with its application and interpretation, in and out of the courts, and thus, in theory, preserving and enhancing the Islamic character of society. In theory but not in practice.

Muslim historians, whether of the right or of the left, find themselves here, surprisingly, in complete agreement on a major thesis: namely, that the *'ulamā'* shirked its responsibilities and let the rulers intervene in the judicial system, levy illicit taxes, and introduce other "innovations" (*bid'a*, a term of opprobrium in Islam). Moreover, the *'ulamā'* are said to have accepted social injustice, and when they tried to correct it they did so usually by mild admonishment (or, like the Ṣūfīs, by withdrawal from the corrupt society). Finally, the *'ulamā'* are alleged to have rarely challanged iniqitous rulers and almost never justified a revolt against them, never tried to develop a political theory, and neglected for centuries the whole field of constitutional law, which needed to be written in accordance with Islamic principles. By the time some of them began to do so—very hesitatingly, it is true—in the eleventh century, the realities of ruler-subject relations were so firmly lodged that they could hardly be rectified; not that the *'ulamā'* actually tried: most political theorists contented themselves with justifying the status quo and adding an Islamic gloss.

## ECONOMIC DEPENDENCE AND SECURITY IMPERATIVE

In answer to the "what" and "how" of *'ulamā'* attitudes and behavior toward the rulers, there is a consensus among the more critical Muslim historians and among most non-Muslim students of Islamic history. There is a consensus, too, as to the cardinality of the problem, i.e., as to the fact that one touches here a focal point explaining why Muslim civil society (led or educated by the *'ulamā'*), while disdaining the political sphere and harboring precious few illusions as to its evil nature, tends on the whole to acquiesce with the way its masters control it. This passivity would readily account for the hurdles Muslim revolutionaries (be they of the left or of the right) face today. We have said "focal point," but should rather have said "raw nerve," for these debates—whether on the part of Muslim fundamentalists and progressivists or of traditionalist *'ulamā'* defending their track record—are always emotional. Both sides know that what is at stake is nothing less than an answer (admittedly, a partial one, for other factors played a role, too) to the question of what went wrong in Islamic history, and whence present development comes from.

To help figure out this intimidating problem, one should pass from the "what" and "how" of the *'ulamā'* question to the "why." Here, for all the plethora of studies conducted recently by Muslims and non-Muslims, progress has been slow, though nonetheless palpable. A major obstacle has been the penury of sources for the early and middle Middle Ages (seventh to twelfth centuries), while the later Middle Ages and the Ottoman era are more amply documented and were, hence, easier to study. On the later Middle Ages, in particular, we possess today a number of excellent monographs that brought forth that combination of slavish subservience and inner alienation characterizing the *'ulamā'* relation to the rulers. Here we are dealing, however, with the phenomenon in its mature form.[5] On the other hand, the *'ulamā'*, who during the first centuries of Islam were a very small class, began to grow from the eleventh century on with the establishment of madrasas and lavish endowments *(waqfs)*. This provided people with job opportunities and fellowships, and, eventually, madrasa graduates were recruited into the expanding bureaucracy. By the late Middle Ages (thirteenth to eighteenth centuries), the class was fully grown but also financially dependent on the rulers more than ever before, and evinced in a more pronounced manner the characteristics of a military caste, alien from the natives in language (usually Turkish) and culture (the *jihād*-imbued frontier culture of central Asia whence most of them came). Some, as in the case of the Mamluks, were of slave origin. The metamorphosis which created this political elite began slowly in the ninth century (with the use of Mamluk praetorian guards in the capital of the Caliphate, Baghdad) and developed momentum with the introduction of the non-native dynasties which ruled the Arabic-speaking Middle East.

*'Ulamā'* subservience (and alienation) in this well-researched era, especially under the Mamluks, is presented as the outcome of material dependence upon the rulers (teachers and scholars living off endowments, civil servants, judges, etc.), of the ruthless and foreign nature of the military caste, but also of the fact that these castes provided a crucial service to society: Islam was on the defensive, invaded by Crusaders and Mongols; the only force which could and did stem that Christian and Pagan tide were the Mamluk regiments, who indeed hoisted their leaders to power after their victories in Manṣūra (1250, over Louis IX of France) and 'Ayn Jālūt (1260, over

the Mongols). The Mamluks kept their tacit pact with the society they came to rule: they put an end to the Crusader Kingdom (1291), repelled later crusades in the following two centuries, blocked Mongol expansion in the early fourteenth century, and began to push it beyond the Euphrates boundary. As the Mamluks kept their side of the bargain, so goes the argument, society kept hers and was subservient, letting herself be fleeced, and later plundered by the rulers.

The *'ulamā'*, the alleged conscience, often the actual spokesmen of civil society, and always a go-between with the authorities, were quite adamant about the need to accept the bargain. Faced with the danger of the Abode of Islam falling under Christian and Pagan rule, and well conditioned by two centuries of *jihād* against the Franks, the *'ulamā'* saw the Mamluks, in the worst of cases, as a necessary evil, the "mighty shield defending Islam." They were ready to pay the price and swallow any number of bitter remedies: Mamluk uncouthness, their contempt for "bloody civilians," for non-Turkish speakers, and for people not of the "most noble," i.e., Turkish, racial stock. They were even ready to close an eye (and sometimes, even two) to dissolute habits (sex and alcohol) of the political elite; they resigned themselves to "administrative" (i.e., non-religious) Mamluk judges (the *ḥujjāb*), taking away the *qāḍīs'* monopoly in certain spheres of justice and employing a written pagan law, the Mongol *Yāsa*. The price for keeping society under Muslim control, however imperfect, seemed to be correct given the bleak alternatives.[6]

The combination of security *(jihād)* imperatives and material dependence was powerful enough to eclipse any other factor. This is both a necessary and sufficient explanation, though perhaps not an exhaustive one.

One wonders, however, whether this double-pronged explanatory model is valid thoughout Muslim history, particularly prior to the thirteenth century. The *jihād* imperative and the alien (and ruthless) character of the elite were relatively late phenomena, and the same holds true for material dependence, which went hand in glove with the growth in size of the *'ulamā'* class. The study of earlier periods may point to other factors that may be relevant also to our understanding of post-thirteenth century, nay even contemporary, Muslim history.

## THE SYRIAN INTERMEZZO

Having broached the major questions, their relevance, and the emerging answers, I do not intend to provide an all-encompassing picture. The state of the art would not justify such a presumption. For what is needed are more case studies, especially of the seventh to twelfth century, placed however in a framework of the major questions delineated above. And as life is lived forward and understood backward (according to Kierkegaard), it might be useful to present here a case study which proceeds backward from the well-researched Mamluk period and focuses on the eleventh to thirteenth centuries. The area we have chosen is Syria, or *al-Shām*, in the Muslim sense of that administrative term (i.e., present-day Syria, Lebanon, Jordan, the occupied territories, and Israel). We shall deal here with a period and an area that represent a privileged intersection of time and space, with as much control of the principal variables as might be available anywhere.

Indeed I have chosen to concentrate upon Syria since it was the last Middle Eastern country to join the club of states ruled by foreign military elites, and did it slowly and with great difficulty at that; moreover, Syria as a whole and its city-states in particular had a long tradition of zeal and ardor in defense of their autonomy within the dismembered Caliphate, a tradition predicated among others upon the existence of local militias *(aḥdāth)*, which were not to be found in a country like Egypt, for instance.[7]

The 1070s marked the era of Turkish penetration into Syria, by regular units of the Seljūqid Empire and in particular by irregular Turkoman bands. This ushered in 850 years of Turkish rule and put an end to a century during which Syria was the theater of a ferocious confrontation between the two regional powers of the day, Byzantium and Fāṭimid Egypt. Both powers were knocked out of the arena in the years immediately preceding the Turkish invasion. Byzantium severely reduced its military presence in Northern Syria following its crushing defeat in Manzikert at the hands of the Seljūqids (1071). Egypt did the same as a result of a complete revision of its foreign policy in the wake of the abortive rebellion fomented in Iraq by its ally Basāsīrī (1060); isolationism replaced adventurism and interventionism all the more quickly as the Egyptian army was soon riven by strife between various ethnic components. Both powers preserved some bases, governors, and puppet rulers in the area: Byzantium in the district of Antioch (until 1084) and the Fāṭimids along the Syro-Palestinian coast and for a while in Jerusalem (until the arrival of the First Crusade). Yet, because of the tiny size of Byzantine and Egyptian military contingents in Syria and the utter indifference of Constantinople and Cairo to developments there, one can say that Syria was now outside of their sphere of influence.

Moving into the Turkish orbit was a more gradual process. The penetration was spearheaded by irregular Turkomans (such as Atsiz, conqueror of Damascus and Jerusalem) and by Seljūqid regiments in the employ of autonomous branches of the ruling family (e.g., Sulaymām b. Qutulmish). Syrian integration into the Seljūqid Sultanate began only in 1085 and required a systematic campaign of conquest opposed at times both by the natives and by Turkish bands and regiments already settled there. Governors appointed by Sultan Malikshāh were imposed upon city after city—an arduous process that took six years to accomplish.

Yet barely a year later (1092) the chief Seljūqid vizier Niẓām al-Mulk was assassinated, the Sultan died, and the Sultanate was thrown again into a whirlpool of instability that soon had its reverberations in Syria as well.

The Byzantines and the Fāṭimids, who had put an end to the short-lived Syrian independence under the Ḥamdānid dynasty, were now gone. The Turks advanced gradually, since their hold was far from being firm. This vacuum created in Syria almost ideal conditions for it to reassert its independence. Two types of indigenous forces were indeed capable of joining the struggle. First was the Arab-speaking dynasties, either military (Mirdāsids and 'Uqaylids in Aleppo) or civilian (Banū 'Ammār in Tripoli, Banū Munqidh in Shayzar) in origin. The second was the *aḥdāth*, who had proved ready and able to defend urban independence and even succeeded in withstanding the onslaught of regular armies (e.g., against the Fāṭimids in Aleppo in 1042 and 1058); these militias were as a general rule led by local notables with a broad-based network of patronage and political and administrative experience, the *ra'īs*. These patrons of the *aḥdāth* soon became local king-makers in their cities (1061 in Aleppo), and quite naturally their role expanded in the period of transition of the the last quarter century. It was the *aḥdāth*, for instance, who deposed the Mirdāsid ruler of Aleppo and gave the city to Muslim b. Quraysh of the Uqaylid family (1079). There were even cases when they hoisted their own *ra'īs* to power (in Jabala in the 1090s).

The upshot of this state of affairs was the development of a sort of "Syrian Intermezzo" (much like the "Iranian Intermezzo," as the historian V. Minorsky describes the Buwayhid era in the Middle East). This "intermezzo" lasted between fifteen and forty years in the various city-states, until the Crusader conquest (along the coast of the Levant and in the hilly areas of Palestine) or the re-assertion of Seljūqid control (in most of present-day Syria) during the first quarter of the eleventh century. During this period, *al-Shām* was fragmented into city-states ruled by natives and fiercely dedicated to their independence, which they defended with tenacity against foreign encroachment, be it Christian (Frankish) or Muslim (Turkish). In some places (such as Shayzar) native dynasties stood their own until the mid-twelfth century.[8]

What part did the *'ulamā'* play in this feverish activity to realize or preserve the local autonomy? Our Arabic sources—few but reliable and independent of each other—provide an almost totally negative answer. There were, it appears, ruling dynasties of *qāḍīs*—Banū 'Ammār in Tripoli and Banū Ṣulayḥa in Jabala—but there is no indication that they came to power as men of religion; neither did their policies as rulers evince any sign that they were *'ulamā'*, nor did they enjoy the backing of segments of this class. It is evident that these were local notables who bolstered their position by taking also the judgeship.

The purely incidental, or politically opportunist, character of their religiosity is borne out by the indifference of these dynasties toward the movement of Sunni "moral rearmament" (to borrow H.A.R. Gibb's phrase), which had by then arrived from Central Asia in the Middle East as well as by their indifference to the anti-Muslim character of the First Crusade. The same holds true for other types of semi-religious notables (e.g., the *sharīf* al-Kutaytī in Aleppo, 1085/6). In other Syrian city-states, the *'ulamā'* failed to intervene on behalf of the *aḥdāth* against local potentates, Seljūqids, or Turkomans. One does not find them also among the supporters of local dynasties trying to extend their borders or to defend them against neighboring city-states or regional powers.[9]

The *argumentum ex silentio* is often a slippery tool, but in this particular case it seems to be relevant and reliable. Against the background of the power vacuum created in Syria there developed a cluster of local forces whose route to political power had been blocked for more than a century (i.e., since the fall of the Ḥamdānids). Thus came to the fore the lower middle class with the *aḥdath*, the middle and upper class with the dynasties of the *ru'asā* (plural of *ra'īs*), local *condotierri* (Mirdāsids, 'Uqaylids), semi-nomad tribes, and clans (e.g., Banū Munqidh). It should be stressed that most of our sources are chronicles written by *'ulamā'* historians who describe extensively the fortunes and the comings and goings of the members of their class. Lack of evidence on the political activity of the *'ulamā'* could not be fortuitous. One may thus entertain some doubts as to whether the relationship between the *'ulamā'* and the bourgeoisie, which seems quite valid with regard to social origin, standard of living, residence, life style, and intermarriage, is actually valid for the political sphere as well. As the Syrian bourgeoisie burst into the political arena, which had been vacated by regional powers, the *'ulamā'*, its putative allies, remained curiously idle.

Moreover, *'ulamā'* dependence of the type studied in the later Middle Ages did not exist in the late eleventh to early twelfth centuries. That dependence was predicated on the "security (or *jihād*) imperative" described above and upon the monopoly enjoyed by the military elites upon the major economic resources of these times—agricultural land parceled out as military fiefs *(iqtā')*, most urban real estate, building materials (defined as "strategic commodity")—and finally on the right to subject the populace to corvées (ostensibly for the *jihād*). Thus, the rulers were the only factor capable of financing religions as well as cultic, juridical, or educational activities, and to expand them. Hence, the virtually complete dependence of the *'ulamā'* upon the political elites of the later Middle Ages, a phenomenon further buttressed by the fact that many of the former were already civil servants. No wonder that their political activity did not exceed the bounds of reporting the subjects' complaints to the ruler and sometimes also admonishing the latter (rather mildly) for his transgressions.[10]

None of these factors operated during the "Syrian Intermezzo." Heterodox Muslim danger was liquidated, and there was no need for *jihād* against so-called apostates. Shīite danger, which once emanated from Fāṭimid Egypt and from southern Iraq, subsided with the former retreating into its cocoon and the latter being subdued by the militant Sunni Seljūqids. Extreme Shīite sects (the *bāṭinīs*, notably the Assassins), who were to loom large in the mid-twelfth century, were still rather circumscribed and met with ferocious resistance even by local Shīites (particularly in northern Syria). And what about the Christian danger? This faded out with the gradual evacuation of Byzantine forces (ending with the fall of Edessa in 1087). Last but not least were the Seljūqids, who certainly could not be construed as a religious danger since they were orthodox Sunnis; while their actual political control was unstable, their hold over economic resources was extremely limited. As there were almost no madrasas and *khānqas* endowed by the rulers and as few *'ulamā'* served in administration, material dependence was a negligible factor.

The comparative method in history is a poor man's substitute for the laboratory experiment of the hard sciences. This is the case where the economic, political-military factors used to explain *'ulamā'* subservience can be said to be negligible, and the same may be true for the social factor. There is no conflict of interest between the *'ulamā'* and the bourgeoisie but also no political cooperation. Is it the factor of *mentalité*—that repugnance toward politics—that is the major driving force? Are all other factors (political, military, etc.) just catalysts? Such a hypothesis can be best tested by analyzing the activities of the Syrian *'ulamā'* during the twelfth century.

## *JIHĀD* AND COUPS D'ÉTAT

While the *'ulamā'* displayed little interest in Syrian politics in the last third of the eleventh century, a resurgence of activity engulfed them in the first third of the twelfth century. The change is to be accounted for by the Crusader invasion of the Middle East (from 1098 on). The *jihād* consciousness, which had been slowly aroused in the area, owed most of its initial impetus to the *'ulamā'* who sounded the alarm, protesting against the indifference of public opinion and rulers alike. They insisted upon the fact that the Crusaders (then popularly dubbed *Rūm*, i.e., Byzantines) were not dependent upon Byzantium, a regional power accepted by the Muslims as part of the natural order of things, but were a new, Christian enemy of Islam (to be distinctly tagged *Faranj*, Franks). These *Faranj* were said to be set upon obliterating *Dar al-Islām* in Syria, and hence should be fought to the hilt, a defensive *jihād* incumbent upon all Muslims. Whereas the rulers, whether Turkish or Arab, paid little heed to these *jihād* sermons and were not inclined to challenge the new status quo established by the Western invaders, the *'ulamā'* were on a collision course with them.

Did the *'ulamā'* undergo a complete change? Not necessarily. The whole *jihād* awakening encompassed just a tiny minority of the *'ulamā'* who did not even succeed in convincing their own class.

Furthermore, the goal of the zealots of *jihād* was (and remained) to exert pressure upon the rulers, be it directly or by manipulating public opinion. They never once attempted to establish a popular fighting force to wage *jihād* outside the framework of the state (like the *aḥdāth* for instance). Rare, if ever, were *'ulamā'* attempts to replace an indifferent or hostile ruler with another one more sympathetic to the cause of the Holy War.[11]

The one exception to this rule was in the city of Aleppo. The *jihād* movement was led there by the *qāḍī* Ibn al-Khashshāb, a moderate *(imāmite)* Shīite who tried unsuccessfully for years to influence the Seljūqid ruler, Riḍwān. After his death the movement called upon the Turkoman chief of Diyarbekir, Īl Ghāzī, a famous *jihād* warrior, to seize power from the hands of Riḍwān's successor, Ibn al-Milḥī (1118). Īl Ghāzī granted Ibn al-Khashshāb's wishes, deposed Ibn al-Milḥī and routed the Franks, who were on the verge of conquering Aleppo after the battle of Darb Ṣarmada (1119). When, after his death (1122), the city-state returned to the hands of Turkish rulers indifferent to *jihād*, the *qāḍī* and his movement launched an appeal to the *amīr* of Moṣul, al-Bursūqī, to reign over Aleppo and lead the fight against the new Frankish siege on the city (1125).

The *qāḍī* did not dare draft his own combat units, perhaps because the balance of power was by then so heavily tilted in favor of the Franks that only a large force of specially trained, armored horsemen could stand any chance against them. But the very readiness of these men of religion to take risky initiatives in order to demote rulers who transgressed what they held to be sacred evinces a behavior quite different from that of the majority of the Syrian *'ulamā'*. Moreover, the *qāḍī* did not act alone; his deputies in the leadership of the movement were the Sunni (Ḥanbalite) *qāḍī* Ibn Jarāda and *sharīf* Zuhra, seconded by other men of religion (especially in the field of propaganda).[12] This resolve of the *'ulamā'* of Aleppo to act against the rulers, to mobilize public opinion and select new rulers who would implement their values seems, at first glance, to weaken the validity of the picture that emerged in the preceding section.

As one takes a closer look at the al-Khashshāb group, one perceives, however, that their activity took place in a rather extreme situation: the Franks were at the gates of Aleppo and on the verge of taking it over (1118, 1124); the deposed rulers were not only indifferent to *jihād* but also were weak in the conduct of domestic affairs; some of them were, above all, partisans of the *bāṭiniyya*, the mortal enemy of moderate Shīites (like Ibn al-Khashshab) and of Sunnis alike. Thus, it is possible to understand that sense of great and immediate danger which pushed the *'ulamā'* of Aleppo into the fray.

This combination of anarchy and *jihād* against the Christian infidels and Shīite heretics was an unusual one indeed. Furthermore, the odds *against* the success of such a course of action were very great. Already in 1111, for instance, Ibn al-Khashshāb carried out an analogous attempt when he invited the commanders of the expeditionary force despatched to Syria by the Seljūqid Sultan to seize power in Aleppo. He failed because Riḍwān, unlike his succesors, was a firm ruler, and because the time was not yet ripe to establish a Sunni-Shīite coalition like the one which was to be set up (after a number of abortive attempts) seven years later and was to be first directed against the *bāṭinī* fortresses in the Aleppo region, and only later against the Franks.[13] The *qāḍī*'s success also emanated from his dynamic and charismatic personality; he was a born propagandist and politician who enjoyed the support of a vast Shīite patronage he had inherited from his ancestors, leaders of the *imāmites* in the city since the mid-tenth century. The *qāḍī* Ibn Jarāda also possessed a broad network of patronage and a first-class power base. It may be no coincidence that the two leaders of the movement were a Shīite and a Ḥanbalite, coming from two minority groups known for their strong ideological commitment and internal solidarity. Their close links with the merchants and tradespeople further consolidated the alliance.

This detailed analysis of the Aleppo phenomenon indicates not only how rare it was—in a time where most Syrian elites were indifferent to the *jihād*—but also that only a rare and extreme combination of circumstances (e.g., multiple dangers to Aleppo, the nature of the opposition) could have prompted the *'ulamā'* to adopt such a course of action.

Finally, the entire "upheaval" consisted of calling upon new rulers who, like their predecessors, were neither Arab natives nor civilians. The *'ulamā'* did not take over. And why not? After all, al-Khashshāb and Ibn Jarāda were not only zealous religious leaders but also local notabilities with solid political experience. Was it due to some repugnance toward the direct exercise of power or to the need for a professional military force that only the Jazīra region could provide? The evidence suggests that both factors were at work.

Even if the military consideration was dominant, there is a paradox involved: only an immense Crusader menace could have prodded the *'ulamā'* to bring about a change of rulers; but in order to counteract that danger one required help from external sources, and this was, of course, at a price. It should be stressed that the new rulers and their armies were by no means pawns in the hands of the two *qāḍīs*. Some friction due to divergent motivations was evident already during the fight against the Franks, as when the uncouth Turkish soldiers made disrespectful comments about Ibn al-Khashshāb, "that guy bearing a turban," who ran among the ranks before the battle of Darb Ṣarmada in an attempt to rouse enthusiasm for the *jihād*.[14]

Even more significant is the fact that Īl Ghāzī and Bursūqī, having removed the immediate danger hovering over Aleppo, chose —for political and military reasons—not to pursue the all-out *jihād* campaign called for by the *'ulamā'*. Both new rulers of Aleppo continued to devote most of their time and attention to their major principality, the Jazīra. Faced with the firm policy of its "liberators," the Aleppo opposition kept quiet.

The story of the *'ulamā'* and the *jihād* in the early twelfth century thus boils down to some agitation among the populace (mostly in Damascus and Aleppo), a number of protests to local rulers and desperate appeals to the Caliph, and two successful attempts to instate a different ruler. The long-term impact of the movement was, however, meager. When, two or three decades later some ruler (such as Zenki and Nūr al-Dīn) adopted a policy of war to the knife against the Crusaders, this was above all for reasons of *Realpolitik* (the Franks as an obstacle to their expansion in Syria, a wedge between Syria and the land of Egypt they coveted). Only secondarily was this policy shaped by the pro-*jihād* spiritual climate created by men of religion.

The *'ulamā'* lack of initiative is evident in other social and political spheres in the first half of the twelfth century. As in the previous century, they took no part in the popular rebellions (led by the *aḥdāth*) against the Seljūqid officers and *condotierri* who took over most of the tiny principalities dotting the fragmented Syrian political map after the dissolution of the empire of Malikshāh. Even the most important insurgency, that of Banū Ṣūfi in Damascus (1150), had no *'ulamā'* in its ranks.[15]

*'Ulamā'* subservience to the powers-that-be is thus not a function

of the size of the principality or of the type of the political elite. The same patterns of behavior apply to the united Syria of the Ḥamdānid era (mid-tenth to mid-eleventh centuries) and to the era of extreme fragmentation we have discussed here. The same dependence exists in a large city-state (Damascus) or a tiny one (Shayzar); the same norms hold in cities ruled by family members of the Seljūqid Sultan (Aleppo and Antioch) and by their senior military commanders, the *Atabeks* (Damascus). A similar situation may be found in the cities governed by Arabic-speaking dynasties (especially along the coast), even when the ruling family was headed by *qāḍīs* (Banū ʿAmmār in Tripoli).

More significant still is the fact that the *ʿulamā'* did very little to spread Moral Rearmament. The Sunni renaissance movement, born in the eastern fringes of the Caliphate in the tenth century as a reaction to the heyday of the *shīʿa*, arrived in Syria in the late eleventh century. Thus, Moral Rearmament was introduced and cultivated in Syria, but only by the Seljūqids who made themselves its paragons in all their territories since the middle of the eleventh century.

In the case of north-eastern Iran and Central Asia—the native land of the Moral Rearmament—this was originally a small but autonomous movement of *ʿulamā'* later mobilized by the (Ghaznawid or Seljūqid) rulers who gave it the backing, impetus, and scope it had not possessed. In Syria this was from the start an arm of the powers-that-be. One cannot find there the private madrasas of the Iranian plateau founded by *ʿulamā'* in order to counteract the activities of extreme Shīite propagandists *(duʿāt)* trained at al-Azhar. (These institutions were to be transformed into public madrasas and squeezed out by the Sultanate.) Indeed, one does not detect in Syria even that (admittedly small) measure of initiative one finds in the Eastern lands. From the outset, Syrian Moral Rearmament was a movement initiated, endowed, and manned by the political elites, and thus inevitably and exclusively for their service. It could never serve as an autonomous basis for *ʿulamā'* activity, as it did for almost a century in the Eastern lands of the Caliphate. Its maneuverability did not have to be curtailed, since from the very beginning it was non-existent.

The two major institutions of the Moral Rearmament—the *madrasa* (seminary) and *khānqa* (Ṣūfī monastery) were founded in Syria and from 1098 onwards served as state establishments. No doubt they provided the *ʿulamā'* with jobs and a measure of influence over the masses, but at the same time they were financially dependent upon the rulers. The relatively meek style of *'ulamā'* criticism of the *Atabeks* of Damascus on the chapter of *jihād* (compared with the behavior of their Aleppo counterparts) may be explained by the fact that the Būrī dynasty of Damascus was a particularly generous and dynamic patron of the Moral Rearmament. Since a number of their demands (e.g., combatting extreme Shīism) were fulfilled by the Būrids, and since many of them entered into Būrid employ as teachers, *imāms* of mosques, and the like), the *'ulamā'* were even less inclined to turn against the rulers. It is by no means fortuitous that Damascus was the most important center of Orthodox activity. This was the major Seljūqid principality of Syria; other Seljūqid-controlled emirates (notably Aleppo) soon followed its example. However, in those city-states ruled by Arabic-speaking native families, no initiative to this effect can be detected; this is true even of cities like Tripoli and Jabala where *qāḍī* dynasties were in power. The Moral Rearmament was clearly a Seljūqid import. And neither in Arab nor in Seljūqid emirates does one find any attempt on the part of the *'ulamā'* to initiate Orthodox activity parallel to and independent of the powers-that-be. Wherever the rulers introduced the Moral Rearmament, men of religion gave it their blessing (and incidentally became its principal beneficiaries) and saw no reason to replicate it by autonomously-based action. In those places where no initiative from above was taken, they never launched it on their own.

Did the rulers monopolize the capital and labor force necessary to build the new institutions and finance their operation? This does not appear to be the case. In the first half of that century many agricultural lands were already fiefs of Seljūqid emirs, while the Syrian bourgeoisie still possessed vast plots (particularly in the vicinity of towns) and most of the urban real estate. Moreover, this class greatly prospered through the commerce of the Levant, which was revitalized by the Crusades. Expropriation of this huge capital would come only during the second half of the century; and finally, the labor force was not yet requisitioned by the state (as would be the case under the Ayyūbids and the Mamluks) and was available at the going market rate.[16] It is not clear why the *'ulamā'* would not (or could not) raise funds for Orthodox activity among the wealthy bourgeois. Was it because the former had misgivings about indigenous action outside the framework of the state (but not *against* it as was the case of *jihād*)? At any rate, it is evident that they did not refrain from doing so out of any aversion to collaboration with the rulers. This aversion seems to have faded somewhat, either due to ideological reasons (the wish to fashion the state in the spirit of pristine Islam and liquidate extreme Shīism) or for opportunistic ones (having to do with endowments and career advancement). Little by little the *'ulamā'* were drawn into the orbits of power, and that on a scope hitherto unknown.

## COLLABORATION AND CONFLICT OF INTERESTS

Collaboration with the authorities became the hallmark of *'ulamā'* behavior in the third quarter of the twelfth century, under Nūr al-Dīn (1146-74), the groundwork having been laid by his father Zenki (1127-46). Syria was united by Nūr al-Dīn, thus enlarging the scope and the intensity of the Moral Rearmament. This intensification was due to the coalescence of the Rearmament with the autonomous movement of *jihād* under the aegis of the sovereign. These movements now represented the internal and the external aspects, respectively, of a deliberate campaign to reassert the Muslim character of the state. Apparently the *'ulamā'* were at the apex of their influence over state affairs: the Franks were being driven from the hilly areas to the coastal plain; the *bāṭiniyya* (and later also the moderate *shī'a*) was destroyed (1147-57); the Shīite Caliphate of Egypt was conquered (1169-71); the establishment of religious institutions and endowments for cultic and educational activity were greatly expanded; *sharī'ā* laws were imposed more stringently (particularly with regard to taxation and to non-Muslims); and men of religion were recruited in large numbers for the civil service, even including the top echelons.[17] There is no doubt that society and polity were now cast in a more orthodox mold. This in turn can be construed as conclusive proof of how right were the *'ulamā'*, who preferred to work *within the system* (and not relying on their own meager forces alone) and to *influence the ruler* without seizing power and exercising it directly. They could, on the face of it, enjoy the best of both worlds: shaping sociopolitical realities while being as minimally involved as possible with the state.

At a second glance, however, certain hitches are noticeable. As the *'ulamā'* were reluctant to campaign on their own for *jihād* and the advancement of Orthodoxy, such activity could come about only with the advent of rulers ready to shoulder these tasks, i.e., the Zengids. The latter, especially Nūr al-Dīn, were imbued with a deep religious conviction and promoted the *'ulamā'* out of respect for the values they stood for. The same holds true for most members of the dynasty that succeeded them, the Ayyūbids (1174-1260). Yet, even the most devout of these sultans were, to begin with, "political animals," and of the military and foreign (Turkish or Kurdish) variety at that. Had the Orthodox platform been incompatible with his overriding politico-military considerations, Nūr al-Dīn would not have done so much to further this platform. Fortunately for the *'ulamā'*, both sets of considerations—the political and the orthodox—overlapped during his reign, a rare occurrence indeed. The Zengid state and the *'ulamā'* shared a common goal: to vanquish their mortal enemies the Franks, the Assassins (a branch of *Ismā'īliyya*, the extremist Shīite sect), and the Fāṭimids.[18] Moreover, the madrasas trained cadres of civil servants and produced men of religion who would inspire the populace with the zeal required for the *jihād* (in order to mobilize manpower and financial resources and maintain the morale of the troops).[19] The prestige of the Zengid state, predicated in part upon the charisma and devout image of Nūr al-Dīn, prodded the *'ulamā'* in many of the independent cities to support the annexation of the latter by Nūr al-Dīn.[20]

Despite the underlying basis of mutual interests, conflicts in certain areas were unavoidable; here, the rulers almost always gave priority to earthly considerations over the more "heavenly" ones. Thus, Nūr al-Dīn postponed time after time the final campaign against the Crusaders (in order to conquer Egypt, to consolidate his Sultanate, and so on). Many of the decrees abolishing non-Koranic taxes were not implemented because of the financial needs of the expanding state. When Egypt was conquered, the discriminatory laws against non-Muslims were not imposed due to the vital services rendered by Copts and Jews in administration, banking, and medicine.

Whenever a conflict of priorities materialized, *'ulamā'* critique was rather limited: many of them had jobs in the civil service they did not want to lose, or lived off endowments controlled by the state; others, less opportunistic, adopted this prudent behavior out of the conviction that it was preferable to cooperate with the state half-heartedly than remain idle regarding issues close to their hearts. The essential dilemma of the *'ulamā'* emerges once again: one cannot exercise influence upon the state from within unless one becomes involved in the affairs of state. Such involvement, however, tied their hands and tongues, constraining their capacity to promote their ideals. What other course of action was open to them? Independent activity (parallel to the state and occasionally against it) was in their eyes loathsome, understandably so in terms of their age-old vision of politics as the realm of evil. Complete withdrawal from political activity was, perhaps, more congruent with the ideals they were reared upon, but this would have had dire consequences in that era where Islam was under siege; it would have brought about moral deterioration, ascendancy of the Shīite heresy, and the prolongation (and possibly expansion) of infidel occupation of Syria-Palestine. There was no evading the dilemma; each solution was fraught with dangers, but that of collaboration with the authorities was deemed the least risky.

At a third glance, the *'ulamā'* predicament appears to be even more poignant. Apart from the areas of explicit conflict of interest, there were other differences which, though implicit, were more basic (and, hence, particularly dangerous). The danger was all the greater due to the progressive weakening of the *'ulamā'* class exactly at a time when it never looked stronger. In order to defend itself against its numerous enemies, Syria needed Turkish (from 1174 on, Kurdish) military rule. The presence of military castes, which was quite loose in the late eleventh and early twelfth century, became firmer and broader under the Zengids; with Nūr al-Dīn they actually strike roots. Virtually all lands were by now military fiefs *(iqtā' istighlālī* and *iqtā' wilāya*). Nūr al-Dīn made these *iqtā'* hereditary and thus created a politico-military landed elite of more than one generation, wielding vast powers. The middle class lost its landed wealth and was on the decline—a decline precipitated by the gradual takeover of commerce by the state (through monopolies, taxes, and customs).[21] This had dire implications for more than this class alone, because the bourgeoisie had always been the mainstay of autonomous economic, social, and political life in Syria. The alienation between the rulers and the ruled was thus exacerbated, catalyzed by the differences in language and origin. At the same time, the *'ulamā'* became even more dependent upon the rulers, who now controlled the economy of the Muslim city.[22]

This period witnessed the death throes of the *aḥdāth*, which had been a manifestation of the Muslim city's capacity for autonomous action in the interval between the dismemberment of the Caliphate and the rise of the military regimes. The Zengids, who did not wish to share their power, replaced it with the *shurṭa*, whose officers (and part of its men) were Turks and later Mamluks, i.e., former slaves whose mentality was even more alien to that of the local population. Thus vanished the sole autonomous military force that could have helped the *'ulamā'* in the struggle for power (and which did aid them in the realm of *jihād*).[23]

Moreover, the anti-Shīite struggle, pushed to its logical conclusion, affected the moderate *shī'a* as well (1147-57), and deprived the *'ulamā'* (at least in northern Syria) of this ally who had been loyal in past struggles against the rulers, the *Imāmites* (Twelvers).

Shorn of allies, lacking an economic basis of its own and the will to initiate autonomous action, the *'ulamā'* thus had to confront the authorities concerning the number one issue (then and today) for this social class: the application of the *sharī'a*. Civilian officials, such as the vizier and the *ra'īs al-aḥdāth* upon whom the *'ulamā'* could wield some influence, since they were considered in the same social class, were not replaced by appointees of the military caste, the *nā'ib* and the *shiḥna*, respectively. These were usually uncouth Turkish officers, ignorant of the niceties and nuances of jurisprudence *(fiqh)* and thus set to naught many of the good intentions of the devout, but distant, rulers. It is true that the *qāḍīs* could in principle invalidate the decisions of these military officials, but having always been hired and fired by the rulers, the *qāḍīs* recruited were of the more pliant *'ulamā'* (and no wonder that folk tradition depicted hell as replete with *qāḍīs*). Furthermore, the *qāḍī al-quadāt* (not chief judge but head of the judicial administration) exercised tight and regular control over their decision making. This official, who was not necessarily a jurist *(faqīh)*, was the one who assigned them to particular cities or slots within each city, and hence dangled the whip of promotion and demotion over their heads. Under Nūr al-Dīn, the *qāḍī al-qudāt* usurped and transferred to his direct control certain functions traditionally fulfilled by the *qāḍīs* and which, though not purely judicial, had greatly bolstered their position (inspections of religious endowments, guardianship of orphans and their assets, and the like).

From yet another direction the powers of the *'ulamā'* were encroached upon by the *muḥtaṣib*, the official in charge of the markets and public morality and who had now been granted most of the municipal civilian tasks of the former *ra'īs al-aḥdāth*. As the *muḥtasib* exercised both juridical and police functions on offences committed in his domain, he took over many of the regular tasks of the *'ulamā'*, and as he was usually present at the market or other public places (either in person or through his aides), he was capable of immediate intervention. Truly enough, he was often a *faqīh* and a madrasa graduate, but he was not supposed to have recourse to the *sharī'a*. Furthermore, unlike the *qāḍīs*, he was not expected in difficult cases to seek out the opinion of the *muftis* (legal authorities), whose legal opinions—albeit couched as recommendations—had, in fact, a binding effect.

Consequently, a sort of hybrid and autonomous judicial system came into existence, half-religious and half-secular. To its above-mentioned officials and devices, one could add the judgment of an offender seized *in flagrante delicto* (which was exercised by the *ra'īs al-shurṭa*, usually a Turkish military officer), and disciplinary proceedings against civil servants presided over by the ruler in person or by his deputy or governor *(nā'ib)* in the city.[24] Finally, religious offences of military people (orgies, alcohol drinking, dance, and music) were out of the reach of either the *qāḍī* or the *muḥtasib* and were left to the discretion of the ruler.

Paradoxically, the domain of the *sharī'a* was curtailed by an innovation originally intended to promote rigorous orthodoxy, namely the institution of *Dār al-'Adl*. This institution was a refurbished version of *al-Naẓar fī-l-Maẓālim*, which had enabled any subject to bring his complaint before the 'Abbāsid ruler on a particular date and place. As this was a mechanism based on equity, a sphere for non-*shar'ī* (though not necessarily anti-*shar'ī*) judicial activity was thus created)—all the more independent of Islamic law, since its masters were unfamiliar with the fine points of the latter.

The *'ulamā'* were on the whole helpless against these developments, but it was only under the Ayyūbid successors of Saladin (after 1193) that they tried to protest against the encroachments: either they had finally understood what happened or they believed that these rulers were weaker and more amenable. They were mistaken. The rulers clamped down on any manifestation of opposition and nipped it in the bud. There is no doubt that, had the *'ulamā'* tried to do so in the second half of the twelfth century, their defeat would have been even more humiliating.

This would explain the mutism of the class as a whole, but what about the higher *'ulamā'* and especially those who were the confidants and mentors of Nūr al-Dīn (and Saladin)? That these *'ulamā'* did nothing to forestall these developments (to the extent that they were aware of them) was due not necessarily to blind obedience or to opportunism. One should not forget that most of them were foreigners brought in by the ruler or attracted by his orthodox renown; their names bespeak their lack of local roots: Iṣfāhānī, Mawṣūlī, Shrazūri, Nīsābūri, Ghaznawī, Balkhi, and so on.[25] Given the cirsumstances of their arrival, it was only natural that they did not develop any organic links to the local *'ulamā'* class and pinned all hopes (for their own careers and for the ideals they wished to promote) upon their rulers.

The yawning chasm between the elite and the plebs was, then, reflected within the *'ulamā'* class itself; the higher *'ulamā'* were not only alienated in mentality, origin, and social status but also in influence and economic power, for the lavish remuneration of top echelon religious jobs (and the fiefs attached to them) were the virtual monopoly of foreign-born *'ulamā'*.

## A COLLECTIVE MENTALITY?

How do the "middle" Middle Ages (eleventh-twelfth centuries), the era of the rise of military regimes, compare then with the later Middle Ages (thirteenth-eighteenth centuries), when these regimes sat firmly in the saddle?

From the viewpoint of the *'ulamā'* motivation and behavior it is clear that the "security imperative" is predominant throughout the thirteenth and early fourteenth centuries: first, due to the Frankish presence, and later due to the Mongol hordes which swept across the Middle East. Material dependence was an important but secondary factor. Their combination more than adequately explains *'ulamā'* behavior. With the Crusader presence liquidated (1291) and the Mongol danger slowly subsiding in the following decades, the "security imperative" declined to a certain extent: subsequent Crusades (such as the one launched from Cyprus in 1368) would still try to reconquer the Holy Land; and fear of such an eventuality led the Mamluks to raze the settlements of the Syro-Palestinian coast where the *Faranj* were expected to land. Material dependence deepened cumulatively, and by the mid-fourteenth century, when the rulers usurped all the land and the capital resources and perfected their labor requisition methods, it became the predominant factor of *'ulamā'* subservience (with a few exceptions like Ibn Tamiyya, which only prove the general rule).

The situation was completely different in the eleventh to twelfth centuries. In the beginning of the eleventh century the "security imperative" played a minor role, the Byzantines having been repelled by the Ḥamdānids of Aleppo. It declined even further as Syria came under the protection of the Seljūqids during the second half of the century. Here one may not speak of material dependence, because the network of madrasas, *khānqas*, and lavish endowments were as yet non-existent, and it was the bourgeoisie and not the ruler who possessed most of the real estate in the town and countryside. The twelfth century ushered in, with the Crusades, the question of security, which grew in importance as the *'ulamā'* became committed to the cause of *jihād* (which only powerful foreign rulers could actually promote). Material dependence, an insignificant factor before Nūr al-Dīn in the third quarter of the century, gained momentum under Saladin, but was still far from the important (albeit secondary) role it was to play more than half a century later.

It is doubtful whether both factors can sufficiently account for *'ulamā'* behavior in the twelfth century (in particular before the rise of the Zengids). They certainly fall wide of the mark in the eleventh century: there was no significant military danger, no need for dependence on the rulers.

The case of the Syrian Intermezzo sharpens the contours of the question even further; in those years (the last third of the eleventh century) the intervention of regional powers receded completely; municipal autonomy blossomed; and the local bourgeoisie (a class closely associated with the *'ulamā'*) held the reins of political and military power. Even then, however, the *'ulamā'* shirked from any meaningful engagement in politics.

Ḍinnāwi's hypothesis that we are dealing here with a mentality shaped by centuries of Islamic history seems to indicate a plausible alternative explanation. It was late in the eleventh century that the eminent Muslim theologian al-Ghazālī (who spent the last years of the century in *al-Shām*) concluded: all power is evil but better have a bad ruler, as long as he is Muslim, than anarchy. Not much different was the message of his contemporary al-Māwardī who thus legitimized the *fait accompli* of Seljūqid seizure of power: anarchy, due to the weakness of the Caliphate, was finally over.

This lesson of the seventh and eighth century traumas had been put quite clearly already in the eras closer to the events. Several decades after the terrible First Civil War, the *qāḍī* Amīr b. Shurḥabil al-Sha'bī of Kufa wrote:

Love the family of the prophet without being Shīite . . . and believe that what is good derives from Allah and what is evil is your own making . . . and obey the Caliph even if he is a black slave.

The great jurist Abū Yūsuf pondering the same question after the turmoils of the 'Abbāsid Revolution argued that evil rulers were nothing but God's chastisement to his community:

Rulers are a scourge through whom Allah punishes those he wants to punish. So do not meet God's scourge with hot temper and anger but with humility and submission.

Even such a puritanical and audacious thinker as Ibn Ḥanbal (d. 855) had this to say about resisting illegitimate power:

You should obey and not rebel against it. If the ruler orders something which implies sin against Allah you should neither obey nor rebel. Do not support the *fiṭna* (civil strife) neither by your hand nor by your tongue.[26]

The specter of *fiṭna* may have haunted the *'ulamā'* to such an extent that it justified almost anything. Especially, as Ḍinnāwī reminds us, when the sovereign rendered at least one constant service to the *'ulamā'* (long before the "security imperative" came to the fore), they combatted the Shīites and other heretics.[27] It was immaterial that they did so less out of religious conviction than because the Shīites considered all power illegitimate other than that of their own *imām*. The Shīites thus justified the "right of resistance" *(Widerstandsrecht)* and were an inherently destabilizing factor. The interests of the Sunni *'ulamā'* thus coincided with those of the rulers between the eighth to eleventh centuries: the former guarded their status as the sole interpreters of the *sharī'a*, and the latter defended their monopoly of power.

This factor would elucidate why most *'ulamā'* did not opt for the alternative conclusion they could draw from their repugnance of politics, i.e., complete withdrawal from the secular world. There were indeed a number of men of religion, especially ascetics and mystics, who argued with Ibn al-Adham that one should even refuse to drink water from public conduits because they might have been funded by non-Koranic taxes. If power is evil, collaboration with it is illicit. Most *'ulamā'* did not go that far for fear this might lead to the loss of the Islamic and Sunni character of society; Islam, they argued, is not a matter of saving one's soul but hinges on applying the *sharī'a*, i.e., molding the behavior of as many believers as possible. To do that, one had only to obey, and try to maintain a minimal cooperation with, all rulers without dirtying one's hands by actually exercising power.

This somewhat contradictory attitude would well explain their behavior all through the eleventh century, including the apparently missed opportunity of the Syrian Intermezzo; it would also account for their predicament during the twelfth century, even as the "security imperative" came to play an important role. From the thirteenth century on the odds were so heavily against the *'ulamā'* (*jihād* and material dependence) that, whatever their mentality, no intervention in politics stood any chance of success.

This hypothesis concerning the crucial role of *'ulamā'* collective mentality is, admittedly, merely just that—a hypothesis. Our knowledge of early Islam is too limited as yet to fully substantiate it. More case studies are needed so that a more comprehensive judgment can be pronounced. Even for the "middle" Middle Ages, where our case is better documented, other countries than Syria should be studied. But, at least, the above study of that period—in a particularly illuminating country—may help lay to rest the notion that military-economic dependency was the sole and exclusive explanation for *'ulamā'* behavior. More than just *jihād* and the standard of living was involved. Mentality *(mentalité)*) should be brought into the explanatory process. And as we are dealing here with an element of "mental structure" (in *Annales'* lingo), Ḍinnāwī and others may be right when they argue that it is valid for the present too; perhaps not only for religious intellectuals in the land of Islam but for some of their secularist counterparts as well.[28]

To say that is not to fall into the trap of reductionism, monocausality, and essentialism. *Mentalité* is neither a sole factor nor even a preponderant one throughout Islamic history. The relative weight of the "bad government is better than no government" notion varies according to time and place. However, it is the only factor which has an uninterrupted existence, a sort of thread running from the second half of the seventh century on, thicker in certain eras, thinner in others. It is but one thread, albeit far from negligible, in the fabric of Islamic culture, which like all cultures is both steadfast and changing. This notion could (and still can) change all the more easily, for it was less the product of Islamic pristine doctrines than a product of a certain traumatic—and cumulative—historical experience. It is indeed at this level of *verités vécues* that *'ulamā'* attitudes toward power are so significant.

## FOOTNOTES

1. H. Ḥanafī, "Arab Nationalist Thought in the Balance," *Qaḍāyā 'Arabiyya,* March-April, 1978, p. 21. Cf. Fu'ad Zakariya interview with *al-Thaqāfa* (Amman) April 1983.
2. Khomeini, *Islamic Government,* Arabic trans., Beirut, 1979; cf. M. A. al-Sammān, introduction to M. 'A. 'Anbar, *Wa-bi-l-Haqq,* Cairo, 1976, p. 19.
3. Z. S. Bayyūmī, *Al-Ikhwān al-Muslimūn*, Cairo, 1979, pp. 261-71; H. Enayat, *Modern Islamic Political Thought*, University of Texas Press, 1979, pp. 118-9, 140-4. Cf. M. M. Shams al-Dīn, *Al-'Ilmāniyya*, Beirut, 1980, pp. 64-6. Cf. my "Ibn Taymiyya: Father of the Islamic Revolution," *Encounter,* May 1983.
4. *Al-Ṭarīq ilā Ḥukm Islāmī,* Beirut, 1970, p. 123. Cf. I. M. Lapidus, *Muslim Cities in the Later Middle Ages,* Harvard University Press, 1967; D. Ayalon, "The Muslim City and the Mamluk Military Aristocracy," *Proceedings of the Israeli Academy of Sciences and Humanities,* Vol. 2, No. 14; idem. "The Great Yasa of Chigiz Khan," *Studia Islamica* (33); pp. 97-141; (36), pp. 113-58; (38), pp. 107-56. S. Humphreys, *From Saladin to the Mongols.*
5. Cf. Cl. Cahen, "Movements populaires et autonomisme urbain dans l'Asie Musulmane du moyen-âge," *Arabica* 5 (1958), pp. 233-50.
6. Cf. Cahen, art. cit.; E. Ashthor-Strauss, "L'Administration urbaine en Syrie mediévale," *Revista Degli Studii Orientali* 31 (1956), pp. 76-128.
7. Cf. Ibn al-'Adīm, *Zubdat al-Ṭalab fi Ta'rīkh Ḥalab,* Vol. 2; Sibṭ b.al-Jawzī, *Mir'at al-Zamān,* ms. Paris, 1506; Ibn al-Qalānīsī, *Ta'rikh Dimashq,* Leiden, 1908.
8. Cf. H. J. Cohen, "The Economic Background and Secular Occupations of Muslim Jurisprudents and Traditionalists," *Journal of the Economic and Social History of the Orient,* 12 (1970), pp. 16-61.
9. Lapidus, op. cit., chap. 2; Cl. Cahen, "L'Evolution de l'Iqtā du X^e au XII^e siecle," *Annales (E.S.C.)* 7 (1953), pp. 25-52.
10. Same sources are in note 7, to which one should add Ibn al-Athīr, *Al-Kāmil fī-l-Ta'rīkh,* Vol. 11, Cairo, A.H. 1303, and Ibn al-Jawzī, *Al-Muntaẓam*, Vol. 9. Cf. "Génèse de la Contre-Croisade," *Journal Asiatique* 254 (1966).
11. Ibn al-Furāt (quoting Ibn Abī Tayyī), *Ta'rīkh,* ms. Vienna, 1702, Vol. 2, fol. 121b ff., 139b ff., 151b ff., 179b ff., 197b ff.; Ibn al-'Adīm, *Zubda,* Vol. 2, pp. 224-8; Ibn al-'Adīm, *Bughyat al-Ṭalab,* ms. Paris, fols. 182b-183a; Al-'Azīmi, "La Chronique Abregée de—" ed. Cl. Cahen, *Journal Asiatique* 230 (1938), p. 380 ff.
12. Ibn al-Qalānīsī, op. cit., pp. 173-5; Ibn Abi Tayyi apud Ibn Furāt, op. cit., Vol. 1, fol. 48a-48b, 54b, 151a-152b; Ibn al-Athir, Vol. 10, p. 170.
13. Ibn al-'Adīm, *Zubda,* Vol. 2, p. 188.
14. Ibn al-Qalānīsī, op. cit.
15. The major sources are Ibn al-Furāt, Ibn al-Qalānīsī, al-'Azīmī, and Ibn al-'Adīm, passim. The best modern account is still Cl. Cahen, *La Syrie du Nord à l'Époque des Croisades,* Paris, 1940.
16. Cf. N. Élisséeff, *Nur Ad-Dīn, un grand prince de Syrie au temps des Croisades,* Damascus, 1967, Vol. 2, pp. 751-79, 843-7.
17. Ibn Abī Tayyī apud Ibn Furāt, Vol. 2, fols. 159a-160a, 195a-195b; Vol. 3, fols.110a-111a; Ibn al-'Adīm, *Zubda*, Vol. 2, pp. 293-4.
18. See, Sibṭ, b. al-Jawzī, op.cit., Vol. 1, p. 322; Abū Shamā, *al-Rawḍatayn,* Vol. 1, pp. 78, 113-20, 215; 'Imād al-Dīn, *Kharīdat al-Qaṣr (Sām)*, Vol. 1, pp. 14-5; Ibn Al-'Adīm, *Zubda,* Vol. 2, p. 315.
19. Abū Shamā, op. cit, Vol. 1, p. 6; Ibn al-'Athīr, op. cit., Vol. 11, p. 113; Ibn al-Furāt, ms. Vienna, Vol. 3, fol. 86b.

20. Ibn al-Qalānīsī, op. cit., pp. 305, 313-5, 320, 327.
21. Abū Shamā, op. cit., Vol. 1, pp. 160-75; 'Imād al-Dīn, op. cit., Vol. 1, p. 277.
22. Cf. Cahen, "Evolution de l'Iqtā' "; Lapidus, op. cit.
23. Cf. Cahen, "Autonomie Urbaine."
24. Cf. Élisséeff, op. cit., pp. 789-90, 824-34.
25. See, Abū Shamā, op. cit., Vol. pp. 11, 13; Ibn al-Furāt, Vol. 3, fol. 166; Subkī, *Ṭabaqāt al-Shāfi'iyya al-Kubrā,* Vol. 4, pp. 74, 238.
26. Ibn 'Asākir, *Ta'rīkh Madīnat Dimashq,* Damascus, 1977, p. 182; Abu Yūsuf, *Kitāb al-Kharāj,* trans. Ben Shemesh, London, 1969, p. 43; Ibn Ḥanbal, *Kitāb al-Sunna,* Cairo, no date, p. 35.
27. Ḍinnawi, loc. cit.; cf. on the Muslim Brethren's critique of modern *'ulamā'*, see al-Bayyūmi, *Al-Ikhwān al-Muslimmūn,* Cairo, 1979.
28. See my "Intellectual Blues," *The Jerusalem Quarterly* 27 (1981).

# Chapter 5:

# EDWARD SAID AND HIS ARAB REVIEWERS

MUCH HEAT (and some light) has been generated in recent years by Edward Said's *Orientalism* (Pantheon Books, 1978). This ongoing debate has been marred by a lot of virulence but has had at least one salutory effect: specialists in Middle Eastern and Islamic affairs —a profession not much given to introspection and certainly not to thinking about the hermeneutical questions underlying its endeavor—were jolted into soul searching. Most notably they found themselves asking the basic question posed by the book: "How does one *represent* other cultures? What is *another* culture? Is the notion of a distinct culture (or race, or religion, or civilization) a useful one?" (Said, p. 325). Said underlines the terms "represent" and "another," for the obvious reason that his is a critique of Western (especially British and French) writings about Islam. It is indeed among such Western observers of Islam that the debate about the book has been taking place.

But what do Muslim and Arab observers of Islam think of the book? Their contribution, coming as it does from the inside, may add some valuable insights to what has become a repetitive cycle of (almost exclusively Western) polemics.[1] Most Arab reviews of Said's book were rather descriptive and cursory. Recently, however, two books have appeared, both dealing with Said and his thesis; one was written by a Syrian philosopher (Ṣādiq Jalāl al-'Aẓm) and the other by an Iraqi scholar (Muḥammad Ḥusayn 'Alī al-Ṣaghīr). Also a Lebanese Muslim sociologist, Nadīm al-Bīṭār, has devoted a detailed chapter to this topic in his most recent book. And my Egyptian and Palestinian friends assure me that an important article by Egyptian philsopher Ḥasan Ḥanafī innocuously called "Arab National Thought in the Balance" should actually be read as a response to *Orientalism*.[2]

Three of the four authors are major figures in Arab intellectual life: Ḥanafī, a Sorbonne graduate, is the editor of *al-Yasār al-Islāmī* (Islamic Left) and a specialist in hermeneutics. U.S. trained al-Bīṭār is one of the most important Pan-Arab thinkers today; a courageous critic of religious traditionalism, he was so vituperatively attacked by Muslim fanatics that, fearing for his life, he had to flee (for a while) to Canada. Yale-educated al-ʻAẓm is the author of the best Arab autocritique after the 1967 war and of a controversial agnostic analysis of Islamic thought that cost him his job at the American University of Beirut and led to court proceedings against him.[3] He is still an influential leftist writer. All three have been directly exposed to Western culture but chose to live in the Arab world where they take an active part in the political and social debate on the left side of the barricade. Finally, al-Ṣaghīr is an authority in Koranic studies.

## SCOPE AND METHOD

It is a measure of the importance attached to Said's book that al-Bīṭār and al-ʻAẓm—the most prominent of the four—are the ones who gave the book the most exhaustive treatment. Both readily agree with Said that knowledge is intertwined with power. Both concur that Orientalism as an intellectual enterprise had close ties with colonial domination in the Middle East. And yet, somewhat unexpectedly perhaps, they are ill at ease with the book. To begin with, this has to do with the scope of Said's subject matter and the research strategy he followed. By Said's own estimate (p. 204) the number of books published about the Arab East alone during the years 1800-1950 is about sixty thousand. But, asks al-Bīṭār,

> How can he, then, generalize and claim that Orientalism as a whole is characterized by hostility [to Islam]. How can he use such absolute terms, neither qualified nor relativized, and allege that his generalizations are scientific? Does it mean he read or perused these sixty thousand books and did not find in them anything running counter to this discovery about the nature of Orientalism with its view of the innate inferiority of the Orient? In fact he claims more than that. He says that what he discovered is the true essence of Orientalism and is applicable to all those who ever wrote about the East, in the broadest sense of the term, that it is not merely about the Arab East. This would mean that Said had read, or at least perused (or read studies about) all those tens of thousands of books published about the Orient in general, and found there nothing running counter to his thesis. This would signify, in turn, that as a scholar Said does constitute a unique phenomenon, so well equipped as to absorb in the intellectual history of humanity and process unlimited quantities of information. . . . For the question is simple; either he read those books or he did not. If he did not, how can he generalize in such absolutist terms about the one and only nature of the

reality he studied. . . . If he did, then surely he accomplished something unheard of: performing in a matter of years what it should have taken others centuries to do. Until now we spoke only about post-1800 Orientalism. What makes Said's claims even more curious is that he drags the writings of earlier centuries also into the bargain.[4]

Al-'Aẓm, who is somewhat less harsh about Said's judgment on modern Orientalism, wonders indeed why he could not satisfy himself with the sufficiently daunting study of modern Orientalism, but rather had to find for it a long genealogy harking back to Homer, Aeschylus, Eurypides, and Dante.[5]

These queries are rendered all the more poignant if one remembers that Said's book seeks inspiration in the methodology of Michel Foucault, which attempts to decode the universe of discourse of an entire field of human endeavor, regardless of the identity, intent, and motivation of specific authors. This would have required at least part of the gargantuan effort al-Bīṭār describes (or a limitation to certain points in time and space as al-'Aẓm suggests). Or, is it, one wonders, that instead of Foucault's structuralism we have here an example of the old-time and now justifiably discredited *Ideengeschichte*, with its vague impressionism and concentration upon a few "landmark authors" (in this case, a couple of dozen Orientalists) supposed to be somehow representative of the totality of this intellectual endeavor, nay even of the *Zeitgeist*, with their biographies (including their often well-substantiated relationships with colonialism) serving to highlight their work?

## DICHOTOMY AND ESSENTIALISM

These methodological questions are less important, say the Arab reviewers, than the actual findings Said comes up with. What bothers them most is the ahistorical, essentialist mode permeating his thesis: Orientalism (with few exceptions such as Louis Massignon) is one and the same throughout history, and even more so in the nineteenth and twentieth centuries. This essentialism is thus both diachronic and synchronic:

Rather than trying to ponder what the specific conditions were in modern Europe which spawned Orientalism, he represents it as having deep roots in Western history, as exemplified by the erroneous, maybe even racist views, harbored vis-à-vis the Orient since the ancient Greeks. Orientalism is, then, a campaign designed to falsify the vision of the East and render it as contemptible as possible in order to reaffirm the notion of Western superiority; as such it is a phenomenon as old as the West.

What all this boils down to is to bring through the back door that very myth about the essentialist, innate properties that Said wants to demolish with regard to the presumed nature of the Orient. He does to [Western] Orientalism what he accuses the latter of doing to the Orient. He dichotomizes it and essentializes it. East is East and West is West and each has its own intrinsic and permanent nature. . . .[6]

Al-'Aẓm who excoriated essentialist tendencies in religious thought, as well as Ḥanafī and al-Bīṭār who upbraided Arab nationalism for its metaphysics ("the eternal Arab nation") and who tried to bring relativism, historical perspective and rigor into the secularist-nationalist camp, thus had the unpleasant surprise of seeing one, who (though living abroad) could be deemed a "progressive" ally of theirs, breathe new life into these detested notions. That he did it with regard to the enemy, "the European mind," which was arrogant and disdainful of Islam and from which Orientalism emanated, does not mollify them. For he who assumes a West assumes an East.

It is this concern for the intellectual health of the Arab world—rather than any solicitude for the Orientalists—that explains the painstaking attention given to Said's arguments—arguments, says al-Bīṭār, characterized by "an unscientific and arbitrary nature." They cloud and mystify realities that should be confronted and simplify what is complex. Orientalism should, he agrees, be understood in its cultural context, which in the nineteenth century was indeed suffused with racism, suprematism, and ethnocentrism. And even then, was this true of all Europeans, he asks?

Anyway, isn't it true that today any thinker evincing racist ideas is liable to be accused by his own peers and compatriots of being plainly stupid, narrow-minded, anti-intellectualist, or Neo-Nazi. For the overwhelming majority of [Western] biologists, geneticists, and sociologists is persuaded nowadays that there is no scientific basis for the notion of racial difference or superiority.[7]

Those who continue to think in terms of distinct cultures rather than races are usually relativists, he says, bearing the imprint of anthropological research in this century.[8] What about the Orientalists, those interpreters of the East to the Western mind? Following Maxime Rodinson—one of the happy few "good Orientalists" in

Said's opinion, who later, however, criticized the book very sharply[9]—Arab reviewers take Said to task for the manner in which he sweeps uncomfortable facts under the rug. As a general rule he either does not place the historical facts in perspective or fails to mention them altogether. Thus, the critical approach to Islam in which Said detects unflinching hostility, though true in some cases is, to begin with, part of the critique of Christianity (and—by extension—of religion in general) born out of the Enlightenment. But one cannot learn this from *Orientalism*. One understands the bitterness of al-'Aẓm, who tried, at great personal cost, to apply this critique to Muslim religiosity from within, when seeing such an approach branded imperialistic not by Lebanese *'ulamā'* but by a fellow leftist and pro-Palestinian writer.

Yet what Arab reviewers find more recurrent (and effective) is Said's sheer disregard for Orientalist endeavor, past or present, which does not conform itself to the picture he draws. At times this leads him to extreme subjectivism, to deny that in principle it is ever possible for virtually any Westerner to describe the East otherwise (i.e., in a distorted manner), nay even that it is ever feasible for any culture to represent another in anything but a totally subjective mode (Said, p. 273). Even Foucault never went so far when speaking of "the cultural archives" we bring into our perception of the Other. Al-'Aẓm notes wryly that this has the boomerang effect of exonerating Orientalism; for if the only cross-cultural discourse possible is totally subjectivist, it would follow that the Orientalists "did just what any other culture would have done in these very conditions."[10]

Such an allegation of the non-feasibility of the whole cross-cultural enterprise is not made explicit by Said in the book, but it renders plausible the virtual non-existence in his pages of disinterested Orientalism (a few good souls like Rodinson, Geertz, Berque, and Massignon notwithstanding). To achieve this result, says al-Bīṭār, Said has to practice sleight-of-hand:

> If indeed Orientalism precedes the nineteenth century and the rise of imperialism. . . what was the aim of all those hundreds and thousands who studied and translated Arabic and transferred the Arabic heritage from Muslim Spain to medieval Europe. . . ? What was, for instance, the aim of all those who studied Ibn Khaldūn (the fourteenth-century North African philosopher of history) and anointed him the founder of modern sociology?[11]

Domination of the Orient as the sole motive for Orientalism—a sort of rudimentary Foucauldianism lacking the insightful nuances of the master—is thus called into question. But moreover:

> Didn't German Orientalism grow up and produce a good many of its great contributions long before Germany turned colonialist in the late nineteenth century. . . ? Here, unlike the case of France and Britain, Said generalizes without any basis, as though the aspects to which we referred did not exist at all.[12]

And what about the Orientalism of the last hundred years? How can one deny, asks al-'Aẓm,[13] for all the services it has rendered imperialism, its numerous achievements in deciphering the Islamic past regardless of whether its great practitioners were sympathetic to Islam (as Massignon), neutral (as most Germans), and even critical or hostile (as Henri Lammens and a good many others were)? When hard pressed to come up with an alternative to Orientalism, Said calls for the study of Arabs and Muslims as individuals, excoriating Orientalism, which is "about texts and not about people." His Arab reviewers are unimpressed: "Does this mean that collective human entities such as nations, social classes, cultures do not exist or are of no importance?" asks al-Bīṭār. "Does [Said] deny the validity of the premises of modern sociology, which studies the patterns of social life and social interaction? Does he reject, then, the basic scientific approach which endeavors to transcend individuals and individual phenomena and discover general relationships, modes or laws which may enable us, in turn, to better understand the individuals?"[14]

And further on:

> [Said] implies that the methodologies predominating today in Western social sciences are bad and erroneous, but that there are three or four scholars—in addition to the author himself, of course—who succeeded in "liberating" themselves from it. And yet never does Edward Said explain to us, be it by hint or otherwise, what is it which make the latter capable of such a "liberation" that so many others failed to accomplish.[15]

Al-'Aẓm comes to the same conclusion regarding Said's hero of the piece, Louis Massignon:

> Massignon appears to be the only virtuous son of the Orientalist establishment, notorious for its metaphysical beliefs, racism, superiority complex, and imperialist connections. Yet one is at a loss to find in the book any objective justification for the distinction it makes between Massignon and

the rest of the Orientalists whom Said criticizes. Why single him out for special treatment? Why lavish praise upon him and attribute to him achievements he does not acknowledge for any of his peers (many of whom had great accomplishments at least as specialists)?[16]

## HONEST MORTICIANS

As against the totalizing, essentializing analysis of Orientalism offered by Said, these reviewers suggest a case-by-case examination of its product. Muḥammad Ḥusayn 'Alī al-Ṣaghīr's book is a good example of such an approach.[17] Sifting carefully through Western studies of the Koran over the last century and a half, he notes that the motivations behind them were a mixed bag: missionary, imperialistic, and strictly scholarly, which would explain the dark suspicions harbored by the *'ulamā'* against Orientalist writings. Al-Ṣaghīr refuses, however, to operate deductively and *a priori* dismiss as flawed a whole branch of intellectual endeavor. He is ready to explore it "warily and cautiously" but with an open mind. His painstaking examination comes up with a number of important lacunae in Western studies of the Koran (on Koranic rhetoric, for instance). Some of the scholars (notably Franz Bull) he finds hostile and prone to distortion in their interpretation. Others (like Nöldeke), while often producing solid research, dabbled at times at "prattle and dubious insinuations unworthy of a scholar of his stature." But on the whole, he finds Western Koranic studies highly valuable, "carefully researched and intellectually honest," their "overall characteristic is purely scholarly." Koranic translations are also weighed and found to be quite useful though not always accurate. Many scholars come out of this scrutiny with flying colors, particularly Régis Blachère. Had the author had recourse to the canons of modern *'ulamā'* (or for that matter of Edward Said), Blachère might have been dismissed for his connections with the French colonial enterprise. But, of course, the bulk of the product al-Ṣaghīr deals with was German, from both before and after the launching of the *Drang nach Osten*. He, however, seems oblivious of dates and possible motivations: only the books and articles exist, judged by their methodology and findings—bad, middling, good, excellent. His generally very positive evaluation is all the more significant as the subject matter—the Koran—is the Holy of Holies, the touchiest taboo, a book not only laying out the fundamentals of the Faith but whose very language is elevated to the rank of a dogma ("the inimitability of the Koran").

The role of the Germans is interesting from another viewpoint too. If there were scholars involved in an "academic effort to embalm Islam" (to use Said's terms), these were the nineteenth-century German Orientalists. Yet this was not because of an imperialist presence in the Islamic lands, which their country barely had. (Paradoxically enough such a presence would likely have had the effect of making them attuned to Islam as a *living* tradition and human experience, if only to answer the questions and needs of intelligence services, commercial enterprises, and so on.) Quite to the contrary, nineteenth-century German Orientalism treated Islam as a classical—i.e., dead but valuable—civilization, to be handled with the same philological care and positivist attention to fact-gathering lavished by German classicists on Ancient Greece and Rome. Whether unwittingly or not, they thereby performed "rites of morticians," laying to rest, so to speak, the remains of a noble but bygone civilization, they did it, however, in a decent, respectful and solid manner. The British and French, while emulating German academicism so hallowed in that century, could not afford to be so purely classicist because of the very imperatives of their colonial empires. They had to study Islam as a living civilization, too. Reality is thus more complex and more ironical than Said makes it to be.

The importance of the cultural context—which Said treats with cavalier disregard—is made even more poignant, if one reflects for a moment on the analogy between nineteenth-century German Islamic studies and their contemporary German "science of Judaism" *(Wissenschaft des Judentums)*. In both fields the Germans admittedly produced the best and most enduring stuff in that century. And yet German-Jewish students of Judaism were even more unabashedly classicist, viewing their own religion as a dead world in an age of enlightenment and assimilation. Some of the major practitioners indeed combined both the Jewish and the Islamic fields: Mauritz Steinschneider, Ignaz Goldziher, Abraham Geiger. Their underlying embalming approach at times puts blindfolds on their eyes, but did not prevent them from producing well-researched monographs and even trail-blazing studies (such as Goldziher's *Mohammedan Studies*). Nor were the "classicist" blindfolds the only ones hampering their sight. The predominant idealism of nineteenth-century Germany—with its liberal Protestant connotations—led to essentialism, as exemplified in terms such as the "essence of Islam" *(Wesen des Islams)*, "the essence of Judaism" *(Wesen des Judentums)*. Imperialism and racism had little to do with it all. Even the early rebels against the "science of Judaism," such as Martin Buber, resorted to a counter-essentialism in their praise of the "Oriental mentality" of Judaism, whose very "kernel" is alien to Western culture.

## ORIENTALISM IN REVERSE

As noted above, it certainly is not anxiety about the professional reputation of Messrs. Goldziher, Blachère, and Co. that bothers Said's Arab reviewers. Their edginess is to be understood in the context of the present concerns of Arab secularist thinkers. Foremost among these is the upsurge of what they dub "Orientalism in Reverse"[18]—the major cultural phenomenon of the seventies and early eighties. It consists of the affirmation of an authentic Islamic or Arab character, harking back to the seventh century, or even earlier, essentially unchanging over time, intrinsically spiritualist and idealist (and diametrically opposed to the materialistic West). Not a new idea, for sure, but one that in the wake of the Islamic resurgence became fashionable in many formerly secularist and modernist circles, disillusioned by the failures of economic modernization and Pan-Arabism. In their quest for a panacea, even erstwhile Marxist thinkers such as Anwar 'Abdel Malek came to see in Islam (also known as "political Islam," "Arabo-Islamism," and so on) the only way out. For leftist and liberal intellectuals cut off from the populace, the success of the Iranian Revolution in mobilizing the supposedly inert masses was the light at the end of the tunnel.

Inadvertently perhaps, a book like *Orientalism*, endowed with the prestige of the author's Western academic credentials, lends itself easily to an all-embracing smear of the West and glorification of the East (or Islam).

Even in "progressive" Arab states one finds many leading writers who are far from being fundamentalist and who attempt to prove in a scientific manner that Arabic is the carrier of certain unique values of Arabhood from times immemorial, as inimitable as the Koranic language, the fount of Arab-Islamic creative genius. Others still speak of the "civilizing mission" of Arabhood to the whole of humanity ("the White Man's Burden in reverse," notes al-'Aẓm).[19] The dichotomy of East-West and spirit-matter only serves to bolster such claims to authenticity. The principal danger, as Arab secularists see it, is that receptivity to modernity will be irreparably reduced. And can a culture grow without being able to borrow? If it boycotts others, does it not run the risk of stagnation, asks al-Bīṭār.[20]

Other dangers are no less unsettling, and here again Said's diatribe against the inherently hostile and distorting West serves—whether he wills it or not—the cause of "Orientalism in Reverse," accentuating in the process certain traits of Arab national thought the secularists had always lamented. The most vigorous critic of these traits (and implicitly of Said) is Ḥasan Ḥanafī. His check list includes all the hallmarks of Orientalism: "impressionism, which consists in vague expressions of states of mind, the one following the other without adding significantly to it"; "preference for the metaphysical rather than the Real. . . for the shadows of things rather than the things themselves"; "deduction rather than induction. . . inferring everything from axioms many of which are anchored in wishful thinking and personal or class interests and are never put to the test of verification." The upshot of it all is "apologetics rather than criticism in. . . support for whatever exists and not to demanding what does not . . . . Indeed the more talented the thinker the greater his ability to cloak unpleasant truth through the intellectual sleight-of-hand, in modish concepts and with the *dernier cri* in slogans."

And he concludes:

> As long as such mystifications are prevalent, the Arab will remain devoid of willpower, deficient in perception and reasoning. Whoever wishes can play with our fate. God, fate and the dictator become one in our eyes. He who questions this is accused of atheism. It is as though the era of science and reason has barely touched us.[21]

It is thus no coincidence that the "Reverse Orientalists" are as hostile to Western Orientalism as traditional *'ulamā'* had been, accusing it of drawing a picture of Islam that is the mirror-image of the one they conjure up.[22]

## COMING TO TERMS WITH THE PAST

Beyond these broad concerns lies a specific bone the reviewers have to pick with Edward Said. No paragraph in his book infuriated them more than the one where he argues that "Orientalism flourishes today. . . . Indeed there is some reason for alarm in the fact that its influence has spread to the 'Orient' itself: the pages of books and journals in Arabic. . . are filled with second-order analyses by Arabs of the 'Arab mind,' 'Islam' and other myths" (Said, p. 322).

Here the Arab reviewers saw themselves attacked. For it became eminently clear as they read further that, for Said, any cultural critique from within Arab society is but a brand of "Arab Orientalism," (a term of abuse in the lingo of Arab conservatives).[23] "If he says that these are second-order analyses. . . shouldn't he explain to us in what way they are so bad," asks al-Bīṭār ironically. "Is it because they try to liberate [the Arab] from the dregs and residues of the past?"[24] In effect what Said objects to is an impressive body of writings produced in Arabic, especially over the last two decades, which tries to come to terms with the Arab past, and more specifically with the impact—not omnipotent, nor even direct, but still important—that this past has upon the Arab present.

Here perhaps lies the primordial divergence between Said and the bulk of Arab liberal and left-wing thinkers. Edward Said seems to share with these thinkers the conviction that modernism has been but a shallow *(fahlawī)* pretense in the Arab countries, limited at best to instrumental borrowing, and at worst to gadget-borrowing. The "*fahlawī* personality" avoids the question of the values of modernity *(mu'āṣara)* that are inexorably linked to technological instruments. It does not relate to the problem of what to do when some of these values clash with the *'aṣāla* (heritage), trying to "reconcile" both by vague formulae. Much like radical thinkers, Said argues that the so-called revolutionary regimes are nothing but a sham, failing to bring about structural change, and finally that the direction that the Arab world should take is that of a cultural revolution, or a complete break with the past.[25]

Yet here similarities end. Said denies the relevance of the Arab-Islamic past to our understanding of the contemporary Middle East. The fourteen-centuries-old tradition and civilization of Islam is no more meaningful in the Arab world, he argued on a PBS talk show in 1977, than seventh-century European events are to our understanding of the United States today. But is it not? Arab modernists have come to perceive in recent years that the past *has* a powerful hold (many of them say "stranglehold") upon Arab society. "One used to believe that this cultural change, the liberation from traditional culture, is imminent," wrote one such modernist. "It has now become unfortunately evident that this was unwarranted optimism, the forces of the past do not manifest any symptoms of attrition or decline."[26]

The relevance of the past is indeed the point where an Arab secularist reading of the present converges with that of most Western Orientalists. Their perspectives are, of course, quite different, each with its own advantages and liabilities. The Arab writers are committed scholars and social critics operating from within; the Westerners are outside observers, once or twice removed, not necessarily involved with the phenomena they monitor. They also have (and had), of course, different audiences. Their methodology, however, is the same: inductive, based on texts as well as on field surveys and anthropological observations, attempting to encompass past and present alike, rigorously respectful of the same rules of evidence, mindful of the historical context. This state of affairs is mentioned by al-'Aẓm while discussing Said's critique of Macdonald and Gibb. The latter were no doubt interpreting Islam for the West in a certain point in time, and more specifically for the needs of the British Empire. This, says al-'Aẓm, by no means invalidates their views *a priori* (as Said would have it), for they had an interest—like any good intelligence agents would—to provide as accurate an assessment of Islam as possible. Al-'Aẓm has strong reservations on the implicit tendency in both writers to "essentialize" the situation they depicted, but as a reading of the twentieth-century Middle East, he finds it valid and dismisses Said's objections:

> I cannot agree with Said that their "Orientalist mentality" blinded them to the realities of Muslim societies and definitively distorted their views of the East in general. For instance: isn't it true, on the whole, that the inhabitants of Damascus and Cairo today feel the presence of the transcedental in their lives more palpably and more actively than Parisians and Londoners? Isn't it true that religion means everything to the contemporary Moroccan, Algerian and Iranian peasant in a manner it cannot mean for the American farmer or the member of a Russian kolkhoz? And isn't it a fact that the belief in the laws of nature is more deeply rooted in the minds of university students in Moscow and New York than among the students of al-Azhar and of Teheran University?[27]

Al-'Aẓm seems to refer here in particular to a number of trailblazing studies by Arab social scientists that had an enduring impact upon liberal and leftist thinkers. Eleven years ago, a team led by 'Imād al-Dīn Sulṭān of the National Research Center for Sociology and Criminology (Cairo) published a research report entitled *Value Conflict Between the Generations*.[28] Based on a field survey of a sample of four social groups (high-school seniors, university students in the arts and sciences, and their respective parents) in well-to-do neighborhoods of Cairo, the Sulṭān team attempted to gauge the generational gap within the Egyptian middle and upper-middle classes. Surprisingly enough, they found the gap to be on the whole insubstantial, all four groups being strongly permeated by traditional Islamic values. Quite unexpectedly, on some issues the male students were more conservative than others (though, usually, females tended to be, within each age group, more past-oriented than males). Male students were particularly hostile to career-oriented female students, a phenomenon explained by the anxiety over the rising number of female students over the preceeding two decades (from a ratio of 1:13 to less than 1:2) and by the fact that only at the university do most of them meet women as fellow students for the first time. (This was some time before the Islamic resurgence, at a time when student associations were still controlled by the Left, but the tension was evident and foreshadowed the emphasis on female seclusion—in buses, lecture halls—and other related themes among fundamentalist students today.)

"It is our finding," wrote Dr. Sulṭān, "that religious faith is deeply rooted in all sectors of Egyptian society." The overwhelming majority of the respondents—regardless of age, sex, and educational achievement—agreed with statements like "a person cannot live without religion," "everyone must believe in life after death," "civilization is bound to collapse without religion" (the latter being a cornerstone of the cultural heritage in which Arab youth, according to eighty-six to ninety-two percent of those interviewed, "should take an active interest").

When these attitudes in principle were tested in specific fields, the prevalence of Islamic norms of behavior (above all in interpersonal relations) was manifest. "God created woman to make man's life easier" elicited a high rate of positive response, as did statements such as "girls should be more strictly treated within the family than boys," "children should be subservient to their families until they marry," with even most youngsters rejecting the proposition that "children should be allowed to leave home when they feel like it without parental interference." Family descent, it was concurred, is the most important criterion in selecting a mate. But with regard to "career orientation and education," traditional norms did not gain the upper hand (and a significant value conflict between generations appeared).

If this is the situation among the educated urban elite—that social group most exposed to modern norms—how much more so in the lower ranks of the socioeconomic scale and outside the Cairo metropolis! Egyptian psychologists Dr. Ḥantūra and Dr. Ṣuwayf found that the overall level in less industrialized Arab countries, such as Jordan and Syria, is analogous to that of rural Egypt. In some areas of life there is no significant difference even between urban and rural milieus. Thus, attitudes toward death, discovered Dr. Sayyid 'Uways, are roughly the same among the Egyptian intelligentsia and *fellahin*, based upon a common belief in life after death and the notion of obligation toward deceased relatives and saintly and pious persons who have died. In a series of imaginative studies—of graffiti, automobile stickers, letters of the devout addressed to the tomb of a famous Islamic scholar, and so forth—he refined and replicated these results, shown time and again to apply to the overwhelming majority of Egyptians. (By contrast, only forty percent of Americans and less than a third of Frenchmen say they believe in life after death.)

When one moves from generalizations to more specific phenomena, one often finds again Arab social critics arrayed on the same side of the barricade as the Orientalists, even though both may draw different conclusions from the same interpretation of reality. Said writes that "Orientalist generalizations about the Arabs are very detailed when it comes to itemizing Arab characteristics critically. . . . Almost without exception, every contemporary work of Orientalist scholarship (especially in the social sciences) has a great deal to say about the family, its male-dominated structure, its all-pervasive influence in the society" (Said, pp. 310-11). But al-Bīṭār retorts: "Said seems to suggest that any criticism directed by an Orientalist at the East (or part thereof) denotes racialism; this amounts in fact to a complete denial of history, for contradictions and divergencies are to be found in any historical phase, culture, and nation. Said seems to say, in effect, that any thinker criticizing the Orient. . .becomes thereby the tool of 'Orientalism' as he understands it."[29] The testiness in the tone implies that the thinker in question is al-Bīṭār himself.

And is it really so untrue, asks al-'Aẓm, that male-female is one of the three major distinctions in Islamic culture (the others being Muslim-non-Muslim and freeman-slave)? (pp.47-9). To say this is so does not mean—as some Orientalists actually used to say (and a few still do)—that this is an unchanging pattern; of course it varied over time, but on the whole the age-old norms of discrimination and male supremacy do remain in force. This point should not be labored upon, perhaps, for those who do not read Arabic now have available the book of a major Arab social critic, Nawal Sa'adawī: *The Hidden Face of Eve* (Zed Press, London, 1980). In it she draws upon her professional experience as a gynecologist to observe that in all key areas (the issue of virginity, the notion of "honor" and premarital sex, legal status, subservience to males, entering marriage as a market commodity, lack of right to initiate divorce and to get lifelong alimony, lower share in inheritance, and so forth), the female condition in both urban and rural Egypt is still governed by the *sharī'a* (Islamic law) and by the social norms it spawned throughout the centuries of total male domination.

The amount of attention given in Arab intellectual circles to the study of women and sexuality is not only a matter for feminists like Sa'dawī, Suhayr al-Qalamāwī, and Amīna al-Naqqāsh, but of numerous concerned male thinkers too. It is part and parcel of their interest in the family as a major bastion of traditional Islamic values—changing and yet steadfast—and as the principal intermediary between the individual and his social and cultural milieu. This is the theme of a 1974 study by Palestinian scholar Hisham Sharabi.[30] The extended urban (and *a fortiori* the rural and nomad) family, contends Sharabi, is essentially a microcosm of society, and thus its structure and relationships reflect and uphold the traditional values of the society-at-large; through its primordial role in child-rearing, the family inculcates these values to its young members, preparing them for their social roles. The family values include: authoritarianism (based upon seniority and male sex), over-dependence vis-à-vis the social milieu, and helplessness as regards the ruling class and lack of personal initiative. Feelings of shame and guilt serve as major vehicles of disciplining the individual, making him subservient to social (and other) authority. Conformity is the rule. Assertiveness is stifled, and the individual is fettered by "fixed norms of speech, behavior, and social discourse." Adaptability as the ultimate goal, says Sharabi, creates a "society where amusement and mutual flattery set the tone, effective action is hardly feasible [and where] it is difficult to thrash out problems."

It is indeed the society-at-large and the negative impact of the past upon it which have preoccupied Arab intellectuals over the last two decades. It is not a monocausal explanation. Other factors (especially the economic dependence of the Arab world) are also taken into consideration, but the heritage—or rather what still remains of it—is a major independent variable. Dedicated to the maxim that their role is not only to understand the world but to change it, Arab social critics did not satisfy themselves with highly specialized empirical research but attempted to wed it to a synthesizing reflection about *la condition arabe*, a theoretical endeavor geared to praxis. If we dub them "left-leaning" it is in the original, nineteenth-century sense of the term as crystallized in France: *les forces du mouvement* (as opposed to *les forces de l'ordre*). They hark back to many a spiritual family (though Marxists in the loose sense of the word are the most prominent, together with the old-fashioned, rationalistic, liberal humanists). Their unifying theme is found in Ṣādiq al-ʿAẓm's *Self-Criticism after the Debacle* (Beirut, 1968), rejecting "the prevailing religious obscurantist mentality which encourages escapism, the traditional behavioral patterns, backwardness and fatalism, lack of initiative and submission to the authorities and their orders."[31] Fine-tuning al-ʿAẓm's generalizations, Lebanese sociologist Ḥalīm Barakāt argued that "religion is an important factor in encouraging [the Arab] to accept rather than confront his situation. The believer is content with his condition, is satisfied with what Allah has allotted to him, and leaves the task of changing the world to the supreme authority." Thus, Man is "powerless in the face of his problems. It has rightly been said that the Arab viewpoint on relations between Heaven and Earth is that 'Heaven has decreed, and earth must obey,' since the Creator has commanded and directed, and his creatures must rejoice in their lot." Contentment, acceptance, and satisfaction are precious qualities to the believing Arab, through which he becomes a virtuous man. These qualities are a bulwark against true revolution, and they prevent the Arab from facing up to his powerlessness and attempting to overcome it. The Arab repeats the statements of the eleventh-century thinker al-Ghazālī that "to maintain silence in the face of Satan throughout one's life is a deed which embodies no harm," that "the believer most beloved by the great Allah is the poor man who is content with little," that hunger is to be found in Allah's treasure house, and "He bestows it only on those whom He loves," and that "if you see poverty approaching, welcome it with the greeting of the righteous." In Arab daily life we find numerous maxims demonstrating the prevalence of this fatalistic approach: "Do not think there is one who manages matters"; "Fate moves men, and the believers can only obey and give thanks"; "Do not be wounded at heart because of livelihood: Only God is responsible for it."[32]

Passivity, claims Edward Said, is one of the traits of Arab society those disingenuous Orientalists just love to write about (Said, pp. 308, 311, 312) and is indeed a factor of great concern to Arab social critics, notably for its political implications—the failure of participatory regimes and forms of political action. Particularly in recent years, many are the symposia and articles dealing with the "passivity of the Arab masses" and their easy manipulation by the ruling classes. Extensive field studies (such as the one carried out by K. al-Manūfī in Egypt)[33] confirmed the prevalence of the "bad government is better than no government" idea preached for centuries by the *'ulamā'*.

Borrowing the concept of the "triple taboo" coined by Syrian sociologist Bū-'Alī Yāsīn (in a 1973 book which carried this title), Ḥasan Ḥanafī endeavors to place all this in a broader perspective:

> The three major taboos of Arab society are God, government, and sex. These are not a matter for discussion but for obedience and repression. At a certain point, all three tend to converge. Sanctuaries and prison cells have the same function; veil and dress come to indicate the special status of womanhood; government relies upon the *sheikhs*, and the latter rely in turn on government; sex films are a safety valve for repressed tendencies as much in this field as in politics, where real participation is banned. The upshot is, of course, enslavement. Allah is thus not one who defends the individual and succors the poor.[34]

Al-Bīṭār, for his part, detected almost a decade ago the main (though not the sole) cause for "Arab political backwardness" in the fact that:

> Attitudes shaped in the sixth century still predominate in Arab culture. The *Weltanschauung* of Arab society is religious and transcendental; it is a holistic philosophy of life through which society defines its place in history and its internal rules of the game. This mystic philosophy creates a man who does not recognize history as an independent truth; a man who is unaware of the fact that there are objective factors and tendencies which exist beyond human aspirations and intentions, and that in order to influence them one should comprehend their logic and dynamics. . . .
>
> This is a society which defines all its activities and the events occurring around it through ritual and relationship to God. The prevailing principle is *peccatis nostris*: if we failed, this is because our relationship with God and other occult forces did not attain the required level of morality or because

the omniscient and omnipresent God had acted against us for an unknown reason or because angels and Satan stood in our way. Modern culture is the exact opposite; it believes that there are objective forces and rules in history and society and that man's freedom is predicated upon his trying to understand them and act in accordance. . . . Arab political action is still largely governed—unconsciously perhaps—by this traditional-mystical mentality. In the best of cases it straddles both the modern and traditional mentalities. It is no coincidence that the major manifestations of Arab political action are idealistic, moralistic, and messianic. . . [inspired] by a typical Third World cultural pattern: transcendental, hierarchic, fossilized, and passive. . . . [Progress] requires an ideology that will extract from Arab mentality that powerlessness, that belief in predestination, which cripple our Arab creative potential.[35]

Politics also imply political economy. More recently, Egyptian philosopher Fu'ad Zakariya, discussing the failure of the Arabs to exploit the oil bonanza as a springboard for economic take-off and sustained growth, laid part of the blame on lack of serious planning. This he ascribed in turn to the age-old notion that the realm of the *ghayb* (the unknown), which includes the future, is a hallowed and forbidden area, better left to God, "He who knoweth," alone. Economists well-attuned to cultural realities, such as George Corm, while emphasizing explanations modelled on the *dependencia* school of Theotonio Dos Santos, attribute an important role to the past-(rather than future-)orientedness ingrained in Arab culture.[36]

Past-orientedness is not only an objective phenomenon but also a subjective one, present at the level of Arab consciousness. One notes this in the preoccupation with the medieval past (or more exactly, with its glorious periods), as we have seen in Chapter 1.

This effort is largely devoted to apologetics and not to a dispassionate search for truth; to praise of one's own culture, not to comprehending it; to blame (others), not to arrive at self-awareness. "We are," writes Fu'ad Zakariya,

alienated from our present and fraught with nostalgia for our past. This is the most negative phenomenon of our cultural life. Our consciousness is so much oriented toward the past, so inexplicably intertwined with it, that it expects the past to do the impossible, namely to solve the problems of the present. Suffice it to mention the great importance attached by Egyptian and Arab writers to the question of cultural heritage *('aṣāla)* and the glory of our past. Our dilemma is how to accommodate both. This dissension with the past is most evident when we speak of the "return of the spirit" whenever we accomplish something of magnitude such as the October War. Present accomplishment is thus intended to resuscitate and vindicate the past. Had we wished to give the present its due share, we would not have interpreted it always from the viewpoint of that return to past glory. Our press and literature do not cease, in fact, to make comparisons between past and present events. They tend to link a modern-day military exploit and another feat of arms dating back several centuries or a twentieth-century revolution and a revolution which took place in antiquity. Such comparisons and analogies have particular significance in our country, because when many of us pride ourselves—quite legitimately, of course—for being the descendents of ancient civilizations, we tend to believe in the existence of latent mystical relationships through which the past influences the present. They claim that he who traces his ancestry to an ancient civilization is bound today to be better, wiser, and nobler than the descendent of a more recent civilization. Truly enough, unity in this vein may be quite agreeable at a purely literary level and may contribute to boost public morale. But can it really stand the test of sober and rational analysis? This would be much like claiming that because twenty-five centuries ago the Greeks had a magnificent civilization, modern-day Greeks are better men than the Norwegians, who are descendents of the lawless viking pirates.

. . . The voice of the past submerges the voice of the present in our thought, literature, and art. We speak of our past more than any other people on earth. The fault is not with our pride in the past, for indeed it is glorious. What callls for soul-searching is that tendency to revert to the past whenever we encounter complex situations in the present, deluding ourselves into believing that solutions inspired by the spirit of bygone days can best tackle contemporary problems.[37]

Spearheading the attempt to come to terms with the past, an impressive body of revisionist historiography has evolved over the last two decades, dedicated to the weeding out of panegyrics, apologetics, and externalization of guilt (see above, Chapter 2, "Arab Revisionist Historians"). It is indeed the support that Said gives—unwittingly or not—to these "religious tendencies" that worries Arab secularists the most. For Said, remarks al-Bīṭār, "all the ills [of the Arab world] emanate from Orientalism and have nothing to do with the socioeconomic, political and ideological makeup of the Arab lands or with the cultural historical backwardness which stands behind it."[38]

By providing ammunition to the defrocked secularists who embraced "Orientalism in Reverse," Said joined what al-ʿAẓm sarcastically called the "Islamanic trend." The dangers the Islamanics *(al-Islāmāniyyūn)* represent—with their transports of enthusiasm for essentialism, authenticity, and Islamic intrinsic spiritual supremacy—lies not only in the severing of cultural links with the rest of the world, thus stifling creativity and chasing away modernity; but also in the fact that it may deal a mortal blow to the (already slim) chances for democracy. In the name of authenticity, the Islamic revivalism the "Islamanics" support rejects democracy as incompatible with "true Islam." It may further strengthen discrimination against women, reintroduce hostility toward that second "inferior social group," i.e., non-Muslims, and, suggests al-ʻAẓm, tongue-in-cheek, may even bring back the Ottoman *millet* and perhaps also slavery (the "third cleavage of discrimination"). Last but not least, it may liquidate Arab nationalism, reducing it to a humble branch of the Islamic tree. Ethnocentrism and obscurantism will reign supreme.[39]

The Arab reviewers are all the more saddened by the fact that it *seemed* as though Said was one of them, a secularist and a modernist. To some extent he is. But unlike Said, Arab liberal and leftist intellectuals face up to realities, do not indulge in wishful thinking, and do not strike out the influence of the Islamic past in verbal *legerdemain*. They know the hold it has on Arab society. They are as harsh with themselves as they are with their society. The Arab left, as they see it, is too fragmented and not liberated enough from the impact of the very heritage it attacks, lacks contact with the masses, and is too weak to conduct an effective fight to capture Arab hearts and minds.[40]

They know that even their fellow intellectuals, the most alienated social class, tend to find refuge in withdrawal from society or in submission to authority rather than in revolutionary action. It is not surprising that in their case, Francis Bacon's dictum has been turned upside down, a better knowledge of their society instilled in them a sense of powerlessness. Their mood is thus tenebrous. It is far removed from Edward Said's exuberant conviction that the future is already there and that it works in the People's Democratic Republic of Yemen. They are far less sanguine about the imminence of the *lendemains qui chantent*, perhaps because they operate from within the Arab world and cannot afford to be caught up in the clichés and fantasies of the outsider and the tourist. Their *Angst* is not the faked one of the radical chic but the real one of people who have a clear perception of their ultimate goal but also of the formidable obstacles blocking the road. In brief, they are serious. Can the same be said of Edward Said?

## FOOTNOTES

[Page references in the text refer to Edward Said's *Orientalism* (Pantheon Books, 1978)]

1. A major exception is Albert Hourani's review essay, *New York Review of Books*, 8 March 1979.
2. S.J. al-'Aẓm, *Orientalism and Orientalism in Reverse (al-Istishrāq wa-l-Istishrāq Ma'kusan)*, Beirut, 1981 (partial translation in *Khamsin* [London] 8, pp. 5-26); M.Ḥ.'A. al-Saghīr, *Orientalists & Koranic Studies (al-Musashriqūm wa-l-Dirāsāt al-Qur'āniyya)*, Beirut, 1983; N. al-Bīṭār, chap. 6, "From Western Orientalism to Arab Orientalism" in his *Ḥudūd al-Huwiyya al-Qawmiyya (The Boundaries of Nationalist Identity)*, Beirut, 1982. Ḥ. Hanafī's article in *Qadāyā 'Arabiyya*, Beirut, Vol. 2 (1978), pp. 17-42.
3. *Al-Naqd al-Dhāti ba'da-l-Hazīma*, Beirut, 1968; *Naqd al-Fikr al-Dīnī*, Beirut, 1969.
4. Al-Bīṭār, pp. 157-8.
5. Al-'Aẓm, pp. 10-11.
6. Al-Bīṭār, pp. 8-9. Here as elsewhere in their writings, the Arab reviewers have close affinities with James Clifford's review essay of Said's *History & Theory* (1980), pp. 204-21, which is perhaps the most perceptive contribution to the *Orientalism* debate.
7. Al-Bīṭār, p. 161.
8. Ibid., pp. 163-4.
9. In his interview with *al-Ḥawādith*, Beirut, 23 Dec. 1980. Some of the other students of Islam praised by Said as exceptions to the general rule were either ambivalent (A. Hourani, loc. cit.) or critical (Clifford Geertz, *NewYork Review of Books*, 12 Aug. 1982) of his approach. Rodinson is quoted *in extenso* by Bīṭār, p. 160.
10. Al-'Aẓm, p. 14.
11. Al-Bīṭār, op. cit.
12. Ibid., pp. 172-3.
13. Al-'Aẓm, pp. 20-21.
14. Al-Bīṭār, p. 163.
15. Ibid., p. 171.
16. Al-'Aẓm, p. 21.
17. Al-Saghīr, pp. 31, 38-9, 88-9, 92. The same argument is made in the special issue of *al-Fikr al-Arabī* (Beirut, January-March, 1983), especially pp. 23-4, 82-93, 112, 338ff.
18. It is al-'Aẓm who coined the term.
19. Al-'Aẓm, p. 34. Another leftist thinker, George Corm, went so far as to dub it "reverse racialism," *Dirāsāt 'Arabiyya*, Jan. 1980, p. 44.
20. Al-Bīṭār, pp. 179, 181.
21. Ḥanafī, pp. 23-4, 28-33.
22. The best discussion of this aspect is to be found in al-'Aẓm's chapter available in English (see note 2). See also, A. Abdel Malek, "L'Orientalisme en crise," *Diogène* 24 (1963), p. 109ff; G.H.A. Juynboll, "The 'Ulamā' and Western Scholarship," *Israel Oriental Studies*, X (1980), p. 173ff.
23. See S. Qudsi, "Arab Orientalists" [Arabic] *al-Ma'rifa*, Damascus, May 1976, pp. 145-8.
24. Al-Bīṭār, pp. 174-5.
25. Other than in his book, Said made the argument with particular vigor in an article in *The New York Times Book Review*, 31 Oct. 1976.

26. N. al-Bīṭār, "Major Causes of Arab Political Backwardness" [Arabic], *Dirāsāt 'Arabiyya*, Beirut, Aug. 1974.
27. Al-'Aẓm, p. 18.
28. Sultān's report in *Al-Majalla al-Itjtimā'iyya al-Qawmiyya*, (Jan 1972); Ḥantūra's study, ibid. (1968) fasc. 1; M. Ṣuwayf, *Al-Taṭarruf Ka-Uslūb li-l-Istijāba*, Cairo,1968; Ṣ.*'Uways Hutaf al-Ṣāmitīn*, Cairo, 1971; idem; *Al-Ḥulūd fi-Hayāt al-Misriyyī al-Mu'asirīn*, Cairo, 1972; idem; *Al-Ḥulūd fi-Turāth al-Sha'bī al-Miṣrí*, Cairo, 1975; On female students, see F. al-Guindi, "Veiling Infitāḥ with Muslim Ethic," *Social Problems* 28 (1981), pp. 465-85. Some of Sulṭān's results were replicated ten years later by 'A.-al-Mashat, "Egyptian Attitudes towards the Peace Process," *Middle East Journal*, Summer 1983.
29. Al-Bīṭār, p. 169.
30. "Family and Cultural Development in Arab Society" [Arabic], *al-Ma'rifa*, Damascus, June 1974.
31. This is the admirably lapidary and precise summary of the message of al-'Aẓm's book coined by Ḥ. Barakat (see article quoted in note 32).
32. "Alienation and Revolution in Arab Life" [Arabic], *al-Mawāqif*, Beirut, 1969, pp. 18-44.
33. *Al-Thaqāfa al-Siyāsiyya li-l-Fallāḥīn al-Misriyyīn*, Beirut, 1980.
34. Ḥasan Ḥanafī; Bū 'Alī Yāsin, *The Triple Taboo* [Arabic], Beirut, 1973 (see above,) chap. 2, n. 48).
35. Al-Bīṭār, passim.
36. Al-Bīṭār, art. cit. (note 26); F. Zakariya "The Future of Arab Futurology," *al-Fikr al-'Arabī al-Mu'āṣir*, Beirut, May 1981; Corm interview quoted above (note 19) and his *Al-Tab'īyya al-Iqtiṣādiyya*, Beirut, 1980.
37. "Till When Shall We Be Alienated from Our Past?" [Arabic], *al-Ahr*ām, Cairo, 28 Nov. 1973; cf. 'Isa, "Arab Cultural Physiognomy," *Qaḍāyā 'Arabiyya*, Beirut, May 1974.
38. Al-Bīṭār, p. 178.
39. Ibid., pp. 179, 181-2, 192-6; al-'Aẓm, pp. 48-53.
40. Ḥalīm Barakāt, "The Arab Intellectuals and the State" [Arabic], *al-Maw*āqif', 1970, pp. 28-48.

# PART III: COLONIAL REPRESENTATIONS OF ISLAM

# Chapter 6:

# COLONIALISM AND POPULAR CULTURE

## A PICARESQUE HERO

One of the traits which make for the uniqueness of the Algerian case in the annals of decolonization is the salient role played by the Pied Noir masses. This sizeable settler community (ca. 980,000, or one-tenth of the overall population) was a major disruptive force, providing the crowds as well as most of the hard-core activists for all the attempts to scuttle *l'abandon de l'Algérie Française:* from the 6 February, 1956, demonstration in Algiers against visiting French premier Guy Mollet, through the events of May 1958, the Barricades Week rebellion (January 1960), the Four Generals' Putsch (April 1961), up to the OAS's final no-holds barred counter-terrorist campaign (1960-62).

While journalistic and fictional descriptions of the fratricidal (and eventually suicidal) Pied Noir psychodrama are legion, no systematic attempt at an in-depth study of their collective mind has been made, apart from Pierre Nora's essay, *Les Français d'Algérie* (1961), based primarily upon observations during his 1958-60 stay as a high-school teacher in Oran.

Source material is not lacking, however, for the study of the popular culture of this overwhelmingly urban community, made up of manual workers, white-collar employees, and small artisans and shopkeepers. The most important among these sources are the cheap mass-circulation novels *(romans à deux sous)* of the *Cagayous* series. Spanning almost three decades of publication (1891-1920) in weekly instalments (usually 16-page fascicles), they were written in the plebeian dialect of the urban Pied Noirs, nicknamed *pataouète*; a French *patois* upon which were grafted vocabulary and syntax forms from Spanish, Italian, Maltese, and Arabic.[1] The prolific author Auguste Robinet (1862-1930), writing under the pen-name Musette, was an Algiers lawyer, journalist, and public official who drew upon his intimate knowledge of the European lower classes (especially as social assistance inspector for children at the Algiers Prefecture) to create the literary hero of the series, Cagayous. "A mixture of Panurge, Guignol, Gavroche. . . and Marius,"[2] this picaresque hero, born in the Bab-el-Oued quarter of Algiers of a French father and a Spanish mother, populist in temperament, floating in his occupations, became immensely popular with the small folk of the French Algerian cities.

The weekly instalments describing his adventures were immediately snatched from the newspaper stalls, according to contemporary eyewitnesses, and were later also sold by mail among the lower classes (the upper classes frowned upon their plebeian vernacular) all through the 1890s and the first two decades of this century. Demand was so strong that many series were re-published in book form (actually collections of brochures).[3] Some of these books were to be published again in the twenties and in the late forties and early fifties, while the anthology *Cagayous: ses meilleures histoires* (edited by Albert Camus's friend and mentor, G. Audisio, and published in 1931 by Gallimard, the well-known Paris publishing house) went through five printings.[4]

If Cagayous came to be a household name, standing in a sense for the city-dweller, lower-class Pied Noir, his popularity is further attested by the numerous imitations of Musette's style and heroes in the Algerian popular press, by the use of a Cagayous trademark for Algiers-made cigarettes, furniture, and *redingote* (modelled after the one worn by the hero in the cover illustration), by Cagayous-style commercial publicity, and by Cagayous numbers in the popular theatre.[5] Popular songs in Algiers would celebrate him (with refrains such as "nous sommes tous des Cagayous"), and during World War I, Pied Noir prisoners-of-war in Germany organized nostalgic *soirées algériennes* where Cagayous stories were told or dramatized.[6] Even before Gallimard consecrated him, the Faculty of Letters of the University of Algiers began to prepare a scientific edition of his *oeuvres* (never published), and a long and erudite chapter was devoted to him in an officially-commissioned study of French colonization in Algeria, published in the series celebrating the centenary of French rule (1930).[7]

Early in 1954, a learned article published in Algiers discussed the question, "Is Cagayous still alive?" and answered it positively both "with regard to the basic psychology and to its mode of expression."[8] Nor were the *oeuvres* published in Algiers on the eve of the 1954 eruption (see note 4), his swan song. The memory lingers to this day among the million Pied Noirs repatriated to France after 1962. In 1971-72, a commercial publishing house successfully launched a series of books, headed by a Cagayous anthology and dedicated to Cagayous-style works and nostalgic recollections about French Algeria, while *pataouète* plays by imitators of Musette have continued to be staged.[9]

In short, if Cagayous "was not a spontaneous emanation of the imagination of the masses. . . but a literary creation," he became "a literary type," a sort of "re-told legend surviving its author" (according to Audisio), "well-rooted in the memory and conversation of the Algero-Europeans. . . quite alive in the manner of Polichinelle and Gavroche"(E. F. Gautier).[10] Whether this popular type of identification with him stems from the way the "type" reflects its audience or whether he in turn fashions it, is an intricate question which needs to be explored.

The Cagayous dime novels do not, however, exhaust the source material for the *mentalité pied noir*, but rather serve to point out where material can be discovered. On the one hand, other popular, mainly humorous, weeklies are to be found—many of them modeled on Cagayous—the most successful among them being *Papa-Louette*.[11] On the other hand, studies of the Pied Noir dialect, based on observations of the real-life vernacular (and not on its somewhat edulcorated literary rendering) provide fascinating insights into the Algero-European collective psyche, much as regional dialects helped Eugen Weber reconstruct the peasant *mentalité* of the turn of the century.[12]

There should also be thrown in a pot pourri of books by other Algero-European humorists writing in *pataouète*,[13] by the more realistic brand of novelists as well as by memorialists describing the *moeurs* of Bab-el-Oued and similar quarters,[14] and also travelogues, especially by Anglo-Saxons, less brainwashed than Frenchmen by the ideology of *la mission civilisatrice*.[15] Last but not least, from a comparative angle, new insights into the Algerian phenomenon may be gained from studies of interracial relations in antebellum (as well as contemporary) United States, the West Indies, West Africa, Madagascar, South Africa, and present-day France.[16]

The bulk of our Algerian sources pertain to the period between the 1890s and World War II, and most particularly to the years 1890-1920, which is just as well for a preliminary study like this one. For these years were the heyday of French rule in Algeria: they followed the crushing of the last traditional rebellion (Mokrani's in 1871) and the bolstering of the colonists' economic and political hegemony (1870-90), contemporaneous with their attainment of a great measure of autonomy (1898-1902) and before the rise of the political challenge of Algerian nationalism (the *Jeunes Algériens* of Emir Khaled, 1919; the Association of the *'Ulamā'*, 1925; and *l'Étoile Nord Africaine*, 1926). They precede by far the abortive, yet modern-style, revolt of May 1945, which gave the Pied Noir community an intimation of its imminent death. In a wider perspective, those were the years of a supposedly impregnable French imperialism, self-righteous and unashamed of its domination, whose apotheosis was marked by the Algerian centenary (1930) and the Colonial Exposition in Paris (1931). And, finally, to come back to Algeria once again, the turn of the century saw there the fusion of the numerous immigrant European ethnicities into one Pied Noir community. It is, thus, a privileged moment in which to seize—in pure state, so to speak—the Pied Noir popular culture.

## LUMPING THE NATIVES TOGETHER

Cagayous, relating how he tries to find his way out of the Palais de Justice in Algiers, stumbles into a room where he sees "a bench, huddled up with men, women, and Arabs."[17] Everything is there in this innocent phrase, dropped (as the context indicates) matter-of-factly, without any intention to elicit a laugh. The Arab is a stranger and belongs to a different human category. The term *arabes*, it should be stressed, refers to all the Algerian-Muslim natives, even though at least one-third of them were Berber-speaking, the proportion being even higher in the city of Algiers, where Cagayous lived, because of the growing exodus from nearby Kabylia. The lumping together of Kabyls and Arabs[18] denotes the influence exercised upon popular perceptions by the new colonial doctrine which evolved in Algeria among *colon* politicians, journalists, and novelists during the quarter-century following the Mokrani revolt and which flatly denied *le mythe berbère-kabyle*, created by colonial administrators and French academics. This alleged that Arabs and Berbers are two completely different races, the former a late-coming conqueror and culturally inferior, the latter the real native and by far superior because of its supposedly Celtic origins.

A whole *divide et impera* policy had been built upon this myth (which of course implied the Frenchification of the Berbers) and was now rejected by Algero-European elites, who considered all the *Islamaélites* as "rigorously unassimilable"; Algeria thus being the terrain of "two societies (European and native) of diametrically opposed *moeurs*, ideals, and religions."[19]

Yet lumping together all natives under one generic noun effaces not only ethnic-cultural distinctions but also individual ones. In Pied Noir dime novels and the colloquial press, a native as a rule does not have a name, a physiognomy, or special characteristics; he is just *l'arabe* or *l'indigène*,[20] addressed indistinctly (as many a memoir confirms) by an irreverent "Ho, Ahmed!"[21]

Here is a scene from the divorce trial of Cagayous at the Palais de Justice:

> *L'arabe chaousse* (usher) became quite angry [at Cagayous' insolent mother-in-law]. Fortunately the judge arrived. . . and the *chaousse* announced that I and my wife should enter the courtroom. My mother-in-law rose up to enter as well, but *l'arabe* blocked her way. "Why can't I accompany my daughter? By what right do you close the door in my face, *moutchou* (Monsieur) Ahmed!", she yelled. "Don't enter," said the *chaousse* who was not called Ahmed [but whose name Cagayous does not bother to note].[22]

Arab women were likewise interchangeably called *fatmas* (and addressed by "Ho, Fatma!") or *mauresques* (and, less frequently, *mouquères*).[23]

Anthropologists argue that "labels of primary potency lose some of their force when they are changed from nouns into adjectives" and that prejudice and stereotypes tend to abate when "we designate ethnic and religious membership. . . with adjectives rather than nouns," thereby adding attributes depicting the subject more truly as an individual.[24] It is precisely this infrequency in the use of the word *arabe* as an adjective (for people) which strikes the reader of Pied Noir sources.[25] It is used, however, to qualify objects, and there usually in a factual ("objective") manner, especially with regard to nouns related to material culture (dress, cooking, furniture, household and marketplace, utensils, etc.). In many cases, however, the attribute "Arab" has an undeniably derogatory connotation: *téléphone arabe* (mouth-to-ear communication), *histoire arabe* (complicated story), *travail arabe* (badly accomplished work), *malle arabe* (enormous, in a jocular sense);[26] and anything *fait à la mode arabe* or *à la mauresque* (diving into the sea, hairdressing, manner of wiping one's nose or washing one's linen) acquires thereby the meaning "inferior, savage, unaesthetic." For the native is not merely the Other, a member of a different and strange society, but also of a backward and dominated society. "Remained Arab" *(resté arabe)* was indeed one of the most damaging notes introduced in the report cards of the Muslim students at the École Normale of Bouzaréah.[27]

The pejorative undertone is even more conspicuous in the colloquial synonyms of "Arabs"—which were of so common a usage (even in the presence of the natives) that they appear matter-of-factly in the press and in popular literature, as well as in glossaries and erudite linguistic treatises.[28] At the beginning of this century the most common among them was *bic*(s) or *bicot*(s),[29] together with *arabicots* and *tronc*(s) or *tronc*(s) *de figuier*.[30] In the years between the wars, and especially after World War II, they were replaced by *ratons, melons, bâtards, nègres, bougnouls*.[31]

The implied attitude toward the Other is brought into sharper focus in another phenomenon, described, somewhat bashfully, in a note appended by A. Lanly, in his *thèse d'état* on "North African French" (1962), to the chapter dealing with the "Encounter Between Arabic and Spoken French":

> Another trait of north African French should, however, be pointed out: the *tutoiement*. It can be attributed, in part, to the Arabic-speakers themselves, since one does not *vouvoie* in Arabic. Those Arabic-speakers who began to use French used *tu* when addressing the Europeans and the latter responded accordingly. It may be said that, prior to the Second World War, *tutoiement* of the natives was the prevailing usage, except in cultured milieux, and perhaps also in government, with regard to important personalities.
>
> The natives, who knew that the French language uses *vous* in polite discourse, came to resent the *tutoiement*, symbolizing the colonizers' superiority. . . and demanded its abolition in the Administration as well as in social life in general. Indeed circulars were issued to all government and public officials prescribing *vouvoiement* of Muslims. In June 1960 the Délégué Général du Gouvernement in Algeria still had to re-invoke these instructions. The colonial *tu* (used in other French colonies or ex-colonies) has thus not disappeared in Algeria.[32]

Written in the very days when the death-knell was ringing for French rule in Algeria, after the anti-*tutoiement* campaigns of Soustelle (1955) and Massu (1957),[33] this note belies the optimism of J. Chevalier, the former Liberal mayor of Algiers, who claimed in 1958 that the "systematic use of *tu* with regard to the natives tends to vanish. Mutual prejudice is fading away." Yet even he had to admit that "a great effort has still to be made in order to introduce courtesy into public manners. There can still be heard on the part of people whose culture leaves much to be desired, impermanent, nay even coarse, words or gestures vis-à-vis the Muslims.[34]

## RIDICULE

The tutoiement, as well as the derogatory epithets and soubriquets, is indeed but the tip of the iceberg, helping us catch a glimpse of a racially hierarchized social structure, where one society (in most cases a minority one) was superimposed upon the other. The "Ho, Ahmed—Bicot—tutoiement" syndrome denotes, in fact, one of the two mechanisms whereby, according to sociological theory, social distance is maintained in such a situation, namely social segregation; the other mechanism being spatial segregation.[35]

Forms of etiquette or ceremonial expression of social roles is a powerful tool geared to the achievement of this aim, confirming our (in this case the Pied Noir's) feeling of superioriy and instilling in the Other (the Muslim) the notion of his inferiority. No wonder that during the heyday of French rule the Algerian Muslim would address the European, either from deference or flattery, as *chef*.[36]

Ridicule is no less effective a method for keeping one's distance from the lower ranks of the social hierarchy. In effect, in Algero-European popular culture the Arab is the eternal laughing-stock. "What is a native for a European?" wrote novelist Mouloud Ferraoun in his diary, "A common labourer, a maidservant, a bizarre creature with ludicrous manners, peculiar customs, an impossible language."[37] And, much as in nineteenth-century France the *patois* of the peasants "was part of their strangeness and ridiculousness" (E. Weber), so in French-ruled Algeria the pidgin French *(sabir)* spoken by the illiterate majority of the natives in their dealings with the Europeans (who did not deign to learn Arabic) was the favorite butt of Pied Noir humorists and chansonniers. The latter used imitations of *sabir* as a standard comic gimmick, particularly in stories poking fun at natives who get into trouble through linguistic misunderstandings.[38]

Following the *feuilles à un sou*, European high-school children used to employ *sabir* to ridicule each other as well as native passers-by.[39] A small but popular literary industry flourished in Algiers and Bône, which specialized in translating French classics *(le Cid,* La Fontaine's fables, etc.) into *sabir*, eliciting laughter and entering in due course into the "Pléiade" of Pied Noir popular culture.[40] Special categories of natives, usually the lowest of the low, would be nicknamed in *sabir: moutchou* (Monsieur) for Mozabite shopkeepers, *porti Madame (Porter? Madame)* for errand boys, and *ciri (cirer?)* for shoe-blacks.[41] The natives (especially the most disinherited) were the frequent target of practical jokes perpetrated by the European urchins and *lycéens*: pranks were played on prostitutes of the Casbah, street-children were teased or sent on imaginary errands, Kabyl oil-vendors had their leather containers pricked, waterdrawers saw their pitchers upset, stones or tomatoes were thrown at *moutchous* and street vendors, crippled beggars were the butt of mischief.[42] A carnivalesque role-reversal, as when Europeans put on Muslim dress ("wrapped up in the *burnous*, or hooded cloak, we looked like real Arabs," "dressed in red like an employee of the *bain maure*"), was considered a comic situation.[43] When the idea of Muslim parliamentary representation was being debated, A. Robinet made Cagayous express his incredulity at such a ludicrous proposition by asking: "Is it true, then, that a man dressed like a *bicot* will be sent as a Deputy to Paris?" And he answered by what he deemed a clinching *trajecto ad absurdum*: "If all it takes to become a grand *mecieu* (monsieur) is to dress up *en arabe*, I'm going to put on a Kabyl or Mozabite costume, go to Paris, and become a street-vendor or *moutchou*."[44]

The second mechanism for maintaining distance between the superior status community and the inferior one, *spatial* (residential) *segregation*, is even more evident in our sources. Practical jokes, it can be noted, took place for the most part in the European marketplace; and it is there in fact that the Muslims (who constituted a minority in all the coastal towns before World War II)[45] engaged in interaction with Europeans.

The Muslim is, as a rule, met there in subservient roles. The checklist is long: *ouled-plaça* (children of the Place du Gouvernement, a combination shoeshine and errand boy), vendors of *beignets* (fritters), *arabes (spondji)*, oil-vendors *(Kebaïlis)*, beggars *(mesquins)*, *moutchous*,[46] all of them dubbed in *pataouète* by names borrowed from Arabic. In addition, there were coal-men, porters (with the *charrette arabe*), pedlars, shoemakers, waterdrawers, fruit and vegetable vendors, etc.[47] As for interaction at the workplace, the dime novels and popular press record less frequent contact, once again limited to the European area of the towns and at the lower range of the occupational ladder: the *chaouch* or *chaousse* (usher)—a job which, as the name indicates, was, in fact, reserved in public administration for the natives, wet-nurse (for the European lower classes), maidservant *(fatma)*.[48]

Indeed, only on the eve of World War I (i.e., towards the end of the period covered by these sources) is it known that Muslims penetrated, at least in Algiers, into the ranks of tramway and railway workers as well as of the *garçons de café*.[49] Muslim vendors and workers thus had to go to the European parts of the coastal towns for their modest trade and low-echelon jobs. Movement in the reverse direction was rare. Europeans, especially of the lower classes, would go to the Muslim sections merely in search of fun: to prostitutes, *médecins arabes* (herbalists, healers, and witch doctors), Kabyl fortune-tellers, or to a *café maure* or Arab restaurant. All these kinds of entertainment—except for the prostitutes—were available even in European areas such as downtown Algiers. Hence the relatively small numbers of those who ventured into the Casbah (usually by night), and the aura of depravity and fascination, that of a *quartier réservé*, which surrounded it in the European imagination.[50] The very name, Casbah—absorbed by the *pataouète* (and later by literary French as well)—is but one of a series of *pataouète* words of Arabic origin designating native sections of cities or parts therof: *médina* and *souk* in the old sections; *derb* or *douar* (as well as the derogatory *village nègre*) for the new shanty towns founded from the inter-war years onwards.[51]

The upshot of all this is, of course, that social interaction was very limited, with residential segregation reinforcing social segregation. Glimpses are caught of Cagayous, Pépète, Papa-Louette, and other folk heroes "playing cards Spanish-style with the Arabs," sipping coffee at the *café maure*, eating *couscous*, *méchoui*, and *loubia* side by side with *bicots* and *arbis*, diving into the sea, in a mixed resort and *à la mauresque*, fishing on the sea rocks near "an Arab that I know a bit."[52] Yet this last sentence is indicative: contact is casual and occasional. No real friendship is created. In a typical episode reported in *La Lanterne* (29 June 1901), ten people are assembled as witnesses to a duel following an exchange of insults between two Europeans: nine of them are Pied Noirs and only one is Arab, whose name is recorded, typically enough, as "Ahmed."[53] Too close a contact was deemed dangerous. When Pépète, the hero of Louis Bertrand's novel about Bab-el-Oued, becomes virtually addicted to playing cards in the Casbah with Kabyl porters, his friends warn him only half-jocosely: "*Cristo*, Pépète, you are soon going to become a real *bicot*."[54] No wonder that ignorance about Arab and Islamic matters was prevalent; it was, of course, easier to feel superior to something little known.

Having the marketplace and the workplace as the sole place of encounter between two residentially segregated communities[55] had yet another result: meeting the Muslim in subaltern roles confirmed, so to speak, the notion of his inferiority, making it a part of the "natural" order of things. Even when after World War I many Muslims moved up the occupational (and, consequently, the socioeconomic) ladder, at most they attained the rank of foreman (i.e., supervisory level) and only rarely managerial level.[56] Linguistic evidence is quite telling on this point: the Muslim foreman was called *caporal* (or *cabo*) in *pataouète* as compared to the (*sergent-*)*chef* for the European manager or boss.[57] As for Maghribi Arab dialects, while they assimilated many words (140 out of 1,665) from the European workplace, almost all of them relate to agriculture, mining, and domestic service, where opportunities for skilled labor were scarce (and where indeed the bulk of the Muslim proletariat was employed).[58] Even more indicative are the Pied Noir colloquial imperatives, borrowed from Arabic and used to address natives: *sir*! (get away!, to beggars, street vendors, shoeblacks, etc.); *chouma* (what a shame!, to servants), *fissa*! (quick!), *jib*! (give me!, to vendors).[59]

The "natural" subaltern role of the Muslims in European eyes is perhaps best perceived in off-the-cuff remarks. Thus, when Cagayous and his fellow-draftees are sent to clean latrines, one of them exclaims: "Why don't they take Arabs to wash these places?" And when going with comrades to attack Jewish shops during the 1898 riots, they are joined by another friend wielding a gigantic bludgeon. "Where did you find it?" asked Cagayous. "If I were you, I would have paid two Arabs to carry it."[60] In another anecdote, Cagayous, separated from his wife, goes to visit their son who is with an Arab wet nurse, and finds out that the latter calls the infant "Youcef" (Arabic for Joseph). "Beware," says a friend who accompanies him, "lest they baptize him *à la mode arabe*. Once arabized, he may prefer to become a shoeblack."[61]

If Algeria is taken as a whole, not only the coastal towns so far analyzed, an even wider range of segregation (spatial and, as a result, social) is found: over nine-tenths of the Muslims lived in the countryside, known as *le pays arabe* (a term which dates back to the early days of French colonization).[62] Once again language here reflects reality and at the same time, by coining it into a linguistic formation, fashions (or bolsters, as the case may be) the mental construction, or vision of the hinterland as native: beginning with *bled* for the whole area (the *colon* is dubbed *blédard* by the European urban dweller) and *tirs* and *hamri* for the soil itself. Elements of the terrain were designated by Arabic terms, such as *djebel* (mountain), *ras* (promontory), *oued* (valley); as were man-made constructions there: *bordj* (fort), *khaïma* (tent), *gourbi* (thatched house), *mechta* (simple stone house), *douar* (hamlet), *foundouk* (inn), etc. As could be expected, a virtually inevitable derogatory meaning came at times to be associated with terms originally borrowed from Arabic in order to denote objective realities: *mentalité de souk* (Muslim-style haggling), *gourbi* for any poor dwelling (compare the racist undertones in *village nègre*, where black means Arab). When Cagayous, for example, is overwhelmed by the great number of Arabs in the Palais de Justice, he yells: "But this is not a *foundouk*!"[63] The identification between countryside and natives necessarily invokes the whole set of essentially negative images associated with the peasantry in French nineteenth-century, urban-dominated perception (savagery, backwardness, etc.); images which at a deeper level may correspond to what Michelet called the "dichotomy history-geography." A recent structuralist-inspired study of French-language Muslim novelists in Algeria also found this very dichotomy "entre deux espaces. . . conflictuels: la Terre et la Cité" as the salient characteristic of this French-language literature.[64] The man-made (and primarily European) city is seen as a creature of history, while the Muslim countryside is still an integral part of nature. Whatever the associations involved, such a dichotomy could only reinforce the cleavage between "hommes et femmes" on the one hand and "arabes" on the other, to use Cagayous's terms.

## THE STEREOTYPES

The "Arabs" or bicots, we have noted, are lumped together; that is to say, they are stereotyped. The stereotype, as an exaggerated (usually negative) belief associated with a category or a human grouping, thus acts as a major justificatory device for prejudice, i.e., "an aversive or hostile attitude toward a person who belongs to that [category or group] simply because he belongs to [it], and is therefore presumed to have the objectionable qualities ascribed to the group."[65]

The composite portrait of the *bicot* in Pied Noir lore is made of five major stereotypes: he is savage, poor, dirty, dishonest, and lascivious.

**Savage**: in the sense of backward, is a stereotype already encountered above, in speaking about *la mode arabe* of doing things. This had nothing exotic or pictureseque about it in Pied Noir eyes; it simply derived from an inferior civilization. "Stupid," "brute," "harking back to the Sahara," "some Bedouin," "fanatics of the forest," "primitive,"[66] are some of the terms in common usage in the popular press. Truly enough, primitivity had its positive traits, especially naïveté; the sympathetic (though still laughable) native innocent is a standard figure in feuilletons.[67] But he is eclipsed by the backward, uncouth, stubborn *(kif-kif bourricot)*[68] and strange *ratons* (rats, i.e., an almost subhuman creature).

The foremost single element in this stereotype of backwardness was language, much as it had been in the nineteenth-century French image of the peasant. Indeed, the term *charabia*, originally designating the patois of Auvergne, was used as a synonym for the pidgin French of *les arabes* (with the pun *charabia-arabe* reinforcing the similitude).[69]

In a typical anecdote, Cagayous and his friends meet a group of black sailors visiting Algiers and remark to their stupefaction that the latter speak English to each other. One of the friends cries indignantly: "Stop all this make-believe! Look at these niggers who came to play Englishmen for us. You had rather *speak Arabic* [emphasis added]. Nobody will believe that fellows blacker than *moutchou* mutton-sellers are English tourists!"[70]

If the *sabir* is at least treated with a mixture of disgust and humor, Arabic is held in utter contempt: "a useless language, difficult, harsh, barbarian."[71] Rare are the characters in Pied Noir folk literature—apart from the Maltese, whose language contains a substantial dose of Arabic—portrayed as able to speak this language. No one betrays the least uneasiness about this fact: Cagayous, Pépète, Embrouillon, and their friends (a good many of whom are of recent Spanish or Italian origin) are so proud of being able to speak French, the language of the masters.[72]

**Poor**: *mesquin* (miserable, beggar) is not the only linguistic evidence for the identification of the native with that creature "more or less dirty, more or less tattered, more or less antipathetic," described by Ferraoun as the prevailing stereotype.[73] Other Arab terms adopted by the *pataouète* might be added: *mesloute* (poor, beggar) and *laouère* (one-eyed, blind beggar) as well as *travaille chômeur* (to be out of work; a literal translation from colloquial Arabic).[74] To "eat the [dry] *pain de dattes* like the Arabs"[75] is a figure of speech denoting the worst stage of destitution. Musette's descriptions of the Algerian scene are full of native invalids and beggars, some of whom are quite sordid (like the "one who creeps on all fours with his arse upwards"), children demanding *bakchiche*, unemployed adults, and stricken children.[76]

**Dirty**: *sale arabe* (later *saligaud*) was one of the most common terms of abuse addressed to Muslims, for indeed dirtiness and poverty (as Ferraoun remarked) go together as stereotypes. Hence also the frequent usage in *pataouète* of Arabic words like *gargaria* (excrement) and *bagali* (filth, rubbish).[77] Here is how a popular satirist and poet depicts "Algiers—Summer Resort"[78]:

> Sordid and stinking Arabs,
> in their native squalor . . .
> infect the streets of Algiers.
> Lice freely rove around,
> in the tram, on benches and elsewhere.
> Some find this picturesque . . .
> for others, it's at least grotesque,
> While I find that disgusting.
> Indeed the town is dirty
> full of rubbish, excrement . . .
> and offensive smells . . . .

Nothing much can be added to this piece of "poetry," only that while Arabs are blamed for squalor all around, the Casbah is most particularly identified with it and even mosques are associated with stench.[79] Small wonder that "in the Arab [or Bedouin] manner" sometimes denotes a penchant for squalour.[80] When individual Arabs are depicted, it is their "dirty burnous" that is highlighted, and the "funny and disgusting" jokes of *Papa-Louette* take as a rule the native (especially the *moutchou*) for hero.[81] *Sale* obviously signifies impurity in the physical sense but has a moral undertone to it, denoting depravity of character, which will be discussed under the last two headings: dishonest and lascivious.

**Dishonest**: In its 19 January 1908 issue, *Papa-Louette* prints the following anecdote about a conversation in the Place du Gouvernement (Algiers) between a "well-dressed gentleman" and a "native porter":

| | |
|---|---|
| *The gentleman:* | Look here! Find me two Arabs who are not thieves to whom I can entrust two bundles of laundry to bring to my house. |
| *The native:* | Such Arabs are not to be found, sir! |

A crude joke, perhaps, yet quite illustrative of Pied Noir humor, peopled by Arab and Kabyl pickpockets, small and big-time thieves, robbers, and the omnipresent *ouled-plaça*, suspected of gaining part of their living out of pilfering.[82] The curse, *grand voleur*!, is reported to have been commonly hurled by European housewives at all kinds of Muslim vendors, particularly the *moutchou*, notorious for his greed.[83] Even during the 1898 riots, when it was the Europeans who were sacking Jewish shops, Cagayous's friends would retort to his reproaches: "We don't steal. An Arab tried to carry away a roll of cloth and some blouses and we stopped him."[84] The burden of the proof is thus on the native, that eternal *sarraqueur* (thief; a *pataouète* word from the Arab root *saraqa*, to steal; hence also *sarraquage*, theft).[85] As one observer rightly noted about Cagayous: "Life is too easy for him to bother to steal; and he is all the more reluctant to do so, as this would mean to resemble the Arabs, that despised race."[86]

The portrait of Arab dishonesty does not stop at that. The native is also a "born liar," a cheat, sly and hypocritical; the main butt of these accuations being those considered by Pied Noirs and Arabs alike as the lowest of the low *(asfal al-sāfilīn)*: Mozabite shopkeepers and the errand boys of the Place du Gouvernement.[87]

**Lascivious**: "It is difficult to find a *mauresque* who is pure and undefiled, at least not in the Casbah." This popular dictum—which could be juxtaposed with the *colon* argument about the "Muslim this sensualist . . . the slave of his primary instincts," whose "sole preoccupation is sex"[88]—sums up this last and probably most tension-laden stereotype. To begin with, the Casbah of Algiers (as well as Muslim sections in other coastal towns) was indeed the *quartier réservé*, the useful function of which could be truly appreciated only in a period when it was out of bounds (especially for soldiers) because of typhus epidemics, and the European press complained that the *filles* *de joie* went into European neighborhoods, bothered respectable citizens, and probably spread "other contagious diseases."[89] As the overwhelming majority of these girls were Muslim,[90] *fatmas, mauresques*, and *mouquères* became more or less synonymous with "prostitutes" (thereby implying a propensity among all Muslim women toward this sinful profession).[91] Hence, also the euphemisms: *faire la noce avec les mauresques, prendre le café avec les mauresques*.[92] Prostitutes were more specifically designated by the Arab words *houris* and *chouarries*, the former a mock-usage of a Koranic term for female creatures of Paradise, the latter, more literal, becoming a common figure of obscene speech among Europeans.[93] *Maison mauresque* likewise became a synonym of *maison de tolérance* and the Arab word, *kif*, which designated pleasure in general, came to stand for this illicit pleasure in particular (as in *faire le kif*).[94] Arab women and old Muslim neighborhoods like the Casbah were thus surrounded by an aura of a somewhat depraved temptation: an attraction all the greater because of the strict code of modesty governing the behavior of the traditionally-minded Spanish and Italian immigrants (at least within their community).[95] A popular weekly printed a *roman feuilleton*—in true Eugène Sue style—entitled "Les Mystères de la Casbah";[96] pornographic postcards featuring all kinds of native women were sold openly, and popular songs and lewd jokes celebrated *chouarries* and *fatmas*.[97]

Nor were these the only attractions. An "enjoyable evening" of European males is depicted as beginning with a massage by a dark-skinned native at the *bain maure*, continuing with a visit to the "museum of little women of the Casbah," and ending with a belly dancers' show.[98] Reminiscences of European adolescence passed in Algiers usually come back to fantasies about "Casbah women." "What fascinated us when coming to stroll there," writes Paul Achard, "was that atmosphere where innocence and debauchery intermingled. . . . We enjoyed being enveloped by the coarse glamor of the shameful streets. . . by the appealing tunes of the guitars. . . by the alluring dresses and make-up of the girls." Any Arab woman passing in the very center of Algiers conjured up in their minds flights of fancy about "Oriental love," which remind one of those entertained by American whites with regard to black female slaves.[99]

The Arab male enjoyed a reputation for complete domination of the female (what Franz Fanon called "the myth of the native woman as slave"). The information available about Islamic laws and customs (easy divorce, low age of marriage, the role of money—*le mariage vente*, polygamy) tended to support this concept and supplied a basis for many a bawdy (and admiring?) story.[100] Moreover, in conformity with his image as savage, the Arab male was presented as hypersexed (physiologically and mentally), "ne pensant qu'à ça," constantly copulating in and out of marriage (and as we shall see elsewhere, out of his community as well), and possessing a powerful sex appeal (not only in the eyes of Muslim women). The super-virile, grossly obsessed, fornicating Arab male is likewise the object of a number of *chansonnettes arabes* in *pataouète*. As with the image of "White [American] over Black," the more swarthy his complexion, the more sexually-driven he was supposed to be.[101] Finally, and rather predictably, Arab terms for sexual organs were most commonly used in curses and oaths.[102]

Heterosexuality did not exhaust the stereotype of the libidinous Arab male. He was reputed to have strong homosexual inclinations and, as such, to be dangerous for young children (especially European). Once again, it was the dark-skinned Mozabite who was the favorite object of more than insinuating jokes, especially about the *batta*, Mozabite children who served at the *moutchou* shops.[103] To round off this picture of depravity, where desire and aversion intertwine, the Arab was associated with commerce in "white slavery" and with hashish smoking.[104]

Broadly speaking, this composite portrait corresponds to the image of the native—an image found to prevail in Saharan Africa, South Africa, or the West Indies (as well as in the anti-bellum United States). The same stereotypes recur: immature, exuberant, impulsive, uninhibited, lazy, fun-loving, or aggressive, oversexed, dirty.[105] The difference from most other colonial situations lies in the size of the colonist group which nourished them.

## IMAGE AND REALITY

These stereotypes are obviously based, to some extent, on colonial realities (especially under the headings of poverty and squalor and even "backwardness" if construed in terms of a lower level of literacy, for example). Yet not only were the grains of truth grossly overblown, but a crucial twist was given to them at the interpretative stage. Thus the wretched situation of the native, which was above all due to the colonization and *cantonnement* policy, was presented as innately characteristic of the backward Muslim: lazy, fatalistic, improvident, impure, etc. An analogous pattern can be detected with regard to sexual mores. Some of the evidence was precise (on divorce, dowry, and low-age marriage), some was slightly exaggerated (polygamy was legal but infrequent), some was decidedly exaggerated (on male sexuality and "white slavery"). But the most salient element, prostitution, while anchored in reality, was curiously distorted. The Casbah was made into a *quartier réservé* for the commercial and hygienic convenience of the Europeans, was managed (in part) by European entrepreneurs, and served a hypocritical European clientele. And, last but not least, nowhere was it mentioned that the "depraved" religion of Islam forbade prostitution and that girls were driven into this profession not because of innate perversion but by the impoverishment resulting from *l'oeuvre colonisatrice*.

According to this view, the stock characteristics of the inferior group being innate, and hence immutable, its present status is not the result of colonization, and it cannot and should not conceivably change in the future. Thus, Arab poverty and destitution are ascribed to backwardness and improvidence; social segregation is supposedly due to discrepancy between "civilized" and "savage" mores; spatial segregation is imperative because the Muslim is dirty, smelly, infectious, and morally depraved; domination (political and otherwise) is necessary because of the native's propensity to revolt or to have recourse to dishonest means, etc.[106] In brief, the colonial *status quo* is almost a "natural order," whereas the Algero-European, according to Governor-General Viollette, "does not concede that the Muslim is a human being equal in essence to himself."[107]

Perhaps the most far reaching implication of such a state of mind is that it engenders insensitivity to suffering and brutalizes human relations. For at the root of the modern colonial dilemma (unlike sixteenth- to eighteenth-century colonialism) lies the fact that it was the offshoot of European societies whose (post-1789) ideals and norms stood in stark contradiction to those of the colonial enterprise. It was thus more imperative than ever to "prove" that the native was a sort of *Untermensch* in order to justify his wretched situation—a situation devoid of liberty and equality and not necessitating any spirit of fraternity on the part of the colonizer.[108] *Colon* children were thus taught that the Arabs, "who are not people like us," do not really suffer from the poverty they live in and from the epidemics which so often attack them; their needs in housing and dress are less, and, on the whole, comparable to those of domestic animals.[109]

Examples of urban Pied Noir insensitivity are legion. Thus the *Papa Louette* satirical weekly proposed in 1909 to reopen the Arab theatre in Algiers, in order to divert from their misery the "famished *bicots*" who were flocking to the town from the drought-stricken countryside and roamed there scratching in the dustbins. The same paper advocated the tearing down of two mosques, those "malodorous" *bâtisses à prier des bicots*, in order to make room for a new boulevard.[110] Paul Achard describes, bemusedly, the tricks played by European children and urchins at the expense of blind beggars, miserable porters, and the like, while Musette's weekly *La Lanterne* has "comic" street invalids as stock characters in its *tchalifettes* (amusing anecdotes).[111] This callous and self-assured attitude also permeates urban catchphrases of *colon* vintage, such as *faire suer le burnous* (or in its more blatant version, *niquer le burnous*), meaning to exploit the natives, or to dispossess (someone) completely.[112]

Colonial domination and its major tool—segregation (both social and spatial)—are thus reinforced by the notion of an "unbridgeable" and "inherent" gap between the superior, fully human group and the inferior, less than fully human one. Ignorance and other barriers to communication between the two groups helped to bolster this superiority complex.[113] The role of ignorance is particularly evident with regard to Islamic culture. Pied Noir notions about Islam were confined to externals (main feasts, prohibitions on wine and pork, and above all, customs and laws related to sex).[114] This very ignorance was not fortuitous, proceeding as it did from the view that nothing much of interest could be learned about the way of thought among that inferior social category, the natives. This basic lack of curiosity may be noted in Cagayous's bemused remarks about tourists, "*ces mecieux* who are so keen on visiting and photographing all kinds of native sites; they insist on viewing the Casbah, each and every ancient gate, each and every old house, nay even each and every donkey."[115] Pied Noir lack of curiosity and ignorance about native spiritual culture are set off by their quite detailed—though instrumentally-motivated—knowledge of native material culture to the extent they interacted with it: food, dress, marketplace, and workplace objects.

The cavalier disregard for the moral foundation of native society accounts for the lack of Pied Noir effort to learn the native tongue. They even declined, out of sheer contempt and apathy, to pick up the smattering of Arabic they could have profitably used. There existed, of course, a feedback relationship here. Disregard breeds ignorance, which in its turn creates further barriers to communication in an already segregated society and so generates further disregard and disdain. Small wonder that *ulémas, muézzins,* and *marabouts* were pejorative terms in *pataouète*, reflecting *colon* prejudice against the traditional elites (which dated back to the days of the 'Abd el-Kader rebellion); mosques were termed lice-ridden; the "Feast of the Immolation" is referred to as "that Feast, if you can call it feast," and disparaging remarks are made about the pilgrims to Mecca.[116] As the Arab proverb has it: "He who does not know you has contempt for you."[117]

## ANXIETY AND PREMONITIONS

Functional analysis runs the risk of presenting a picture which is too static, too stable—in other words, too complacent. The system in question works; it is organically constructed; tensions and contradictions—so far as they exist at all—are absorbed into the system, their edge blunted by compromises and countermechanisms. This danger is all the greater in regard to the 1890-1920 period discussed here, since that was the "false apogee" (to borrow J. Berque's terms) of French rule in Algeria. Never was the Algerian countryside calmer and more secure. The traditional Muslim elites (*caïds*, *marabouts*, etc.) ceased to be the carriers of the banner of *jihād* and became subservient collaborators of the Gouvernement-Général. Modern Algerian nationalism was not even in an embryonic phase. Nevertheless, deep-running crosscurrents of fear and anxiety can be detected in Pied Noir popular culture. We have noted in passing a few such examples—fear of job competition, of homosexual assaults, of contagious diseases—but it may be rewarding to probe this phenomenon a little further.

The sexual domain—the domain of ultimate intimacy—is the one where such anxieties can be most readily discovered (as the last two examples indicate). The subsuming notion is the native danger to the preservation of colonial hierarchy. As students of interracial relations have found out in other case studies, such a hierarchical social structure is not really called into question by contact with prostitutes because of the mercenary character of the relationship, and the fact that the natives involved are women (and of a lowly nature and status at that). Such a contact can even be construed as a case in which male and European domination is reaffirmed. On the other hand marriage—even between a European man and a Muslim woman (hypergamy)—creates a danger of loss of status, due in particular to the narrow socioeconomic gap between poor whites and Muslims; and the danger is multiplied considerably when it is a relationship between a native man and a European woman. The mere existence of an ethnic (or color) line creates, however, not only aversion but also attraction and temptation, rendered all the more troublesome by the inaccessibility of the veiled, house-bound Arab woman and the relative "availability" of the more liberated—yet presumably defenseless—European woman.[118]

This explains the strand of anxiety running through many Pied Noir *tchalèfes* (funny or lewd anecdotes). In one such story, a bantering Spanish maidservant is trying to pull Cagayous's leg: "Your *novia* [fiancèe] has run away with an Arab waterdrawer!"; another anecdote appeared in *La Lanterne* in the form of an advertisement: "Attention please! Ramonette, alias Tonto, diver at the port of [Algiers] . . . wishes to announce to all and sundry and to the banks in particular that he is no longer responsible for the debts that his wife is liable to contract, since she has fled her *domicile conjugal* with an indigenous coalman."[119] The combination of low status (native) male of a lowly profession is of course particularly explosive, subverting a social order based on hierachy and domination (as it was, for instance, in the antebellum American South vis-à-vis the slaves).[120] Sexual aggression on the part of Muslim men is the subject of many tales (e.g., Cagayous's meeting with his future wife for the first time when he rescues her from the attack of "a *bicot* armed with a club"),[121] humorous *chansons* in *sabir* (such as one about an Arab who prides himself on his virility as proved by his conquest of "a girl called Annette"),[122] or anecdotes (for example, an Arab trying to touch European women "inadvertently" during the hurly-burly of a May Day demonstration).[123] "Fruits of Passion" (in Jordan's words) between an Arab male and a Pied Noir woman are quite often the topic of jokes or insults: The "social register" in *La Lanterne* features an advertisement in which a certain Madame Louis, a widow, denies the rumor that she has given birth to twins, one black and one white; and Aunt Tonia of Bab-el-Oued is looked down on by her neighbors for giving birth to a child "whose father is an Arab."[124]

These not-so-funny jokes betray a lot of uneasiness. Without venturing into the slippery ground of psycho-historical analysis, it is evident that it is European domination and superior status which are the issue here. As long as the colonial subject "knows his place," however, such fears—which reveal a vague notion of the frailty of the colonizer's position—can remain latent and be worked out through safety-valves such as the *tchalèfes*. But what if more open and direct challenges to domination begin to materialize? As O. Mannoni has put it in his study of Madagascar:

> What is bad about the [colonial subject] is not his physical traits, his "stupidity," not even his "depraved" instincts. One is proud to possess big monkeys or dangerous beasts. What is unbearable is that the [native] presents himself as a fully-fledged human being and proves to have a will of his own.[125]

In the quarter of a century preceding World War I, several pointers in that direction did appear, challenging, however indirectly, Pied Noir conceit. The most unsettling phenomenon was the mass exodus of landless Muslims from the *bled* into the heavily-European coastal towns (Algiers, Oran, Bône, Philippeville, etc.). Algiers could still be dubbed "a great European city" and the "fourth town of France,"[126] but the proportion of natives, primarily Kabyls, was rising, approaching a quarter of the population, concentrated in the already overpopulated Casbah. The overall European urban population was beginning to be overtaken by Muslim town dwellers: at the end of World War I, the respective numbers were 600,000 to 500,000; exact parity (708,000 each) was achieved by 1936.[127] The idea of "Ici, la France" was further challenged by the alarming statistics propagated by publicists concerning the all-Algerian "demographic problem": European immigration was coming to a standstill by the turn of the century, the birthrate of the progressively-Frenchified Spanish and Italian immigrants was falling, while the growth rate of the natives (a combination of the high traditional birthrate and the progress of hygiene) was beginning to soar. In the whole country, the proportion was 700,000 Europeans compared to 5,000,000 Muslims (a ratio of 1:7) by the end of World War I.[128] Numerical ratios, it is well-known, have a virtually magic ring in multiethnic societies, closely linked to perceptions of the security of (or challenge to) the dominating race.[129]

Qualitative indicators generated analogous feelings of malaise. The early twentieth century saw the rise of the first generation of Muslim *évolués*, a new and modernized elite, the product of French high schools, Écoles Normales, and (to a lesser extent) universities; completely assimilated, vying for mid-echelon (and soon upper-echelon) posts and thus tilting the "ethnic [or racial] line" in a dangerous manner.[130]

Socioeconomic status and ethnic origin were becoming much less congruous than in the past. Moreover, the assimilated *évolués* raised a whole new series of demands, seeking to achieve the *fusion des races* and *droit de cité* of nineteenth-century colonialist ideology now fallen into disuse in Algeria, and to some extent in metropolitan France as well. The major demands were the extension of French education to Muslims, voting powers (municipal, departmental, and ultimately parliamentary), equality in military service. Disquieting shadows began to gather over the complacent horizon of the Pied Noirs.

The alarm and virulence of their reaction are readily perceived, particularly in the recurring sexual symbolism in which it was embodied (even when the matter in hand could hardly relate to that domain of the most sensitive taboos). Thus the hordes of "frightening and starving natives," Kabyl beggars, ruffians, and *yaouleds* (street-children) flowing into the towns, quite plausibly account for the growing preoccupation with the poverty of the natives;[131] yet it is only by a leap of the Pied Noir imagination that the swarming Kabyl peddlers could be considered potential sexual aggressors or the protagonists of those jokes told about European housewives who supposedly succumbed to their "charms."[132]

The "fusion of races" with the growing Muslim population became an unsettling prospect. Hence, fusion was presented, in a mock-lecture "delivered" by a pompous *évolué* to a naive *yaouled*, as the fusion of libidinous Muslim men and coveted European women; universal franchise for the Muslims without renunciation of "Koranic" personal status (based on the *sharīʿa*) was termed a legitimization of polygamy; and granting French education to Muslim girls "was bound to lead them to prostitution."[133] If the native was so depraved, it followed that equality superseding domination would inevitably corrupt the Pied Noir society, morally and, above all, sexually. A chansonnette about the *fusion des races* describes with a wealth of disgusting details "proud [Spanish] hidalgos, bantering Neapolitans, squinting Arabs, and stinking Mozabites" licking ice cream from the same cup, indulging in all kinds of promiscuity, with the result that, "once the Arabs intermingle with the Europeans, all the inhabitants of Algeria will contract syphilis."[134]

Blatant incongruity of status—or the perceived danger thereof—was bound to breed strong status anxiety. Anxiety was violently expressed, as in the rage of Cagayous's mother-in-law against the *chaouch* who gives her orders, or in the hero's exasperation ("this is not a *foundouk*!") at finding the Palais de Justice, symbol of French rule, teeming with Muslim litigants and clerks and his evident relief when a "French judge" passes by and "rescues" him. Perhaps Cagayous is not all that sure of his inherent superiority; after all he ruefully observes time and time again: "*les bicots sont plus louettes* [clever] *que nous autres*." Small wonder that he uses this argument *inter alia* in order to explain why one "should not proceed with the assimilation of the natives."[135]

The most sensitive topic (i.e., Pied Noir privilege) relating to assimilation was, of course, the franchise. In the story quoted above, *The Muslim Deputy*, Cagayous expresses his disbelief in the mere possibility of such an incongruity of status: a man "dressed like a *bicot*" coming to sit at the Holy of Holies, the French Parliament, repository of sovereignty and domination. The alleged "absurdity" of that haunting spectre pushes him to a flight of fantasy, with the inevitable erotic undertones: our hero declares that he too will dress "like a *bicot*, go to Paris, become a Kabyl peddler and so amass a fortune playing dirty tricks on those poor slobs, the Parisians," who are so easy to manipulate that "a squalid waterdrawer, that we here would never touch with a thirty-foot pole, is the coveted attraction for the rich women [of Paris], those silly geese, who vie with each other in bringing him to their homes . . . "[136]

The educational and professional implications of assimilation were likewise beginning to be perceived in the persons of the *évolués*, those "loquacious natives" with their much ridiculed "doctoral tone." Their manner of speech was all the more infuriating as their impeccable French had nothing to do with the *sabir* and shamed the *pataouète*, the supposed symbol of superior Pied Noir culture.[137] If, at the working-class level, competition for mid-echelon jobs was barely appearing (among dockers, tramway drivers, railwaymen, etc.), those professions where Muslims had already made their entry at that level witnessed a degree of conflict. The attitude of European medical orderlies and judges' clerks has already been noted, and added to it was the blatant antagonism between future European schoolteachers and their fellow Muslim comrades at the (segregated) École Normale of Bourzaréah: racist insults and practical jokes, refusal of contact in sport and at parties, etc.;[138] all these were surefire mechanisms to work out status anxieties. For it was not their jobs that those Muslims, designed for a separate educational system, were liable to take from them but their superiority of culture and status as propagators of the *mission civilisatrice*. In blue-collar work, ethnic problems were bound to be worse, inasmuch as jobs were more mixed. The railwaymen, for example, despite their left-wing tendencies, wrote in their newspaper:

> The native belongs to an inferior race . . . and cannot raise himself through his own efforts to the level of the European. . . . The native is a cheat, dirty, thieving, sly, ungrateful. To do him good is like giving jam to pigs. To injure him is to teach him to become submissive and civilized.[139]

The Army presented yet another threat to the hierarchy: the despised Muslim was granted arms, a measure of status and power over European civilians (in some situations), or, as an NCO, over European soldiers. As early as 1898, the anti-Jewish rioters expressed their stupefaction at having their demonstrations dispersed—pinnacle of humiliation—by the *turcos*, the Muslim fusiliers; forced to obey the latter, they took revenge by ridiculing their *sabir*.[140] If the Muslims are given arms, it was argued, they might revolt or, alternatively but not very logically, they might become French citizens and voters.[141] Once again, the almost ineluctable note of sexual jealousy crept in: during World War I, Pied Noir soldiers in military hospitals would protest at the "excessive solicitude" shown by the "naive" French nurses toward wounded Muslim fellow-soldiers.[142]

The ultimate nightmare, native insurrection, is barely evoked in the popular culture bred by the secure urban setting of pre-World War II Algeria. Cagayous even mocked the isolated *colons* of the countryside with their ever-present musket and deep sense of physical insecurity.[143] City dwellers like Albert Crémieux, a former trade union activist who conjured up this spectre, were rare indeed. In his novel, *Le Grand Soir*, he depicts a Muslim uprising in Algiers in which "all the hatred accumulated for over a century explodes in terrible savagery and vandalism." Fanatic Arab mobs run amok, setting the town on fire, massacring the Europeans, and pillaging their houses, before being crushed and massacred in their turn by French troops.[144]

This was in 1929, a year before the centenary celebration, the apotheosis of French colonialism. Colonial conceit and complacency were still, on the whole, maintained. It was only with the Muslim jacquerie of May 1945 that the simmering anxieties and nightmares erupted in full violence.

## NOTES

1. The first *feuilletons*, later to be assembled in *Pochades Algériennes* (Algiers, 1895), appeared in the weekly *Le Turco* in 1891-92 (according to the author's letter to *Papa-Loueete*, 4 April 1909). The last publication is *Cagayous Poilu* (Algiers, 1920).
2. G. Audisio, Introduction to *Cagayous: ses Meilleures Histoires* (Paris, 1931), 8. (This includes a very useful section on the language of Cagayous.) On Musette and his work, ibid., 8; P. Mille, "Quand Panurge Resuscita" in *Cahiers de la Quinzaine* IX/16 (30 June 1908), 146-56; idem, "L'Illustre Cagayous" in *Nouvelles Littéraires*, 19 April 1930, 68-72; and A. Dupuy, "Les Enfances de Cagayous" in *Journal des Instituteurs de l'Afrique de Nord* (1947), No. 5, 66-7, 79.
3. In addition to the collections mentioned in notes 1 and 2, the major Cagayous books (all published in Algiers) are: *Les Amours de Cagayous* (1896); *Cagayous Antijuif* (1898); *La Sortie de Barberousse* (1898); *Cagayous à la Caserne* (1899); *Cagayous à l'Exposition; La Lanterne de Cagayous* (newspaper, June-September 1901); *Cagayous Partout* (1905); *Cagayous au Miracle* (1905); *Cagayous à la Fête* (1905); *Cagayous à la Course* (1905); *Cagayous Philosophe* (1906); *Le Mariage de l'Aviateur* (1906); *Le Divorce de Cagayous* (1906); *Coups de Tête* (1907); *Cagayous Aviateur* (1909); *Cagayous Chauffeur* (1909): to which should be added occasional *feuilletons* in *La Dépêche Algérienne, Les Nouvelles, L'Illustration Algérienne.*

   For data on distribution and sales, see the P. Mille articles as well as indications interspersed in the numerous collections of brochures (especially *Les Amours de Cagayous*) and in *Papa-Louette*, 3 July 1909. According to Audisio (Introduction, 15), one such brochure sold 12,000 copies on one day.
4. *Le Mariage de Cagayous* (second ed., 1924, third ed., 1949); *Les Amours de Cagayous* (second ed., 1949); *Cagayous à la Caserne* (second ed., 1950); *Cagayous à la Mer* (anthology of earlier pieces) (1952): The 1949-52 editions were part of *Les Oeuvres de Cagayous* published by Baconnier, Algiers (in the *Méditerranée Vivante* series). On the Audisio anthology, see note 2.
5. Introduction (signed: Fly) to *Les Amours de Cagayous*, 16-7; *Le Mariage de Cagayous* (1906), fasc. 1, 4.
6. P. Achard, *Salaouetches* (second ed., Paris 1972), 239. Audisio, Introduction to op. cit., 8 (note 1).
7. E.F. Gautier, *Un Siècle de Colonisation* (Paris 1930), 113-22. Audisio, op. cit., 14.
8. J. Pomier, "Situation de Cagayous Type Populaire Algerois" in *Afrique* (January 1954), 7-15.
9. The series *Et Alors? Et Oilà,* published by Ed. Balland, is directed by the well-known journalist R. Bacri of *Le Canard Enchaîné* fame, himself the author of a

book of childhood memoirs bearing the name of the series and a *pataouète* tongue-in-cheek dictionary, *Le Roro de Bab el-Oued* (Paris, 1969). Other books published are the Audisio anthology and works by E. Brua and P. Achard. For plays, cf., e.g., A.-P. Lentin, "Le Cid, Pataouète et Rapatrié," *Jeune Afrique,* 23 March 1964.

10. Audisio, Introduction, op. cit., 8; Gautier, op. cit., 121.
11. This weekly appeared for eight consecutive years (1906-14) and had a circulation of around 12,000. Other weeklies perused were: *Le Cochon, La Cravache, Le Diable à Quatre, Le Cocu Algérien* (all from the years 1898-1912).
12. The most comprehensive study is A. Lanly, *Le Français de l'Afrique du Nord* (Paris, 1962). See also idem, "Notes sur le Français de l'Afrique du Nord" in *Le Français Moderne,* July 1955, 197-211; P. Pérégo, "Quelques remarques à propos du français parlé en Algérie" in *La Pensée* (1955), 90-959; G. Audisio, "Essai sur le Langage de Cagayous" in op. cit., 17-40; Audisio, "Lexique" in ibid., 251-65; A. Dupuy, "Le Français d'Afrique du Nord" in *Vie et Language, 94* (1960), 2-11; *Révolution Africaine* No. 110, 6 March 1965 (article signed A.M.); ibid., No. 111, 13 March 1965 (signed M. Bourboune). On a comparative basis see for the Algerian Muslims: L. Brunot, "Sabirs" in *Journal des Instituteurs d'Afrique du Nord* (April 1948); M. Hadj Sadok "Dialects Arabes et Francisation Linguistique en Algérie," in *Annales de l'Institut d'Études Orientales* (Algiers 1955), 61-97. Cf., E. Weber, *Peasants into Frenchmen* (Stanford, 1976), Chapter 6.
13. E. Brua, *Fables Bônoises* (Algiers, 1938); idem, *La Parodie du Cid* (Algiers, 1941); idem, *Les Fables de Kaddour* (Paris, 1972); A. Dupuy, *Fables en Sabir* (Algiers, 1947); R. Bacri, *Le Roro; Les Sabirs de Kaddour ben Nitram* (Tunis, 1952).
14. L. Bertrand, *Pépète le Bien Aimé* (Paris, 1904, second ed., renamed *Pèpéte et Balthazar,* Paris, 1920); J. Pelegri, *Les Oliviers de la Justice* (Paris, 1958); H. Kréa, *Djamal* (Paris, 1961); L. Lecoq, *Pascalouète l'Algérien* (Paris, 1934); F. Duchêne, *Mouna, Cachir et Couscous* (Paris, 1930); L. Favre, *Bab el-Oued* (Paris, 1946); idem, *Dans la Casbah* (Paris, 1937); A. Memmi, ed., *Anthologie des Écrivains Français du Maghreb* (Paris, 1964). Works by R. Randau and J. Pomier are not cited here because they were too vehemently addicted to "Algerianist-Latinist" propaganda. For memoirs, see H. Klein, *Feuillets d'El-Djézaîr* (Algiers, 1921); Achard, op. cit.; R. Bacri, *Et Alors? Et Oilà!* (1968); cf. M. Baroli, *La Vie Quotidienne des Français de l'Algérie (1830-1914)* (Paris, 1967).
15. E. Ayer, *Motor Flight Through Algeria* (New York, 1913); M.D. Stott, *The Real Algeria* (London, 1914).
16. Particularly useful were W.D. Jordan, *White Over Black: American Attitudes Toward the Negro (1550-1812)* (Chapel Hill, 1968); G.S. Allport, *The Nature of Prejudice* (Boston, 1954); O. Mannoni, *Psychologie de la Colonisation* (Paris, 1950); P.H. Maucorps and others, *Les Français et le Racisme* (Paris, 1965); P. Van den Berghe, *Racism and Ethnicity* (New York, 1970); M. Banton, *Race Relations* (New York, 1967). Many insights can also be gained from T. Zeldin, *France (1848-1945),* 2 vols. (Oxford, 1973, 1977).
17. *Le Divorce de Cagayous,* 34; cf. J. Roy in *L'Express,* 29 September 1960 (memories of childhood).
18. Kabyls are sometimes mentioned as a subcategory of "*les arabes*" or "*les indigènes*." *Papa-Louette,* 21 May 1911, 1 August 1914; Achard, op. cit., 75; *La Lanterne de Cagayous,* No. 1, 16; ibid., No. 11, 9; No. 13, 7; *Le Mariage de Cagayous,* 147; *Cagayous: ses Meuilleures Histoires,* 95.
19. Quoted by Ch.-R. Ageron, *Les Algériens Musulmans et la France* (Paris, 1968), 52, cf. 47ff., 576-7; 874ff, 990-7.

20. E.g., *Le Mariage de Cagayous,* 15; *La Lanterne de Cagayous,* No. 3, 12, 15; No. 6, 12; No. 11, 9; *Le Divorce,* 8, 174. Achard, op. cit., 82, 91; *Cagayous Antijuif,* 134; *Cagayous à la Caserne* (second ed.), 20, 89, 106. Achard, op. cit (second ed.), 244. *Papa-Louette,* 4 and 11 August 1907; 15 November 1908; 13 December 1908; 30 October 1910.
21. *La Lanterne de Cagayous,* No. 2, 9; Achard, op. cit. (second ed.), 9, 39, 78, 87, 246, 280; Lanly, op. cit., 51. P. Nora, op. cit., 128; Brua, *Fables,* 45.
22. *Le Divorce de Cagayous,* 31, "Moutchou" is pidgin Arabic used in a pejorative sense (v. Audisio, "Lexique," 260).
23. *Cagayous: ses Meilleures Histoires,* 52; *Cagayous Antijuif,* 157, 159; *Papa-Louette,* 4 and 18 August 1907; 24 November 1907; 14 March 1909; 1 and 24 October 1909; 19 March 1911. Achard, op. cit., 86; Bacri, *Et Alors? Et Oilà!,* 45; Bacri, *Roro,* 13, 78, 84; Lanly, op. cit., 42 (note 5).
24. Allport, op. cit., 1955, 181.
25. But note "*l'arabe chaousse*" mentioned above, "le médecin arabe," *La Lanterne de Cagayous,* No. 10, 8; No. 13, 15).
26. Lanly, op. cit., 52-3. Bacri, op. cit., 127; Lentin, op. cit., 39. See in *colon* press; *Dépêche Algérienne,* 9 May 1924 (letter from Algiers' voters). For similar use of the adjective "African" in Sub-Saharan Africa, see Banton, op. cit., 253; *Le Divorce de Cagayous,* 197; *Cagayous: ses Meilleures Histoires,* 68 (note 5); *Cagayous à la Caserne* (second ed.), 20, 89, 125; *Les Amours de Cagayous,* 29, 71.
27. See the study of these report cards (dating from the turn of the century and preserved in the school's archives) in F. Colonna, *Instituteurs Algériens (1883-1939),* 163, 165, 172.
28. See the glossaries appended to *Cagayous: ses Meilleures Histoires,* and Brua, *Fables;* cf. Lanly, op. cit., 51, 52.
29. For the origins of this term—a diminutive of *arab(icots)*—Lanly, 51 (note 5); cf. *Cagayous Antijuif,* 143; *Le Divorce de Cagayous,* 175. *Cagayous à la Caserne* (second ed.), 150; *La Lanterne de Cagayous,* No. 3, 12; No. 6, 5, 8; *Papa Louette,* 25 October 1908; 15 November 1908; Brua, *Fables,* 39-40; Bertrand, *Pépète et Balthazar,* 155, 282; Achard, op. cit., 38. For use by *colon* press see *Dépêche Algérienne,* 5 November 1907. For use by Muslim notables (protesting against their inferior status) v. Ageron, op. cit., 1,089.
30. *Papa-Louette,* 24 November 1907; 5 August 1910, 2 October 1910, 1 November 1910, 21 December 1912, 9 August 1913; Brua, op. cit., 40, 57; J. Roy in *L'Express,* 29 September 1960 (on usage by *colons* in the countryside); Achard, op. cit. 63, 83.
31. Brua, op. cit., 40, 44; Colonna, op. cit., 177; J. Roy, *La Guerre d'Algérie* (Paris 1960), passim; Lanly, op. cit., 177. The term *bougnoul* (fritter), which is of military origin, was used in a derogatory sense to designate the natives in Indo-China and West Africa.
32. Ibid., 217 (note 1).
33. J. Soustelle, *Aimée et Souffrante Algérie* (Paris, 1956); J. Massu, *La Vraie Bataille d'Alger* (Paris, 1971).
34. *Nous, Algériens* (Paris, 1958), 54. For his own campaign against "abusive terminologies" see the Manifesto of the Intergroupe des Libéraux, which he founded (May 1951), reproduced ibid., 109.
35. Cf. Van den Berghe, 42-6.
36. Lanly, op. cit., 192. Cf. the South African "baas."
37. *Journal (1955-62)*, Paris, 1962, p. 45.
38. Weber, op. cit., 87; *Le Diable à Quatre,* passim; *Papa-Louette* 27 January 1907; 18 September 1907; 1 September 1907; 22 March 1908; 13 December 1908; 11 July

1909; 16 and 23 October 1910; 13 May 1913; 11 October 1913; 1 and 8 November 1913; 1 August 1914; *Cagayous Antijuif,* 71; Achard, op. cit., 228. On the *sabir,* see article by Brunot (note 12).

39. Achard, op. cit., 16, 27, 33, 71, 90, 163, 240, 248. On pidgin in other colonial situations, v. A. Burgess in *The Times Literary Supplement* 25 November 1977.
40. See Brua, whose *La Parodie du Cid* and *Les Fables de Kaddour* (supra note 9) were republished by Balland as a Pied Noir classic. Cf. *Fables en Sabir* (Algiers, n.d., but before 1954); *Les Sabirs de Kaddour ben Nitram* (Tunis, 1952).
41. Audisio, "Lexique," 260; Achard, op. cit., 248; *Papa-Louette,* 11 July 1909. The *Moutchou* is a recurrent comic figure in Pied Noir lore; see, e.g., *Le Mariage de Cagayous,* 180; Achard, 131, *Papa-Louette,* 1 September 1907. *Le Divorce de Cagayous,* 18, 134.
42. *Cagayous Antijuif,* 157-61; *La Lanterne de Cagayous,* No. 6, 4-5; No. 14, 11; *Cagayous: ses Meilleures Histoires,* 79, 81, 95; Achard, op. cit., 9; idem, *L'homme de la mer* (Paris, 1931), 107; *Cagayous au Miracle,* 3; *Cagayous à la Caserne,* 92.
43. *Le Divorce de Cagayous,* 59, 66, 72; *Le Mariage de Cagayous,* 171. *Les Amours de Cagayous* (second ed.), 129; Dupuy "Les Enfances de Cagayous," 67. Cf. N. Zemon-Davies, *Society and Culture in Early Modern France* (Stanford, 1975) on sexual role-reversal.
44. *Cagayous Antijuif,* 143-4. The *pataouète* term *mecieu* usually designated metropolitan Frenchmen.
45. A. Nouschi, "Le sens de quelques chiffres: Croissance urbaine et vie politique en Algerie (1926-1936)," in *Études Maghrébines, Mélanges Ch.-A. Julien* (Paris, 1964), 199ff.
46. Duchêne, *Mouna, Cachir et Coucous,* 202-09; Achard, *Salaouètches* (second ed.), 26, 248; Hadj-Sadok, art. cit., 91 (on the term *Wlad el-Blasa,* reborrowed by North African French from the *pataouète*); *Papa-Louette,* 11 July 1909; *Le Mariage de Cagayous,* 118; *Cagayous Antijuif,* 145; *Cagayous à la Fête,* 15; Lanly, op. cit., 72-3.
47. *La Lanterne de Cagayous,* No. 2, 15, No. 3, 15, No. 6, 12, No. 11, 8-9, No. 13, 5; *Le Mariage de Cagayous,* 118; *Le Divorce de Cagayous,* 134, 171; Lucas and Vatin, op. cit., Audisio, "Lexique," 260; *Papa-Louette,* 25 October 1908; *Papa-Louette,* 21 May 1911.
48. *Le Divorce de Cagayous,* 169, 177; Lanly, op. cit., 72-3, 192 (in the countryside, *chaouch* signifies foreman); Baroli, op. cit., 182. The upper classes and part of the upwardly mobile bourgeoisie continued to employ European girls (of Spanish origin), cf. *Les Amours de Cagayous,* 108-09; *Cagayous à la Caserne,* 44, 110, 143; *La Lanterne de Cagayous,* No. 13, 11.
49. Ageron, op. cit., 849 (and notes 4, 5); Hadj-Sadok, art. cit., 76 (*garçon* in North African Arabic denotes the servant of a European).
50. See *Papa-Louette,* 20 November 1911; *La Lanterne de Cagayous,* No. 10, 8; No. 11, 14, No. 13, 15, No. 14, 9. *Les Amours de Cagayous* (second ed.), 11; *Le Mariage de Cagayous,* 69; *Cagayous au Miracle,* 7, 14; *Cagayous à la Caserne,* 43, 125; Bacri, op. cit., 23-4. On the Casbah, see infra.
51. Lanley, op. cit., 66-8.
52. *Cagayous: ses Meilleures Histoires,* 60, 68, 83; *La Lanterne de Cagayous,* No. 10, 5; *Cagayous Antijuif,* 10; *Le Mariage de Cagayous,* 213. *Papa-Louette,* 30 April 1911; *Cagayous à la Caserne,* 132; *Pépète et Balthazar,* 128, 208, 267, 353.
53. *La Lanterne de Cagayous,* No. 2, 9.
54. *Pépète et Balthazar,* 155.
55. Residential segregation was best described by urban geographers such as: R. Lespès, *Algier, Étude de Géographie et d'Histoire Urbaine* (Paris, 1930); E.F. Gautier, op. cit.; J. Pelletier, *Alger 1955: Essai d'une Géographie Sociale* (Paris, 1959).

56. On the socioeconomic structure of the Muslim and European communities, see A. Nouschi, *Naissance du Nationalisme Algérien* (Paris, 1962), 34-5; S. Amin, *L'Economie du Maghreb* (Paris, 1966), 145-53; R. Barbé, "Classes Sociales en Algérie, 11, in *Économie et Politique*, 62-3, Sept.-Octo 1959; cf. Ferraoun, quoted supra.
57. Lanly, op. cit., 192; Baroli, op. cit., 123.
58. Hadj-Sadok, art. cit., 74. Only six words came from industrial work, cf. ibid., 65.
59. Lanly, op. cit., 90-92. They could be used—but only jocularly—among Europeans.
60. *Cagayous à la Caserne,* 67; *Cagayous Antijuif,* 20.
61. *Le Divorce de Cagayous,* 168-79.
62. Cf., e.g., Ageron, op. cit., 132.
63. Ibid., 814; Lanly, op. cit., 49, 59, 64-70, 71; *Le Divorce de Cagayous,* 34; Duchêne, op. cit., 127. *Douar* was also later employed for "shantytown."
64. Weber, op. cit.; Ch. Bonn, *La Littérature Algérienne de Langue Française* (Ottawa 1974), Part I; Pelegri, op. cit., passim.
65. Allport, op. cit., 191, 7.
66. E.g., *Papa-Louette*, 4 August 1907; 18 August 1907; 8 November 1908; *Cagayous à la Caserne,* 27, 89; *Le Divorce de Cagayous,* 31; Brua, *Fables,* 57; *Demain* (Socialist), 18 September 1920. Pied noir counterterrorism in the 1950s resorted to the same cliché: a menacing postcard sent to an FLN agent calls him "*ancien sauvage du bled arabe*" (J. Coersten, *The Red Hand* [London, 1962]). Cf. R.-J. Clot, *Empreintes dans le sable* (Paris, 1950), 21-5.
67. *Papa-Louette,* 13 December 1908; 21 December 1912; 13 October 1913; 1 November 1913; 8 November 1913.
68. E.g., ibid., 27 January 1907, cf. Weber, op. cit., ch. 6.
69. Lanly, op. cit., 56; *Cagayous Antijuif,* 144.
70. Musette, "Cagayous Indigne," in *Les Nouvelles* quoted in *Papa-Louette,* 29 September 1907.
71. Hadj-Sadok, art. cit., 65, 67.
72. *Papa-Louette,* 9 May 1914; *Cagayous Antijuif,* 159; *Cagayous à la Course,* 12, 16; *Cagayous: ses Meilleures Histoires,* 118, 125; *La Lanterne de Cagayous,* No. 13, 4; *Le Divorce de Cagayous,* 34, 87.
73. Loc. cit.
74. Lanly, op. cit., 76, 103, 105, 259; *Papa-Louette,* 20 June 1909; *La Lanterne de Cagayous,* No. 3, 12, 13.
75. Ibid., No. 1, 2.
76. Ibid., No. 1, 15; No. 4, 12; No. 14, 11; *Cagayous au Miracle,* 3; *Cagayous à la Caserne,* 106.
77. Achard, op. cit., 82; *Papa-Louette,* 27 January 1907; 24 January 1909; 22 May 1910; *Cagayous: ses Meilleures Histoires,* 52-3, 95; Audisio, "Lexique," 257, 262. Lanly, op. cit., 107; *Cagayous Antijuif,* 158; P.-H. Maucorps, op. cit., 156 (and note 1).
78. *Papa-Louette,* 29 August 1909.
79. Ibid., 3 June 1909; 30 October 1910; *Cagayous: ses Meilleures Histoires,* 52; *Cagayous Antijuif,* 158-60; cf. Bertrand, *Pépète,* 259.
80. *Cagayous à la Caserne,* 27, 67, 89; *Les Amours de Cagayous,* 71; *Cagayous Antijuif,* 37. On the association of filth with savagery, cf. Weber, op. cit., chap. 1.
81. *Papa-Louette,* 3 November 1907; 24 January 1909; 28 March 1909; 10 May 1913.
82. Cf. ibid., 4 August 1907; 11 July 1909; Brua, *Fables,* 44; *Cagayous à la Caserne,* 150; *La Lanterne de Cagayous,* No. 11, 9.
83. Achard, op. cit., 79, 83, 131, 246; Brua, op. cit., 43.
84. *Cagayous Antijuif,* 40.
85. Achard, op. cit., 78; *Papa-Louette,* 4 August 1907; 23 May 1909; Lanly, op. cit., 105, 119.

86. Audisio, "Introduction," 10.
87. *Papa-Louette,* 2 February 1908; Colonna, op. cit., 246; Achard, op. cit., 27; *Le Mariage de Cagayous,* 118, cf. P.H. Maucorps, op. cit., 156; Ageron, op. cit., 560 (note 4). The *moutchous* were aptly defined as "the Jews of the Arabs" (Achard, *L'Homme de la mer, 107).* Cf. N.A. Stillman, "Muslims and Jews in Morocco," in *The Jerusalem Quarterly 5* (1977), 78.
88. *Papa-Louette,* 14 March 1909; *Le Radical,* 16 February 1896; M. Vivarez, *Transmutations Algériennes* (Algiers, 1891), 20.
89. *Papa-Louette,* 23 July 1909; 10 October 1909; Saadia and Lakhdar, *L'aliénation et la résistance de la famille algérienne* (Lausanne, 1961), 121, 125; Achard, op. cit., 48, 60; "A la Casbah," in *Cagayous Antijuif,* 157ff; Achard, op. cit., 241; Bacri, op. cit., 53-4.
90. Baroli, op. cit., 182; Saadia and Lakhdar, op. cit., 124-5; Achard, op. cit., 59; *Papa-Louette,* 10 October 1909.
91. *Papa-Louette,* 4 August 1907; 7 March 1909; 10 January 1909; 29 August 1909; 24 October 1909; 19 March 1911; 1 August 1914; *Cagayous Antijuif,* 159; *Cagayous à la Caserne,* 136; Achard, op. cit., 232.
92. *La Lanterne de Cagayous,* No. 2, 9; *Cagayous à la Caserne,* 41, 136; *Cagayous à la Fête,* 6; *Cagayous Antijuif,* 51.
93. *La Lanterne de Cagayous,* No. 2, 8, No. 11, 4; *Cagayous Antijuif,* 53; *Le Divorce de Cagayous,* 17; *Cagayous à la Caserne,* 14, 144; *Le Mariage de Cagayous,* 42, 48, 150, 170; *Papa-Louette,* 18 August 1907; 10 October 1909; Lanly, op. cit., 102, 103; Achard, op. cit. 241.
94. Audisio, "Lexique," 258, 264; *La Lanterne de Cagayous,* No. 6, 16, No. 7, 13; *Les Amours de Cagayous,* 143, 146; *Cagayous à la Caserne,* 21. It should be noted that Maghribi dialects absorbed French words like *putana* (putain), *bordîl* (bordel), and *fîzît* (*visite*, medical inspection of prostitutes); cf. Hadj-Sadok, art. cit., 89, 92; *Papa-Louette,* 11 July 1909.
95. Cf., e.g., *Les Amours de Cagayous,* 29, 100, 110, 125; *Le Mariage de Cagayous,* 112; *La Lanterne de Cagayous,* No. 2, 9.
96. *Papa-Louette,* 19 September 1909 to 14 November 1909. Cf. the series of stories, à la Maupassant, about Arab women, ibid., 26 January 1908; 2 and 9 February 1909; and cf. ibid., 18 September 1907.
97. Saadia and Lakhdar, op. cit., 125; *Le Divorce de Cagayous,* 125; *Cagayous Antijuif,* 77; Achard, op. cit., 230-1, 241, *Papa-Louette*, 18 August 1907, 10 January 1909, 9 February 1908, 12 August 1912.
98. Ibid., 25 October 1913. On belly-dancers, cf. also ibid., 23 April 1911. *Cagayous à la Caserne,* 92; Achard, op. cit., 229.
99. Ibid., 48, 60 (Algiers *ca.* 1900); and v. Bacri, op. cit., 23-4 (Algiers *ca.* 1942); cf. Bertrand, *Pépète*, 157-9 (describing Algiers *ca.* 1900); W. D. Jordan, op. cit., 138, 144ff.
100. Van den Berghe, op. cit., 24, 30f.; O. Mannoni, op. cit., 109, 115; Jordan, op. cit., esp. part I: Banton, op. cit., 155, 185.
101. *Papa-Louette,* 4 August 1907, 23 May 1909, 24 October 1909, 5 December 1909; Achard, op. cit., 45-48. Cf. Ageron, op. cit., 45 (note 5); A. Bertrand, *L'Algérie* (Paris 1929), 88; F. Fanon, *An V de la Révolution Algérienne* (Paris, 1959), 53; and the 1871 text of Pomel quoted by Lucas and Vatin, *L'Algérie des Anthropologues* (Paris 1975), 130.
102. *Papa-Louette,* 1 August 1914; "Aventure arabe," 4 August 1907 and March 1909; "Noce Arabe," 23 July 1909; "chansonnette arabe," in ibid., 19 March 1911; ibid., 15 August 1910. On the relationship "Dark = (sexually) Evil," see Jordan, op. cit., 32ff, 143, and cf. the fascination with *Ouled Naïl (Naïlia)*, the dark-skinned Mus-

lim women from the Sahara (*Cagayous à la Caserne,* 92; *Cagayous Antijuif,* 160; Saadia and Lakhdar, op. cit., 121; *Papa-Louette,* 9 February 1908, 12 December 1909).

103. Audisio, "Essai," 27; idem., "Lexique," 258, 263; Lanly, op. cit., 95, 101; Bacri, *Roro,* 42; *Papa-Louette,* 15 October 1908; 1 August 1914.
104. Achard, op. cit., 52, 57; Audisio, op. cit., 258.
105. *La Lanterne de Cagayous,* No. 3, 6-7; Achard, op. cit., 26; Saadia and Lakhdar, op. cit., 121. Cf. E. Morin, *Rumour in Orleans* (New York, 1971).
106. Maucorps, op. cit., 78-102; Banton, op. cit., 270, 315-6, 324; Mannoni, op. cit. 118; Van den Berghe, op. cit., 46; Cf. the examples of *colon* lore in Ageron, op. cit., 47, 556, 576, 760, 968, 972, 1,084.
107. *Journal Officiel, Débats, Sénat* (1935), 347; cf. Hugonnet, *Souvenirs d'un Chef de Bureau Arabe* (Paris 1858), 70.
108. Cf. Van den Berghe, 25, 28. Consciousness of this contradiction was sometimes clearly formulated at the elite's level (e.g., by the Algiers prefect Lutaud, quoted by Ageron, op. cit., 1,000, 1,107).
109. J. Roy's childhood recollections in *L'Express,* 29 September 1962. Cf. Ageron, op. cit., 53, 999.
110. 20 June 1909; 30 October 1910.
111. Achard, op. cit., 11-12; *Cagayous au Miracle,* 3; *La Lanterne de Cagayous,* No. 3, 12, No. 13, 5, No. 14, 11.
112. Lanly, op. cit., 102; Ageron, op. cit., 639; Bacri, *Roro,* 33. *Niquer,* of course, introduces a sexual undertone into the notion of domination.
113. Cf. Allport, op. cit., 226; Mannoni, op. cit., 311.
114. E.g., Achard, op. cit., 84; *La Lanterne de Cagayous,* No. 5, 7; *Le Mariage de Cagayous,* 19; *Cagayous à la Caserne,* 67; *Papa-Louette,* 13 October 1907.
115. *Cagayous á la Fête,* 6, 15.
116. E.g., *Papa-Louette,* 13 October 1907; 15 August 1909; 30 October 1910. *La Lanterne de Cagayous,* No. 3, 12; *Cagayous Antijuif,* 114. Note the derogatory use of *houris.* For *colon* attitudes of M. Kaddache, *La vie politique à Alger (1919-1939)* (Algiers 1970), 92; Ageron, op. cit., chap. 11.
117. Stillman, art. cit., 83.
118. Cf. Mannoni, op. cit., 109 (note 1), 113; Banton, op. cit., 107, 150; cf. Nora, op. cit., 174ff; A.-P. Lentin, *Le dernier Quart d'Heure* (Paris, 1963), 38-39; on Muslim reaction cf. H. Kréa, *Djamal,* 68, 80-81, 88, 111, 115-16.
119. *Les Amours de Cagayous,* 108; *La Lanterne de Cagayous,* No. 2, 15.
120. Jordan, op. cit., 139, 158.
121. *Le Mariage de Cagayous,* 10, 15.
122. *Papa-Louette,* 4 August 1907.
123. *Le Divorce de Cagayous,* 174-5.
124. *La Lanterne de Cagayous,* No. 4, 9; *Le Mariage de Cagayous,* 50, Cf. on mulattoes, Jordan, op. cit., 154ff., 167ff.
125. Mannoni, op. cit., 115; cf. Van den Berghe, op. cit., 24.
126. Gautier, *Un Siècle de Colonisation,* 245; *Bulletin mensuel de l'Afrique Française* (1930), 299.
127. Gautier, *Un Siècle,* 243-54; Nouschi, "Le sens de qqs. chiffres," 200ff.; idem, *Naissance,* 34; Kaddache, op. cit., 127. The preponderance of Kabyls in Algiers explains why no distinction was made in their favor by Pied Noir urban dwellers.
128. Nouschi, *Naissance,* chap. 2; V. Demontès, *Le Peuple Algérien: Essais de Démographie Algérienne* (Algiers, 1906); Gaunier, op. cit., 91-2; R. Lespès, *Pour comprendre l'Algérie* (Algiers, 1937), 31.
129. Jordan, op. cit., 141-3; Allport, op. cit., 227-8.

130. B. Saadallah, "The Rise of the Algerian Elite 1900-1914," in *Journal of Modern African Studies 1* (1967); 1-11; J.-C. Vatin, *L'Algérie Politique: Histoire et Société* (Paris, 1974), 126-36, 144-54.
131. *La Lanterne Algérienne,* 21 July 1989; *Papa-Louette,* 3 June 1909; 20 June 1909; Ageron, op. cit., 576, 808, 849, 885; Kaddache, op. cit., 127.
132. *Papa-Louette,* 1 March 1913; cf. 21 May 1911.
133. Ibid., 13 December 1908; A. Bernard, *L'Algérie* (Paris, 1929), 88; Ageron, op. cit., 535; V. Confer, *France and Algeria* (Syracuse, 1966), 14.
134. *Papa-Louette,* 18 August 1901.
135. *La Lanterne de Cagayous,* No. 3, 7; cf. No. 7, 3.
136. "Le Député musulman" in *Cagayous Antijuif,* 145.
137. Ageron, op. cit., 1,049; *Papa-Louette,* 13 December 1908.
138. See interviews with former students conducted by Colonna, op. cit., 136-9, 144, 177, 190.
139. *Le Cheminot Algerien,* 1 April 1928.
140. *Cagayous Antijuif,* 69-71, 233-4.
141. *Papa-Louette,* 1 November 1908.
142. Soldiers' letters quoted by Ageron, op. cit., 1, 187-88. The same fears were generated by the mobilization of Muslim workers for the military industry in France during these years (ibid., 1,158, note 1).
143. *La Lanterne de Cagayous,* No. 1, 6.
144. A. Crémieux, *Le Grand Soir* (Paris, 1929), 212ff.

# Chapter 7:

# HATING THE JEW AS AN ARAB

IN COLONIAL Algeria, the Jews inhabited the grey zone between the two major communities: on the one hand, natives whose ancestors settled that land long before the Muslim conquest; on the other, others coming from Muslim Spain during the fourteenth the fifteenth centuries. By virtue of the Crémieux Decree (1870), which conferred upon them French citizenship, the Jews were elevated as a group into the "colonizer stratum," but never fully accepted by either community. To the Muslims, they were former second-class subjects, a protected people *(ahl al-Dhimma)*, protected yet inherently inferior for not sharing in the one true faith. To the Pied Noirs, they had the dubious distinction of having greatly contributed to the rise of anti-semitism as a mass movement in France in the early 1880s, thus testifying to the umbilical cord linking the three Algerian *départments* and mainland France. Indeed, the Dreyfus Affair (1897-1902) was one of the first occasions when colonial Algeria actually set the pace, to some extent, for events in metropolitan France, a harbinger of things to come in the 1950s and early 1960s. In 1897-98, the Algerian Jews were the victims of the first pogroms in the history of modern France; four anti-semitic representatives (including Edouard Drumont, the master theoretician of French anti-semitism, author of the immensely popular treatise *La France Juive*) were elected to parliament, and an anti-semitic mayor, Max Régis, was elected in Algiers. Not only was the popular basis of anti-semitism particularly broad in Algeria, but its successes (the boycotting of Jewish stores, the victories at the polls) set an example and accelerated developments in mainland France.[1]

"Anti-semitic feeling lies dormant at the heart of every Frenchman in Algeria," said the anti-semitic socialist, F. Grégoire, even before the Dreyfus Affair. Soon afterwards the French essayist, J. Hess, made the assessment that "nine-tenths of French Algerians have an anti-semitic mentality," an evaluation which was supported by the historian G. Esquer regarding the 1940s. The hero of French popular literature in Algeria, Cagayous, whom we have met above, was defined by his creator as "anti-Jewish from the top of his head to the tips of his toes."[2] It is illuminating to examine this early and widespread phenomenon of modern, popular anti-semitism against its colonial background, not only at the level of statements made by leaders, but primarily at the level of beliefs and opinions, that is, the popular culture of the Pieds Noirs. This may be yet another way of elucidating the dynamics of a colonial situation in an Islamic land. The source material consists of the Cagayous dime novels and of the popular literature in *pataouète* used in the former essay, to which one should add the local anti-semitic press *(La Silhouette, L'Antijuif)* supplemented by the recollections of people who lived in turn-of-the-century Algeria.

The popular mentality of the Pied Noirs regarding foreigners did not focus on the Jews because the foreigner *par excellence* was naturally the Muslim native. It will be useful, therefore, to discuss the popular image of the Jew compared to that of the Muslim. The image of the Muslim was based on five stereotypes: barbaric, impoverished, filthy, dishonest, and lecherous.[3] How did the Jew measure up against these characteristics? And what relation was there between the images and colonial reality? The general resemblance is readily apparent when we encounter the portrait of the Jew as depicted by August Pomel, a member of Parliament from Oran (1871):

> Lying, hypocritical, deceitful, dirty, low. . . always restless, imbued with superstitions, his religious customs have something idolatrous about them, He worships the golden calf. . . . That is how we found the Jews when we conquered Algeria, and that is how most of them have remained to this day.[4]

The resemblance grows stronger, though more complex, when we examine each of the five stereotypes separately.

## THE IMAGE

**Barbaric.** This is how the Jews appeared to the Pied Noirs, primarily because of their language. A popular song from the late nineteenth century mocked the Jews:[5] "They're uneducated, they don't speak French." The anonymous author was exaggerating, but there is no doubt that there was a basis for this accusation. Among themselves, most of the Jews continued to speak a Judaeo-Arabic dialect that sounded to the Pied Noirs—as indeed it was—

like the language of the natives, and hence inferior, despised, and incomprehensible. Part of the advantage enjoyed by the Jews over the Christian tradesmen lay in the fact that they could bargain with the natives, something that greatly annoyed the French. Like the natives, the Jews (except for a few youngsters who had received a French education) spoke *Sabir*, a Mediterranean *lingua franca* based on French, which contained Arabic, Italian, and Spanish words, in their negotiations with the Europeans. The Jewish variant of *Sabir* was less incorrect as regards its morphology and syntax (and even included Hebrew words), but sounded like gibberish to the French; and their accent (such as substituting z for s, *zézaiement*) made it sound even more inferior and ridiculous.[6] Inferior and ridiculous, that is how the popular attitude toward both the Arab-Berber and the Jewish languages can be defined, since regarding something as ridiculous is a status-determining device, particularly when the French culture, where purity of language is a central component, is involved. Thus, the European humorists used a pastiche of the Jewish *Sabir* as a tried and tested routine for bringing a smile to their readers' lips, "reproducing" monologues or dialogues of so-called Jews, while also revealing the speakers' ignorance of the modern world.[7] The Arabic *patois* used by the Jews was regarded as a reflection of their stiff-necked isolation ("Among themselves, the Jews mock the French") or as an expression of their ridiculousness and inferiority. In an advice column for newly-arrived Europeans, a humorous journal ressures them: "Don't be afraid of the chap calling out *hendu harakeh kedimeh el-biheh*. That's just a Jew buying and selling old hides."[8]

Second in importance in this context was the Algerian Jews' adherence to their religion, which in itself constituted a characteristic of cultural backwardness for a population as fundamentally indifferent, if not downright hostile, to religion as were the Pied Noirs. Many Pied Noirs had come to find refuge in the colony as Jacobins and democrats during the monarchic and imperial periods of the nineteenth century, while others had lost all connection with religion as a result of the materialistic ethos which had gained preeminence among the colonists, despite the efforts of the Catholic church to give colonialism a missionary nature as the restoration of Christianity to "the country of Saint Augustine." The continued existence of traditional Jewish schools, of Jewish religious marriage ceremonies (particularly of very young girls), the "barbaric" strangeness of the circumcision ceremony, and so on, were evidence of "the Jews' religious backwardness." This impression was heightened by the fact that many of the Jewish customs (removing their shoes before entering the synagogue, the mode of prayer, wailing at funerals) closely resembled practices of Islam, which was the epitome of "Oriental barbarism" as far as the Europeans were concerned.[9] It is hardly surprising, therefore, that "rabbis" and *marabouts* (Muslim holy men) were expressions denoting derogation and contempt.

Beyond these two features, the barbaric image derived from the fact that the vast majority of Jews during the first years of the French conquest, and to a lesser but still considerable extent later on in the nineteenth century, stubbornly refused to accept many facets of modern culture (in education, preventive medicine, and so forth). Jewish resistance to "the benefits of French civilization" was on the whole weaker than among the Muslims—and was soon to fade away—but the popular image was influenced by the memory of the bitter opposition in the period before 1870, and also by the traditional sector of the Jewish community in the late nineteenth century, and was reinforced by emigration from Morocco and Tunisia. The fact that in their material culture the Jews generally remained quite similar to the Muslims (dishes such as *couscous* and *lubiya*, the dress of women and old people, among others) also played a part in this context. Thus, this stereotype embodied a certain incompatibility between the image of the Jew and the reality, but in contrast to other stereotypes, which follow below, there was an inner inconsistency within it. The barbarism of the Jew was commensurate with that of the barbarian *par excellence*, the native.[10]

**Impoverished**. This stereotype is somewhat more problematic, since it reflects a complex reality. A satirical feuilleton about "The Jews on the Sabbath Day" describes them going one by one to spend their day at the synagogue, "nasally intoning verses from the psalms and the Talmud: first comes the peddler (of local origin), who sells matches and dirty postcards, wearing faded festive garments and shabby, though polished, shoes; after him comes the travelling salesman (of Alsatian origin) of needles and sewing implements, wearing slightly better clothing; then comes the bottle and rag merchant, in more respectable garb, and finally the expensive silk clothes, made up according to the latest fashion, of the wealthy cloth merchant."[11] This is a basically fair description of the Jewish community, many of whose members still lived in abject poverty and depended on charity. Most of the Jews were petty tradespeople and only a small minority, prominent by virtue of its conspicuous consumption and political power, was really wealthy. Thus, the image of the Jew varied from the poor, traditional, culturally-backward Jew, an image very close to that of the Arab *miskīn* (miserable, a word which passed into French as *mesquin*), to that of the wealthy Jew like S. Kanoui, "the Rothschild of Oran," who had considerable clout in his community, particularly on the way it voted at elections. The impoverished Jew, often the Moroccan Jewish immigrant, tends to appear together with associations of barbarism (stereotype 1) or filth (stereotype 3). The economic stereotype, with which we are dealing at present, tends to emphasize the wealthy Jew, the complete opposite of the unfortunate Arab ("supreme pleasure" in *pataouète* is *kif rodchile*, from the Arabic "like Rothschild," and "vast wealth" is *rodchilerie*).[12] The various versions share the assumption that every Jew (and every Jew is "of course" a tradesman) is motivated by greed, whether he is a small merchant or a large one. This characterization is not found with regard to the natives, except for the Mozabite petty traders who came from the borders of the Sahara to the coastal towns. The origin of this similarity is perfectly clear: it stems from the competition between the Jews and the Mozabite, on the one hand, and the Pied Noir tradesmen, on the other, and the fact that the former two (i.e., a large part of the Jewish community, a marginal section of the natives) were engaged in daily buying and selling activities with the Pied Noirs (principally grocery stores and peddlers).

The typical joke about Jews (and also about Mozabites) deals with their money grubbing, which knows no bounds (to not observing Sabbath, to extending beyond the grave and involving small children, and even to selling a member of the family into prostitution, and so on). Thus, one joke concerns a Jew who has been gravely injured in a traffic accident; a priest (who does not know him) offers him the last sacrament, and the Jew says: "What is your last price for the crucifix on your hand?" Another joke tells about a father, Mardochée (Mordechai, a stereotype name for a Jew, like Schloumou, Shlomo), who made his three sons promise to put money in his coffin. When he died his two younger sons each put a thousand franc note in his coffin, while the oldest one took the two notes and replaced them with a crossed cheque for three thousand francs.[13]

The similarity between the Jew and the Mozabite as upwardly mobile elements in a traditional society, which compete with the ruling colonial society, is reflected in Pied Noir proverbs, such as: "Who is a Jew? An Israelite *(Israélite)* who climbs the ladder of success. Who is an Israelite? A Jew who has become wealthy. And who is a Mozabite? A Jew times two."[14] Like the Mozabites who, after all, were not wealthy and were prominent only against the background of the general poverty of the natives, the Jewish petty traders were a nuisance in comparison to the status of their co-religionists in the past, for there is no doubt that the situation of this Jewish intermediate stratum was steadily improving. It was against it that the boycott of Jewish stores was directed in 1897-98, and the antisemitic "Hooligans' Song" had attacked it in these words:

> Get out, Semites
> Get out, dirty Jews
> Sellers of matches,
> And traders in rabbit skins
> Drive the Schloumous out![15]

**Filthy**. This refers primarily to the impoverished Jew, his clothing, and his home, and also to a great extent to the peddler and petty trader, at least in his dress and personal hygiene (an image which recurs in connection with the Mozabite, too, who became the favorite subject of "sick jokes"). Expressions such as "dirty peddler" and "stinking merchant" abound in characterizations of Jews. At least with regard to the poor Jews, as well as to those who had recently immigrated from Tunisia and Morocco, there was certainly a great deal of veracity in this, since in former generations the Jews had stubbornly resisted French-introduced hygiene and medicine. This explains, perhaps, why diseases that were rife among the natives (such as smallpox) were also attributed by the Pied Noirs to the Jews, at least as a relic of the past, which had become a stereotype. The same image recurs in *pataouète*, where the phrase "oursins juifs" denoted inedible black sea-urchins.[16] It happens quite frequently with stereotypes that the generalization is rapidly extended from a small sector to the entire group and from the past to the present. Thus, for example, the Jewish women hurrying to synagogue on the Day of Atonement "totter on their filthy feet," in the eyes of a popular humorist; and in the words of a popular song: "The Jews have dirty faces/They smell of oil and fat."[17] It is not surprising that like *sale arabe* (dirty Arab), *sale juif* (dirty Jew) became a common imprecation. The avowedly anti-semitic press gave the image a demonological extension, supporting the demand to "sweep out Algeria and cleanse it of Jews"; "These descendants of the scapegoat smell of their ancestor. . . . God created the Jews on a day of drunkenness and shame. He fashioned them of dung, vomit, urine, and spit. Then he handed them to Satan, who licked them with enjoyment. Hence the Jew's rottenness of body and soul."[18]

This leads to the fourth stereotype, from physical to moral lack of cleanliness.

**Dishonest.** *Liar, cheat, sly, thief*—these epithets, as in the Arab image, explain how a creature who is inferior by birth and culture can exist and sometimes (like the Mozabite) even compete with the Pied Noirs. Because of the occupations of the Jews, the image focuses on unfair business practices: cheating in weight, price, and quality; setting fire to the premises in order to get insurance money, usury; obtaining money under false pretenses. This image differs from that of the Arab who steals from the colonizer's farm because of the difference in the actual situation (where the Arab is generally a dispossessed tenant farmer), but contributes to the atmosphere of suspicion, which inevitably exists in intergroup relations based on inequality.

It is hardly surprising that an accusation of this kind is raised with particular ferocity in a period of general crisis, as in M. Régis's propaganda of 1897-98 ("An abominable race for whom theft is laudable and work shameful; in their stores you are cheated from the very outset"). Like the jokes about the Jews' avarice, a category of feuilleton developed about the *juif louette* (the wily Jew, an expression in *pataouète*) usually vis-à-vis a recently arrived European (such as a Spaniard), who is the *roulé* (the dupe). Feuilletons of this kind were meant to be both instructive and amusing.[19] A typical satirical song, "le youpin volant" (a play on words: the "flying Jew"—the stealing Jew; the French word *voler* means both to steal and to fly) describes him as always stealing, remorselessly and incessantly, even from corpses and wounded men on the battlefield. Popular jokes tell about a Jewish lad who steals money from his employer by swallowing it, or about a Jew who protests to the judge: "I'm not guilty; a thief and myself are two different things," and the judge replies: "Right, they're two thieves." And the picaresque hero, Cagayous, describes in passing a street scene in Algiers where a vendor of soft drinks is surrounded by Jewish men and women; the Jews snatch his cups and drink, and cheat the vendor, who does not know who has paid and who has not.[20]

**Lecherous.** Sex is one of the most sensitive taboos and is inevitably intertwined with images, as in other areas of intergroup relations; its saliency indicates the intensity of hatred and suspicion.[21] This stereotype is, indeed, quite prominent, although not to the same extent as in the relations between Europeans and Muslims. This is partly because "the oldest profession in the world" was dominated by Muslim women, and the redlight area was usually in the Muslim part of the mixed towns. This virtual identity between prostitution and a certain community was naturally grist for the mill of those who condemned the Muslims for being corrupted. If the Muslim generally appears in popular sex mythology as the inferior sexual partner (except in instances of aggression, such as rape), the Jew—because of the same ambivalence in his status—appears in two situations: as both the inferior (prostitution) and the superior partner (pimps, prostitute's customers, and the like).

Nevertheless, the Jew's heterosexual tendencies are presented as being essentially similar to those of the Muslim, and the same applies in describing perversions of various kinds (e.g., homosexuality, sodomy). The difference is solely one of emphasis: among Muslims it is first and foremost an animal-like sexual lust, among Jews a commensurate (if not greater) craving for money, which reaches such an extent that they are prepared to prostitute their wives and daughters.[22] The same applies to the subject of sexual aggression (which is also an indicator of fear of aggression by another social group). Muslim aggression is animal-like and physical, often involving the threat or use of force, while with Jews it is based on purchasing favors with money (mistresses) or its equivalent (in stores, for example) and only rarely on physical rape. A comedy in three acts published in a satirical journal tells the story of a flighty Christian girl who is seduced by the wealthy banker, Shlomo, until, with the help of her sweetheart, a student called Raoul, they get the better of him and "fix" him.[23] The danger from the inferior social group is, therefore, primarily physical in one case and economic in another, but it is from an inferior group whatever happens. A European prostitute is described in a popular newspaper as giving her favors to all and sundry: "Jews, Arabs, Kabyls and Mozabites, anything was good enough for her"; and another is condemned for sleeping with "Jews and Mozabites."[24]

## THE LOGIC OF THE COLONIAL SYSTEM

Our discussion of the stereotypes thus indicates that the image of the Jew is fundamentally that of a native *(indigène)*, as he was legally until 1870 and culturally still after that (at least among the older generation, in the towns of the hinterland and amongst immigrants from Morocco and Tunisia). He was not merely a native but someone who was regarded prior to the French conquest and also after 1830 as far as the Muslims were concerned, as *asfal al-sāfilīn* (the lowest of the low). Consequently, the Jews were hated because they were classed as Arabs *(indigène–arabe* in colonial terminology) and of the most inferior kind, worse even than the dark-skinned Mozabite. "They are inferior and degraded beneath the burden of Muslim intolerance and despised by the natives to such an extent that women do not bother to wear veils in their presence, since association with them is in any case impossible; they humbly accept insults and shame of every possible kind"—that is how Auguste Pomel described the Jews at the time of the conquest, in the portrait cited above, while another observer noted that basically "the Jew remains a native," and this applied even more to his brethren, the recent immigrants from the neighboring Maghreb countries.[25] Idioms reinforced the image: *Arabes israélites*, and, more clearly, *youdis* (from the Arabic *yahūdī*) were the derogatory terms used by the Pied Noirs for Jews, and they were no less common than their mainland parallels, *youtre* and *youpin*.[26] It is characteristic that when a Pied Noir satirist related a prophecy about the future of the colony which was supposedly made to the first French governor of Algeria, he put the words in the mouth of an "old Jew."[27]

The colonial situation is built on a clear hierarchy of status, with a clear dividing line between the settler, who has the political monopoly and the superior socioeconomic position, and the native. The function of the stereotypes is to justify and reinforce this state of affairs (in the settler's mind and, if he accepts them, also in that of the native). The concomitant residential segregation constitutes a physical parallel to social segregation, allowing for interaction only at public places and primarily for the purpose of essential economic transactions.[28] As long as "the native knows his place" the relations are quite relaxed and paternalistic. As soon as the hierarchy begins to break down, however, a sense of unease and even anxiety is created in the settlers' psyche.[29]

In this respect the Crémieux Decree (1870) constituted an act which broke the hierarchy by granting an entire section of natives full civil rights. In contrast to the *Senatus Consultus* of Napoleon III (1865), which opened the way for natives to receive citizenship on an individual basis while relinquishing their "personal status" (i.e., the right to be judged by Islamic or rabbinical courts), under the Decree Jewish natives were allowed to receive citizenship without even becoming assimilated (i.e., without severing their connection with their "barbaric" religion). The complaint voiced so frequently in Algerian anti-semitism about the electoral strength of the Jews and their influence on the governors and prefects reflects above all the settlers' anxiety at the sight of "voters in turbans," which was a contradiction in terms according to colonial logic. And if this was done for one group, was there not a danger that it would serve as a precedent for the Muslims? The colonists' claim that the Mokrani revolt (1870-71) broke out because of the natives' anger over the Crémieux Decree does not fit the facts, but it contains a grain of colonial logic: the moment the hierarchy is broken in one place the other natives may demand similar rights.[30] The persistance of the myth concerning the link between the Mokrani revolt and the Crémieux Decree is reasonable on the basis of this logic.

Even without this myth, however, there was absolutely no compatibility, as far as the settlers were concerned, between the social position and cultural background of most of the Jews and their new legal status. The ameliorated educational and economic status of some of them only complicated the picture and created the tensions reflected in the first two stereotypes. The political status appeared to give the Jews opportunities they did not "deserve," thereby also hinting at the possibility that the fears and anxieties of the settlers regarding their position vis-à-vis the natives in general would materialize.[31] Moreover, the Jews' ascent on the educational and economic ladder brought them into competition with (or in positions of authority over) the middle and lower strata of the Pied Noir community, who were in any case the most sensitive about their colonial status. This is mirrored by the almost complete disappearance of Jewish maids from Christian homes at the turn of the century and the appearance of Christian maids (generally of Spanish origin) in Jewish homes, the virtually total disappearance of Jewish street urchins and messenger boys *(yaouleds)*, and their replacement by Muslims, the expansion of the stratum of Jewish petty tradesmen and the emergence of Jewish civil servants and members of the free professions.[32]

A change in social status (or at least in the Jew's perception of himself) was inevitable, and hence the complaint often voiced by the Pied Noirs regarding the Jews' arrogance. This was particularly difficult to stomach because it came from creatures "whose forefathers were not considered worthy of even polishing the slippers *(babouches)* of the Muslims" (according to Morinaud, a notable from Constantine).[33] As might have been expected, this complaint was expressed in sexual symbols, mentioning the bold way Jews looked at Pied Noir women,[34] just as the threat of Jewish competition was reflected in the fourth stereotype, which stressed the purchase of favors with money, rape, etc. The typical relationship was almost always one in which the man was Jewish and the woman Pied Noir, namely, where the degradation in status (which is determined by the male) was particularly clear. The danger of education and upward mobility was also expressed in similar symbols; thus, an anti-semitic journal claimed that "under the pretext of becoming civilized," Jewish girls became prostitutes and "reached the pits in cynicism and moral depravity. [They] thus considered themselves French and European and worthy of fitting into our society."[35] (Incidentally, the same argument was used, as if to point out potential dangers, against the education of Muslims.)

## ANTI-SEMITISM AND INTEGRATION

The colonial situation made its mark on Algerian anti-semitism in many other ways too. The colonial society was a multi-ethnic one of immigrants, only half of whom were French and the rest of Spanish, Italian, and Maltese origin. Although the Enfranchisement Law of 1889 had granted automatic citizenship to the children of non-French immigrants, the ethnic differences, which were due primarily to the sense of superiorty of the French, were still so evident at the turn of the century that even the offspring of mixed marriages (predominantly Spanish-French) were not considered to be *français naturels* (genuine French) and were given the nickname *champoreaux* (a mixture of coffee and rum). Ethnic loyalties and rivalries between non-French sections of the population were still quite fierce, both vis-à-vis the French and among themselves, being intensified by separate areas of residence and economic competition (between Spaniards and Italians, for example).[36]

Their common sociopolitical status as colonizers confronting a native Muslim majority, whose presence was always regarded as a sword of Damocles, was undoubtedly an integrative factor; but their coalescence was helped greatly by popular anti-semitism. Hatred of the natives was supplemented by hatred of the Jews as natives who had exceeded their "rightful" position. This formed a common bond among the new, non-French immigrants, principally the Spaniards, who were imbued with a traditional, religious hatred of the Jews and the French, most of whom were not religious. This applied particularly to immigrants who were at the bottom of the occupational scale and were in fierce competition with the Jews.[37] A somewhat ironic description of the *naturalisés* (naturalized citizens) and their attitude to the Jews was given in the dime novels of the Cagayous series eight years after the anti-semitic riots. Cagayous, who is himself the product of a mixed marriage, and his associates, meet a street urchin of Neapolitan origin "who calls out in a mole-like accent, *En bas les tchouifes* [Down with the Jews!]." Cagayous demands "Tell me in what school you learned to speak French like that?" and there is an exchange of insults. In order to prove his Frenchness, the lad declaims the "Anti-Jewish Marseillaise" of the period of the riots, as sung by the Neapolitans (i.e., Italians) in their foreign accent and on the basis of the principle that people are generally blind to their own faults:

| | |
|---|---|
| Sonent batriotes. . . | We are patriots. . . |
| mendja gagouette. . . | We eat peanuts. . . |
| Bevent anisette | And drink anisette. |
| Ah! que ganailles sonent les tchouifes | What scoundrels the Jews are! |
| Mal edouqués | They're uneducated |
| No parlent frantchais. | They don't speak French. . . |
| A bas les tchouifs! | Down with the Jews! |
| La Frantche aux Franchais! | France for the French![38] |

Another popular song was the "Anti-Jewish Marseillaise" of the Bab-el-Oued quarter of Algiers, whose inhabitants were of Spanish, French, and mixed origin, which in 1898 expressed another variation on the theme of integration against the Jews:

| | |
|---|---|
| C'est à Madagascar | To Madagascar |
| Que partent les Youdis. | We'll send the Jews. |
| Là ces sales cafards | The dirty bastards will go there |
| Portent leur viande cachir. | Taking their kosher meat with them. |

| | |
|---|---|
| Le Grand maître Drumont, | Drumont, our great leader |
| Et Max Régis | Together with Max Régis |
| A grands coups de bâton, | Will drive the Jews out |
| Feront partir les youdis. | Beating them with sticks. |
| Débout Français | Onward, Frenchmen! |
| Et vous braves Espagnols, | And you, brave Spaniards! |
| C'est assez subir le joug | We've suffered enough under |
| de Youdis. | the Jewish yoke! |
| | |
| Dans la ville d'Alger, | In the city of Algiers |
| Il n'y a plus qu'un cri | Only one cry is heard |
| Patrie, fraternité | Motherland! Fraternity! |
| A bas les youdis. | Down with the Jews! |
| C'est a Bab-el-Oued, | In Bab-el-Oued |
| Quartier travailleur, | The workers' quarter |
| Dames et fillettes | Women and girls |
| Chantent toutes en choeur. | Sing in chorus. |
| Les hommes, les garçons, | Men and boys |
| Pour acclamer Drumont | Applaud Drumont. |
| Français, Espagnols | Frenchmen and Spaniards |
| Sont d'une gaieté folle. | Are mad with joy.[39] |

Max Régis, who was himself of Italian origin, harped on the same theme in his election poster addressed to "Naturalized voters," (1898) and whose refrain was "You are French and shall remain French!" A third version of the Anti-Jewish Marseillaise addressed "the descendants of Clovis (king of the Franks) and of Charles V."[40] The active role played by the Spaniards and Italians in the riots of 1897-98, which was etched on the collective consciousness of the settlers, and the persistence of their hostility to the Jews in the years that followed (as expressed in the humoristic press), all indicate the power of the integrative motif in colonial anti-semitism.[41]

Our study of this motif has already hinted at another, final aspect of the influence of the colonial situation. The collective identity of the settlers did not only generate negative feelings (toward Jews and Muslims) but also had a positive content which was focused on France. This did not refer solely to the issue of the civil rights of French citizens (as is reflected in the term *citoyens français* as a synonym for settlers). The culture of the settlers was defined as French, hence the pride of Algerian-born Europeans of the first generation (such as Cagayous)—who constituted the majority of the settlers after 1885—in their ability to speak French, the scorn they heaped on the incorrect French of the new immigrants, and their umbrage when mainland Frenchmen were unable to understand their speech and regarded it as *pataouète*, that is, as a barbaric, inferior *patois*.[42]

The historical associations which peppered popular literature referred primarily to French history, particularly post-1789. The influence of the primary schools of the Third Republic, where three-quarters of the European children received their education, is very apparent here.[43] French patriotism and its symbols (the army, the Marseillaise, the presidency) were admired by the mass of settlers, and even the most lowly among them were proud of their ability to enjoy French culture (from food to the opera).[44] Thus, France was the normative reference group of the settlers, as well as the guarantee of their cultural superiority over the natives. Above all, however, France was the political and military guarantor of the continued presence of the Pied Noirs. The governor-general and the prefects, rather than the mayors and the M.P.'s, were regarded as the highest political and social authority; in the popular view the solution for injustices was to apply to the French parliament or the president of the republic. It is hardly surprising that the settlers, most of whom had not set foot in mainland France before World War II, attributed such prestige to a visit to the "motherland."[45]

Even though Algeria was legally an integral part of the mainland, relations with it were not devoid of tensions, largely because of the regional particularism of the settlers, the geographical distance, and the ethnic composition. The *français de France* (mainland Frenchmen) were not only regarded as different but were also given nicknames, such as *francaoui* (Frenchman in Arabic) or *patos* (ducks in Spanish). The tourist and the colonial official, the two kinds of mainland Frenchmen whom the settlers met most often, were objects of scorn because of their ignorance of local customs and their effeminate, "Parisian" characteristics, contrasting with the virile dynamism of the settlers. Pied Noir dynamism was regarded as French regional particularism, an expression as it were of French features that were degenerating on the mainland (risk-taking, creativity, machismo) and which had persisted in an area of frontier-culture.[46]

The network of love-hate relationships of this kind explains not only some of the eagerness of the new immigrants to "become

French," but also, and primarily, the view prevailing in Algerian anti-semitism that the settlers proved themselves as true Frenchmen —and even as superior to the mainland French—by their enthusiastic defense of the Republic against Dreyfus and his ilk. The popular novel *Cagayous the Anti-Jew* clarified this:

> The Jews are always sticking their noses in the affairs of the government. The [mainland] Frenchmen are like ants, continuing quietly with their affairs, without reacting. Meanwhile the Jews utilize the opportunity, invent all kinds of tricks and sow disharmony and strife, wars and distress. If the Algerians [i.e., the Pied Noirs] had not raised their voices in bitter protest in the Dreyfus affair, the mainland Frenchmen would have thought we were all foreign immigrants or French or Italian *champoreaux*. But we hate Jews even more than they do, blood is hotter here than in France![47]

The Dreyfus affair (in which Algeria did, in fact, and for the first time, influence events in France) and even more than that, anti-semitism in general, helped the integration of the colony with the mainland, preserving the sense of being different (and even superior) of the Algerian *départments*. This did not apply to France only. In 1904 a satirical journal wrote that all Europe was becoming degenerate, "and Jewish gold sullies the honor of the motherland." Fortunately, he adds, Algeria had proved itself (in 1898) as being bolder and more courageous than Europe. This motif was also worked into a fourth variation *(l'Antiyoutre)* of the "Anti-Jewish Marseillaise."[48] The European motif was rare, however, and most of the integrative function was directed towards France. "One cry will be heard above all others, and that is Algeria's demand to remain French; Down with the Jews." "All of us, all France, cry: 'Down with the Jews.' " These are typical and recurrent phrases, which also embody a note of criticism of "those (mainland) French who no longer have an iota of masculinity."[49]

The ways of history are strange. In view of the later developments of our century, it is rather ironic that the birth of anti-semitism as a modern mass movement, in a most enlightened Western country, was closely connected with the hatred of Jews as Arabs.

## FOOTNOTES

1. For an up to date discussion of this subject, see *Histoire de l'Algérie Contemporaire (1871-1954)*, Vol. 2, Paris, PUF (1979), pp. 60-6.
2. C. Martin, *Les Israélites algériens de 1930 à 1902,* Paris, 1936, p. 283; J. Hess, *La Vérité*

*sur l'Algérie,* Paris, 1905, p. 227; G. Esquer, *8 novembre 1942,* Algiers, 1945, p. 40; Musette (pseud. A. Robinet), *Cagayous antijuif,* Algiers, 1898, p. 5.

3. *Supra,* pp. 168-72.
4. *Des races indigènes de l'Algérie,* Oran, 1871, p. 73.
5. Quoted in Musette, *Le Divorce de Cagayous,* Algiers, 1906, p. 181.
6. M. Cohen, *Le Parler arabe des juifs d'Alger,* Algiers, 1910; C. Martin, op. cit., p. 60 ff., 244 ff., 286 ff.; H. Chemouilli, *Une diaspora méconnue: les juifs d'Algérie,* Paris, 1976, p. 78. Cf. on Jewish cooking, J. Bahloul, "Le double langage alimentaire des juifs algériens," *Les Annals ESC* 38/2 (1983).
7. For example, *Papa-Louette,* 28 Dec. 1912, 6 Nov. 1910, 19 Dec. 1909, a popular song (from circa 1900) quoted in P. Achard, *Salaouètches,* Second edition, Paris 1972, p. 229 ff.; *L'Antijuif,* 26 Aug. 1897.
8. Musette, *Cagayous Antijuif,* p. 96; *Lanterne de Cagayous* (1901), No. 13, p. 15; ibid., No. 8 ("monologue en juif").
9. *Papa-Louette,* 31 May 1908; 9 March 1911; *Le Cochon,* 27 April 1902; 4 May 1902; *Antijuif,* 26 Aug. 1897; cf. M. Baroli, *La vie quotidienne des français d'Algérie (1830-1914),* Paris, 1967, p. 221 ff; Martin, op. cit., pp. 66, 170; Ageron, op. cit., p. 48; E. Brua, *Fables Bônoises,* Algiers, 1938, p. 51.
10. Cf. Y. Turin, *Affrontements culturels dans l'Algérie coloniale,* Paris, 1971, passim; Martin, op. cit., passim; *Papa-Louette,* 6 Nov. 1910; Achard, op. cit., p. 230; G. Des Illiers, *Les juifs algériens et la question antisemite,* Algiers, 1897, pp. 7-10.
11. *Papa-Louette,* 10 May 1908.
12. *Papa-Louette,* 7 May 1908; 15 Nov. 1908; 15 Aug. 1909; 20 Oct. 1909, Ageron, op. cit, p. 584; Musette, *Les Meilleures histoires de Cagayous,* Paris, 1931, p. 69; *Le Cochon,* 30 March 1902; *Cagayous antijuif,* p. 26; *Laterne de Cagayous* (1901) No. 7, p. 13; *L'Antijuif,* 8 Aug. 1898; Musette, *Les Amours de Cagayous,* Algiers, 1896, p. 92; *Le Divorce de Cagayous,* Algiers, 1906, p. 47; *Cagayous Antijuif,* p. 26.
13. *Papa-Louette,* 30 Oct. 1910; 30 Aug. 1913; 14 Feb. 1914; 18 Aug. 1907; *Le Cochon,* 5 June 1902; 9 March 1902; *L'Antijuif,* 27 Jan 1898; cf. D. Bensimon, "Les Juifs d'Algérie . . . leur évolution socio-economique," *Yod* (I.N.L.C.O.), 1976, pp. 59-81.
14. A. Lanly, *Le Français de l'Afrique du Nord,* Paris, 1962, p. 135 (note 5); *Papa-Louette,* 20 June 1909.
15. *L'Antijuif,* 22 July 1897; 24 Feb. 1898; *Cagayous Antijuif,* p. 121. It is true that the boycott was also directed against Jewish manual workers, low-rank civil servants and servants (*L'Antijuif,* 11 Dec. 1897; 13 Feb. 1898; 24 Feb. 1898), but they were not among the wealthy or upwardly-mobile groups, were not considered important, and were pushed to the side of anti-semitic thinking. Too many nuances would have complicated the necessarily simplistic nature of the prejudice which was the end-product of the stereotypes.
16. Musette, *Le Divorce de Cagayous,* Algiers, 1906, p. 21; *Les Meilleurs histoires de Cagayous,* p. 70; *L'Antijuif,* 10 Feb. 1897; *Le Cochon,* 27 April 1902.
17. *Papa-Louette,* 16 Oct. 1910; *L'Antijuif,* 12 Sept. 1897.
18. La Silhouette, 1 March 1896; anon., *L'Oeuvre des antijuifs d'Alger,* Algiers, 1899, p. 141. Cf. *L'Antijuif,* 8 Aug. 1897.
19. *La Lanterne de Cagayous* (1901), No. 1, p. 9; *Le Télégramme Algérien,* 21 Feb. 1898; Brua, op. cit., p. 52; *Papa-Louette,* 19 Dec. 1909; 14 Feb. 1914; 1 Aug. 1914; *L'Antijuif,* 10 Feb. 1897; 29 Aug. 1897; Des Illiers, op. cit., pp. 10-s, 40; *Le Cochon,* 1 May 1902.
20. *Le Cochon,* 24 April 1902; *Papa-Louette,* 30 Oct. 1910; 3 June 1909; Musette, *Les Meilleurs histoires de Cagayous,* p. 74.
21. Compare O. Mannoni, *Psychologie de la colonisation,* Paris, 1950; W. D. Jordan, *White Over Black: American Attitudes Towards the Negro (1550-1822),* Chapel Hill, 1968; P. Van Berghe, *Racism and Ethnicity,* New York, 1970.

22. *Papa-Louette,* 31 May 1908; 31 June 1909; 13 Oct. 1909; 20 Oct. 1909; *L'Antijuif,* 11 Jan. 1891; 10 Feb. 1897; 26 Aug. 1897; 7 Oct. 1897; *Le Cochon,* 17 Nov. 1901, 24 Nov. 1901; 29 Dec. 1901; 6 June 1902; 22 April 1902; 9 Jan. 1902; 4 May 1902; P. Achard, op. cit., p. 229 ff; *Cagayous antijuif,* p. 96; Hess. op. cit., p. 212 ff., 217, 226 ff.
23. *Papa-Louette,* 15 Aug. 1909.
24. *Le Cochon,* 8 April 1902; 27 March 1902.
25. Pomel, op. cit., p. 74; Des Illiers, op. cit., p. 40; cf. E. F. Gautier, *Un siècle de colonisation,* Paris, 1930, p. 98.
26. Ageron, op. cit., p. 17 (note 5); *L'Oeuvre des antijuifs d'Alger,* p. 141.
27. *Papa-Louette,* 1 Sept. 1908.
28. Cf. Mannoni, op. cit., Van den Berghe, op. cit.; A. Memmi, *Portrait du colonisé,* Paris, 1970.
29. Mannoni, op. cit., p. 115; Van den Berghe, op. cit., p. 24.
30. *Papa-Louette,* 15 Nov. 1908; 28 Feb. 1909; *L'Oeuvre des antijuifs d'Alger,* p. 32 ff.; Martin, op. cit., pp. 110, 124, 146, 150, 157, 259, 264; *L'Antijuif,* 30 Jan. 1898; 24 Feb. 1898; *Le Cochon,* 1 May 1902; *La Lanterne de Cagayous,* No. 1, p. 2. The governor-general, Lépine, was called "Isaac Lepine" during the Dreyfus affair, and even in 1955 Soustelle (a non-Jew), who was not trusted initially by the settlers, was called "Ben-Sousan."
31. On this point see the last part of chapter 6.
32. Musette, *Les Amours de Cagayous,* Algiers, 1896, pp. 101, 108, 123; M. Baroli, op. cit., p. 89 ff.; D. Bensimon, art. cit.; *L'Oeuvre des antijuifs d'Alger,* pp. 32 ff.; Des Illiers, op. cit., pp. 16-17.
33. For example, *La Depêche Algérienne,* 4 Jan. 1898; *Le Télégramme Algérien,* 22 April 1899; for similar reactions by Moslems see: Ch. R. Ageron, "L'émeute antijuive de Constantine (août 1934)," *Revue de l'Occident musulman et de les Méditerranée*, pp. 13-14 (1973), pp. 36-7.
34. For example, *Le Cochon,* 4 May 1902; *Cagayous antijuif,* p. 96.
35. *L'Antijuif,* 7 Oct. 1897.
36. *Les Meilleures histoires de Cagayous,* pp. 57, 118, 125; *La Lanterne de Cagayous,* No. 1, p. 10; No. 4, p. 14; No. 6, p. 4; No. 10, p. 13.
37. See the last chapter of J. B. Vialar, *Emigracion española a Argelia (1830-1900),* Madrid, 1975.
38. *Le Divorce de Cagayous,* pp. 180-1.
39. *L'Oeuvre des antijuifs d'Alger,* p. 141.
40. Ibid., p. 140; *Papa-Louette,* 2 April 1911.
41. Martin, op. cit., p. 270 ff.; *Papa-Louette,* 19 Jan. 1908; 19 Dec. 1909; 12 Aug. 1912; 1 Aug 1914; *Cagayous antijuif,* p. 120.
42. *Le Divorce de Cagayous,* pp. 8, 28-31, 24-35, 180-181; *Papa Louette,* 25 Aug. 1907; 10 Nov. 1907; *Le Mariage de Cagayous,* Second edition, Algiers, 1924, pp. 14, 24, 78, 136; *La Lanterne de Cagayous,* No. 5, pp. 9-10; *Cagayous a la Caserne,* Second edition, Algiers, 1950, pp. 10-11.
43. *Le Mariage de Cagayous,* pp. 29, 45; *Cagayous à la Caserne,* p. 122; *Le Divorce de Cagayous,* pp. 161, 162, 188, 194; *Cagayous à la Caserne,* pp. 66, 72, 111; *Cagayous antijuif,* p. 17; *Les Meilleures histoires de Cagayous,* p. 121; Cf. Lanly, op. cit., p. 323 (note 3); F. Colonna, *Instituteurs algériens, (1983-1939),* Paris, 1975.
44. *Papa-Louette,* 2 April 1911; *Les Meilleures histoires de Cagayous,* pp. 243-9; *La Lanterne de Cagayous*, No. 1, p. 10; No. 2, p. 2; No. 3, p. 5; *Cagayous antijuif*, pp. 16-7, 65, 96; *Cagayous à la Caserne*, p. 44; *Le Mariage de Cagayous*, pp. 84-5.
45. *Les Meilleures histoires de Cagayous*, pp. 68, 88, 117-22, 126; *La Lanterne de Cagayous,* No. 3, pp. 1, 3; *Les Amours de Cagayous*, pp. 34-6, 81, 103; *Papa-Louette,* 5 April 1913; Achard, op. cit., p. 252 ff.; *Cagayous à la Caserne,* p. 146; *Le Mariage de Cagayous,* p. 73; Colonna, op. cit., p. 135; Baroli, op. cit., p. 87.

46. Lanly, op. cit., p. 52; Ageron, op. cit., p. 572 (note 2); *Les meilleures histoires de Cagayous,* p. 78; *Le Mariage de Cagayous*, p. 212; *Cagayous antijuif*, pp. 24-5; *Les Amours de Cagayous*, pp. 38-44, 90-1; *Papa-Louette,* 18 Aug. 1907; 8 Sept. 1907; 15 Aug. 1910; *La Lanterne de Cagayous,* No. 6, p. 7, No. 13, p. 15; Cf. Camus, *Actuels,* vol. 3, p. 140 ff.; E. F. Gautier, *Conférences des Sciences Politiques,* Paris, 1929, p. 220; J. Olivieri, in *Le Monde,* 25 Feb. 1960.
47. *Cagayous antijuif,* pp. 24-5.
48. *Le Cochon,* 18 April 1902.
49. *La Dépêche Algérienne,* 12 Jan. 1899; *Cagayous antijuif,* pp. 17, 97; *Le Cochon,* 28 April 1902.

# Chapter 8:

# SLAVE DEALER MENTALITY AND COMMUNISM

## INITIAL MISUNDERSTANDINGS

In the spring of 1921, a few months after the foundation of the French Communist Party, a confidential poll was conducted among its Algerian federations on their attitudes towards "the native question." Sample answers were:[1] "We should campaign resolutely against nationalist tendencies among the educated minority of the natives and discredit them by all possible means in the eyes of their co-religionists"; "nationalism must be denounced and the indigenous populations must be impressed by [French] force"; "an insurrection of the natives at present, if successful, would have most tragic consequences for the Europeans: the Muslims . . . would not hesitate to massacre all the men and enslave all the women and children"; [such a revolt] "would result in a defeat for socialism and in the regression of civilization." These answers clearly contradict the eighth of the twenty-one conditions of admission to the Communist International, which had been accepted by the majority of French (and Algerian) Socialists in December 1920:

> Every party which wishes to join the Communist International is obliged to . . . support every colonial liberation movement not merely in word but in deed, to demand the expulsion of their own imperialists from these colonies, to inculcate among the workers of their own country a genuinely fraternal attitude to the working people of the colonies and the oppressed nations, and to carry out systematic agitation among the troops of their country against the oppression of colonial peoples.[2]

This contradiction is the natural point of departure for a discussion of Communism in Algeria. That Algerian Communists—almost exclusively Europeans—should hold such views is scarcely astonishing. After abandoning in 1902 their support of extremist *colon* demands for Algerian autonomy in which the privileges of European settlers would be guaranteed, Algerian Socialists became firm believers in assimilation. The essence of assimilation, to their mind, lay in linking Algeria directly with metropolitan France, and the subsequent abolition of independent organs of government such as the *gouvernement général* and the *délégations financières*.[3] However, they also regarded it as a solution, both political and cultural, for the "native question." Consequently, they advocated a wide range of reforms: the abolition of all repressive emergency laws directed against the natives, known as the *code de l'indigénat*; equal taxation, with abolition of the so-called *impôts arabes*; expansion of educational facilities in the Arab-Berber sector; equal pay for equal work, notably the granting to Muslim civil servants of the *quart colonial*; and, last but not least, the progressive extension of the Muslim franchise to local assemblies and, eventually, to the French Parliament.[4] Bold as such positions were for that time, it should be stressed that they were self-restricting because of the overall objective of assimilation. French sovereignty was, of course, never called into question; abuses of the colonial system were attacked, but not the situation itself. It is most revealing, for instance, that the 1902 Congress devoted much of its time to defending the interests of the small *colons* against the big landowners. The term "Algerian proletariat" in these resolutions denotes only workers of European origin, in contrast to the "natives, our subjects."[5] The latter were to be progressively integrated into the European community (and, through it, into France), winning, in the process, a growing measure of equality. Yet all this hinged upon one explicit condition: deculturation; "natives" must relinquish their "backward civilization" and "attain emancipation" through the assimilation of French culture. Indeed, the 1902 Congress believed that the most urgent step was to enjoin the natives to speak only French, even in Muslim worship, and to prohibit the appearance of books, newspapers, and signboards in Arabic. In order to achieve this hegemony of "the national language," French schools were to be forcibly implanted in the Muslim sector and Muslim denominational schools closed. However, some doubt seems to have remained in the minds of those socialists as to whether the natives could ever attain the level of Frenchmen. Schools to be established for natives were to be vocational and only "in exceptional cases will deserving subjects be admitted to the lycées."[6]

This policy did not mar the relations of Algerian Socialists with their comrades in France. Apart from Jaurès and a few occasional *délégués à la propagande* the SFIO (French Socialist Party) was indifferent to Algerian problems, and even had it taken notice of the resolutions adopted at Algerian congresses, it is doubtful whether it would have condemned them. From 1907, all-out opposition to colonial possessions, predicated upon orthodox Marxist theory, became a minority opinion in the party, with the pendulum swinging quite distinctly towards the reformist position. The reformists saw no reason to abandon colonies "prematurely," as they would simply fall into the hands of other (and worse) powers; they considered colonization a positive factor of modernization and social progress, and simply recommended that indigenous populations be granted greater latitude for self-improvement under the benevolent tutelage of France.[7] When, after World War I, the SFIO became very active in the campaign for the extension of Muslim franchise in local assemblies, a campaign which led to the February 1919 reforms, it was merely catching up with the policy advocated by the Algerian federations before the war.[8]

Given these attitudes of the Algerian Socialists on the colonial question, how can the fact be explained that most of them joined the Communist International at the moment of the split (December 1920)?

The explanation was not simply ignorance. It is true that the shift in the strategy of the Communist International to a greater emphasis on colonial revolution occurred only in June 1920 with the new Lenin theses, at a time when the Algerian SFIO was already leaning heavily towards the Bolsheviks.[9] It is also true that the Twenty-One Conditions were formulated in August during the Second World Congress. There was thus little chance for discussion of this unexpected "flaw" in Communist ideology. Yet it is an established fact that from September 1920 the problem was clearly perceived by the Algerian federations.[10] It was actually taken into account in some of the discussions held prior to, and during, the sectional and federal congresses (in November-December) which were to formulate instructions to be given to Algerian delegates at the Tours Congress. However, enthusiasm for the Communist International did not abate; 34 out of 41 Algerian mandates were cast in favor of the Cachin-Frossard motion, which recommended affiliation to the Third International.

The Algerian rift, like the split in the SFIO in metropolitan France, took place because the bulk of the pro-Communist International faction misunderstood the nature of the world organization they were about to join or the new party model it wished to create.

The basic misunderstanding, in the case of both the Algerians and the "Centre" faction of the SFIO, was of the character of the

Twenty-One Conditions. Lenin viewed them on a take-it-or-leave-it basis; the centrists, however, thought it feasible to join the Communist International while voicing serious reservations about several conditions which were actually tantamount to rejection. The Algerians could therefore deem themselves eligible for admission while rejecting the Eighth Condition. It is true that the leader of the French "centrist faction," Frossard, expressed reservations on different conditions (such as conditions over trade unions, illegal activity, or the expulsion of minorities) but once the right to express qualifications was accepted in principle it could evidently be invoked in the case of the "colonial condition" as well. The Oran section even found "implicit reservation" on the colonial issue in the Frossard-Cachin motion.[11] So important was the qualification on Article 8, that it was not confined to Algerian centrists. Thus one of the leaders of the extreme left, who was present when proposing to vote for the leftist motion of Heine, hastened to add that the motion, which advocated unconditional acceptance of Communist Interantional discipline, "should be amended on the chapter of native policy."[12]

A second line of defence consisted in the interpretation of the Sixteenth Condition, namely "Consideration must be given to the individual varying conditions in which individual parties have to combat; [the Communist International] must take decisions of general validity only when such decisions are possible"—thus implying that decisions on colonial policy in Algeria were in the domain of the local federations.[13] There were two basically erroneous assumptions here: that federations would be granted an autonomy analogous to that they had enjoyed in the SFIO; and that colonial (and hence Algerian) affairs would continue to be of marginal interest for the Communist International, as they had been for the SFIO. The same interpretation had even greater relevance for the Algiers section, the only section which had endorsed Lenin's "theses on national and colonial policy" presented to the Second World Congress. As the 1921 poll was to show, while Algiers favored the principle, it certainly did not think that it could be applied to Algeria in the forseeable future.[14]

Finally, the Lenin theses had been conceived in terms broad enough to allow of different interpretations, permitting the Algerians to assume that colonial doctrine, being in a state of flux, could still be maneuvered in a direction acceptable to them. There was, to begin with, Lenin's hostility towards most nationalist movements (as well as pan-Islam). Better still, it was possible to point to the all-out Europocentric stand defended in the Second Congress by Serrati and supported by a Frenchman, Rosmer, which held that only a successful revolution in the imperialist countries could liberate the colonies, with the obvious result of postponing the prospect of colonial insurrection to the remote future. Serrati found himself in the minority at the Second Congress, but was neither expelled nor condemned. It was therefore quite possible to assume that a good Communist could hold these or similar views, and even to hope that the Communist International might adopt them.

All these misunderstandings are evident in the speech prepared by would-be historian Ch.-A. Julien, then an Algerian delegate to the Tours Congress.[15] He made no bones about the fact that his colleagues in Algeria did not subscribe to all of the Communist International views on colonial questions, and claimed the right to act as befitted local conditions, "which do not square with standards established mainly on the basis of Asian experience." He depicted them—quite accurately—as "clearly opposed to any revolt or colonial movement of nationalim." There were two reasons for this opposition: such an insurrection in Algeria had no chance of success and would end in a senseless massacre; even if successful, it would only replace colonial rule by a Muslim oligarchy, thus increasing the exploitation of the indigenous masses. Furthermore, such an "independent" state would be too weak to fend for itself and was bound to fall into the hands of another imperialist power. Practical arguments aside, Julien strove to prove that even on the theoretical plane, he was not overstepping the bounds of orthodoxy. Claiming that Communist colonial doctrine was not yet cast into a rigid mold, he cited as proof contradictions between various official documents of the Communist International in the previous twenty months. Surveying the gamut of opinions, Julien declared that Algerian Socialists opted for the Serrati thesis.

In a candid moment some of his comrades admitted: "We may not be taking the conditions of admission to the Communist International too literally," only to add, "but we are sure of our fidelity to the spirit of . . . the October Revolution" (resolution of the Federation of Constantine, November 1921.)[16] Nowhere is the conviction of their being orthodox Communists more transparent than in this text, nor the use of Leninist analysis to legitimize their prejudices more sophisticated. Consider, for example, this defense of imperialism: "From a Marxist viewpoint, colonization is a necessary process through which backward nations arrive at the capitalist phase of organization from which Communism is to be born." Or their attack on nationalism in the colonies:

> Nationalist agitation would result in the replacing of a society with an advanced capitalist concentration, and acute class consciousness, i.e., ripe for a collectivist organization, by a society where hostile races will be embroiled in a fierce struggle; in the latter case it is the ruling classes which will regain popularity and power.

One of the first observers to detect the Algerian deviation from Communist International norms was Robert Louzon, a Frenchman who had founded the Tunisian Communist federation. He argued that "A Communist must have a Communist mentality and not an Algerian mentality."[17] The Algerian federations attempted to prove that it was possible to have both. The "Algerian mentality" is particularly evident in the accepted views on Muslims revealed in answers to the poll quoted above, and in articles in the party organ, *La Lutte Sociale*.[18] These views were largely the half-truths and prejudices shared with their fellow Pieds Noirs and with Algerian Socialists of the turn of the century. The composite image of the Muslims is that of a fanatical, ignorant and retrograde population: "The natives of North Africa consist, for the most part, of Arabs who resist the economic, social, intellectual, and moral evolution indispensable to individuals in order to form an autonomous state."[19]

Their fervent religiosity implied the partial or total abdication of reason, and the alliance of ignorance and religion constitutes an ever-present threat to the Europeans. "Fanaticism," writes *La Lutte Sociale*, "is as violent among the natives as in early Islamic times; the smallest *marabout* who preaches the holy war finds supporters. Women, through their ignorance, maintain in the Muslim family hatred of the *roumi*" [European].[20] "After seventy years of colonization the Arab remains what he had always been: simple-minded, primitive, his spirit tied up by custom and tradition."[21]

The same image is reserved for the Muslim elites—either traditional or modernized—who constitute the spearhead of "Muslim nationalism" [sic]. Concurrently, oppression and exploitation of the "native proletarians" are attributed not only to the colonists but "above all to their bourgeois coreligionists, their religious leaders . . . their landed proprietors."[22] The obvious solution is therefore (a) *repression:* "one should combat the influence of [Muslim] clergy and chiefs who fan the smoldering embers of the "surviving national feelings," these "prejudices which wither away very slowly,"[23] and (b) *assimilation:* "indigenous schools must be abolished for they inculcate children with racial pride"; and pupils must "be compelled to go to French schools." But "education granted to them should be essentially agricultural and practical."[24] Even when pointing out the areas where the alleged "Muslim mentality" offers some hope for Communism, Algerian Communists simply evoke one of the basic notions of their fellow Pied Noirs: the presumed collective ownership of land once practiced by the Muslims, and their alleged innate inclination to community of property.[25]

The Communist declaration (after a by-election success in Algiers, October 1921) that they had acquired *droit de cité* there,[26] was correct—and not only in the limited political context. For they were an integral part of the European community, sharing its basic beliefs and committed to its survival and predominance, while giving vent to the aspirations for social change prevalent in the lower strata of this community, as among their counterparts in metropolitan France. And by every available yardstick the party was prospering. Membership, which increased after the war (actually doubling to 750)[27] was virtually unaffected by the crisis of December 1920. Only a handful of members abandoned the federations of Oran and Algiers, though in Constantine one-half (about 100) left. The losses were quickly replaced and by mid 1922 the three federations had the pre-1920 figure,[28] reaching one thousand in 1925;[29] and that at a period when PCF (French Communist Party) membership was on the decline. Electoral results in the First (almost exclusively European) College were impressive: one-sixth in Oran (June 1921), one-fifth in Algiers (November 1921);[30] and no sizeable changes occurred in the 1924 (parliamentary) and 1925 (municipal) elections.[31] Right-wing and Socialist rivals reminded the voters of the Eighth Condition and concentrated on the Communist danger to the empire.[32] But the electorate, and especially the working class constituencies which gave the Communist Party massive support (Belcourt and Bab-el-Oued in Algiers, Marine in Oran, etc.), seemed unperturbed; for them the Communist Party expressed their socioeconomic demands. This was understandable, as Communist platforms contained no allusion to decolonization, and the scant references to "native reforms" were in accordance with the old liberal-socialist line—abrogation of the *code de l'indigénat*, extension of education and of the right to vote, equality of wages and taxation, etc.[33] The SFIO, aware of the failure of its attacks, indeed flayed the PCF for deliberately deluding voters by maintaining silence at its rallies about the Eighth Condition "which demands the evacuation of the colonies by the invaders, i.e., by precisely those European workers and small *colons* to whom they are holding forth."[34] This was an unjustified accusation for, as we have seen, the Algerian Communists were quite sincere, if mistaken, in their belief that their views were compatible with Leninist dogma. When pressed to the wall and asked to comment on articles in *l'Humanité*, which spelled out the decolonization theory, Communist candidates in Algiers disclaimed any responsibility for them.[35]

It seemed, therefore, that nothing could undermine the integration of the CP into the European community, nor detract from the aura of respectability it enjoyed there, an image confirmed by independent observers.[36] Its status was bolstered by the fact that its leadership consisted of prominent local intellectuals: the historian Ch.-A. Julien, the Batna physician L. Laurens, and the school principal Maurice Guillon, of Sidi-Bel-Abbès. Amongst the lower middle class and the proletariat, the party profited from the prestige of E. Mazoyer, the hero of the workers for his role in directing the railwaymen's strike in 1920 and from the long-time leader of the Bône proletariat, Giovacchini.

The most glaring paradox in the genesis of Algerian Communism is the fact that admiration for Bolshevism and what was to be labeled "slave-owner mentality"[37] could maintain a robust coexistence for five (or even six) years. No pressure for change could be expected to emerge from within, so steeped was the membership in *colon* prejudices. Why was none forthcoming from the Communist International and the PCF?

In a sense, the three misunderstandings accompanying the birth of Algerian Communism were not altogether illogical (at least on a short-term basis). Although the Comintern could not conceivably repeal the Eighth Condition, or even accept the Serrati thesis, it was some time before it shed its belief in an impending European revolution, given the continued fermentation in Central Europe. Thus, the Third World Congress (June 1921) dealt almost exclusively with European questions. While it began to consider the Third World as an equally, or even more, promising arena for the Revolution—a process marked out by a session of the Executive Committee (ECCI) (February-March 1922), the Fourth Congress (November-December 1922), and the Fifth Congress (July 1924)—actual Comintern activity in this direction was far from substantial, tactics were still under debate, and apparatus meagre. At any rate, the brunt of its interest was on south and Southeast Asia and, to a much lesser degree, the Middle East. North Africa lagged far behind, scarcely entering into the deliberations. Moreover, by virtue of an ECCI resolution of March 1922—laying down a pattern of organization and action which was to be followed for over thirty year—the PCF was put in charge of propaganda in the French Empire and of "establishing closer contact with the oppressed colonial masses."[38] The Comintern kept overall control in its hands, but rarely exercised it.

The PCF, in the tradition of the pre-war SFIO, was virtually indifferent to colonial affairs, not withstanding perfunctory lip service in *l'Humanité* to "liberation of the colonies." As Ho Chi Minh (then called Nguyen Ai-Quoc) was to point out in 1922, the party was still at the stage of "purely sentimental expression of position, leading to nothing at all" and had not yet attained that of "a well-defined working program, an effective and practical policy."[39] It was only through the initiative of several French members who had lived in the empire and a few colonials residing in France that a *Comité d'Études Coloniales* (CEC) was founded in August 1921. Even this would not have come into being were it not for Paul Vaillant-Couturier who was the only PCF leader interested in colonial problems, and who backed the group. The very title of the CEC indicates acceptance of the cautious view of Ch.-A. Julien, who was a cofounder, that the colonial issue was so complex that a detailed region-by-region study was essential for hammering out a program of action.[40] The balance sheet of CEC activity was negative. The only tangible result of its efforts was the weekly colonial forum in *l'Humanité*, designed to arouse interest and foster debate and study; yet it disappeared after less than a year of existence (May 1922-March 1923). By its own admission,[41] the CEC failed to draw the attention of the party leadership to the colonial question, and even in persuading one of the higher authorities to conduct a comprehensive discussion as to strategy and tactics in that field.

The Algerian federations thus enjoyed wide autonomy on Muslim policy, all the more secure as the men whom the party nominated as *délégués à la propagande* for North Africa were the Algerian-reared Ch.-A. Julien (1920-21) and native son E. Mazoyer.[42] They had little to fear from occasional French visitors; for even a man like Vaillant-

Couturier, who toured Algeria in 1922, was converted to many a belief held by local Communists.[43] Incendiary declarations in *l'Humanité*, which sometimes contained critical allusions to the positions of colonial federations, could thus be dismissed as "impatient . . . and blind theories worked out in Parisian clubs."[44] Thus Condition Sixteen was valid for Algerian affairs, *de facto* if not *de jure*. Likewise, the *actual* Europocentric orientation of PCF (and, to some extent, of the Comintern as well) lent credence to the assumption that the Serrati doctrine was perfectly orthodox—if unlikely to gain immediate predominance. The state of flux of PCF and Comintern colonial policy even made it plausible to believe that the Eighth Condition might one day be repealed.

## THE SIDI-BEL-ABBÈS AFFAIR: A STORM IN A TEACUP?

The serene picture presented by Algerian Communism in its first five years is marred by one episode, the Siddi-Bel-Abbès affair, which, due to a combination of circumstances, became an affair of some notoriety in the international Communist movement and beyond. We shall therefore examine it closely, and try to place it in its true perspective.

The affair was sparked off by a "Manifesto for the Liberation of Tunisia and Algeria" promulgated by ECCI on May 20, 1922. Its key paragraphs were:[45]

> The dawn of emancipation has appeared before the Arab proletarians, subjected to the shameful exploitation of the native aristocracy and the French conqueror. The imperialist war awakened a spirit of unrest in Tunisia and Algeria. . . . And, together with the nationalist demands, class demands are being mingled ever more frequently and urgently . . . . For the first time since the conquest of North Africa by French capitalism, the natives . . . are finding strong and reliable allies among the compatriots of their exploiters, who have made the natives' cause their own and will support it until victory is won, that is the . . . PCF . . . The struggle for the liberation of Algeria and Tunisia is only beginning. It will end only when the slaves have triumphed!

The Manifesto was evidently the result of the February-March session, where the ECCI resolved to enhance the importance attached to activity in the colonies, but its very nature dictated the limits to such activity. All the ECCI did, at this early stage of its recognition of the prospect of non-European revolution, was to launch, through *ad hoc* committees, several manifestos aimed at various regions. While this demonstrates that the colonies were no longer lumped together, and regional differences were beginning to be perceived, the act was purely symbolic, a kind of declaration of intent published, moreover, solely in the Comintern weekly *(Correspondence Internationale)*. No leaflets were printed for dispatch to the "oppressed populations" themselves. The Manifesto laid down no guidelines for action in the "struggle" it proclaimed, all this presumably being left to the European party put in charge, that is to the PCF. Needless to say, there was no follow-up to verify implementation. No organ of the PCF published the Manifesto, and it is clear this frustrated the success of the whole venture. The *Correspondence Internationale* did, however, reach Algeria, and so, three weeks after its publication, waves of shock were triggered off in the three Algerian federations.[46] Of their own accord several sections held assemblies to discuss it; later, presumably upon the initiative of the interfederal secretariat—a loose coordinating body—congresses of the three federations were held, culminating in an interfederal congress on 24 Septmber.[47]

Only one sectional resolution, apparently also the earliest, is known to us in full. It was issued by the section of Sidi-Bel-Abbès, the strongest in the Oran federation, which—deservedly—was dubbed the "Communist Mecca": the town's European working-class population ensured it the unrivalled score of more than one-third of the vote in every postwar election.[48] The kernel of the resolution is a *verbatim* reproduction of that adopted a year earlier, in response to the internal poll; this in itself constituted the reassertion of positions and assumptions held at the time of the Tours Congress. In order to "dot the i's," an extensive introduction was drawn up, commenting on the 1921 theses, and as a rejoinder to the Manifesto.[49] The three major assumptions are of course reiterated:

(a) No uniform thesis is possible on the colonial question, [for the latter] is characterized by its absolute and necessary lack of unity. [Hence] the Communist federations of the colonies alone are qualified to decide upon local tactics.

(b) The liberation of the native proletariat of North Africa will be the fruit only of the revolution in the mother country. . . . A victorious revolt of the Muslim masses of Algeria which would not be posterior to a similar victorious revolt of the proletariat of the mother country would inevitably bring Algeria back to a regime close to feudalism.

(c) Consequently, the best way in which to "aid . . . every liberating movement" in our colony, is not to "abandon" this colony, as it is stated in the [Eighth] Condition of admission to the Third International, but on the contrary to remain there, on condition that the Communist Party increases propaganda in favor of trade-unionism, communism, and the cooperative system.

The strange brew typical of Algerian Communism is easily detectable: on the one hand, repetition of Pied Noir beliefs ("in the case of premature Arab sovereignty . . . slavery will be extended because slave ownership, in the strict sense of word, is a Muslim tradition in Algeria"); on the other hand, use of Marxist dialectics and affirmation of belief in the tenets of the faith:

> Colonial insurrection at present . . . is a dangerous folly which the Algerian . . . Communists, who possess above all the Marxist sense of situations, do not wish to become accomplices before the judgment of Communist history. . . . Indeed, . . . any revolutionary movement must mark a step forward in the historical development of humanity . . . and not a reaction towards a . . . stage already condemned by history.

The vehemence of the reaction is best perceived in the peremptory demand that the CI refrain from propagating the manifesto in Algeria, since "its letter and spirit engage the responsibility [of local Communists] without being endorsed by them."

The excerpts of other resolutions[50] available to us are too fragmentary for reconstruction of the whole, but they do not seem to have been written in a different vein. The significant fact is that the interfederal congress unanimously adopted a resolution presented by the Oran federation, unmistakably written by Maurice Guillon, secretary of the Sidi-Bel-Abbès section.[51] Tempers in Sidi-Bel-Abbès had probably cooled in the meantime, and other sections (probably Algiers) may have brought pressure to bear in order to tone down the response.[52] The end result was a resolution removing some of the edges of the Sidi-Bel-Abbès text, but the essential elements were retained. The first three paragraphs of the interfederal resolution, dealing with "the absolute and inevitable lack of unity" of the colonial problem, are taken almost word for word—with the omission of one provocative sentence—from the Sidi-Bel-Abbès resolution.[53] The three assumptions are spelled out, although less rigidly formulated: The Eighth Condition "is wrong in being too general . . . and not taking into account the specific conditions [of the colonies] and the means for party action in each of them;" in Algeria no prospects for locally initiated insurrection and "expulsion of imperialists" are in view, since the Muslim bourgeoisie, standard bearer of the "deeply-embedded hereditary nationalism" is "devoid of resolution and energy . . . and fearful of retaliatory acts on the part of the administration." The paragraph on decision making revived a formula advanced in *La Lutte Sociale* a year before.[54] Supreme authority was to rest with the Directory Committee of the PCF (but not the CI!), with the Algerians cast in the role of senior advisors.

> It is our imperative duty to criticize the policy followed and point out its errors and omissions, for we are well placed for that; it behooves us as well to supply the party with the information it lacks on the particular conditions in our area and suggest methods one should have recourse to in order to avoid gropings and mistakes which are liable to have serious consequences.

Because of the desire to avoid a head-on clash and to confine the affair to the sphere of the PCF, the manifesto was not even mentioned. Likewise, not a tract was left of the haughty demand of Sidi-Bel-Abbès that "the colonial program of action of the CP be established in common consent with the Socialist federations."

As was rightly claimed in the 1926 purge, the interfederal resolution signified "a return to the spirit of Sidi-Bel-Abbès."[55] It certainly reflected the general consensus which had prevailed among Algerian Communists from the outset, and down to the smallest detail, of the stereotypes of the "natives"; their "ignorance and illiteracy maintained by their religious or administrative leaders," and their "fatalism and religious fanaticism." The fact that Guillon was elected by the congress as interfederal secretary[56] set the seal on Sidi-Bel-Abbès as a genuine, if rather outspoken, representative of Communist Pieds Noirs.

The reaction that followed is hardly surprising, for such articulated and public statements called for some response. But it is worth noting the source and the form of the reaction. Only the Sidi-Bel-Abbès resolution came under fire, and even that only from the Comintern. This gave the affair the flavor of a struggle against a small deviant group, while Algerian Communism could emerge virtually unscathed. The interfederal resolution remained unknown to the Comintern; the PCF published it (without any comment) in its theoretical organ *Bulletin Communiste*, and it was criticized only once, by a Tunisian militant;[57] the French Directory Committee remained completely oblivious (or indifferent) to the matter.

It is worth describing in some detail the sequence of events, in order to illustrate the dismal plight of the CI and PCF colonial apparatus and their activity. The Sidi-Bel-Abbès affair might never have occurred had not the section decided at its late-June assembly to bring its views to the attention of authorities outside Algeria, though it is not clear which it had in mind. The resolution was sent to Ch.-A. Julien, then teaching in Montpellier, probably because he was the sole Communist activist in France whom they knew well, and because they expected him to plead their cause. In mid-July Julien sent the letter to Frossard, the PCF secretary-general, without any effort to enlighten him further.[58] Frossard, completely indifferent, passed it in turn to "Moscow's eye in Paris," Jules Humbert-Droz. This permanent CI representative, although possessing "plenipotentiary powers to intervene in PCF life" did not consider the matter to be of any consequence, and moreover deemed colonial affairs, much as before the 4 March resolution, to be within the jurisdiction of Comintern colonial experts. He dispatched the Algerian letter to the praesidium of the Comintern recommending that "the Comintern secretariat for the colonies establish close contact with these federations in order to expound CI colonial tactics to them and to take into account, as far as possible, the situation and conditions of their struggle."[59] His letter arrived in Moscow on the eve of the Fourth World Congress, which consecrated colonial action as a major CI undertaking, and also took the PCF to task for its numerous faults. The Sibi-Bel-Abbès document was recognized by Safarov and Trotsky, the CI specialists on colonial and French affairs respectively, as useful material for the assertion of their views on matters within their responsibility. Safarov, aided by the Tunisian delegate, used it to demonstrate that "chauvinist ideas, foreign and hostile to proletarian internationalism," prevailed in Western CP's on the colonial question. Trotsky cited the occurrence in the course of his diatribe against the PCF and its internal crisis; he regarded it first and foremost as an attempt—characteristic of a Socialist-ridden party—to refute the right of the CI to intervene in the internal affairs of its national sections.[60] This was in no way an indictment of Algerian Communism as a whole, though Sidi-Bel-Abbès expressly claimed to represent the entire Algerian party; moreover, had CI colonial experts paid more attention and been better equipped to deal with Maghribi affairs, they could have easily found out—merely by reading *La Lutte Sociale*—that the phenomenon was widespread and deeply rooted. But even had they developed any interest in Algerian or Sidi-Bel-Abbès Communists per se, it is doubtful whether any practical consequences would have emerged.

For the CI the internal crisis of PCF leadership was of greater importance than colonial affairs; and in the latter sphere, the emphasis was on global strategy (the Roy-Lenin debate), and insofar as tangible regional problems at all interested CI specialists, they did not include those of North Africa.

Consequently, the World Congress resolutions on the "French question" and the "Eastern question"[61] referred only to Sidi-Bel-Abbès—in the latter resolution obliquely—and to Algerian Communism not at all. It was categorically condemned as evidence of (1) the PCF's duty to put an end to its indolence as regards "the struggle against colonial slavery . . . and revolutionary activity in the colonies"; (2) the need "to combat quasi-socialist tendencies towards colonialism in some well-paid categories of European workers in the colonies."

On the second point, the Comintern hints for the first time at the real question, that of Algerian Communism, but left implementation entirely to the French party, in accordance with the 4 March resolution, and—worse still—did not try to ascertain whether it had been put into effect. It is significant that when Manuilsky mentioned the Sidi-Bel-Abbès affair at the Fifth World Congress (July 1924)—citing it as an example of "social-imperialist survivals" in Western parties—he enquired whether the section leaders had been expelled.

The PCF certainly had other preoccupations: it was engrossed in the developing crisis with the Frossard group and was to become engrossed with that of Souvarine. Even such an elementary Comintern demand as the transformation of the CEC from an advisory to an executive organ was not carried out,[62] and the Third Party Congress (1922) as well as the 1924 National Council, were as oblivious of the colonial question as their predecessors had been.[63] In 1924 Manuilsky was obliged to reiterate most of Safarov's accusations on the PCF's colonial activity.

At first in Algeria the mere condemnation of Sidi-Bel-Abbès seemed to spark off the process foreseen vaguely at the World Congress. Guillon submitted his resignation from the party in late December, "grieved to death" as he wrote in his letter, and protesting his fidelity to Communist doctrine.[64] His act was followed by a mass secession, mainly in western Algeria—though it may also be ascribed in fact to the defection of the Frossard group early in January. A major crisis might have developed had it not been for the Algerian federation which promptly stepped into the breach. A federal congress was summoned in mid-January to discuss the "implementation of the decision of the Fourth Congress," and it endorsed a "program of action" on native affairs. The program was dispatched to the *Bulletin Communiste* in order to dispel the impression created by the publication there the month before of the interfederal resolution.[65] On the face of this was an effort to comply with CI exigencies and perform a *volte face*; an Algerian leader, Mouillard, the nominated provisional secretary of the interfederation, even declared that the program was a repudiation by the federation of the 24 September theses.[66] In fact, his aim was to ward off future conflicts with the Comintern while maintaining intact the core of the Algerian position.

The Algiers Program avoided the problem by refraining from discussing either the Eighth Condition or the Serrati thesis. It dispatched the whole strategic chapter in one passage: "the CP possesses the key" to understanding the phenomenon of imperialism; believing that "the sufferings of the colonized are caused by the appetites of capitalism and will disappear only with the abolition of the capitalist regime itself and the establishment over the whole globe of a Soviet regime." This final goal—couched in terms so vague that nobody could find fault with them—was however dismissed as "purely theoretical" and "lifeless." "If the CP wants to exercise real influence over the masses it must create easily comprehensible catchwords." Strategy, the source of all the strife, should thus be shelved and tactics reign supreme. "Communist parties in the colonies, while never ceasing to proclaim their real aim, should, as the action develops, compose varying slogans, always adopted to immediate situations." The importance of tactics is reflected in the fact that more than four-fifths of the document is devoted to them. On the whole they follow the lines laid down by the prewar SFIO: demanding an end to expropriation, the abolition of emergency laws, equal terms of military service, and the extension of education (French, not Muslim). This signified, first of all, that Algeria was not ripe for revolution in the foreseeable future (i.e., until after the revolution in France); secondly, that the Algerian federations intended to remain the sole judges of any changes in the situation and any action which might have to be taken. On the last point, the Program was slightly more outspoken: "in every colony local members must define tactics."

The three main assumptions laid down on the eve of the Tours Congress were therefore reintroduced surreptitiously. The Algerian leadership conceded that they had erred in gauging Comintern attitudes, at least as regards the first two points, but only as to matters of principle and not from a pragmatic viewpoint. They seemed to think that the colonial aspect was a minor plank which the Comintern was not too keen to implement, at any rate not in Algeria. If they refrained from provoking the Comintern on the question, as Sidi-Bel-Abbès had done, they believed they could still remain Pied Noirs and Communists. The CI did not, in fact, react to the publication of the interfederal resolution and the Algiers Program, either through lack of information, or simple indifference. No danger was anticipated from the PCF, given its notorious lack of interest in the colonies. The French even appeared to endorse the Algerian interpretation of the Sixteenth Condition in principle, when *Bulletin Communiste* entitled the Algiers Program "The Colonial Question and the Algerian Thesis"—without of course, taking the trouble to discuss it.

No formal discussion is known to have taken place in the other two federations. They seem, however, to have accepted the Program. It should be recalled that the Algiers department accounted for at least half the Communist membership in Algeria.[67]

How little the Algerian outlook changed is illustrated by an article written by Victor Spielmann and published in *La Lutte Sociale* on the very day the Algiers Program was elaborated:

> . . . given the revolutionary situation in present day Europe . . . it is highly possible that in 1940 Europe will be . . . a Bolshevik federation. Whereas present day Algeria is composed of heteroclite elements: Kabyle, Arab, French, foreigners (Italian, Spanish, Maltese) . . . incapable of governing themselves for want of common accord, the chances are that in 1940 Algeria will be a European, America, Bolshevik, or Turkish colony.[68]

In short, we have the Serrati position coupled with a version of the French thesis on the Algerian "congenital incapacity for independence." The fact that Spielmann, an old-style *indigénophile* who had joined the CP at its foundation,[69] continued to be its mentor on Muslim affairs speaks for itself. His articles in the party organ concentrated on attacking injustice, for example expropriation, and advocating piecemeal reforms, especially partial Muslim representation in the French parliament. The independent weekly *Le Trait d'Union*, which he had founded to gain a wider audience for his views, was not only tolerated, but even warmly recommended to party members.[70] It is most revealing that this paper was highly praised by the local Socialists, and Muslim assimilationists, e.g., the young Ferhat Abbas, were among its regular contributors.[71] *La Lutte Sociale* even published the manifesto of *Cercle Franco-Indigène*, the new association Spielmann had launched, in order to foster racial rapproachment between "Frenchmen" and "natives" "in the framework of *French* North Africa" (italics added).[72]

Though former tactics were maintained, the Algiers Program did incorporate two items insisted on by the Comintern. However they were neither particularly unpalatable from a Pied Noir viewpoint, nor of any practical consequence. "Expansion of the recruitment of natives" was promised, and several means to that objective were outlined: neither the prewar Algerian SFIO nor the Communist sections had been opposed in principle to this goal.[73] Even the Sidi-Bel-Abbès letter speaks only of the obstacles impeding party propaganda among the Muslims. In any event, the promise was never fulfilled. None of the innovations suggested, such as the publication of articles in Arabic in *La Lutte Sociale* or the nomination of Muslim candidates for elections, was really carried out.[74] The overall effort directed at the Muslims remained trivial, and new members scant in number.[75] Such failure may have been due in part to resistance (not necessarily muffled) by some of the rank and file, or to the (at best) unenthusiastic welcome reserved for Muslim recruits. Even in the Communist-dominated labor union, the CGTU, one of the arguments frequently voiced was "trade unionism is O.K., but not for the Arabs."[76]

The second point—"determined support to be given to the democratic aspirations" of the "educated minority of the natives" and "establishment of contacts" with them—was even less of a novelty. The notion was perhaps intended to placate the Comintern, which had ruled in favor of tactical alliances with progressive nationalist movements (Lenin's thesis in his debate with Roy). But the Algiers section had already been of that opinion at the time of the 1921 poll.[77] The congress of the Algiers federation held in September, 1922, distinguished two kinds of nationalism: "the one progressive, hence revolutionary, the other conservative and regressive."[78] They had in mind the *Jeunes Algériens* movement led by Captain (alias "Emir") Khaled. Khaled was an advocate of *association* and sought to win for Muslims a substantial voice in the management of Algerian affairs and representation in the French parliament, to abolish Algerian colonial institutions, and to create direct *rattachement* to France, without however renouncing personal status based on Muslim law.[79] The

Algiers Program had required that this embryonic form of nationalism gave expression to the "popular yearning for emancipation," but could still be acceptable to the Communists as it was content to operate within the framework of French sovereignty. It is true that most sections in eastern and western Algeria, and even some in the Algiers department, were inclined to lump Khaled together with the hated *chefs indigènes*. In the discussions before the Tours Congress and during the 1921 poll—which bear the mark of *colon* press campaigns against the Emir—Khaled's doctrine was usually depicted as a variant of the dangerous "native nationalism," and he himself was regarded as the incarnation of the spectre of Arab-Berber domination over the Pieds Noirs.[80] That the change of attitude began in Algiers is easily accounted for by the fact that the Khaled phenomenon was mostly confined to this city and its vicinity. Communists there thus came to distinguish clearly between the modernized Mulsim elite which backed Khaled and the traditional elites (religious, feudal, or bourgeois), the *vieux turbans*. As it became better known, his program was perceived to be one of constitutional reform in the Tunisian Destour style, and his protestations of loyalty to France were no longer thought hypocritical. As noted in the 1923 program, the Communists found themselves taking the same positions as the Young Algerians on most practical issues—for instance on the extension of education, or the abolition of the *code de l'indigènat*. Inevitably contacts between the two movements were established, probably through Spielmann on one side and Touili Ben Amar on the other,[81] and indirect collaboration soon developed. According to a 1922 article in *L'Ikdam* (Khaled's organ), during the campaign for the parliamentary by-election in Algiers (1921), the Young Algerians had supported E. Mazoyer, the CP candidate, "with our money and our influence." The reason was that all the other candidates had called for the abolition of the February 1919 reforms, which extended the Muslim franchise, while Mazoyer supported their implementation. The author of the article (as might have been expected, Touili Ben Amar) went on to say that at the time of writing (June 1922), the movement, while remaining neutral as regards Communist doctrine in general, did not seek to conceal its "sympathy" for the CP as "defenders of natives" who "treat us on an equal footing."[82]

Why the Algiers federation did not insist on including support for "democratic nationalism," enunciated in its September, 1922, resolution, in the interfederal resolution debated a fortnight later, is not clear. Possibly the federation attached little importance to this concept. In view of the conclusion of the Roy-Lenin debate in the Fourth World Congress, a revival of the concept would have been not only natural, with Guillon's tougher line discredited, but also useful. In fact Lenin's term "anti-Imperialist alliance" was borrowed by the Algiers Program for the new tactic.

However this alliance failed to materialize. The CP launched the idea at a time when the fortunes of the Young Algerians were already in deline. Khaled himself was losing faith in his political perspectives in the face of violent *colon* propaganda against him and of administration pressure on the Muslim electorate to vote for "loyal" candidates; furthermore, the French government was impervious to his pleas for immediate reforms. In mid-1923, he gave up all political activity and went into voluntary exile in Egypt. What remained of his movement soon collapsed.[83] The Communists called for his "return from exile," claiming that the administration had forced him to leave,[84] and succeeded in making political capital out of the issue in the Muslim community.

The episode is of some importance in accounting for the *colon* myth of Khaled as a crypto-Communist, and in explaining why the Emir later agreed to ally himself publicly with PCP: Paris rallies were held under their aegis in 1924, and he appeared on a Communist-sponsored list in Algiers elections in 1925,[85] at the initiative of the PCF;[86] finally it expalins why the Communist electorate did not defect at these elections.

Quite apart from its negligible practical results, the issue had no sizeable impact on Algerian Communist thought: nationalist "separatist" aspirations were condemned as before, most of the Muslim elite remained suspect, and native particularism was still abhorred. Albert Crémieux, *délegué à la propagande* of the CGTU, wryly remarked in 1923: "in Algeria, if one scratches lightly at the anarchist, the Communist, or the trade unionist, it is extremely rare not to find the European conqueror underneath."[87] It is not surprising, therefore, that the Algerian federations weathered the storm quite easily. Defections ceased, the rise in European membership continued, and in the 1924 elections, even in Sidi-Bel-Abbès, the party maintained its previous position.[88]

In retrospect it is clear that the Sidi-Bel-Abbès affair was no more than a storm in a teacup.

## THE SHOCK AND THE PURGE

What the Comintern dubbed "slave-dealer Communism" in Algeria—that is, belief in most tenets of Leninism but adherence, too, to outright *colon* racialism—was severely shaken by the impact of the Rif War and ensuing purge. In the years 1925-27 it suffered a heavy blow but did not perish completely, a good indication of how deeply rooted the phenomenon was. According to Barbé, PCF delegate at the Sixth Comintern Congress,

> [The Rif War] was the first occasion on which a section of the International was confronted with the necessity of carrying out Lenin's principles of the struggle against imperialist policy and against the colonial policy of a big imperialist power.[89]

The boast remains valid, even if one is forced to admit that pacificism and antipatriotism played at least as important a role as anti-colonialism in the PCF campaign against the war, and that the defects of the campaign were quite evident, such as no action in Morocco and in the French army, or the failure to sway the pro-Communist proletariat.[90] The break with the "reformist heritage of the Second International" on colonial matters was perhaps not yet apparent when a militant Muslim emigrant in France hailed it in late 1924.[91] It became incontestable only when the campaign was properly launched in May 1925, after the French army had joined the Spanish in fighting the Moroccan rebels.[92] For the Algerian federations, whose fundamental assumption had been that the policies of the Second International would persist, this was the moment of truth, particularly as the territory in question was now not only French but bordering on Algeria. The slogans "clear out of Morocco," "fraternization (with the Rebels)," "Moroccan independence," and so on, had an ominous ring in the ears of the Europeans in Algeria; and the local and French press spelled out, for those who were slow to grasp them, the possible implications of "Moroccan independence," dwelling constantly on the "collusion" between Abd el-Krim and the Comintern.[93]

That the erosion of traditional positions of Algerian Communism was neither immediate nor total was due in part to the very ambivalence of the campaign. It could be considered primarily as an antimilitarist venture, of a kind quite popular in the party, especially among those of the *génération du feu*, who had reached Communism through their wartime experiences, which had caused them to revolt against the army and the values it fostered.[94] In fact *le travail anti*, as it was called in party cant, had been one of the salient features of CP activity in Algeria.[95] One could still stick posters, distribute leaflets, or harangue passers-by against the war in Morocco, as *La Lutte Sociale* sought to depict the campaign. It is significant that only a negligible part of this propaganda was conducted in the Muslim community and virtually none in army units stationed in Algeria or passing through to the field of combat.[96] Late in June the Colonial Commission of the PCF (as the CEC had recently been renamed) concluded in a secret document: "In Algiers, the Committee of Action [against the War] has a false concept of its mission."[97]

Whether the Algerian leadership was really mistaken, or merely pretended to be so in order to weather what they judged another ephemeral storm, its tactics could not prevent the impending crisis. For one thing, the PCF attitude was now too widely publicized and too clear-cut for the Algerian militants to be able to play it down. The party organ had to publish such anticolonial PCF documents as the May 1925, manifesto, and several incendiary leaflets were smuggled from France.[98] Moreover, the party front was not so monolithic. Several groups of militants—JC (Communist Youth) for the most part—had been touched by the anticolonialist zeal of the JC generation rising to prominence in France, and stressed this aspect in their activity, which was in any case usually bolder than ordinary party effort.[99] On the other hand, Governor-General M. Viollette harassed the Algerian CP with unprecedented severity: *La Lutte Sociale* was banned several times, party offices and the homes of militants were searched, activitsts caught engaging in propaganda against the Rif War were arrested, and afterwards given harsh sentences. Others were subject to police and employers' pressure, *inter alia*, to divulge information, or, as in the case of railwaymen, were transferred to distant places in the hinterland.[100] All were branded by Viollette as "bad Frenchmen," subverting the security of the State and the survival of French Algeria.[101] The respectability of the party was thus severely undermined; for the first time it was becoming isolated from the broad consensus of Pied Noir opinion. Their isolation grew after the arrest in mid-July of three delegates the PCF tried to infiltrate into Algeria and the confiscation—and subsequent publication—of the written instructions they had carried with them.[102] Objectives laid down there were "to win over the indigenous populations, conduct propaganda in rural areas, disorganize the army . . . coordinate the struggle of the [European] proletariat with that of natives against imperialist oppression," and ultimately achieve "the revolutionary insurrection of the natives" and "the foundation of an Algerian Republic." The "practical means" recommended for bringing about this final phase were: "(a) refusal to pay taxes; (b) return to brigandage, robbery, and other crimes which will engender disobedience to the *caïd*, the judge, and the administrator; (c) sequestration of the *gendarmes*." Two months later, the unsuccessful attempt of Doriot to infiltrate into Morocco from Algeria got full coverage in the press,[103] and further enhanced the image of Communism as the enemy of the empire and Algeria.

These developements shocked a membership convinced hitherto of the compatibility of being both a Communist and Pied Noir. The evasions and euphemisms of the party press betray the malaise which resulted: "The misapprehension of our militants as regards the native question"; "too many members do not understand the reason for the arrests, and see our activity in a false light."[104] In more candid moments, the origin of the dilemma was stated bluntly: hostility towards collaboration with the national liberation movement; "many European members say that they have left our organizations because we incite the natives to rebel and thrust them into the sea."[105] Indeed mass defection was the most obvious consequence of the crisis, brought about largely by official persecution, and the climate of animosity and seclusion which surrounded the party. At first it tended to dismiss defectors as "timorous elements" but soon had to acknowledge the importance of the crisis of faith. It became doubly difficult to evade the issue when some of its leaders resigned and gave full publicity to their reasons for doing so. V. Spielmann, who could be charged neither with cowardice nor with lack of compassion for the Muslims, said that the slogan of "independence for the colonies" was composed of "verbiage . . . bluff and outbidding."[106] D. Giovacchini, whose resignation severely shook the Bône section of the Party, claimed in a *mot célèbre* that had he been living in France he would have remained a Communist, but could not do so in Algeria, as the party there was working for the destruction of the French presence.[107] Whole cadres were as vulnerable to the virus as the rank and file.[108] Even among the JC (hard hit, it is true, by repression) "only a few comrades remain at their post of revolutionary struggle," lamented one activist, "and the cadres are crumbling."[109]

In one year, overall membership dropped from one thousand to four or five hundred,[110] with many cells disappearing altogether.[111] The party periphery showed similar signs of collapse. Circulation of *La Lutte Sociale* fell away, aggravating the financial difficulties inflicted by recurrent seizures.[112] In the departmental elections of autumn 1925, all the CP candidates in Algeria suffered severe losses. The most telling defeat was that of R. Cazala, the JC secretary who had been arrested for conducting propaganda against the Rif War in the ranks, who stood in Algiers and received only 86 votes.[113]

Perhaps the most vivid illustration of the fears and disillusion which the campaign against the Rif War engendered in the CP membership and its sympathizers is a work of fiction, *Le grand soir*, written several years later by Albert Crémieux. In it Crémieux, who had meanwhile left the party, describes an abortive Communist revolution in France. The final act is staged in Algiers with the outbreak of a Communist-instigated insurrection of the Muslims, which soon gets out of hand. An unruly and fanatic Arab mob sets the city on fire, lynching Europeans and plundering their houses before being in turn massacred mercilessly by French troops.[114]

That hallowed myth, the proletarian revolution, was suddenly perceived to stand in stark contradiction to the interest for self-preservation of the European colonists—for the majority of Communists their most significant reference group. The genie of "Muslim fanaticism" was about to be released from its bottle by the party it had hitherto placidly backed and fought for.

Traumatic as the effect of the Rif War was, it did not scotch all its illusions, or eliminate from the party all those loyal to the old tenets of Algerian Communism. It seems unlikely that the 40 or 50 per cent who remained members had always believed in, or had suddenly been converted to, Leninist decolonization theory. The arguments advanced by party members are sometimes barely distinguishable from those of the defectors. For example, a secretary of a Bône cell denied that the CP was advocating (as Giovacchini claimed) that the small *colons* be thrust into the sea,"since this will signify the destruction of civilization and the perspectives of progress in Algeria."[115] Not surprisingly, when the *région algérienne* (that closely-knit structure which had replaced the loose interfederation in 1925)[116] held its March 1926 conference, ten out of twenty-four delegates voted for a motion which was almost a carbon copy of that of the Algiers congress of January 1923.[117] They had experienced a powerful shock, but were slow to draw the conclusions from it. With the tide turning against

Abd el-Krim on the battlefield in August-September 1925, and the antiwar campaign brought to a virtual standstill after the failure of the 12 October general strike, many an Algerian Communist could be forgiven for assuming that the storm had passed, and that the PCF's sudden anticolonialist zeal was dying down.

This was to reason without the Colonial Commision elected at the Fourth PCF Congress in January 1925. Its very composition bespeaks the alliance which was to attack old-style Algerian Communism: Doriot and Lozeray of the JC, Ḥadj 'Ali 'Abd el-Kader and Benseman for Algerian migrant workers.[118] The alliance began to take shape early in 1923 during the campaign against the occupation of the Ruhr when Doriot (masterminding the operation from Paris) and Lozeray (conducting it in the field), undertook to preach insubordination to French troops stationed there. It was because of the need to woo the Algerian and Moroccan regiments among these forces that the JC took up the colonial question, and became vividly aware of the relationship between the struggle against European capitalism and that against colonialism. Leaflets prepared for distribution among the Muslim troops were aimed at conveying this feeling:

> Comrades, Friends! Despite your resistance and that of your ancestors, French imperialists invaded your country. They . . . demolished your homes, plundered your villages, made themselves masters of the immense wealth of your country, bringing you in exchange nothing but misery and slavery. . . . Moreover, French imperialists draft you by force and send you to faraway battlefields . . . to usurp the land of Germany. German workers and peasants suffer from the occupation of their country just as the workers and peasants of the colonies suffered and still suffer under the boot of French imperialism. . . . If you are given the order to fight and kill . . . *do not shoot!* Hold out your hand to the German workers for *they are your friends.*[119]

In order to translate this and other leaflets into Arabic, to help prepare the issues of *al-Kazīrna* (Barracks), the French-Arabic antimilitaristic paper,[120] and to conduct oral propaganda in the units, recourse was had to Algerians living in France (under the supervision of Mahmoud Ben Lekhal, a graduate of the Moscow Cadres School) for the Toilers of the Orient.[121] Most of the Algerians (such as Benseman and Ḥadj 'Ali)[122] came through the *Union Inter-coloniale,* a front organization for colonials living in metropolitan France, founded in 1922 and in which immigrants from Indochina and the Antilles predominated. The movement, led by Ho Chi Minh, was the only one in the PCF sphere which was genuinely concerned with colonial problems and openly advocated their independence.[123] From 1923 onwards it was gradually taken over by Algerian migrant workers, who were the largest group of colonials in France.[124] Other propagandists came through the JC such as Bourahla[125] or from the CGTU as did Issad, a cofounder of the *Étoile Nord Africaine*.[126]

The JC-Algerian immigrants alliance outlived the Ruhr campaign, and its mark is evident in the substantial space accorded to colonial affairs, in 1923-24, by *l'Avant-Garde* (the JC organ), in close collaboration of the Doriot group with the *Union Inter-coloniale* (led, after Ho Chi Minh's departure for Moscow, by Ḥadj 'Ali), and in the organization of mass rallies in honor of the emir Khaled during his visit to France (July 1924).[127]

With the rise to prominence of the JC generation at the time of the Bolshevization of the PCF, in late 1924, and the outbreak of the Rif War (which supplied an ideal target, combining as it did, antimilitaristic and anticolonial issues), the alliance became a force to be reckoned with. Furthermore, the new Colonial Commission was action prone, advocated radical solutions for the colonial system as well as within the party, and possessed executive capacities which the defunct CEC had lacked.[128] Unlike the latter, both components of the Commission attached great importance to Algeria and its *région* and were well briefed on what went on there, being independent of Algerian Communist sources of information. For the JC activists Algeria was important because it bordered on the theatre of war, and because of the dubious value of its Communist organization, an idea impressed upon Doriot and Chasseigne by Manuilsky's speech.[129] The interest of the Algerian immigrants in their homeland is self-evident, and people like Ḥadj 'Ali, who according to his own testimony joined the PCF because of the Eighth Condition," were naturally sensitive to the deviations from the condition so pervasive in the *région algérienne*.[130] The constant flow of migrants to France, and the periodical return of workers for vacations or to help during the harvest, kept Muslim activists in the PCF well-informed, while Lozeray and his comrades drew their information from the secret delegation under Célar, a JC leader, who had been dispatched to Algeria to launch action in and around the battle area.[131]

It took the Commission barely a month from the moment the Rif campaign was launched to decide that Algerian Communists were neglecting to carry out the tasks allotted to them. Impatience with Algerian Communism had been mounting since the Comintern Congress, and, now that solid proof was available, the Commission was spurred into direct action. At first it had let itself be deluded by Algerian verbal acrobatics; on the eve of the Founding Congress of the *région algérienne* in March 1925, the Commission persuaded the French Politbureau to send a cable exhorting the delegates "to ascribe greater importance to the colonial question," to which the Congress reacted, as in January 1923, by adopting a vague resolution on the "liberation of indigenous masses from the yoke of imperialism" associated with a run-of-the-mill list of reforms.[132] This was, however, before the Rif campaign entered high gear, kindling the Commission's zeal and facing the *région* with difficult and specific challenges. It was typical of the Commission's frame of mind that it immediately sent to Algeria a delegation headed by one of its members, Henri Lozeray. The delegation's most urgent task was to control subversive activity in Algeria among Muslim troops and peasants.[133] But at the same time, and partly in order to further the central aim, Lozeray was to take the *région* in hand. The main objectives were the "intensification of activity among the natives," particularly among the young, who were thought to be more amenable; the foundation of a "Leninist School" in Algiers, presumably modelled on the PCF Bobigny School, in order to train a new "hard core" of cadres to take the helm and indoctrinate the rank and file; and to establish stable contacts with the "Khaled movement."[134]

Whatever hopes were pinned on this delegation were shattered when all three members were arrested upon arrival. However, the determination and efficiency of the Colonial Commission were such that two months later a new delegation was dispatched consisting of two young *apparatchiki*, Louis Campiglia and André Schneider.[135] In view of the declining fortunes of Abd al-Krim and the failure of Doriot's mission, the disillusioned Commission now modified its expectations: the delegation was to abandon subversive activities related to the war, and embark upon the long-term task of the "internal regrouping of the party (in Algeria)."[136] Articles in *La Lutte Sociale* presented a new version of the Lozeray plan: first and foremost, the intensive indoctrination of cadres and members on the theoretical foundations and practical consequences of Comintern Colonial policy; the aim was to dispel "misapprehension" (probably those analyzed above), to liquidate "prejudices inculcated by the bourgeoisie among European workers concerning the racial inferiority of the natives." Only then could the party "exert itself to penetrate the indigenous populations" thus eradicating the "mistrust harbored by the natives towards all French political formations," a feeling easily understandable in view of the meager party work among them in the past.[137]

Campiglia, the first of the French *missi dominici* who were to preside over the destinies of Algerian Communism for the next quarter of a century, seems to have enjoyed powers of supervision and intervention much like those of Humbert-Droz in France, which led on to a key post within the regional hierarchy, that of *responsable à l'appareil*, later known as organizational secretary. In this capacity he was in charge of the lynchpin of the organization, the training and selection of cadres. He started work almost immediately and nominated a provisional regional committee composed of trustworthy men, with the post of secretary going to M. Garau, a JC leader who had proved his mettle in the campaign against the Rif War.[138]

With the apparatus under control, a massive indoctrination campaign was launched, culminating in conferences of the seven *rayons* (regional subdivisions) in February 1926, and a conference of the *région* the following month. In both rounds the "Theses on Algerian Colonial Policy" were adopted, but by unimpressive majorities.[139] The initial plan was to exploit the conferences to force a showdown on the opposition, offering them a choice between falling in with the Comintern line or exclusion, but it had to be abandoned in the face of the minority's unexpected strength. Indoctrination was thus launched anew, under Marcel Joubert, a new delegate who joined the former two. Though young, he had considerable experience in anticolonial action,[140] and formulated party positions more precisely, on several points setting more ambitious goals. This "radicalization of our political orientation" was probably deliberate and designed to scare off many vacillating members and drive moderate oppositionists to the other extreme, hence making the choice unequivocal. By deft maneuvering Joubert succeeded in driving a wedge between moderates and *ultras* in the opposition, forcing a showdown on the latter in January 1927, on the Muslim right to vote, an issue on which they were isolated from the moderates.[141] Only after the representatives of the *rayon* of Blida, the stronghold of the extremists, had been ousted, did Joubert turn against the much enfeebled members of the moderate wing, bringing about the expulsion or defection of many.[142]

The intricacies and fluctuations of this tortuous struggle are too confused for general interest; the brief summary sketched above may suffice to prove the durability of the old tradition as well as the determination of the PCF delegation. It should also be emphasized that, at least at the cadre level, this was a struggle between generations. One camp consisted of "youngish puritans aged 23 or 24" (as one oppositionist scoffed);[143] the Delegation itself, composed of French JC activists; its main allies, Garau, Cazala and E. Cormon (all formerly JC secretaries), and finally the great majority of their disciples who were in their twenties, and had come to the party after the 1920 split.[144] Though several veteran low level activists (Estorges, Poquet) did remain in the party after the 1927 purge, it is significant that only one long-standing leader, Pierre Larribère of Oran, did so.[145] When the official party history was written two decades later, it was Larribère who was singled out as the founder of Algerian Communism at the time of the Tours Congress, the names of other co-founders being consigned to oblivion.[146] The opposition, on the other hand, was led by—and for the most part composed of—veterans of the Socialist party, either members of pre-war SFIO,[147] or those of the *génération du feu* who joined in the wake of war.[148] Pre-split divergencies did not count as regards the colonial question. Much as the Sidi-Bel-Abbès section had been ultra-leftist before Tours, Lemédioni, the 1926-27 opposition leader, had been a Zimmerwaldian during the War.[149]

During the Rif campaign official party spokesmen had tried to avoid spelling out the final aim, and dissenters could only suspect it. Now the French delegates made it clear from the outset. While short-range claims might be brought forward, "these should by no means serve to obscure the ultimate objective we are fighting for, *the independence of Algeria*" (Campiglia's italics).[150] Yet even the partial reforms were expanded. The party, which since Khaled's Paris rallies had openly supported his demand for Muslim representation in parliament, now tried to outbid the emir by asking for representation based not on a limited electorate from among those maintaining Muslim personal status but on universal suffrage.[151] To this was later added the demand for universal suffrage within a single electoral college (i.e., no more guarantee of European predominance), in all Algerian elective assemblies.

Three main preconditions were laid down:

*(a)* "The national composition of the party must tend to be in

keeping with the national composition of the colony." A Muslim majority in membership and cadres would transform it into "an Algerian party with ancillary activity among the Europeans in lieu of a European party with ancillary activity among the natives."[152]

*(b)* Once "Arabicized" (as the process was later to be called), the CP must create a united front with the nationalists. In case of failure or lack of eligible partners, it should utilize "nationalist aspirations" in order to create a sort of front organization to be infiltrated and led by the Communists.[153]

*(c)* The prime target of the Communist-Nationalist front was to be the abolition of the *délégations financières*. This was an old assimilationist (and socialist) idea now converted into the stepping stone for independence; the *délégations* were to be replaced by an Algerian parliament elected by a single electoral college and by universal suffrage, and having full sovereign and constituent powers.[154] The intermediate reforms in local assemblies could be viewed as a preparatory stage, giving the Muslims a growing role in Algerian affairs.

In the face of this intransigent and monolithic stance, the opposition was deeply divided, though it succeeded at the March 1926 conference in forming a short-lived alliance and so foiled Campiglia's bid for a "definite resolution."[155] It was the heavily working-class *rayon* of Blida, led by the trade unionist Constant, that replaced Sidi-Bel-Abbès[156] in propagating the extremist, openly racialist, and procolonialist stand. Fervently singing the praises of French colonization which had brought civilization and progress to Algeria,[157] they claimed that Muslims "could only benefit from continuation of French rule."[158] The obverse of the picture was conjured up with the help of *colon* clichés about Muslim unruliness, violence, and fanaticism, and subservience to a reactionary elite. They regarded the proposed emancipation as "untimely," for it would merely augur a return to the old-time (i.e., pre-1830) anarchy, and would be achieved by "spilling the blood of our compatriots." Independent Algeria they dubbed "an Arab Kingdom," an obvious allusion to Napoleon III's famous phrase in the speech announcing his bold plan of Algerian reforms in 1863, the abhorred memory of which still lingered among the Pieds Noirs. In a similar vein, the short-term demand for voting rights for Muslims in local elective bodies was rejected:

> If Europeans sell their votes, *a fortiori* the natives![159] Worse still, if they are given political equality in the same college (as the Europeans) all the *marabouts* will be elected, and religious fanaticism will hold full sway. They are six times as numerous as we are! . . . What will become of the European workers and

civil servants if elective assemblies are dominated—as they are bound to be—by the natives?

The influence of the arguments is proved by the ferocity with which the PCF delegates combatted them. Hence a *La Lutte Sociale* forum ("Questions and Answers") aimed at allaying the fears of the rank and file, dealt with questions such as:

> When Algeria is independent, will the indigenous populations know how to maintain self-rule?;
> What will be the fate of the European workers if the natives themselves administer their country?;
> If the natives are given the right to vote, will religious intolerance reign supreme and all *marabouts* be elected?[160]

The moderate sector of the opposition for the most part followed the line traced by the Algiers section in the September 1922, and January 1923, federal congresses; Algiers, and in particular the popular quarter of Bab-el-Oued, was in fact its bastion, and two top-ranking local activists, Lemédioni and Salomon Ben Amar, its foremost representatives. Of the three initial misapprehensions, that concerning the Serrati thesis had been relegated to oblivion—inevitably so after the decision at the Fourth and Fifth World Congresses to shift focus to the East. The Eighth Condition and its theoretical premises were admitted, but the Sixteenth Condition remained the chief focus of discord. The 1922-23 resolutions had been definite and taken by the sovereign body—it was claimed in the 1926 conference of the Algiers *rayon*—and Campiglia was in no position to demand that they be repealed. As for the substance, "independence" and "land for the peasants" could not be taken as "blanket formulae" and applied to Algeria, since "the situation there is not the same as in China and Egypt; Algeria bears the impact of a century of colonization and has no organized national movement." As for Khaled and his followers, they did not contest French sovereignty.[161]

What gave the Sixteenth Condition its particular edge in this context was that it was now directed at a specific target: the "caste of salaried officials [i.e., the Delegation] who hold the party under their dictatorship and drown the voice of the opposition";[162] if colonial policy was to be reexamined it should be done in an atmosphere free of "outside intervention."[163] The polemics were thus injected into the debate which had raged in the party ever since the beginning of the

Bolshevization process in the second half of 1924—and catalyzed by the Rif War—over such questions as the tightly controlled cellular organization, autonomy and initiative at the grass-roots level, the right to free criticism, and over the very principle of democratic centralism. Lemédioni even professed all-out support for the famous "Letter of the 250" drawn up by the "rightist opposition" in France, which condemned the wholesale imposition of anticolonialist slogans and instructions upon the membership.[164] The high-handed behavior of the Paris emissaries, as for instance, in imposing an electoral program for a departmental by-election in Blida without consulting the *rayon*,[165] gave the Algerian opposition ample ammunition. But the most effective plank of the French "rightists" was only tenuously connected with the colonial problem: it was the protest against the rigorous party control over the CGTU, this being utterly alien to the tradition of the French Left. In particular it was expressed through the curbing of the autonomy of professional federations (the principle of *direction unique*), and the direct subjection of Communist trade unionist cadres to the party. On this issue Lemédioni succeeded in marshalling the support of CGTU veteran cadres including the Regional Secretary and dockers' leader Schiavo,[166] and the moral backing of the Monatte Anarcho-Syndicalist group in France.[167] In fact during the 1927 split and purge most of the followers of the moderates came from the CGTU. Its short-lived journal, *Combat Social*, was preoccupied with the fierce struggle for hegemony in the Algerian CGTU, culminating in the summer of 1927 in the defection of the ex-Communists, and of the minority of unions they led, to establish an autonomous—but minority—trade unionist movement.[168]

Eager as they were to extend their base, the moderates were not ready for compromise, even on the colonial question. Their stand was apparently one of principle and not tactics. True to the traditions of Algiers Communism and its support for Khaled's demand of parliamentary representation, they found embarrassing the extremists' rejection of the principle of the Muslim right to vote.[169] Joubert hastened to widen the rift by declaring in February 1927 that the "party may discuss the question of independence with the opposition . . . but the question the party cannot and will not discuss is that of the political rights of the natives."[170] It was this dividing line between the two clusters of dissident opinion which brought about their rapid rout, and probably also their failure to establish a new political force.

The party emerged from the protracted crisis, claimed its organ, "feeble numerically, perhaps, but pure."[171] Of the loss in membership there is no doubt. The most prudent estimate would put the 1927 losses at 150 at the very least, added to the heavy toll of the Rif crisis, and the slow erosion during the indoctrination process supervised by Campiglia and Joubert.[172] The small party (200-250 members) was to pass seven years in the political desert before growing again during the Popular Front era, and to an even larger extent in the post-World War II years. Arabization was to expand (reaching almost half the membership in the late forties), electoral and trade unionists victories were to be won.[173] Yet what party lingo euphemistically dubbed "colonialist remnants" surfaced in an almost cyclical regularity. They were, ultimately, to tear the CP in Algeria asunder during the early years of the Algerian revolution. The "slave-dealer mentality" had the final word. "Left-wing colonialism" (the "colonizer who refuses," to borrow Memmi's term) was to prove an abortive experiment.

## FOOTNOTES

1. The poll has been studied by Ch.-R. Ageron, "Les Communistes français devant la question algérienne de 1921 à 1924," *Mouvement Social,* no. 78, January-March 1972, pp. 13-23.
2. J. Degras, *The Communist International: Documents,* vol. 1, London, 1956, p. 170.
3. L. Paoli, "Autour de quelques manifestations économiques et sociales à Alger," *La Revue Socialiste,* XXV, 1902, pp. 457-8, 462-4, 473-5; A. Juving, *Le Socialisme en Algérie,* Algiers, 1924, pp. 191-206; Ch.-R. Ageron, "Jaurès et la question algérienne," *Mouvement Social,* no. 42, 1963, pp. 8-21; *A. Nouschi,* in G. Haupt and M. Reberioux, *La Deuxième International et l'Orient,* Paris, 1967, p. 442ff.
4. Major resolutions were adopted in the Congress of Constantine in 1902—see L. Paoli, "Les congrès socialistes algériens," *La Revue Socialiste,* XXVI, 1903, pp. 57-64; and the Congress of El-Affroun in 1912—see *La Lutte Sociale,* 7 and 14 Jan. 1912; Juving, pp. 227, 240-1; Ageron, pp. 24-5; Nouschi, pp. 449-56. Cf. *La Lutte Sociale,* 21 Jan. 1912; 11 and 18 Feb. 1912; 12 May 1912.
5. Paoli, pp. 58-9; Nouchi, pp. 446-8, 449, 451.
6. Paoli, p. 60-4; Nouschi, pp. 451-6, 458.
7. Haupt and Reberioux, pp. 19, 30-3, 44-5, 136ff; R. Thomas, "La Politique socialiste et le problème colonial de 1905 à 1920," *Revue Française* d'Histoire d'Outremer, XLVII, 1961, pp. 214-32. On Socialist indifference to the Algerian question before World War I, see Ageron, and the *Compte-rendus sténographiques* of the Seventh Congress of the SFIO, 1910, pp. 109-10, 143-5, 480, the Ninth Congress, 1912, pp. 194-5, and the Eleventh Congress, 1914, pp. 120-2.
8. Cf. *Demain* (organ of the SFIO in Algiers), 26 June and 10 July 1920; *La Lutte Sociale* (then organ of the SFIO in Oran), 22 June and 6 July 1919.
9. See the votes of Algerian delegates in the SFIO Congress of Strassbourg, February 1920—*Compte-rendu,* pp. XVIII-XXIII; cf. *Demain* and *La Lutte Sociale,* 1919 and 1920, *passim.*

10. The earliest mention of the "colonial condition" (then no. 2) is to be found in *Demain,* 18 Sept. 1920, presumably following *L'Humanité,* as this draft was not published in Algerian SFIO papers. The second draft, comprising twenty-one conditions, was published by *La Lutte Sociale,* 18 November 1921.
11. Ibid., 4 December 1920. It is true that the paragraph on colonies in that motion was somewhat milder and spoke vaguely of the need to "denounce colonialism" and to "side actively with the populations subjugated by European capitalism in their struggle against oppression."
12. *L'Humanité,* 7 Jan. 1921 (Julien's article).
13. Ageron in *Le Mouvement Social.*
14. Text of the resolution and commentary in *Demain,* 16 September, 18 October, and 13 Nov. 1920; 11 Dec. 1921.
15. The speech could not be delivered because of the tumult resulting from the arrival of the celebrated Zinoviev telegram. Julien published it, in article form, in *L'Humanité,* 1 and 7 January 1921.
16. *Demain,* 22 Oct. 1921.
17. *Bulletin Communiste,* III, 1923, p. 16.
18. It became the organ of the three Algerian federations (Algiers, Oran, and Constantine), when *Demain* was closed down in March 1921.
19. Excerpt from the answer of the Sidi-Bel-Abbès section to the poll, published in *La Lutte Sociale,* 7 May 1921; cf. H. Carrère d'Encausse and S.R. Schram, *Marxism in Asia,* London, 1969, p. 197.
20. Ageron, loc. cit.
21. *La Lutte Sociale,* 23 June 1921; cf. ibid., 22 Oct. 1921.
22. Ageron, loc. cit.; and the Sidi-Bel-Abbès resolution (n. 19).
23. *La Lutte Sociale,* 18 June 1921.
24. Ageron, loc. cit.
25. Ibid.
26. *La Lutte Sociale,* 5 Nov. 1921.
27. See the *Compte-rendus sténographiques* of the SFIO National Congress of February 1920 and December 1920; Juving, pp. 115-8.
28. The party took 920 cards from PCF headquarters, but the number of those distributed must have been somewhat smaller. Cf. the *Rapports du Secrétariat Géneral* to the SFIC (PCF) Congresses of 1921 and 1922; Juving, loc. cit. The Algerian SFIO had half this membership figure.
29. This figure denotes actual members and is based on a speech by the Algerian delegate Schiavo in the Fifth Congress of the PCF (5° Congrès National. *Compte-rendus sténographiques,* Paris, 1926, p. 252). The 1,500 figure indicated by PCF Secretary General P. Sémard (report to the Sixth Plenum of the ECCI to be found in the supplement to PCF/CC, *Rapport moral au 5e Congrès,* Paris, 1926, p. 11) probably refers to the number of cards taken from headquarters.
30. *L'Echo d'Oran,* 6 May 1921; *L'Echo d'Alger,* 3 Oct. 1921.
31. Juving, loc. cit., pp. 220-3; Kaddache, *La vie politique à Alger de 1919 à 1939,* Algiers, 1970, pp. 110-11, 119; *La Depêche de Constantine* and *L'Echo d'Oran,* 12 May 1924. In 1924, except for failure in Oran, the CP polled between 10 and 12 percent in most urban centers (more than the overall PCF percentage), one-fifth in Algiers and one-third in Sidi-Bel-Abbès.
32. *L'Echo d'Oran,* 5 June 1921; *Le Travailleur* (Socialist), 29 Oct. 1921, 16 April 1927; *L'Echo d'Alger,* 29 April 23.
33. Ct. *La Lutte Sociale,* 18 Jan. 1924.
34. *Le Travailleur,* 27 April 1924; cf. ibid., 28 Sept. 1921, 22 Oct. 1922, 25 April 1924.
35. *L'Evolution Nord Africaine,* 22 Feb. 1924.
36. Ch. Houel in *Cahiers de l'Afrique du Nord,* passim.
37. *Mentalité des possesseurs d'esclaves.* The term was coined in Trotsky's article (or

rather note) in *Bulletin Communiste,* IV, 1923, p. 34 (see *infra,* nos. 60, 61).

38. J. Degras, *The Communist International,* Oxford, 1956, vol. 1, pp. 325-7. The British and Italian CP's were put in charge of parties in their respective empires.
39. *L'Humanité,* 25 May 1922; cf. his speech in the Fifth World Congress, Carrère d'Encausse and Schram, pp. 199-200.
40. *L'Humanité,* 28 May and 7 July 1921.
41. *La Lutte Sociale,* 27 April 1923; PCF, 3e Congrès National, *Compte-rendus sténo.,* p. 66; *Bulletin Communiste,* 1924, pp. 597-8, 615.
42. Ageron, pp. 11, 24; *La Lutte Sociale,* 5 Jan. 1921, 20 April 1924.
43. Ageron, pp. 26-7.
44. L. Laurens, secretary of the Constantine federation, in *La Lutte Sociale,* 17 Sept. 1921.
45. Degras, vol. 1, pp. 351-3.
46. The manifesto was endorsed on 20 May and published on 6 June in *La Correspondence Internationale.* The first known Algerian reaction (that of Sidi-Bel-Abbès) came on 27 June. As the first non-Communist reference to the Manifesto is the parliamentary speech of E. Morinaud, deputy of Constantine on 4 July (JO, *Ass. Nationale, Débats,* pp. 2304-5) it seems that the Sidi-Bel-Abbès Communists learned about it from the *Correspondence Internationale* and may have passed the information to other sections.
47. At least two section assemblies are known: Sidi-Bel-Abbès (n. 46) and Algiers (n.d.). On 10 September congresses of the federation of Oran and Algiers departments were held, the latter endorsing a motion put forward by the section of Algiers. The Constantine federal congress was held on 17 September. See *La Lutte Sociale,* passim.
48. Cf. *L'Echo d'Oran,* 16 Nov. and 15 Dec. 1919, and 29 Oct. 1922. The section thus preserved its pre-split strength, unlike its main rival, the section of Oran (*La Lutte Sociale* 9 April and 3 Dec. 1921, and supra n. 31).
49. The original version is to be found in an appendix to the letter whereby the resolution was brought to the attention of the PCF. S. Bahne (ed.), *Archives de Jules Humbert-Droz,* vol. 1, Dordrecht-Holland, 1970, pp. 256-61. English translation in Carrère d'Encausse and Schram, pp. 196-8.
50. That of the Algiers section is quoted in *La Lutte Sociale,* 15 Sept. 1922. E. Morinaud quoted in his 4 July speech (n. 46) from a brochure "The Native Question and Communism," published recently in Bône. The tone of the excerpts is pro-Serrati. The brochure may have been a reaction to the Manifesto or (if published beforehand) at least indicates the position that Bône, the biggest section in Eastern Algeria *(La Lutte Sociale,* 12 Nov. 1921) would adopt in Summer 1922. *L'Evolution Nord Africaine*, 6 Nov. 1925, claimed that the author was Giovacchini, the sectional secretary.
51. Published in *Bulletin Communiste*, III, 1922, pp. 939-40. According to *La Lutte Sociale*, 26 Feb. 1926, only three delegates attended the Congress.
52. According to *La Lutte Sociale*, ibid, only one delegate at the Algiers federal Congress voted for the "Sidi-Bel-Abbès motion.
53. The phrase left out was "If an Egyptian sovereignty is necessary, a sovereignty of cannibals is undesirable; if a Gandhi can become a head of state, a Batouala cannot."
54. *La Lutte Sociale,* 17 Sept. 1922.
55. Regional Secretary M. Garau in the 1926 Algiers federal congress, *La Lutte Sociale,* 26 Feb. 1926. The same argument was advanced by Guillon after he left the party (*Le Travailleur,* 11 Feb. 1923).
56. The interfederation was a loose body, coordinating activity of the three Algerian federations.
57. R. Louzon, "Une honte," *Bulletin Communiste,* III, 1923, p. 15ff.

58. N.N. [illegible signature] (Montpellier), to Frossard (Paris), 10 July 1922, *Archives Humbert-Droz,* vol. 1, p. 256. N.N. must be Julien, who had been transferred there by the Ministry of Education from his post in an Oran *lycée* because of his Communist activities. Julien's continued contacts with the Algerian federations are demonstrated in his candidacy in the departmental election in Oran later that year *(L'Echo d'Oran,* 9 Oct. 1922).
59. Humbert-Droz (Paris) to CI Praesidium (Moscow), 31 August 1922, ibid., p. 319. For H.-D.'s powers see his mandate (signed by Zinoviev, 17 Sept. 1921, ibid., pp. 91-2).
60. Carrère d'Encausse and Schram, p. 193; *The Fourth Congress of the CI,* London, n.d., pp. 213-14.
61. *Bulletin Communiste,* IV, 1923, pp. 33-4. In a note appended to this French publication of his speech Trotsky deals with the *esclavagiste* character of the Sidi-Bel-Abbès letter.
62. Degras, vol. 1, pp. 405, 392-3. The "French Resolution" was conceivably formulated by Trotsky (sees the use of the term *esclavagiste* in the paragraph on Sidi-Bel-Abbès, *Manifestes, thèses et resolutions des quatre premiers congrès de l'IC,* Paris, 1934, p. 198; cf. supra n. 60).
63. Carrèr de'Encausse and Schram, p. 193; Another demand to include "natives" in the CEC, was to be implemented only in 1924, when Hadj Ali Abd el-Kader, future ENA founder, was nominated to it (*Bulletin Communiste,* 1924, p. 597).
64. See n. 41.
65. Letter to Frossard dated 22 Dec. 1922, reproduced in *Le Travailleur,* 11 Feb. 1923.
66. The Congress was summoned in the week following Guillon's resignation (*La Lutte Sociale,* 29 Dec. 1922). The Program was in fact published in *Bulletin Communiste,* III, 1923, pp. 47-8, three days before it was adopted in Algiers on 14 Jan. 1923.
67. Ibid., III, 1923, p. 61. This was an answer to the sharp criticism levelled by R. Louzon. Franco-Tunisian Communist leader (ibid., pp. 16-7), against the interfederal theses, which had been published there the month before.
68. In 1922 membership in the Algiers Federation was 450 (out of less than nine hundred, see n. 28, and PCF, *2e Congrès National, Rapport du Secretariat National*). Two years later they numbered 600 (out of 1000, see n. 29 and *La Lutte Sociale,* 9 Jan. 1925). According to Mouillard (*Bulletin Communiste*, 1923, p. 61), the other two federations were to debate the program, but it is not clear whether they actually did.
69. *La Lutte Sociale,* 26 December 1922.
70. Spielmann answered the 1921 poll in the name of the Algiers section and wrote extensively in *La Lutte Sociale* (and also in the Colonial Forum of *l'Humanité* in 1922-3). On his former career see Ageron, *Les Musulmans algériens et la France,* Paris, 1968, pp. 671, 1036 (n. 1), 1085, 1154.
71. *La Lutte Sociale,* 8 June 1925. His brochures, *La Colonisation algérienne et la question indigène,* I, II, III, Algiers, 1922, 1923, were printed in a CP controlled co-operative and recommended to party members. A collection of *Le Trait d'Union* is to be found in the periodicals section of *Archives d'Outremer* (Aix-en-Provence). See in particular the leading article in the 5 June 1923 issue. Because of financial difficulties, it ceased publication in January 1925. *Colon* press considered it a sham CP publication (*L'Evolution Nord Africaine*, 15 June 1923, 4 Jan. 1924; *L'Afrique Latine,* March 1924, p. 394).
72. *Le Travailleur,* 10 June 1923. F. Abbas wrote there under the pseudonym Kemal Abenseradj (*Trait d'Union,* 20 April, 5 May and 20 May 1924). Cf. F. Abbas, *Guerre et revolution d'Algérie: la nuit coloniale,* Paris, 1962, pp. 117-8, 121 (n. 1).

73. *La Lutte Sociale,* 11 Jan. 1924.
74. Ageron, p. 20; *La Lutte Sociale,* 7 January and 4 August 1912 (debates of pre-war local congresses).
75. The presentation of Khaled and other Muslims in a CP sponsored platform for the Algiers municipality in 1925 (see *infra*) heralds a new period beginning with the campaign against the Rif War.
76. Based on confidential documents. According to a party report seized during searches in 1925, *La Lutte Sociale* had only 89 Muslim subscribers.
77. A. Crémieux, *A.B.C. du Syndicalisme,* Algiers, 1924, pp. 27-8. Crémieux tried to refute this argument, but one may doubt his success. *Le Réveil Ouvrier* (organ of the Departmental Union of Oran) fails to mention its antiracist streak in a fulsome review devoted to the work (issue of 1 May 1924).
78. Ageron, pp. 16-7.
79. *La Lutte Sociale,* 15 Sept. 1922.
80. Cf. Ch.R.. Ageron, "L'Emir Khaled petit-fils d'Abd el-Kader fut-il le premier nationaliste algérien," ROMM, II, 1966, pp. 9-39; Idem, "Le Mouvement Jeune-Algérien de 1900 à 1923," *Etudes Maghrébines—Mélanges Ch. A. Julien,* Paris, 1964, pp. 217-43.
81. For instance, *Demain,* 16 Oct. 1920.
82. Spielmann was a frequent contributor to *L'Ikdam* and Ben Amar wrote occasionally in *La Lutte Sociale* (see, for instance, 8 Oct. 1921).
83. *L'Ikdam,* 23 June 1922. The author of the article, "La question algérienne et le communisme," was Touili Ben Amar. Cf. ibid., 16 June 1922 (article in Arabic).
84. Ageron, "L'Emir Khâled," pp. 36-41. For another interpretation of his departure, portrayed as an expulsion by French authorities, see M. Kaddache, "Al-Amir Khäled wa-nashatuhu al-siyasi bayna 1919 wa 1925," *BHCM* (Arabic part), no. 4, January 1968; B. Sa'adallah, *al-haraka al-wataniyya al-jaza'iriyya,* Beirut, 1969, p. 415.
85. E.g., *La Lutte Sociale,* 3 May 1924, 15 March 1925. For a defense of Khaled before his departure, ibid., 12 Jan. 1923.
86. Cf. Ageron, "L'Emir Khaled"; Kaddache, *La vie politique à Alger,* p. 78ff.
87. Ibid.; on PCF role see *La Lutte Sociale,* 1 May 1925.
88. *La Vie Ouvrière,* 21 Dec. 1923. Cf. the letter of an Arab complaining of signs of racial hatred by European workers towards their Arab fellow workers (*La Lutte Sociale,* 14 Nov. 1924). His observation concerning the anarchists may be confirmed by even casual reading of their Algerian organ, *Le Flambeau.*
89. *L'Echo d'Oran,* 12 May 1924.
90. Cf. N. Le Ghennec, "Le PCF et la guerre du Rif," *Le Mouvement Social,* LXXII, 1972, pp. 43-7; J.R. Perry, *Soviet policy towards North Africa,* Ph.D. thesis, Columbia University, 1972, pp. 219 ff.
91. El-Djazaïri, pseudonym of Ḥadj 'Ali 'Abd el-Kader, founder of the *Etoile Nord Africaine* (ENA), in *La Lutte Sociale,* 5 Dec. 1924.
92. During the first phase of the campaign Algerian leaders passing through Paris even took part: Spielmann, who left the party at the second phase, presided over a meeting of the *Union Intercoloniale* held to celebrate the Doriot-Sémard telegram (*Le Trait d'Union* 5 Oct. 1924; *L'Humanité,* 13 Nov. 1924). J. Labrevoit, secretary of the federation of Constantine, addressed the Congress of North African Workers in Paris (*L'Humanité,* 8 Dec. 1924), *L'Etincelle* (organ of the Bône Communists), 21 Dec. 1924.
93. See *L'Echo d'Alger, L'Evolution Nord Africaine* and *La Dépéche Algérienne, passim,* and even the Socialist weekly *Demain,* 15 June and 4 July 1925. Cf. Perry, pp. 222-3.
94. Cf., for example, *L'Echo d'Alger* and *La Lutte Sociale,* April-May 1922, passim.

95. See, for instance, the May 1922 incidents in Algiers (antimilitarist rally of the CP broken up by the police, the Communists in reply turning on a funeral of World War soldiers). Detailed account in *L'Algérie,* 25 May 1922.
96. Based on: *L'Echo d'Alger,* 9 through 14 June 1925; *La Lutte Sociale,* passim; confidential docments; and the accusation brought in the trials of Communist militants (as reported in the press in the following months).
97. Document seized during the arrest of the clandestine PCF delegation (*infra,* n. 102). It was made public at the moment of their trial (*La Dépêche Algérienne,* 6 Sept. 1925). The main grievance raised in the document was the lack of activity among Muslims.
98. *La Lutte Sociale,* 22 May 1925.
99. Most of those brought to trial were JC members. JC secretary R. Cazala was the only one condemned for propaganda among the troops.
100. *La Lutte Sociale,* passim; *La Dépêche de l'Est,* 25 May 1925; *L'Avant Garde* (JCF), 19 Sept. 1925; PCF, *5e Congrès, Compte-rendus sténo,* Paris, 1926, pp. 252-4; J.O., *Ass. Nat. Débats,* 18 Dec. 1926, pp. 4333; Parti Communiste (SFIC), *Quatre ans de répression,* Paris, 1928, p. 15. Cf. n. 111.
101. *L'Echo d'Alger,* 16 July 1925.
102. Excerpts were published by *La Dépêche Algérienne,* 6 Sept. 1925; *L'Evolution Nord Africaine,* 21 May 1926 (also 8 Dec. 1934 and 3 May 1939).
103. *L'Echo d'Oran,* 1 and 4 Sept. 1925; *L'Evolution Nord Africaine,* 7 Sept. 1925. Cf. the accounts of Doroit (*L'Avant-Garde,* 10 Oct 1925) and Barbé (*Souvenirs de militant et dirigeant communiste,* MS. Institut d'Histoire Sociale, Paris, pp. 59-63).
104. *La Lutte Sociale,* 25 Sept. and 20 Oct. 1925.
105. Ibid., 18 June 1926; Anon., "The revolutionary movement in the East," *The Communist International,* Dec. 1925, p. 111; Cf. the letter of an ex-Communist to *L'Evolution Nord Africaine,* 18 Dec. 1925.
106. *Demain,* 12 June 1926; Cf. *La Lutte Sociale,* 30 June 1928.
107. *L'Etincelle* (Giovacchini's organ), 2 August 1925.
108. For example Chiosy, leader of the railwaymen of Mennerville (*La Lutte Sociale,* April 1932). Leaders of East Algerian Communists, Lebrevolt and Laurens, seem to have left during this period.
109. *La Lutte Sociale,* 25 Sept. 1925.
110. In a report to the ECCI Sixth Plenum (March 1926) PCF secretary general P. Sémard alleged that three quarters of the members left (supplement to *Rapport moral au 5e Congrés du PCF,* p. 10). As previous membership is estimated by him at 1,500 (ibid., p. 11), fewer than 400 must have remained in the ranks. The 1,500 figure (given also in the *Communist International,* Dec. 1925, p. 111) was contested in the PCF Fifth Congress by the Algerian delegate, who maintained that the party had only 1,000 members (*Compte-rendus sténo.,* p. 252).This seems plausible, for the federation of Algiers (which used to account for half the party's strength) had 600 members in 1925 (note 68). Sémard must have been referring to the numbers of cards delivered by the PCF to the Algerian federation, and the Algerian to the actual number for which dues were paid. Sémard seems however to have been quite accurate as regards the 1926 figures. *La Revolution Prolétarienne,* 15 June 1927, p. 121, claimed, on the basis of information from Algerian opposition, that prior to the 1927 purge the party had 500 members. Membership thus declined to 400-500, and the defection rate was 50-60 percent.
111. This was the result, *inter alia,* of the transfer of key members (e.g., railwaymen) to distant places in the countryside (PCF, 5e Congrès, *Compte-rendus sténo.,* p. 253).
112. Loc. cit.
113. *Demain,* 17 Oct. 1975; *La Lutte Sociale,* 16 Oct. 1925.

114. *Le grand soir,* Paris, 1929, p. 212ff. On Crémieux as party activist see *L'Evolution Nord Africaine,* 1 Feb. 1925.
115. In a letter to Giovacchini's paper *L'Etincelle,* 2 August 1925. Note the affinity with the arguments of Constant (infra, p. 192).
116. Introduced during the late 1926 Bolshevization. The *"régions"* took the place of the former SFIO-inherited organization based on federations (or *"départments"*) and usually regrouped several *départments* in one *région.* Algerian federations adopted the principle in Jan. 1925 and held a Unification (or First Regional) Congress two months later (*La Lutte Sociale,* 9 Jan. and 27 March 1925).
117. Ibid., 12 March 1926.
118. PCF, *4e Congrès national, Compte-rendus sténo.,* pp. 52, 368-9. Benseman's name (known from *Le Paria,* see infra) was erroneously rendered Bersman (and Belseman). The commission also included two members whose initials only are given, probably because they were Algerian temporary residents and hence liable to expulsion. (Hadj Ali, according to a biographical notice in *Archives de la Préfecture de Police,* Box 57, was a naturalized French citizen.)
119. Manifesto "To the Soldiers of Algeria and Morocco" (in French, Arabic, and German): copy in the Institut Maurice Thorez (Paris).
120. This organ "defending the rights of Maghribi soldiers" (according to the subtitle) was published at least until June-July 1924 when the Bibliothèque Nationale collection ceases. Many of the articles were borrowed from *Le Conscrit,* the JC-controlled antimilitaristic paper. *Al-Kāzirna* was smuggled occasionally into North Africa (*L'Evolution Nord Africaine,* 10 Oct. 1924; *Le Flambeau,* 23 May 1924).
121. Biography in Kaddache, p. 78 (note 2). On his studies in Moscow see *L'Avant-Garde,* 6 March 1926, *Le Paria,* June 1926. On his activity in the Ruhr see *Le Journal* (Paris), 24 Jan. 1924. He was arrested together with another Algerian, Bourahla, and numerous JC militants, including Lozeray, and court-martialed and sentenced to five years imprisonment, but was released late in 1924.
122. *Le Paria* passim. According to A.P.P. (note 117), Hadj Ali had been writing for *al-Kāzirna* and probably edited it after Ben Lekhal's arrest.
123. An example of the *Union*'s stance: *Le Paria,* Nov. 1923, published the Colonial Appeal of the Peasants International, which *L'Humanité* failed to publish. Ho Chi Minh criticized the latter on that score (*On revolution,* New York, 1967, p. 60).
124. Cf. growing frequency of articles on Maghribi problems in *Le Paria,* many of which were written by Hadj Ali under various pseudonyms (Ali Baba, El-Djazairi, etc.; see A.P.P., Box 57). On Algerian workers see J.-J. Rager, *Les Musulmans algériens en France et dans les pays islamiques,* Paris, 1950, pp. 286-7.
125. Bourahla, JC activist in Algiers where he took part in the 1922 antimilitaristic demonstrations (note 95). He later came to France and was one of those who fought there for a more active campaign against colonialism (*L'Avant-Garde,* 1 June 1923).
126. See A.P.P., Box 57 and infra.
127. *L'Humanité,* 3, 13, and 20 July 1924; 30 Sept. 1924; M. Lebajaoui, *Verité sur la révolution algérienne,* Paris, 1970, pp. 19-21; Ageron, "L'Emir Khaled," p. 42-3.
128. Hadj Ali, who rose in the CP hierarchy after Ben Lekhal's arrest, was nominated to the CEC in 1924 and was its rapporteur at the National Council in June delivering a devastating attack on party indifference *(Bulletin Communiste,* 1924, pp. 597-8).
129. Cf. declaration of Chasseigne upon his return from the World Congress (*L'Humanité,* 18 Aug. 1924) and articles of A. Marty, a JC supporter on anticolonialism. (*La Lutte Sociale,* 23 Jan. and 13 Feb. 1925). Cf. the telegram sent in March 1925 to the Algerian Regional Congress (infra, p. 187).

130. A.P.P., Box 57; Cf. his article in *La Lutte Sociale,* 5 Dec. 1924.
131. Barbé, *Souvenirs,* MS. I.H.S., p. 61. Other members were M. Joubert, the JC colonial "expert" and P. Villière.
132. *La Lutte Sociale,* 27 March 1925.
133. Supra, note 102. The other members of the delegation were also JC activists: V. Arrighi, born and reared in Algeria, then IRA secretary in Paris, left the party in 1929 after being compromised in the scandal of the Workers' and Peasants' Bank and later joined Doriot's PPF and served as its delegate for North Africa; and Accouturier, the JC secretary in Montluçon.
134. Reconstructed from fragments leaked to the press (see note 103).
135. *La Lutte Sociale,* 26 Feb. 1926; *Combat Social* (organ of the dissenters), 31 March 1927. Campiglia was signing his articles L. or Louis.
136. The term is used in *The Communist International,* Dec. 1925, p. 111. Sémard in his report to ECCI (appendix to PCF, *5e Congrès national, Compte-rendus sténo.,* p. 11) writes in the same vein.
137. *La Lutte Sociale,* 25 Sept. 2, 9, and 23 Oct. 1925.
138. Garau (b. 1899) was active in the Algerian JC as early as 1922, notably in the antimilitaristic demonstrations (*L'Algérie,* 23 May 1922), later becoming the JC secretary (*La Lutte Sociale,* 8 March 1924). He was one of those arrested during the Rif campaign, and was subsequently promoted to secretary of the Algiers *rayon.*
139. Ibid., 19 and 26 Feb. and 12 March 1926.
140. Joubert was active in Tunisia in 1922 editing the Communist organ *L'Avenir Social* after the arrest of the local leadership, before being arrested himself (*Bulletin du Comité de l'Afrique Française,* XXXII, pp. 107, 193). He was one of the first who tried to draw the JCF to anticolonialist activity, presenting a report in this spirit to the 1923 congress (*L'Avant-Garde,* 1 June 1923). In 1925 he was a member of Célar's clandestine delegation (note 131). His 1926-27 articles in *La Lutte Sociale* are signed L. Boiroux.
141. Infra, p. 194.
142. *La Lutte Sociale,* 14 and 21 Jan., 25 Feb., 25 March, 1 and 15 April 1927; *Combat Social,* 31 July 1927.
143. *Le Combat Social,* 31 March 1927.
144. The JC organization was founded in Algeria in 1921 by Camille, P. Larribère's son (see note 145 and *La Lutte Sociale,* 16 Dec. 1927). Most sections were even more recent and constantly thought back to 1924 (*L'Avant-Garde,* 1 Nov. 1924). Only in extremist Blida did the JC back the opposition (*La Lutte Sociale,* 23 July 1926). On the generation gap in the CGTU see infra, note 166.
145. *La Lutte Sociale,* 12 March 1926. A veteran Socialist, Larribère, was among the few activists who came on tour with Doriot during his Sept. 1925 mission. (v. Barbé, *Souvenirs).* His two sons were high-ranking cadre members of the Algerian CP after World War II.
146. Ecole Elementaire du PCA, "Cours no. 4," *Le Parti,* Algiers, 1947, p. 3
147. E.g., E. Lemédioni who joined in 1913 (*Révolution prolétarienne,* 1927, p. 122); S. Ben Amar, secretary of the Algiers section before World War I (*La Lutte Sociale,* 3 Oct. 1909, 6 March 1910).
148. Such as Constant (*Le Combat Social,* 31 March 1927).
149. Loc. cit. Sidi-Bel-Abbès was the section which in 1920 had suggested voting for Heine's motion with a "colonial amendment" (supra, p. 158).
150. *La Lutte Sociale,* 19 Feb. 1926.
151. *La Lutte Sociale,* 17 Dec. 1926, 21 Jan. 1927.
152. Ibid., 31 Dec. 1926, 18 Feb. 1927. This is Joubert's formula. Campiglia had spoken merely about "improving the ethnic composition of the party."

153. Ibid., 26 Feb. 1926.
154. Ibid., 21 Jan. 1927.
155. Lemédioni persuaded the Constant group not to present a motion of their own but to vote for his.
156. Sidi-Bel-Abbès and Oran were now among the staunchest supporters of the Delegation and the Provisional Committee.
157. Ibid., 12 March 1926.
158. This quotation and all the following in the paragraph are taken from a motion adopted by the *rayon* of Blida on 24 Jan. 1927. No complete version exists. Excerpts are to be found ibid., 27 Feb. 1927, 1 April 1927; *L'Evolution Nord Africaine,* 15 April 1927.
159. Cf. the 1914 speech of *colon* deputy Cuttoli affirming the existence of a *mentalité indigène* which accounted for the Muslims being "unruly, intemperate and inclined to bribery and fraud" (quoted in V. Confer, *France and Algeria: The problem of civil and political reform,* Syracuse University Press, 1966, p. 89).
160. *La Lutte Sociale,* 11 and 18 Feb. 1927.
161. Ibid., 26 Feb. and 12 March 1926. The "blanket formulae" paragraph is a paraphrase of criticism levelled by French oppositionist Lariot against the Rif campaign (*L'Humanité,* 5 Jan. 1926).
162. *La Lutte Sociale,* 26 Feb. 1926.
163. Ibid., 25 Feb. 1927 (resolution of cell 89).
164. Cf. Le Guennec, pp. 59-63.
165. *La Lutte Sociale,* 26 Feb. 1926.
166. Together with other veteran leaders, such as Andréani, Nieto, Laulom, Lagrange. Cf. ibid, 14 Jan., 21 Feb., and 1 April 1927; *Le Combat Social,* 31 March 1927.
167. Their organ, *Révolution Prolétarienne,* published dissident views, and the latter's autonomous unions were in touch with the analogous organization founded by P. Monatte after his expulsion from the PCF in 1924.
168. The battle for the Algerian CGTU was lost when the Communists assured themselves of predominance in the key professional federation, the railwaymen (*Le Cheminot Algérien,* 1 July 26), but not as the result of substantial financial aid from France and a number of prestigious CGTU leaders coming for propaganda tours (see *La Lutte Social* and *Le Combat Social,* passim: *L'Algérie,* 29 March and 12 April 1927; CGTU, *4e Congrès National, Compte-rendus sténo.,* pp. 315-7). The opposition group was financially weak, and *Le Combat Social* had to stop publication by mid-June. Most autonomous unions finally joined the CGT (*Révolution Prolétarienne,* 1930, p. 84; *Demain,* 22 Feb. 1930).
169. Cf. Lemédioni's letter to Constant, which was intercepted by the CP and published by *La Lutte Sociale,* 1 April 1927, and his letter of resignation from the party (*Le Combat Social,* 14 April 1927).
170. *La Lutte Sociale,* 25 Feb. 1927.
171. Ibid., 15 April 1927.
172. According to the opposition (*Révolution Prolétarienne,* 1927, p. 121), no more than 150-200 members remained in the party. This may be a somewhat biased underestimate. On the other hand the opposition disposed of the entire *rayon* of Blida (about 60, v. loc. cit.; PCF, *5e Congrès, Compte-rendus*, p. 253), the 15-strong cell of Lemédioni (*Le Combat Social,* 3 March 1927), and a dispersed following, hard to gauge accurately but surely at least 100-120.
173. See my *Communisme et Nationalisme en Algérie,* Paris 1976.

## INDEX

[The definite article, al-, has been deleted]

DS 37 .S57 1985

Sivan, Emmanuel.

Interpretations of Islam

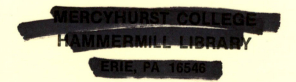